rick stein's
complete seafood

rick

stein's
complete seafood

TEN SPEED PRESS
Berkeley

photography by
james murphy

All rights reserved. Published in the United States by Ten Speed
Press, an imprint of the Crown Publishing Group, a division of
Random House, Inc, New York.
www.crownpublishing.com
www.tenspeed.com

Ten Speed Press and the Ten Speed Press colophon are
registered trademarks of Random House, Inc.

Originally published in the U.K. by BBC Books, in 2001. First
published in hardcover in the United States by Ten Speed
Press, in 2004.

Library of Congress Cataloging-in-Publication Data on file with
publisher.

Paperback edition ISBN-13: 978-1-58008-914-2

Commissioning Editor: Vivien Bowler
Project Editor: Rachel Copus
American Editor: Norma MacMillan
Art Director: Lisa Pettibone
Designer: Paul Welti
Home Economist: Debbie Major

A NOTE ABOUT THE RECIPES
Recipes give both standard American cups and spoons and
metric measures. The two sets of measurements are not exact
equivalents, so use one or the other and not a combination.

Set in RotisSemiSans light
Printed and bound in Singapore by
Tien Wah Press Pte Ltd
Colour separations by Radstock Reproductions Limited,
Midsomer Norton

BBC

11 10 9 8 7 6 5 4 3 2

First American Paperback Edition

contents

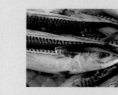

introduction

I'M VERY PLEASED that *Seafood* is being published in North America. The project grew out of an idea to put the techniques and recipes that we teach at my seafood school in Padstow, Cornwall, in England, into a book. I wanted to create the definitive, how-to-prepare-it-and-cook-it book with well-designed, step-by-step photography—a book that would educate and inspire at the same time. I was very influenced in this endeavor by the excellent *Time-Life* series that came out in the late 1970s under the editorship of one of my food-writing heroes, the late Richard Olney.

I have always felt that a book like this could be universal because I could see from wandering around fish markets and fishing ports, and eating in restaurants and from street vendors all over the world, that fish cooks the same wherever you are. Why not, I reasoned, write a book that would be just as useful in Padstow as in Portland, Oregon? So I embarked on a mammoth but completely enjoyable task of forming fish into families with close relatives all around the world, and I made sure that all the recipes and techniques were relevant to fish that you could buy in San Francisco or in Sydney.

I was much aided when dealing with fish from North America by two books: *The Encyclopedia of Fish Cookery* by A.J. McClane and—most particularly—*Fish* by Mark Bittman. Mark not only writes extremely well, but has also been to my restaurant in Padstow a couple of times, which makes him both a scholar and a gentleman. I also must thank Johnny Apple for his great influence on the subject of American fish. His encyclopedic knowledge of fish dinners he has had across the length and breadth of the country led me to insist we film on the

Eastern Seaboard for one of my British TV series; it was while there that I finally realized that Maine lobsters are every bit as good as Cornish ones.

buying fish

My recipes are generally rather simple and require the excitement of truly fresh fish to make them shine. Buying the freshest fish is therefore essential. I worry that my recipes will not work as well if people only have the average fish counter at a supermarket to rely on. But even faced with a limited selection of fish, there's always going to be something good to buy. The cardinal rule is to be flexible. Most of my recipes can be made with lots of different fish and I have given alternatives for many recipes. Large john dory, for example, can be used instead of brill or turbot, and monkfish dishes can be made with swordfish. Rather than slavishly going for the fish in the recipe, choose the best-looking fish on the counter and use that. Go for the brightest eye, the most sparkling skin. Like wine-tasting, it's easier to make a judgment of quality by contrasting one fish with another.

look particularly for the following signs of quality:

- EYES: these should be clear and bright, not cloudy and sunken or blotched with red.
- SKIN: the skin should be shiny and vivid. Colors such as orange spots on plaice, the green and yellow flecks on cod, and the turquoise, green, and blue lines on mackerel should be bright and cheerful. Slime on fish is a good sign.
- FINS: these should be clearly defined and perky, not scraggy and broken.
- GILLS: the gills should be a startling, lustrous pink or red, moist, and a delight to the eye, not at all faded or brown.
- SMELL: fresh fish doesn't smell of fish, just of the sea. It should be appetizing—something you want to eat, not something the odor of which you hope will disappear when you cook it. It won't.

- FEEL: good-quality fish should be firm. Obviously some fish is softer than others, but all fish goes slack and feels flabby as it goes stale.

farmed fish

Farmed fish have one advantage over wild: Freshness can be perfectly controlled as the fish are kept alive until they are ordered. Otherwise, the quality is not quite as good as that of wild, mainly because the fish tend to be sold when they are too small and the flavor has not had a chance to develop. There are signs, however, that fish may be allowed to mature in the future, and as long as the fish are fed nothing to rid them of any of their flavor before they are dispatched, the quality can be excellent. Salmon are harvested in larger sizes, but there is a vast difference between the best and worst. If you can select your cut from a whole fish you will notice that the top-quality fish are much sleeker and firmer than the cheaper ones, which are stubby and quite often have truncated fins—an indication of overcrowding in the fish pens. When buying prepared fillets of salmon, look for firm flesh and leave the flabby stuff alone.

filleted fish

It's more difficult to tell the freshness of fish fillets because there are fewer indicators to go by. But, as with whole fish, fillets should look bright and shiny. The flesh should be white, pink, or off-white, depending on the species. Fillets that are going stale will have a yellow or—worse—brown tinge. Fresh fillets should be firm to the touch and should not smell.

A simple rule I follow when buying fillets is to ask myself if I would like to eat them raw, sliced and served as sashimi.

storing fish

Domestic refrigerators are not ideal for storing fish as they are set at about 41°F (5°C) and fish should be stored at 32°F (0°C). If possible, you should use the fish the day you buy it. If you must store it for a short time, put the fish in a shallow dish or tray, then wrap the container in plastic wrap and place it in the coldest part of the refrigerator.

thawing frozen fish and shellfish

Always thaw fish in the refrigerator, on plenty of paper towels or in a colander set in a bowl, so that it doesn't end up sitting in water into which it will leach out lots of its flavor.

buying crustaceans

Lobsters and crabs are sold either live or cooked. They are never sold dead and uncooked because the flesh deteriorates very quickly and becomes mushy and tasteless. Cooking stops this process. Live lobsters or crabs should be obviously alive, with clear signs of muscular activity, whether aggressive waving of the claws in crabs or snapping of the tail in lobsters. Claws, tails, and legs should not be dangling limply.

Whether cooked or raw, crustaceans should feel heavy for their size as this is an indication of good muscle quality. Compare the weights of two similarly sized lobsters or crabs by weighing them in each hand and opt for the heavier as it will have more meat.

It's hard to get consistent quality in cooked lobsters or crabs because you are dependent on your fishmonger as the cook. How much salt, if any, did he or she use? How long did he or she cook the crustaceans for? What was the quality like before cooking? It's really a question of sticking to a fishmonger whom you know and trust.

shrimp

Shrimp are sold either raw ("green") or cooked and can be bought whole with their heads still on or as "tails" (headless), either peeled or unpeeled. Shrimp tails are better value for money than whole shrimp, but whole shrimp are usually better quality. The shells preserve the flavor and, once removed, can be used to make nice stocks and flavored oils.

Shrimp are normally sorted by size and sold by the average number per pound (occasionally per kilo). If the fishmonger is offering 31 to 35 shrimp per pound they will be large enough for most purposes. The lower the number of shrimp per pound, the bigger the shrimp (which might then be called prawns) and the more expensive they will be.

With the exception of local catch, the majority of shrimp available will be frozen. "Fresh" shrimp will almost always have been frozen and then thawed at their destination. Shrimp freeze well, but do not travel well chilled, which is why they are usually boiled at sea if they are not to be frozen. Like lobsters, shrimp deteriorate after death and become soft and tasteless very quickly. Unless they are local, or I can get them still alive, I always prefer to buy frozen raw shrimp of the best quality as it gives me complete control.

Once the shrimp are thawed they deteriorate quickly. So when buying "fresh," make sure they feel firm and that the shells are taut, intact, and not dull-looking. Make sure, too, that they smell fresh—definitely not of ammonia—and avoid any that have signs of darkening or black spots around the head.

langoustines

These crustaceans, also known as lobsterettes, langostinos, Dublin Bay prawns, or scampi, are more like lobsters. Care should be taken if buying them raw because, like raw shrimp, they deteriorate rapidly (see above). When buying cooked langoustines, give the tails a flick; there should be some spring left in them, indicating the muscle was in good condition when the langoustine was cooked.

buying live shellfish

All uncooked shellfish, whether in two shells (bivalves) or one shell (univalves), should be alive.

The shells of bivalves, such as oysters, cockles, mussels, and clams, should be closed or should close when tapped or squeezed together. Broken shellfish and those that don't close should be discarded. It's advisable not to buy from a

batch where many of the shells are open because it's a sign that they have been out of the sea too long and won't taste fresh.

Univalves, such as whelks, periwinkles, and abalone, are alive if you can see the creature moving inside the shell, if the shell moves, or if there is foam on the shell opening.

Live shellfish that you buy from a fishmonger will have health certification. If you are gathering your own, be aware that they can present a health risk if taken from a polluted area. Shellfish taken from the seashore are safer than those found in estuaries and harbors because any pollution is likely to be diluted by the open sea, but whenever gathering your own shellfish it is advisable to ask for advice locally.

cleaning and storing shellfish

Wash shellfish in cold water to remove sand and mud, and scrape away any barnacles or weed. With mussels, just before cooking remove the threads that attach the mussel to the rocks. Mussels don't keep well once this has been removed.

Shellfish can be stored, covered with seaweed or a damp cloth, for a few days in the bottom of the refrigerator.

how much fish and shellfish to buy

As a rule of thumb, you will be able to eat slightly less than half the weight of any whole fish you buy. Lobsters, crabs, and shrimp will give you much less, about one-third of the weight you buy.

For whole fish, therefore, an 8½-oz (240-g) fish is about right for a first course; a 14- to 18-oz (400- to 500-g) fish will be generous for a main course. Good portion sizes of fillet are 4 oz (100 g) for a first course and 6 oz (175 g) for a main course.

The minimum size of lobster per person should be 1 lb 2 oz (500 g) for a whole one, 14 oz (400 g) for half a larger one. For crabs I would suggest l lb 2 oz (500 g) of whole crab per person.

useful equipment for fish cookery

• KNIVES – a large cook's knife with a 10-inch (25-cm) blade for chopping and cutting lobsters in half • A thin, flexible-bladed filleting knife that will allow you to feel both the fillet and bones while using • A small-bladed, 3-inch (7.5-cm) knife for opening raw clams, etc. • A very sharp, long-bladed knife for thinly slicing salmon, smoked salmon, and tuna

• A FISH POACHER – for poaching not only salmon, but other fish such as sea bass and trout, too. It can also double up as a steamer

• A DEEP-FAT FRYER – these are thermostatically controlled and are therefore safer to use than ordinary pans, and are essential for fish cookery

• A FISH SCALER – you can use a knife, or even a scallop shell, but this makes the job much easier

• A SLOTTED FISH TURNER

• A CONICAL STRAINER, LADLE, AND FINE SIEVE – vital for straining soups and stocks

• A MORTAR AND PESTLE – for making harissa and charmoula, for example

• KITCHEN SCISSORS – for cutting off fins

• A LOBSTER PICK

• FISH PLIERS or TWEEZERS – for pin boning

• PERIWINKLE PICKERS (very fine, short skewers or long pins) – for removing periwinkles and cockles from the shell

- LOBSTER CRACKERS – for lobsters and crabs
- A LARGE, HEAVY-BASED FRYING PAN – with a well-seasoned surface
- A PETAL STEAMER – for steaming fish and vegetables
- A FISH-SHAPED WIRE CLAMP – for grilling
- A PAIR OF LONG-HANDLED TONGS
- A CLEAVER AND MALLET – for portioning whole turbot
- A RIDGED CAST-IRON GRILL PAN
- A WOK OR DEEP CHEF'S PAN
- A LARGE, SHALLOW PAN WITH A WELL-FITTING LID – for steaming and braising
- A THERMOMETER
- A LARGE ROASTING PAN – for baking whole fish
- A FOOD PROCESSOR – for making light work of soups, mayonnaise, purées, and pastes
- CHEAP WOODEN CHOPSTICKS and a SUSHI MAT – for home-smoking fish
- A VERY LARGE POT – for cooking crabs, lobsters, and langoustines

a few handy pantry ingredients

- A bottle of Pernod or Ricard
- A dry, white vermouth such as Noilly Prat
- Some herb fennel, growing in the garden or in a pot
- Capers
- Vinegar – sherry, white, red, and balsamic
- Fennel seeds, crushed dried red pepper flakes, coriander seeds, cumin seeds, ground turmeric, paprika, cayenne pepper
- Thai fish sauce (*nam pla*)
- Saffron

- Good-quality anchovy fillets in olive oil
- A well-flavored extra-virgin olive oil
- Toasted sesame oil
- A block of tamarind pulp
- A bottle of dark soy sauce
- Good-quality, whole black olives
- Maldon sea salt flakes
- Some good-quality dried pasta
- A jar of sun-dried tomatoes in olive oil
- A few dried porcini mushrooms
- Sichuan peppercorns
- Chinese salted, fermented black beans
- Dried, fine rice noodles

a note about the recipes in this book

The recipes in this book are grouped under the following categories: Soups, Stews, and Mixed Seafood; Large Meaty Fish, Skate, and Eels; Large Round Fish; Small Round Fish; Flatfish; Crustaceans; Mollusks and other Seafood. Some of these need explaining. By small round fish I mean any fish under 1¼ lb (550 g), i.e. a fish that would feed one person. Large round fish are larger than 1¼ lb (550 g) and less than 11 lb (5 kg), i.e. fish that could be cooked whole, but will sometimes be filleted, and any fish larger than 11 lb (5 kg) that will always need to be filleted, being too large ever to cook whole. By large, meaty fish I mean fish such as tuna, shark, and swordfish, which will always be sold in steak or fillet form. Skate and eels also usually come ready-prepared.

chapters 1/4

4 techniques

techniques
chapter 1

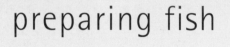

preparing fish

---

technique 1

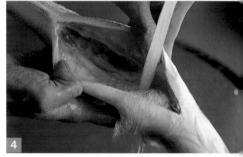

1 Work under cold running water or over several sheets of newspaper. Grip the fish by its tail and scrape it from the tail toward the head, working against the direction in which the scales lie, using a fish scaler or the blade of a blunt, thick-bladed knife.

2 Cut away the dorsal, pelvic, and anal fins using a strong pair of kitchen scissors.

3 Slit open the belly of the fish from the anal fin up to the head and pull out the guts.

4 With a small knife, cut away any remaining pieces of gut left behind in the cavity, then wash it out with plenty of cold water.

14

scaling and gutting small round fish for grilling

GRILLED WHOLE SEA BASS (for full recipe see page 163)

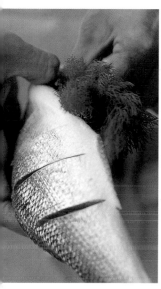

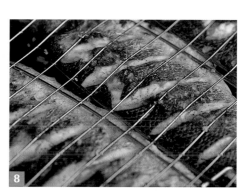

5 Slash the flesh of each fish four or five times down each side. Rub them with oil and season with a little salt and pepper.

6 Season the inside of the gut cavity, then push in a small bunch of herb fennel.

7 Put the fish into a wire clamp and close it up. Grill for 6 to 8 minutes on each side, sprinkling the fish with some Pernod just before turning.

8 When the fish are cooked through and the skin is crisp and golden, sprinkle them with a little more Pernod, then serve with some fennel mayonnaise (see page 224).

preparing small oily fish for broiling

SPLIT HERRINGS WITH SALSA (for full recipe see page 158)

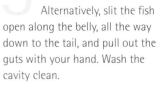

3 Alternatively, slit the fish open along the belly, all the way down to the tail, and pull out the guts with your hand. Wash the cavity clean.

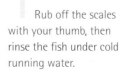

1 Rub off the scales with your thumb, then rinse the fish under cold running water.

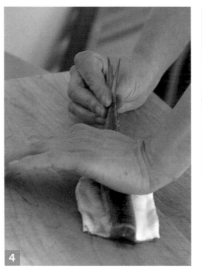

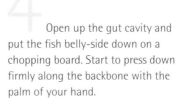

2 Cut off the head and discard. If you want to remove the guts without slitting the fish open, give the belly a gentle squeeze. Trap the exposed guts under the blade of a knife and drag them out.

4 Open up the gut cavity and put the fish belly-side down on a chopping board. Start to press down firmly along the backbone with the palm of your hand.

5 Continue pressing firmly all along the backbone until the fish is completely flat.

6 Turn the fish over and pull away the backbone, snipping it off at the tail end with scissors. Remove any small bones left behind in the fillet using fish pliers or tweezers. Season inside and out, then push back into shape.

7 Cut the tomatoes into small dice. Mince the garlic; roughly chop the parsley; and rinse the capers. Mix all the ingredients together in a bowl with some seasoning.

8 Broil the fish, close to the heat, for 2 minutes on each side. Serve with a large spoonful of the salsa alongside.

skinning and pan-frying a whole flatfish

DOVER SOLE À LA MEUNIÈRE (for full recipe see page 181)

1 Using a pair of kitchen scissors, cut away the frills from either side of the fish, close to the edge of the flesh. Snip off all the other little fins.

2 Make a shallow cut through the skin across the tail end of the fish with a sharp knife. Push the tip of the knife under the skin to release a small flap that you can get hold of.

3 Dip the fingers of your left hand in some salt and grab hold of the tail. With your other hand, take hold of the skin using a dish towel and, in one swift, sharp movement, pull the skin away along the entire length of the fish. Repeat on the other side.

4 Dip the skinned fish into some flour that has been seasoned with salt and pepper, making sure that it becomes well coated on both sides.

5 Lift up the fish and pat it on either side to remove the excess flour.

making a *beurre noisette*

Discard the frying oil from the pan and wipe it clean. For each fish add 4 teaspoons (20 g) unsalted butter and let it melt over a moderate heat (1). When the butter starts to turn light brown and smell nutty (2), add 1 teaspoon of lemon juice (3) and ½ tablespoon of chopped parsley. Immediately remove from the heat and quickly pour the butter over the fish.

For each fish, heat 1 tablespoon of canola oil in a large, well-seasoned or nonstick frying pan. Add the fish, lower the heat slightly, and add ½ tablespoon (7 g) unsalted butter in pieces.

Fry for 4 to 5 minutes over a moderate heat until richly golden on the underside. Carefully turn the fish over and cook for 4 to 5 minutes longer.

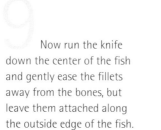

Lift the fish onto a board. Working down first one side of the fish and then the other, trap the lateral bones, which run all around the outside edge of the fish and into the fillets, with a thin-bladed, flexible knife, and drag them away.

Now run the knife down the center of the fish and gently ease the fillets away from the bones, but leave them attached along the outside edge of the fish.

Take hold of the bones at the head end and carefully "unzip" the fish. The bones will come away cleanly and the fillets will fall back into place.

Transfer the fish to a warmed serving plate and slightly part the fillets at what was the head end so that you can just see the underlying fillets. Spoon some *beurre noisette* over the fish and serve.

filleting a large round fish and broiling thick fish fillets

COD WITH RED WINE SAUCE (for full recipe see page 126)

FILLETING
A LARGE
ROUND FISH
AND BROILING
THICK FISH
FILLETS

1 Scale the fish. Remove the head by cutting diagonally just behind the gills on both sides from under the pelvic fin around to the top of the head. This will retain all the fillet.

2 Starting at the head end, cut through the skin slightly to one side of the backbone along the whole length of the fish, using a sharp, thin-bladed, flexible knife.

3 Return to the head end and gradually cut the fillet away from the bones, keeping the blade as close to the bones as you can. When you reach the rib cage, if the bones are thick, continue to cut close to them until the fillet comes free. However, if the bones are fine, cut through them and remove them from the fillet with fish pliers or tweezers afterward.

4 As you near the tail end, get the whole blade of the knife under the fillet. Rest the other hand on top of the fish and cut the remainder away in one clean sweep. Turn the fish over and repeat on the other side.

5 Remove the thick bones from the fillets with fish pliers or tweezers.

6 Trim up the edges of each fillet and cut away the thinnest part of the belly flap. Cut the rest of the fillet across into portion-sized pieces weighing 6 to 8 oz (175 to 225 g).

7 For the sauce, sauté some finely diced vegetables and spices in butter over a high heat until well browned.

8 Add some red wine, stock, sugar, and a pinch of salt, and simmer until well reduced and concentrated in flavor.

9 Strain the sauce through a fine sieve into a clean pan. Bring it back to a simmer, then whisk in a little *beurre manié* to thicken. Adjust the seasoning, if necessary.

10 Brush each portion of cod with melted butter and season on both sides with salt and pepper. Broil, skin-side up, about 4 inches (10 cm) from the heat, for 8 minutes. Serve on some cooked lentilles de Puy, with a little sauce spooned around.

filleting small round fish for poaching

MACKEREL WITH MINT AND BUTTER SAUCE (for full recipe see page 158)

TWO WAYS OF
FILLETING
SMALL ROUND
FISH

1 With the back of the fish facing you, make a cut behind the back of the head, down to the backbone, using a sharp, thin-bladed, flexible knife.

2 With the knife still in place, turn it toward the tail and start to cut away the fillet. As soon as the whole blade of the knife is underneath the fillet, put your other hand flat on top of the fish and cut it away in one clean sweep, keeping the knife as close to the bones and as flat as possible.

3 Lift off the fillet, then turn the fish over and repeat the process.

4 Make a hollandaise-style sauce: put the egg yolks, water, and a sherry vinegar reduction into a large heatproof bowl. Rest it over a pan of simmering water and whisk vigorously until pale and voluminous. Remove the bowl from the pan and whisk in some clarified butter, lemon juice, seasoning, and chopped mint.

5 Poach the fillets in simmering, lightly salted water for 3 minutes, turning them over halfway through. Then lift them out and let the excess water drain off. Serve with the warm butter sauce.

filleting small round fish for stuffing

HERRING RECHEADO (for full recipe see page 160)

1 Remove the head of the fish. Start to cut away the top fillet until you can get the whole blade of the knife underneath it. Rest a hand on top of the fish and cut the fillet away from the bones until you are about 1 inch (2.5 cm) away from the tail.

2 Turn the fish over and repeat on the other side.

3 Pull back the top fillet and snip out the backbone close to the tail with scissors. The fillets will still be attached by the tail.

4 Spread the cut face of one fillet with a little masala paste, then put the fish back into shape.

5 Tie the fish in two places with string. Grill or broil for 3 minutes on each side.

preparing flatfish for broiling

BROILED, SCORED PLAICE WITH ROASTED RED PEPPER

(for full recipe see page 178)

1   Remove the lateral bones that run through the frills and part way into the flesh of the fish by cutting very close to the underlying fillet with scissors.

2   This will remove the frills and about ½ inch (1 cm) of the adjacent flesh.

3   Score the fish on both sides like the veins of a leaf, using a sharp knife.

4   Broil or roast a red bell pepper until the skin is black and blistered all over. Let cool, then break in half and remove and discard the stem and seeds. Peel off the skin and cut the flesh into very small dice.

5   Mix the roasted red pepper with chile pepper, garlic, oregano, olive oil, lemon juice, salt, and pepper. Pour this over the fish and work it into the cuts with your fingers. Leave for 1 hour. Broil the fish, dark-side up, 4 to 6 inches (10 to 15 cm) from the heat for 7 to 8 minutes.

preparing flatfish for deep-frying

GOUJONS OF LEMON SOLE (for full recipe see page 180)

1 To fillet the fish, cut around the back of the head, down to the backbone, using a sharp, thin-bladed, flexible knife. Then make a cut down the center of the fish, from head to tail.

2 Starting at the head, slide the knife under one fillet and carefully cut it away, keeping the blade as flat and as close to the bones as possible. Remove the adjacent fillet, then turn the fish over and repeat.

3 Lay the fillet skin-side down, with the narrowest end facing you. Hold the tip of the skin with your fingers and, angling the blade of the knife down toward the skin and working it away from you, start to cut between the flesh and the skin. Firmly take hold of the skin and continue to work away from you, sawing the knife from side to side, keeping the blade close against the skin until the fillet is released.

4 Trim the frills away from the edge of the skinless fillet to give it a neat finish.

5 Slice the fillets diagonally into goujons about the thickness of your little finger.

6 Bread the goujons, then drop them one at a time into hot oil. Fry in small batches until crisp and golden.

CUTTING
LARGE
FLATFISH AND
ROUND FISH
INTO STEAKS

cutting large flatfish into steaks

TRONÇONS OF TURBOT WITH SAUCE VIERGE

(for full recipe see page 182)

1 Cut away the frills of the fish with scissors, then cut close around the back of the head, down to the backbone, so that you retain as much of the fillet as you can. Cut through the backbone using a cleaver and mallet, then cut away the head.

2 Cut through the flesh along the backbone of the fish, down to the bone, with a sharp knife. Cut through the bone with the cleaver and mallet, then finish cutting the fish in half with the knife.

3 Cut each half into portion-sized tronçons, cutting through the backbone when necessary with the cleaver and mallet.

cutting large round fish into steaks

Scale the fish and trim off the fins with scissors (1). Rinse out the cavity with plenty of cold water (2). Cut the fish across, through the backbone, into steaks about 1½ inches (4 cm) thick, using a large, sharp knife (3).

4 For the sauce vierge, put the olive oil, lemon juice, tomato, black olives, anchovies, and garlic into a small pan. Warm through just before serving.

5 Mix together some olive oil, chopped rosemary, thyme, and bay leaf, crushed fennel seeds and peppercorns, and some sea salt flakes in a small roasting pan. Add the tronçons of turbot and turn them once or twice to coat.

6 Put the tronçons dark-side down into a smoking-hot ovenproof frying pan and sear until the skin has taken on a good color. Turn them over, transfer the pan to the oven, and roast for 8 to 10 minutes. Add chopped parsley and seasoning to the sauce vierge. Lift the fish onto warmed plates and spoon some of the sauce around.

cutting escalopes from a salmon fillet

ESCALOPES OF SALMON WITH SORREL SAUCE (for full recipe see page 141)

PREPARING
DIFFERENT
CUTS FROM A
WHOLE
SALMON

1 Fillet the salmon as described for cod on page 20. Put the fillet skin-side down on a board with the narrowest (tail) end pointing toward you. Angle the blade of the knife down toward the skin and start to cut between the skin and the flesh, keeping the blade as close to the skin as you can. When the released fillet starts to get in the way, fold it back, take a firm hold of the skin, and continue.

2 Remove the pin bones, which lie hidden in the flesh down the center of the fillet; run your thumb along the line of bones in the opposite direction to which they are lying—they will then poke out of the flesh. Pull them out with fish pliers or tweezers, or by trapping them between the point of a small, sharp knife and your thumb.

3 Put the fillet skinned-side down on a board. Hold a long, thin-bladed knife at a 45-degree angle and cut the salmon into large slices about ¼ inch (5 mm) thick—these are called escalopes or scallops.

4 Brush the escalopes with oil and season them, then broil, 1 to 2 inches (2.5 to 5 cm) from the heat, for 30 seconds, until only just firm. Arrange on top of the sorrel sauce and garnish with more chopped sorrel.

preparing a pavé of salmon

PAVÉ OF SALMON

(for full recipe see page 142)

1 Put the fillet skinned-side down on a board. Remove the thinnest part of the belly flap, then neaten up the edges of the fillet with a sharp knife. Now cut the fillet across into neat rectangular pieces known as pavés (slabs), each weighing about 6 oz (175 g).

2 Lightly oil and season the pavés, then put them skinned-side down on a smoking-hot, ridged cast-iron grill pan. Cook over a high heat, pressing them down gently now and then with a metal spatula, until they have taken on rich golden bar marks underneath.

3 Sprinkle some wine over the pavés and let them cook for a few more seconds, then turn them.

4 Cook on the other side for just 30 seconds or so, then remove the grill pan from the heat and let the pavés continue cooking in the residual heat of the pan for 30 seconds. The salmon will remain quite rare inside. Serve on top of the roasted vegetables with the warm red wine vinegar and fennel seed *sauce vierge*.

filleting thin-bodied fish for broiling

JOHN DORY WITH LEEKS (for full recipe see page 169)

PREPARING
THIN-BODIED
AND
ELONGATED
FISH FOR
BROILING AND
PAN-GRILLING

1 Make a cut around the back of the head and under the sharp, bony gill flaps using a sharp, thin-bladed, flexible knife.

2 Snip off all the spiny fins with strong scissors.

3 Lay the fish on a chopping board and run the tip of the knife vertically all around the outside edge of the fish, close to the raised ridge of sharp little spines.

4 Flatten the blade of the knife slightly and start to cut the fillet away from the underlying bones, keeping the blade of the knife as close to them as you can. The fillet from this side of the fish will come away in one piece. Turn the fish over and repeat on the other side.

5 Neaten up each fillet by cutting away the belly flap, then cut each fillet diagonally across into two similar-sized pieces. Brush with melted butter, season, and broil, skin-side up, for about 4 minutes.

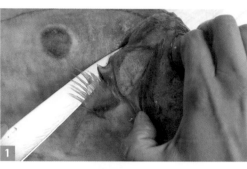

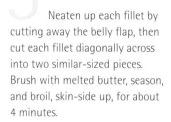

to assemble the dish

Pan-grill the blanched leeks until nicely marked on both sides. Arrange them in the center of each plate (1) and put the john dory fillets on top (2). Add the halved soft-boiled eggs and drizzle some vinaigrette over (3). Scatter on some Parmesan shavings and serve.

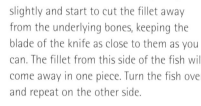

preparing elongated fish for pan-grilling

SALAD OF PAN-GRILLED GARFISH (for full recipe see page 167)

1　Don't bother to gut small fish. Cut around the back of the head with a sharp, thin-bladed, flexible knife.

2　Turn the blade of the knife toward the tail and start to cut away the fillet, keeping the blade as flat against the bones as you can.

3　As soon as the whole blade of the knife is under the fillet, rest your other hand on top of the fish and cut the fillet away in one clean sweep, down toward the tail. Turn the fish over and repeat on the other side.

4　Make a marinade of olive oil, lemon juice, thyme, lightly crushed fennel seeds, dried red pepper flakes, and some seasoning.

5　Brush some of the marinade over both sides of each fillet. Let marinate for 5 minutes so the flavors can permeate the fish a little.

6　Heat a flat or ridged cast-iron grill pan until smoking hot. Add the garfish fillets and cook them for 1 to 1½ minutes on each side. Transfer them to a plate to stop them cooking any further.

7　Arrange the fish fillets and strips of sun-dried tomato in among some mixed baby salad leaves. Deglaze the pan with the leftover marinade and a little sherry vinegar. Spoon this sauce over the salad and around the outside edge of the plate.

SPECIAL
TECHNIQUES
FOR SMALL
ROUND FISH

a special technique for preparing gurnard

PAN-FRIED GURNARD WITH SAGE AND GARLIC (for full recipe see page 175)

2 Turn the blade of the knife horizontally toward the tail and take the dorsal fin in the other hand.

4 Cut through the backbone where it joins the back of the head, but not all the way through the fish.

1 Place the fish belly-side down on a chopping board. Make a shallow, vertical cut just behind the head of the gurnard, where the spines of the dorsal fin begin.

3 Slice just under the skin through the bones of the dorsal fin, right the way along the entire length of the fish, and lift them away.

5 Push your thumbs underneath the skin on either side of the head and pull it away slightly.

preparing whiting for deep-frying whole

MERLAN FRIT EN COLÈRE (for full recipe see page 166)

2 Push a toothpick up through the soft part of its under-mouth, through the tail, and out through the top of the head. Season the fish inside and out with salt and pepper.

1 Scale, gut, and trim the whiting. Twist the fish into a circle so that the tail goes into its mouth.

3 Coat the fish well on all sides with flour seasoned with salt and pepper, then tap off the excess.

6 Take hold of the head in one hand and the body of the fish in the other, and pull the head down toward the belly.

7 As soon as the head becomes free, use it to help pull away the skin from the body of the fish

8 Pull the skin off the whole fish and right over the tail.

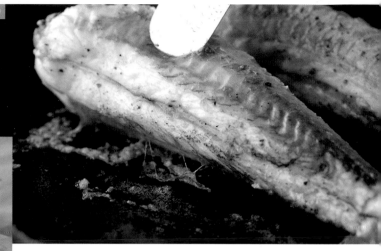

9 Pan-fry the prepared fish in a little oil and unsalted butter until golden. Remove to a plate and wipe the pan clean. Melt the remaining butter, add a little garlic and the whole sage leaves, and cook gently for 30 seconds. Add some lemon juice and seasoning, then pour this over the fish.

4 Dip the floured fish in beaten egg, making sure that it is well covered.

5 Finally, coat the fish in fresh white breadcrumbs, pressing them on well to make sure that it is covered with a thick, even coating.

6 Deep-fry the fish, one at a time, at 325°F (160°C) for about 5 minutes until crisp, golden, and cooked through.

skinning a whole skate and roasting the wings

ROASTED SKATE WINGS (for full recipe see page 123)

SKINNING A
WHOLE SKATE,
REMOVING
THE CHEEKS,
AND
ROASTING THE
WINGS

1 Put the skate on a large chopping board. Using a sharp, thin-bladed, flexible knife, make a cut 1 inch (2.5 cm) behind the nose, all the way through the fish. Cut around both sides of the head and then down either side of the backbone, to the tail. Separate the head from the backbone and tail, and set aside. Discard the rest.

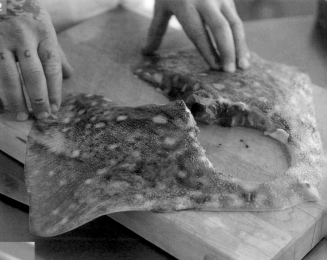

2 Separate the two wings where they are joined at the nose. Work with them one at a time.

3 Push the tip of the knife under the skin at what was the nose end to release a large flap that you can get hold of. Turn the wing over and release a flap on the other side.

4 Grab hold of the flap of skin with fish pliers and start to tear it away from the surface of the wing.

5 Once you have released a small amount, hold the wing down with a dish towel and sharply tear the skin away completely, using the pliers. Turn the wing over and remove the skin from the other side. Repeat with the second wing.

6 Trim about 1 inch (2.5 cm) away from the thinnest edge of each wing.

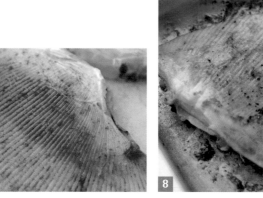

7 Dry the skate wings on paper towels, then sprinkle them on both sides with some paprika and coarsely crushed black pepper.

8 Lightly brown the wings in some butter in a small roasting pan on top of the stove. Season with salt, then transfer to the oven to roast for 10 minutes.

9 Lift the roasted skate wings onto the plated chile beans. Deglaze the roasting pan on top of the stove by adding a little sherry vinegar and chicken stock, and stirring with a wooden spoon to release all the juices that have baked onto the bottom of the pan.

10 Strain the juices through a fine sieve into a clean pan. Season to taste, then spoon the juices over the skate wings.

removing skate cheeks

Lay the head dark-side down on a board and pull back the jaw to open up the mouth (1). Slice diagonally under the jaw down toward the nose (2) and remove the mouth piece, which will have the skate cheeks attached (3). Cut around the spherical cheek meats with the tip of a small, sharp knife and remove (4). These will still have a small piece of bone in the very center, which you can remove if desired (5), although it is easier to get it out once the cheeks have been cooked.

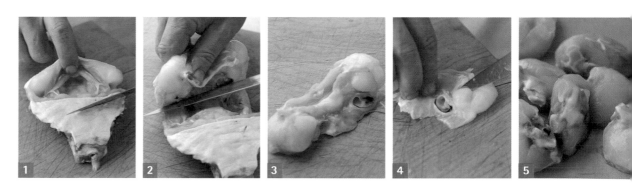

skinning freshwater eel for stir-frying

STIR-FRIED EEL (for full recipe see page 125)

1   Cut through the skin around the back of the head with a small, sharp knife.

2   Using fish pliers, pull away about 1 inch (2.5 cm) of skin from all the way around the head.

3   Hang the eel up by the head, with a meat hook or a piece of string, from something very secure and with plenty of room in which to work. Using a second pair of pliers, grab hold of some skin on either side of the eel and start to pull it away.

4   As soon as the skin starts to come away more cleanly, firmly and steadily pull it down toward the tail. As you near the tail it will start to get a little harder, but just give it a vigorous final tug and it will come away completely, over the tail.

5   To fillet the eel, lay it on a chopping board and cut off the head. Using a sharp, thin-bladed, flexible knife, make a shallow cut along the backbone of the fish, just above the line of bones. Start to cut away the fillet, keeping the blade of the knife as close to the bones as you can.

6   As soon as you can get the whole blade of the knife under the fillet, rest your other hand on top of the fish and cut the fillet away in one clean sweep, down toward the tail. Turn the eel over and repeat on the other side.

7 Cut the eel fillet diagonally into pieces that are 1 inch (2.5 cm) wide.

8 Put the pieces of eel into a bowl and add the cornstarch and a pinch of salt. Toss together so that the eel is well coated in the cornstarch.

9 Heat a wok over a high heat until smoking hot. Add the sesame oil, garlic, ginger, and chile pepper, and stir-fry for a few seconds.

10 Add the black bean paste, quickly followed by the eel pieces. Stir-fry for 1 minute, then add the rice wine, soy sauce, and water. Stir-fry for 2 minutes until the eel is cooked through.

11 Add the green onions and stir-fry for 1 minute, then tip out onto a warmed serving dish. Serve with some steamed rice.

techniques
chapter 2

cooking fish

technique 19

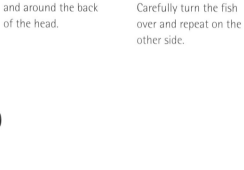

1 Make a court-bouillon in a fish poacher. Add the salmon. Bring back to a gentle simmer, then poach for 16 to 18 minutes. Lift out the salmon on the rack, rest it on the side of the pan, and let the excess liquid drain away.

2 Lift the fish onto a serving plate. Make a shallow cut through the skin along the backbone and around the back of the head.

3 Starting at the head end, peel back the skin and remove it. Carefully turn the fish over and repeat on the other side.

technique 20

1 Put some milk, or a mixture of milk and water, into a large, shallow pan and add some bay leaves, onion, and black peppercorns.

2 Bring to a boil, then add the smoked haddock or smoked cod fillets and bring back to a gentle simmer.

poaching whole fish in a court-bouillon

POACHED SALMON (for full recipe see page 144)

4 To serve, run a small knife down the length of the fish between the two fillets. Gently ease them apart and away from the bones.

5 Lift off the fillets in portion-sized pieces, then turn the fish over and repeat. Serve with mayonnaise, cucumber salad, and new potatoes.

poaching fish fillets in milk

3 Poach the fish for 3 to 4 minutes until it is firm to the touch and the flesh has turned opaque, then remove. If serving in one piece, peel back the skin and discard. Otherwise, leave on a plate until cool enough to handle, then break into large flakes, discarding the skin and bones.

poaching fish in oil

TWO WAYS OF
POACHING
FISH IN OIL

1 Fillet the fish as described on page 20, then skin the fillets as described on page 28. Cover both sides of the fish in a thick layer of salt. Leave for 10 minutes, then rinse well and dry on paper towels.

2 Prepare a bed of aromatic vegetables on which to put the fish: gently cook some sliced onion and garlic in olive oil until very soft but not colored, then add some bay leaves, lemon slices, and thyme.

3 Lay the fish fillets in a single layer on top of the vegetables.

4 Pour some inexpensive olive oil over the fish so it is completely covered. Place the pan over a low heat and slowly bring the temperature of the oil up to 212°F (100°C)—this will take about 15 minutes. Remove the pan from the heat and let the fish cool in the oil. Then remove the fillets, drain off the excess oil, and use to make *tonno con fagioli* on page 118, for example.

poaching fish in oil at low temperature

HALIBUT POACHED IN OLIVE OIL (for full recipe see page 183)

Pour a thin layer of inexpensive olive oil into a shallow pan just large enough to hold the fish in a single layer. Add the pieces of seasoned fish to the pan and add enough oil just to cover them.

Place the pan over a low heat and let it heat very slowly until it reaches 130° to 140°F (55° to 60°C). Agitate the fish very gently with a metal spatula now and then so that the oil and the fish heat evenly.

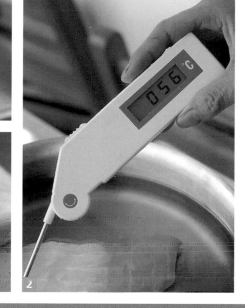

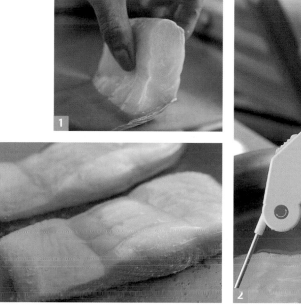

When the oil reaches temperature, poach the fish for 15 minutes, taking the pan on and off the heat when necessary to maintain the correct temperature.

When the fish is cooked it will be firm and opaque and will have a meltingly tender texture.

braising a whole large flatfish

MYRTLE'S TURBOT (for full recipe see page 182)

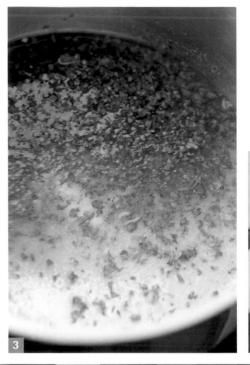

1 Cut through the dark skin, all the way around the fish, close to the frill-like fins. This will make it easy to remove before serving and prevent it from splitting during cooking.

2 Season the fish lightly and place it in a large roasting pan with just enough water to prevent it from sticking—about 2½ cups (600 ml). Braise, uncovered, in a hot oven for about 30 minutes.

3 Prepare a sauce with some melted butter and chopped fines herbes, to which you can add the reduced cooking juices when the fish is done.

4 Transfer the fish to a warmed serving dish and carefully remove the top skin. Reduce the remaining cooking juices to a few tablespoons, then add to the pan of herb butter.

5 Pour the sauce all over the fish and take it to the table to serve.

6 Remove portion-sized pieces of the top fillets by sliding a metal spatula under and lifting them off the bones.

7 Lift off the bones to give you access to the two bottom fillets.

braising fish fillets

BRAISED SEA TROUT (for full recipe see page 149)

BRAISING
FISH FILLETS

1 Melt a generous amount of butter in a shallow pan large enough to hold the fish fillets in a single layer. Add some sliced carrots, celery, and leeks.

2 Stir the vegetables well, then cover tightly and "sweat" (cook gently in their own steam) over a medium heat for about 3 minutes, until beginning to soften. Then uncover and add some dry white wine.

3 Next, add some chicken stock and bring to a gentle simmer.

4 Cook the vegetables gently in the uncovered pan until almost all the liquid has evaporated but the vegetables are still moist. This makes a well-flavored base, or "fondue," on which to rest the fish.

5 Lay the fish fillets skinned-side down on top of the "fondue" and sprinkle with some seasoning and finely shredded basil leaves. Cover with the lid and simmer gently for 8 to 10 minutes, until the fish is just cooked through.

6 Carefully lift the fillets off the "fondue" with a metal spatula and put them on warmed serving plates.

7 The fish will have released some liquid back into the vegetables, so increase the heat and simmer rapidly until it has reduced once more and the sauce is glistening. Add some more butter and shake the pan until it has amalgamated with the vegetables. Season to taste with a little lemon juice, salt, and pepper, then spoon this over the fish and serve.

TWO WAYS OF
STEAMING
WHOLE FISH

cooking fish in a steamer

STEAMED GRAY MULLET (for full recipe see page 171)

1   Pour about 1 inch (2.5 cm) of water into the bottom of a shallow pan with a well-fitting lid. Put a basket steamer into the pan and bring the water to a boil, then lay the prepared fish on the steamer.

2   Sprinkle the fish with some julienned fresh ginger. Cover with the lid, reduce the heat to medium, and steam for 10 to 12 minutes.

3   Carefully lift the fish off the steamer onto warmed plates and scatter on some sliced green onions. Make a sauce with some of the steaming juices and some soy sauce, and pour it over the fish.

4   Heat some sesame oil in a small pan. Add some thinly sliced garlic and let sizzle for a few seconds, then pour this over the fish.

steaming fish over seaweed

BLACK BREAM STEAMED OVER SEAWEED (for full recipe see page 164)

1 Spread some washed fresh edible seaweed over the bottom of a large, shallow pan with a well-fitting lid.

2 Add about 1¼ cups (300 ml) water, put the prepared and seasoned fish on top, and cover with the lid.

3 For the sauce, sweat some sliced fennel, onion, and garlic in butter until soft. Add the stock, white wine, and seasoning, and simmer gently until the liquid has evaporated and the vegetables are very tender. Cool slightly, then scrape into a blender and add the Pernod, lemon juice, and egg yolks. Blend until smooth.

4 With the machine still running, gradually add melted butter to make a smooth hollandaise-like sauce.

5 Pour the sauce into a bowl and add some chopped herb fennel and seasoning to taste. Keep warm.

6 Place the pan of fish over a high heat. When steam starts to escape from under the lid, lower the heat and steam for 5 minutes. Take the uncovered pan to the table to serve, if desired, so that everyone can appreciate the aroma when the lid is lifted.

roasting whole large fish in the oven

BAKED SEA BASS WITH ROASTED RED PEPPERS (for full recipe see page 148)

1 Cut five or six shallow, diagonal slashes along the length of the prepared fish, first in one direction and then in the other so that it becomes marked with a series of crosses.

2 Turn the fish over and repeat on the other side. This will help the heat to penetrate to the center of the fish more quickly.

3 Arrange the vegetables over the bottom of a large roasting pan and bake for 30 minutes until par-cooked.

4 Put the fish on top of the vegetables. Sprinkle it with oil, sea salt, and pepper and rub these well into the slashes. Return to the oven and roast for 35 minutes, until the fish is cooked through to the backbone. The temperature next to the bone should be about 120°F (50°C).

gently cooking fish fillets in the oven

TETSUYA WAKUDA'S CONFIT OF SALMON (for full recipe see page 144)

Cut a thick piece of skinned salmon fillet across into four pieces, each 2½ to 3½ oz (65 to 90 g). Turn them in a marinade of grapeseed and olive oils, ground coriander, white pepper, garlic, thyme, and basil, and refrigerate for 2 to 3 hours.

Lift the pieces of fish into a shallow roasting pan sprinkled with some finely diced vegetables—these prevent the fish from coming into contact with the hot pan.

Bake the fish in a very cool oven—225°F (110°C)—for 10 minutes. It will cook very gently so that it retains its bright orange, almost raw-looking color and will only get lukewarm, but will be meltingly tender.

baking fish in a pastry casing

SALMON EN CROÛTE (for full recipe see pages 140–1)

1 Prepare two even-sized, thick pieces of skinned salmon fillet (see page 28). Spread the inner face of one fillet with the flavored butter and lay the second fillet on top.

2 Put a sheet of puff pastry on a greased baking sheet and place the salmon in the center. Brush a wide band of beaten egg around the salmon.

3 Roll out a second piece of puff pastry into a rectangle roughly 2 inches (5 cm) larger than the first one, and lift it on top of the salmon.

4 Press the pastry tightly around the outside of the salmon, taking care not to trap in too much air or stretch the pastry—this might cause the pastry to shrink and the parcel to pop open during cooking. Press the edges of the pastry together very firmly.

5 Neatly trim the edges of the pastry and mark all the way around with a fork—this will help ensure an even better seal. Decorate the top of the pastry with "scales" made with an overturned teaspoon. Chill for 1 hour, then brush with egg and bake at 400°F (200°C) for 35 to 40 minutes. Serve hot, cut into slices.

baking fish in a salt casing

SEA BASS BAKED IN A SALT CRUST (for full recipe see page 150)

1 Mix about 4 lb (1.75 kg) of cooking salt with 2 egg whites. The mixture will look very much like wet sand.

2 Spread a thick layer of the salt mixture over the bottom of a shallow baking dish or pan and put the fish on top.

3 Completely cover the fish with the remaining salt mixture, making sure that there are no gaps. Don't worry if the tails are still exposed. Bake the fish in a hot oven—400°F (200°C)—for 20 minutes.

4 Remove the fish from the oven and crack the top of the salt crust with the back of a large knife. Lift away the crust so that you can carefully lift out the fish.

5 Put the fish on a serving plate. Make a shallow cut through the skin along the backbone and behind the head of the fish.

6 Pull the skin away from the top of the fish and lift off the two fillets. Turn the fish over and repeat on the other side. Serve with the lemon sauce and potato confit.

baking whole fish in foil

WHOLE SALMON BAKED IN FOIL WITH TARRAGON

(for full recipe see page 140)

1 Put a prepared salmon into the center of a large sheet of foil that has been brushed with lots of melted butter.

2 Bring the edges of the foil up around the sides of the fish and scrunch them together at either end to form a canoe-shaped parcel. Carefully lift the parcel onto a large baking sheet.

3 Pour a mixture of melted butter, tarragon, white wine, lemon juice, and seasoning into the cavity of the fish and over the top. Bring the sides of the foil parcel together over the top of the fish and seal really well to make a loose but watertight parcel. Bake in a hot oven—425°F (220°C)—for about 30 minutes.

4 Remove the fish from the oven and open up the parcel. Carefully lift onto a serving plate and serve as described on pages 38 to 39 (technique 19).

baking fish fillets "en papillote"

HAKE EN PAPILLOTE

(for full recipe see page 135)

1 Cut out four 15-inch (38-cm) squares of parchment paper and foil. Put the foil squares on top of the paper ones and brush the centers with olive oil. Put three pieces of oven-roasted tomato slightly off-center on each one, sprinkle with basil, and top with a piece of seasoned hake.

2 Bring the other side of the square over the fish so that all the edges meet. Starting at one end of the opening, fold over about ½ inch (1 cm) of the edge, doing about 1½ inches (4 cm) at a time. Work your way all around the edge to make a half-moon-shaped parcel. Then fold all around again to make an even tighter seam.

3 Give the folded edge a good bash with a rolling pin. Put the parcels on a baking sheet and bake in a very hot oven—475°F (240°C)—for 15 minutes.

4 As the fish cooks, the steaming juices will make the tightly sealed parcels puff up. Remove them from the oven, quickly transfer them to a warmed serving dish, and take them to the table.

5 Slit open the parcels with the tip of a sharp knife.

6 Pull back the paper and foil from the baked fish.

7 Lift the fish and tomatoes onto warmed plates. Pour the cooking juices from the parcel over the fish. Spoon a little tapenade around the fish and serve.

making a fish stew

CACCIUCCO (for full recipe see page 102)

1 Prepare and fillet the fish (see pages 22 and 30). Cut the fillets across into pieces 1½ inches (4 cm) wide. Clean the squid, reserving the ink sac (see page 92, steps 1 to 6). Remove the meat from the cooked lobster, reserving the shell (see page 76). Cut the lobster meat into small chunks.

2 Make a well-flavored stock for the base of the stew: sauté some minced onion, carrot, and celery in olive oil until lightly browned. Add the red wine and lobster shell, and boil vigorously for 3 to 4 minutes.

3 Add some chopped tomatoes, fresh bay leaves, hot red chile peppers, and water, and bring back to a boil.

4 Put the squid ink sac into a small dish with a little water and mash with a teaspoon to release all the ink.

5 Add the ink to the pan, then let the stock simmer for 45 minutes.

6 Strain the stock through a fine sieve into another pan, pressing down with the back of a ladle to release as much liquid as possible. If necessary, boil rapidly to concentrate the flavor, until the stock is reduced to about 5 cups (1.2 liters).

7 Slice the body pouch of the squid into rings. Heat some olive oil in a heavy casserole in which you can finish the stew. Add the squid along with some garlic and whole sage leaves, and fry quickly until lightly golden. Lift onto a plate. Cook some prepared mussels with a little wine or water in a large, covered pan until just opened (see page 88, steps 1 to 4). Tip into a colander set in a bowl to reserve the cooking liquid.

8 Pour the stock and mussel liquid into the casserole and bring to a boil. Add the pieces of fish and simmer for 2 minutes.

9 Add the lobster meat, mussels, and squid, and simmer for 1 minute until heated through. Put 2 slices of olive-oil-baked ciabatta into the bottom of each large soup plate, ladle in the stew, and serve.

deep-frying small fry

DEEP-FRIED WHITEBAIT WITH LEMON AND PERSILLADE

(for full recipe see page 166)

(for full recipe see page 166)

DIFFERENT
WAYS WITH
SMALL FRY

1 Rinse the whitebait, then drain in a colander, shaking well. Dry on paper towels. Tip into a bowl of flour seasoned with cayenne pepper and salt.

2 Toss the whitebait in the flour until they are all well coated. Drop a large handful of fish into the frying basket and shake off the excess flour.

3 Lower the basket of whitebait into a pan of hot oil and fry for 2 to 3 minutes, until crisp and golden.

4 Remove the basket from the oil and drain the fish briefly on paper towels. Repeat. Tip them onto a warmed serving dish, sprinkle with the persillade, and serve with lemon wedges.

2

broiling small fish

BROILED SMELTS   (for full recipe see page 160)

Thread the prepared smelts onto bamboo skewers that have been soaked in cold water for about 1 hour. Lay them on a lightly oiled baking sheet.

Sprinkle them with olive oil, salt, and pepper, then broil close to the heat for 2 minutes until cooked through.

Lift the fish onto warmed plates and sprinkle with a mixture of minced lemon zest, rosemary, parsley, garlic, green olives, and capers. Drizzle a little olive oil around the plate and serve.

removing bones from small whole fish such as anchovies

Pinch the head between your thumb and forefinger and pull it off, taking the guts with it. Pinch along the top edge of the fish and pull out the backbone. The flesh is so soft it will come away easily. Open the double fillets out flat and proceed with the recipe. (For instructions on marinating anchovies in chile, lemon, and garlic, see full recipe on page 161.)

making fish quenelles

POACHED QUENELLES OF GURNARD

(for full recipe see page 174)

1 Everything must be as cold as possible before you start. Put the fish pieces, bread, milk and butter paste, egg, lemon juice, and nutmeg into a food processor.

2 Blend the mixture for at least 1 minute so that everything breaks down to form a very fine paste.

3 Transfer the mixture to a bowl and set the bowl in a slightly larger one of well-iced water. Add the cream a little at a time, beating vigorously between each addition.

4 The finished mixture should be light and quite thick in texture. Cover and chill for 30 minutes.

Bring some lightly salted water to a gentle simmer in a wide, shallow pan. Mold the mixture into quenelles using two wet spoons: take a heaped spoonful of mixture on one spoon and scoop the mixture onto the other spoon by tucking the front edge of the empty spoon under the back edge of the mixture on the front one. Do this two or three times until you achieve a nice football-shaped quenelle with a slight ridge running along the top. Drop them off the spoon into the water and poach gently for 3 to 4 minutes, turning them over halfway through.

Remove with a slotted spoon and drain briefly on a clean dish towel. Transfer the quenelles to individual gratin dishes and cover with the prepared shrimp sauce. Broil close to the heat for 1 minute or until lightly browned.

techniques
chapter 3

preparing raw, smoked, and cured fish

1 Flavor the cooked Japanese sticky rice with a sweet and salty vinegar mixture; add it gradually, lifting and folding the rice, so that it takes on a glossy sheen.

2 Wet your hands with lightly vinegared water. Take 3 tablespoons (20 g) of the rice mixture and shape into a small, rectangular block.

3 Cut the slices of fish into small rectangles slightly larger than the tops of the blocks of rice. Put a very small dot of wasabi paste on your finger.

Keta
The Japanese name for the large, orange-red eggs of the salmon.

making sushi NIGIRI SUSHI (for full recipe see pages 105–6)

6

7

8

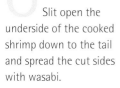

6   Slit open the
underside of the cooked
shrimp down to the tail
and spread the cut sides
with wasabi.

4   Spread the
wasabi along the
underside of each
piece of fish or along
the top of the blocks
of rice.

5   Lay the
pieces of fish on
top of the blocks
of rice and press
down lightly.

7   Open the shrimp
out flat. Lay a shrimp
on top of each block
of rice and press
down lightly.

8   Spoon some keta onto the
remaining blocks of rice. Arrange
the sushi on each plate and serve
with some pickled ginger and the
dipping sauce.

preparing monkfish for serving raw

CEVICHE OF MONKFISH (for full recipe see page 155)

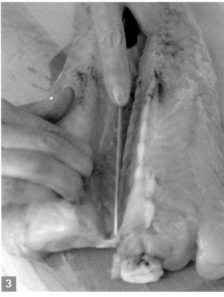

1 First, remove the skin from the monkfish tail: Put the monkfish tail belly-side down on a board. Release some of the skin at the wider end of the tail and pull back so that you can get a sharp, flexible-bladed knife underneath to cut through the fine dorsal spines.

2 Grab hold of the wider end of the tail in one hand and the skin in the other, and briskly pull the skin away, down over the tail.

3 Remove the two fillets by cutting along either side of the thick backbone using a sharp, thin-bladed, flexible knife, keeping the blade as close to the bone as you can.

4 Pull off the thin membrane that encases the fillets, releasing it with the knife where necessary.

5 Cut the fillets across into thin slices and put them into a large, shallow dish.

8 Add some extra virgin olive oil and seasoning to taste, and mix once more. Serve with thinly sliced avocado.

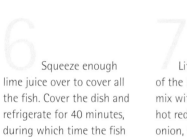

6 Squeeze enough lime juice over to cover all the fish. Cover the dish and refrigerate for 40 minutes, during which time the fish will turn white and opaque.

7 Lift the fish out of the lime juice and mix with thinly sliced hot red chile pepper, red onion, tomato, and chopped cilantro.

preparing tuna carpaccio (for full recipe see page 117)

Wrap the tuna in plastic wrap so that it takes on a neatly rounded shape. Freeze until very firm but not completely frozen; this will make it easier to slice thinly. Unwrap the tuna (1) and slice very thinly using a sharp, long-bladed knife (2). Arrange the slices on the plates and sprinkle with olive oil, sea salt, and black pepper (3). Add some thinly shaved Parmesan cheese (4). Pile some arugula leaves into the center and serve (5).

hot-smoking fish

GRILLED, LIGHTLY SMOKED ARCTIC CHAR (for full recipe see page 151)

1 Put the skinned fish fillets into a light brine and let cure for 20 minutes.

2 Put a 1-inch (2.5-cm) layer of hardwood sawdust into the bottom of a wok and rest six wooden chopsticks over the top to act as a platform. Place the wok over a high heat until the sawdust begins to smoke. Then reduce the heat to low.

3 Rest a sushi mat (or something else that is permeable and will allow the smoke through) on the chopsticks. Lay the fillets of fish on top. Cover the wok with a lid and smoke the fish for 3 to 4 minutes.

4 Uncover the wok and lift out the sushi mat and fish. With a metal spatula, carefully lift the fish off the mat and onto a board. Cut each fillet into four equal pieces..

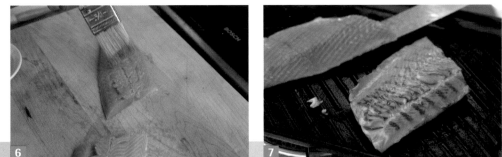

5   Make a dressing of minced shallot, chopped chives, olive oil, vinegar, and salt.

6   Brush the pieces of smoked Arctic char with some olive oil.

7   Heat a ridged cast-iron grill pan until smoking-hot. Place the pieces of fish diagonally on the grill pan and cook for 30 seconds on each side or until lightly marked by the ridges. Spoon a little dressing into the center of each plate, put a piece of fish on top, and serve warm.

hot-smoking fish in a box smoker

A box smoker is a metal box, with a tight-fitting lid, that sits on top of the grill. Wood chips are placed inside of the box, and the fish is placed on top of the lid; the heat of the grill causes the chips to smoke and, through the holes in the lid, infuse the fish with flavor. Box smokers are ideal for small, cleaned, trimmed, and slashed whole fish weighing 6 oz to 1 lb (175 to 450 g), such as mackerel, herring, and trout, and 4- to 12-oz (100- to 350-g) steaks or pieces of thick fish fillet such as salmon, cod, sea bass, barramundi, snapper, and tuna. The fish can be eaten hot or cold.

a scandinavian cure for salmon

GRAVLAX (for full recipe see page 143)

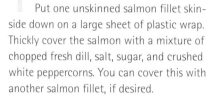

1 Put one unskinned salmon fillet skin-side down on a large sheet of plastic wrap. Thickly cover the salmon with a mixture of chopped fresh dill, salt, sugar, and crushed white peppercorns. You can cover this with another salmon fillet, if desired.

2 Tightly wrap the fish in two or three layers of plastic wrap, then lift it onto a large, shallow tray.

3 Place a chopping board on top of the fish and weigh it down with cans of food. Refrigerate for 2 days, turning it every 12 hours so that the briny mixture bastes the outside of the fish. Replace the board and weights each time.

4 Unwrap the salmon and place it on a board. Slice at a 45-degree angle into very thin slices, using a very sharp, long-bladed knife .

5 Carefully lift off the almost see-through slices as you cut them. Arrange a few slices on each plate and serve with the traditional horseradish and mustard sauce.

salting fresh cod

BRANDADE DE MORUE (for full recipe see page 130)

1 To salt your own cod, pour a ½-inch (1-cm) layer of salt over the bottom of a shallow, plastic container. Put a thick piece of unskinned cod fillet on top and cover with another thick layer of salt. Cover and refrigerate overnight.

2 The next day, lift the now rigid piece of cod out of the salt and rinse under cold water.

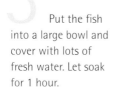

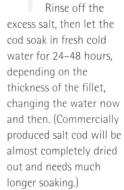

3 Put the fish into a large bowl and cover with lots of fresh water. Let soak for 1 hour.

4 Rinse off the excess salt, then let the cod soak in fresh cold water for 24–48 hours, depending on the thickness of the fillet, changing the water now and then. (Commercially produced salt cod will be almost completely dried out and needs much longer soaking.)

5 To make the brandade, drain the soaked cod and remove the skin and bones. Simmer gently in water for 5 minutes, then lift out, drain well, and put into a food processor.

6 Bring a mixture of heavy cream, garlic, and olive oil to a boil in a small pan.

7 Add the hot cream mixture to the fish, turn on the processor, and blend to a thick, smooth paste. Season to taste with lemon juice and pepper. Spoon the mixture into a warmed dish and garnish with some croûtons, black olives, and chopped parsley. Serve warm.

DIFFERENT
USES FOR
FISH ROE

using caviar in a sauce

GRILLED MULLOWAY WITH ASPARAGUS AND A CREAM AND CAVIAR SAUCE

(for full recipe see page 145)

1 Prepare a sauce of reduced fish stock, vermouth, and cream. Brush portion-sized pieces of mulloway fillet with melted butter, season, and broil, skin-side up, for 7 to 8 minutes. Lightly steam some asparagus until tender.

2 Arrange the asparagus in the center of warmed plates and place the mulloway fillets on top.

3 Reheat the sauce and stir in some lemon juice and 1 teaspoon of caviar. Season to taste. Spoon the sauce around the outside of each plate.

sautéeing fresh roe

PAN-FRIED HERRING ROE ON TOASTED BRIOCHE

(for full recipe see page 159)

1 Dust the herring roe lightly in flour seasoned with salt and pepper.

2 Melt some butter in a frying pan and, as soon as it begins to foam, add the roe.

3 Fry them over a medium-high heat for 2 minutes, turning once, until lightly golden.

4 Spoon the roe onto warm toasted brioche and serve with some dressed salad leaves, beurre noisette (see page 18), and capers.

making taramasalata

(for full recipe see page 130)

Scrape the roe away from the thick outer skin using a knife (1). Put the roe, soaked bread, garlic, onion, and lemon juice into a food processor (2) and blend to a smooth paste. With the machine still running, gradually add some olive oil as you would for mayonnaise. Spoon the mixture onto a shallow plate and garnish with some lemon wedges, black olives, and chopped parsley (3).

techniques
chapter 4

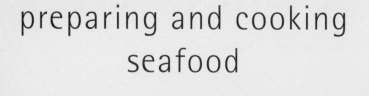

preparing and cooking seafood

techniques 46a and 46b

1 To butterfly peeled shrimp, remove the head, if necessary, and peel off the shell, leaving the last tail segment in place (see page 72). Make a deep cut down the back of each shrimp with a small, sharp knife, about halfway down into the meat. Pull out the intestinal vein if dark and visible.

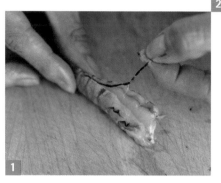

2 Brush the shrimp with oil or melted butter, season, and lay them on their sides on a lightly oiled baking pan. Broil for 2 minutes until cooked through.

technique 47

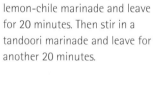

2 Toss the shrimp in a lemon-chile marinade and leave for 20 minutes. Then stir in a tandoori marinade and leave for another 20 minutes.

1 Make three little slits in both sides of each unpeeled shrimp, between the segments of the shell. This will let the marinade penetrate the shells and flavor the shrimp.

butterflying raw shrimp for broiling

2 Open up the shrimp and lay them with the meat facing uppermost on a lightly oiled baking pan.

1 To butterfly shrimp in the shell, remove the head, if necessary (see page 72), then put the shrimp belly-side up on a board. Cut each shrimp in half lengthwise, through the shell, to within ½ inch (1 cm) of the tail.

3 Brush them with oil or melted butter and season, then broil, 2 to 3 inches (5 to 7.5 cm) from the heat, for 2 minutes, until cooked through.

marinating raw shrimp for the grill

TANDOORI SHRIMP (for full recipe see page 200)

4 When the fire is ready, place the skewers on the rack above the glowing coals.

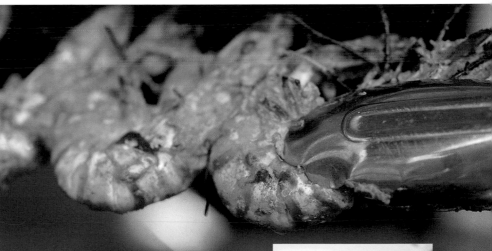

3 Thread the shrimp onto metal or soaked bamboo skewers, piercing them just behind the back of the head and down through the tail.

5 Grill the shrimp for 2 minutes on each side, until cooked through and nicely colored. Serve with the katchumber salad.

PREPARING AND COOKING SEAFOOD

technique 48

PREPARING
RAW SHRIMP
FOR CURRIES
AND
STIR-FRIES

preparing raw shrimp for curries and stir-fries

SHRIMP CALDINE (for full recipe see page 197)

1 Hold the body of the shrimp in one hand and firmly twist off the head with the other. Save the heads for making stock, if desired.

2 Break open the soft shell along the underbelly of each shrimp and peel it away from the flesh. You can leave the last tail segment of the shell in place for some recipes.

3 Run the tip of a small, sharp knife along the back of the shrimp and pull out the intestinal vein if dark and visible (deveining is not always essential).

4 Mix the shrimp with a little vinegar and salt, and set to one side. Heat some oil in a medium-sized pan, add some sliced onion, slivered garlic, and chopped fresh ginger, and fry gently for 5 minutes, until softened.

5 Grind some turmeric, black peppercorns, coriander seeds, cumin seeds, and white poppy seeds together into a powder. Add to the softened onion and fry for 2 minutes to cook out some of the raw flavors.

6 Add some coconut milk, tamarind water, and water, and bring to a simmer.

7 Add some salt and some seeded and finely shredded mild green chile peppers. Stir, then simmer for 5 minutes.

8 Add the shrimp and simmer for 3 to 4 minutes, until they are only just cooked through but still moist and juicy inside.

9 Stir in some more shredded green chiles and chopped cilantro.

10 Spoon into warmed bowls and serve with steamed rice.

cooking langoustines

BROILED LANGOUSTINES WITH A PERNOD AND OLIVE OIL DRESSING

(for full recipe see page 190)

1 Bring some salted water or the prepared shellfish bouillon (see page 223) to a boil in a very large pan.

2 Add the langoustines to the pan and bring back to a boil.

3 Cook the langoustines for 2 to 5 minutes, depending on their size. Let cool.

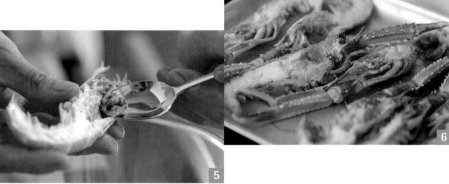

4 Put each langoustine belly-side down on a board and cut it in half lengthwise.

5 Scoop out the creamy contents of the head (the tomalley or liver) with a teaspoon and mix it with the prepared dressing.

6 Arrange the halved langoustines cut-side up on a baking pan and brush with melted butter. Broil, 2 to 3 inches (5 to 7.5 cm) from the heat, for 1 to 3 minutes, until heated through. Arrange on warmed plates and spoon the dressing over them.

removing the meat
from a cooked lobster
LOBSTER THERMIDOR

(for full recipe see page 194)

to cook a lobster from raw

Put it into the freezer 2 hours before cooking; this will kill it painlessly. Bring a large pan of heavily-salted water to a boil (i.e. ½ cup/150 g of salt to every 10 pints/4.5 liters of water). Add the lobster and bring back to a boil. Cook those up to 1½ lb (750 g) for 15 minutes and those up to 2½ lb (1.25 kg) for 20 minutes. Remove and let cool.

1   Put the lobster belly-side down on a board and make sure none of the legs is tucked underneath. Cut it in half, first cutting through the middle of the head between the eyes. Then turn either the knife or the lobster around and finish cutting it in half through the tail.

2   Open it up and lift out the tail meat from each half.

3   Remove the intestinal vein from the tail meat.

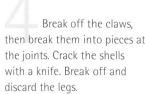

4   Break off the claws, then break them into pieces at the joints. Crack the shells with a knife. Break off and discard the legs.

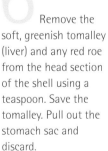

5   Remove the meat from each of the claw sections in pieces as large as possible.

6   Remove the soft, greenish tomalley (liver) and any red roe from the head section of the shell using a teaspoon. Save the tomalley. Pull out the stomach sac and discard.

7

8

9

9 Sprinkle with some freshly grated Parmesan cheese and broil, 2 to 3 inches (5 to 7.5 cm) from the heat, for 4 minutes, until the lobster meat is heated through and the cheese is golden.

7 Cut the tail meat into smaller pieces. Transfer the cleaned half shells to a baking sheet and evenly distribute the tail and claw meat between them along with any roe.

8 Make a fish stock and cream reduction (see page 194). Stir the tomalley into the sauce. Spoon about 3 tablespoons of the sauce into each half shell.

removing the tail meat in one piece

Pull the tail away from the head (1). Turn the tail section over and cut along either side of the flat belly-shell using strong scissors (2). Lift back the flap of shell (3). Lift out the tail meat (4). Remove the intestinal vein either by cutting the tail into thin slices and removing it from each slice with the tip of a small sharp knife, or by running the knife down the back of the meat and removing the intestinal vein in one piece.

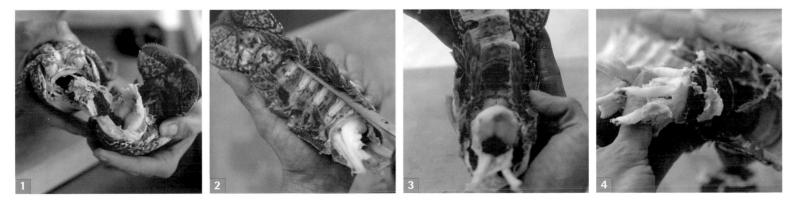
1 2 3 4

PREPARING AND COOKING SEAFOOD

techniques 51 and 52

CUTTING UP
RAW LOBSTER
FOR STIR-
FRYING AND
BROILING

cutting up raw lobster for stir-frying

LOBSTER WITH GINGER, GREEN ONIONS, AND SOFT EGG NOODLES (for full recipe see page 193)

1 Kill the lobster painlessly, as described on page 76. Cut it in half and remove the stomach sac and intestinal tract as described on page 79, steps 1 to 3. Cut each tail half into three pieces.

2 Chop the claws from the head and cut each one into two pieces through the joint. Crack the shells with a large knife.

3 Snip off the antennae close to the head using scissors, and discard.

4 Cut off the feeler-like legs as close to the shell as you can using scissors, and discard them. Then cut each head section into two pieces.

halving a raw lobster for broiling

BROILED LOBSTER WITH FINES HERBES (for full recipe see page 192)

1 Kill the lobster painlessly, as described on page 76. Lay the lobster belly-side down on a board and cut it lengthwise in half.

2 Remove the stomach sac, a slightly clear pouch that will now be cut in half, from the head section of each half.

3 Remove the intestinal vein from the tail section.

4 Put the lobster halves on a baking pan and brush the meat with melted butter. Season with salt and pepper, then broil, 6 inches (15 cm) from the heat, for 8 to 10 minutes.

5 Prepare a sauce of fish stock, Thai fish sauce, lemon juice, butter, and chopped fines herbes. Spoon this over the cooked lobster and serve.

PREPARING AND COOKING SEAFOOD

technique 53

REMOVING
THE MEAT
FROM A
COOKED CRAB

removing the meat from a cooked crab

to cook a crab from raw

Turn the crab onto its back with its eyes facing you. Drive a thick skewer between the eyes into the center of the crab. Then lift up the tail flap and drive the skewer down into the center of the body. When the crab is dead its legs will go limp. Bring a large pan of heavily-salted water to the boil (i.e. ½ cup/150 g salt to every 10 pints/4.5 liters of water). Add the crab and bring back to a boil. Cook those up to 1¼ lb (550 g) for 15 minutes, those up to 2 lb (900 g) for 20 minutes, those up to 3¼ lb (1.5 kg) for 25 minutes, and any larger for 30 minutes. Remove and let cool.

The amount and type of meat you'll get will depend on the crab: Dungeness, for example, will yield more chunk or lump meat than blue crab. Shown here is a European brown crab, which contains both white and creamy brown meat. If the meat is put back into the shell, the crab is described as "dressed."

1 Put the crab back-shell down on a board and break off the claws.

2 Break off the legs, taking care to remove the knuckle joint too.

7 Scoop out any brown meat from the center of the body section using a teaspoon and keep it separate from the white meat.

8 Cut the body section in half using a large knife.

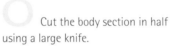

9 Remove the white meat from all the little channels using a crab pick.

3 Lift up and break off the tail flap.

4 Push the blade of a large knife between the body and the back shell and twist the blade to release it.

5 Place your thumbs on either side of the body section and press firmly upward until it comes away.

6 Pull the feathery-looking gills, known as the "dead man's fingers," off the body and discard.

10 When all the meat has been removed you should be left with a hollow and much lighter piece of shell.

11 Crack the shell of the claws with the back of a knife and remove the meat. Remove the thin piece of bone concealed within the meat of the pincers. Break the shell of the legs with crackers and hook out the white meat with the crab pick.

12 Put the back shell on a board with the eyes and mouth facing you. Press on the little piece of shell located just behind the eyes until it snaps. Lift out and discard the mouth piece and stomach sac.

13 Scoop out any brown meat (this is sometimes quite wet and more solid) from the back shell using a spoon and add it to that from the body.

making crab cakes

MARYLAND CRAB CAKES (for full recipe see page 187)

3 Fold this into the crab meat, taking care not to break up the lumps of crab too much, then stir in some chopped parsley.

4 Shape the mixture into eight 3-inch (7.5-cm) patties. Put them onto a plate, cover, and chill for at least 1 hour to help them firm up.

1 Add some finely crushed cracker crumbs to the crab meat to absorb any excess moisture in the meat.

2 Make a binding mixture of beaten egg, mayonnaise, mustard, lemon juice, Worcestershire sauce, and seasoning.

6 Add the crab cakes and fry them over a medium heat for 2 to 3 minutes on each side, until crisp and golden.

5 Pour some clarified butter into a well-seasoned or nonstick frying pan and let it get hot.

7 Lift two cakes into the center of each warmed plate and spoon some of the tarragon butter sauce around them.

how to prepare soft-shell crabs

SAUTÉED SOFT-SHELL CRABS WITH GARLIC BUTTER
(for full recipe see page 188)

Cut straight across the face, about ¼ inch (5 mm) behind the eyes, to remove the eyes and mouth. Push your finger into the opening and hook out the stomach, which is a small, jelly-like sac. Turn the crab over and pull off the little tail flap. Turn it back over again and lift up the sides of the soft top shell to pull out the gills, or "dead man's fingers." The crabs are now ready to cook.

preparing raw crabs for steaming or stir-frying

STEAMED CRAB WITH LEMONGRASS DRESSING (for full recipe see page 184)

PREPARING
RAW CRABS
FOR STEAMING
OR STIR-
FRYING

1 Kill the crabs as described on page 80. Then put each crab back-shell down on a board and break off the tail flap. Break off the claws close to the body.

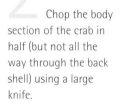

2 Chop the body section of the crab in half (but not all the way through the back shell) using a large knife.

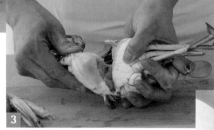

3 Grab hold of the legs and gently tug on them to pull the body sections away from the back shell. Use a knife as an added lever if necessary, but they should come away quite easily, with the legs still attached.

4 Turn each piece over and pick off the feather-like gills ("dead man's fingers"). Discard the back shells or save them for making stock.

5 Cut the claws in half at the joint. Crack the shells of each piece with a hammer or the back of a large knife.

4

6 Bring about 1 inch (2.5 cm) of water to a boil in a wide, shallow pan. Pile the pieces of crab onto a petal steamer, lower it into the pan, and cover with a well-fitting lid. Steam for 8 minutes.

7 Uncover the pan of now cooked crab pieces and lift out the petal steamer.

8 Transfer the crab to a serving dish and spoon the prepared lemongrass dressing over it.

EXTRACTING
THE FLAVOR
FROM
CRUSTACEANS
FOR SOUPS

using crab shells and meat for making a bisque

SHORE CRAB BISQUE (for full recipe see page 101)

1 Wash the crabs well under running water. Prepare them and cook in a pan of well-salted boiling water (see page 80) for 2 minutes, then drain.

2 Chop up the crabs very roughly into smallish pieces using a large knife.

3 Add the crab pieces and a splash of Cognac to a pan of lightly sautéed vegetables.

4 Fry the crab pieces for 3 to 4 minutes, stirring now and then, until all the liquid has evaporated.

5 Add some tomatoes, tomato paste, white wine, tarragon, and fish stock to the pan. Bring to a boil, lower the heat, and let simmer, uncovered, for 30 minutes.

6 Briefly blend the soup, in batches, until the shells have broken down into pieces about the size of a fingernail. It should not be completely smooth. Then strain through a conical sieve into a clean pan.

7 Press as much liquid as you can from the debris with the back of a ladle, then discard everything that is left in the sieve.

8 Strain the soup once more through a fine sieve to remove the finer debris. Bring it back to a boil, and reduce a little to concentrate the flavor, if necessary. Add some cream and season to taste with lemon juice, cayenne pepper, and salt.

4

making a clear crab soup

SEAFOOD IN A CRAB AND GINGER BROTH

(for full recipe see page 104)

1 Flavor a pan of chicken stock with fresh ginger, lime zest, lime juice, lemongrass, chile, and Thai fish sauce. Add the pieces of prepared crab (see page 84) and shrimp shells.

2 Bring the stock to a boil, then cover, and let simmer gently for 25 minutes, to extract the flavor from the crab.

3 Strain the stock into a clean pan and let it cool. Meanwhile, remove the meat from the crab claws; set aside.

4 Add some minced inexpensive white fish fillet, such as pollock, some thinly sliced leek, and 2 egg whites to the cooled stock.

5 Return the pan to a medium heat and whisk steadily until the mixture comes back to a boil. Stop whisking immediately and let simmer very gently for 5 minutes, during which time a crust will form on the top of the soup.

6 Slowly pour the stock through a cheesecloth-lined sieve into a clean pan. Finally, let the crust slide into the sieve and leave until all the liquid has dripped through. Briefly cook the shrimp, some thinly sliced monkfish, and some prepared vegetables in the clarified stock. Finish with noodles and the reserved crab meat.

clarified soups and stocks

As the fish and egg whites cook and coagulate, they will entrap all the fine particles in the stock. When the crust is parted it should reveal a crystal clear stock beneath.

PREPARING
MUSSELS AND
CLAMS FOR
COOKING AND
SERVING RAW

cleaning and steaming mussels

MOULES MARINIÈRE

(for full recipe see page 213)

1 Wash the mussels under plenty of cold water. Discard any that are open and won't close up when lightly squeezed. Pull out the tough fibrous beards, or "byssus," protruding from between the tightly closed shells.

2 Knock off any barnacles with a large knife, then give the mussels another quick rinse to remove any little bits of shell.

3 Put the mussels into a very large pan with the butter, minced onion, and white wine. Make sure that there is plenty of room in which the mussels can be moved around. If the pan is overcrowded, those at the bottom will overcook before the heat can reach those at the top, so never more than half-fill the pan.

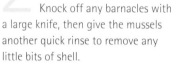

4 Cover and cook the mussels over a high heat, shaking the pan vigorously every now and then, for 3 to 4 minutes, until they have all just opened.

5 Immediately remove the pan from the heat and spoon the mussels into warmed deep bowls, discarding any mussels that have remained closed. Add the parsley to the juices in the pan and pour the broth over the mussels.

opening mussels for serving raw

Push the tip of a small knife between the shells on the straighter side. Run the tip all around the edge (1). Ease back the top shell (2) and run the tip of the knife around its inside edge to release the meat, taking care not to tear the mussel. Pull back the top shell (3) and snap it off, if desired.

removing the meat
from large clams

NEW ENGLAND CLAM CHOWDER

(for full recipe see page 204)

1 Wash the clams under plenty of cold water. Put them in a single layer into the bottom of a large, shallow pan and add a little water.

2 Cover the pan with a tight-fitting lid and cook over a high heat for 2 to 3 minutes, until the clams have opened just enough for you to get them out of the shells. You don't want to cook them completely.

3 Remove the clams from the pan, reserving the liquid if it's required, and let them cool slightly. Then slide a small, sharp knife into each shell and cut through the two muscles on either side near the hinge, which hold the two shells together.

4 Remove the clams from the bottom shells and chop them into small pieces.

preparing small clams for serving raw

CLAMS WITH SAUCE MIGNONETTE (for full recipe see pages 204–5)

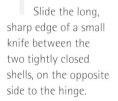

1 Slide the long, sharp edge of a small knife between the two tightly closed shells, on the opposite side to the hinge.

2 Draw the blade of the knife back so that only the tip is inside the clam. Run just the very tip of the knife all the way around the edge of the shell, so as not to damage the clam inside. You will eventually feel the resistance give way.

3 Run the blade around the top inside edge of the shell to release the clam from the top shell. Carefully pull back the top shell so as not to damage the clam, releasing it where necessary if still attached. Release the meat from the bottom shell and snip off the shell, if desired.

4 Arrange the clams on their half-shells on a plate of crushed ice and seaweed, and spoon the sauce over them.

PREPARING
SCALLOPS AND
OYSTERS

preparing scallops and searing

SEARED SCALLOPS WITH IBÉRICO HAM (for full recipe see page 215)

1   Wash the scallops to remove any sand and weed from the shells. Hold a scallop in one hand, with the flat shell facing uppermost, and slide the blade of a sharp, thin-bladed, flexible knife between the two shells.

2   Keeping the blade of the knife flat against the top shell, feel for the ligament that joins the meat of the scallop to the shell. Cut through it and lift off the top shell.

3   Pull out the frilly "skirt" and black stomach sac that surrounds the white scallop meat and pink coral. Rinse away any sand from inside the shell.

4   Slide the knife under the scallop meat, keeping the blade close to the shell, and cut it away. Pull off and discard the small white ligament attached to the side of the scallop meat.

5   Rub the bottom of a nonstick frying pan with cold butter. Set the pan over a high heat and, when the butter starts to smoke, add the scallops. Sear them for 2 minutes on each side, pressing down on them lightly with a metal spatula so that they take on a good color.

6   Transfer the scallops to the plates of ham and salad leaves. Remove the pan from the heat, add some sherry vinegar, and scrape up all the browned residue from the bottom. Return the pan to the heat and whisk in some butter, chopped parsley, and seasoning. Spoon this dressing over the scallops and salad leaves, and serve.

opening oysters

WARM OYSTERS WITH BLACK BEANS, GINGER, AND CILANTRO (for full recipe see page 213)

1 Wrap one hand in a towel and hold the oyster in it, flat shell facing uppermost. Push the point of an oyster knife into the hinge, located at the narrowest point.

2 Work the knife back and forth quite forcefully until the hinge breaks and you can slide the knife in between the two shells.

3 Twist the point of the knife upward to lever up the top shell and locate the ligament that joins the oyster meat to it. It will be slightly right of the center of the top shell. Cut through it with the knife and lift off the top shell. Keep the bottom shell upright so as not to lose any of the juices, although for this dish you need to pour away half of the juices.

4 Release the oyster from the bottom shell, but leave it in place. (Remove it completely if you are shucking the oysters.) Pick out any little pieces of shell. Arrange the oysters on their half-shells on a heatproof serving platter covered in a thick layer of coarse salt and sprinkle with some ginger. Broil for 3 minutes. Sprinkle the cucumber, cilantro, and chive mixture into each shell, add the black bean dressing, and serve warm.

preparing squid for stir-frying

STIR-FRIED SALT-AND-PEPPER SQUID (for full recipe see page 221)

1 Hold the squid's body in one hand and the head with the other, and gently pull the head away from the body, taking the milky white intestines with it.

2 Remove the tentacles from the head by cutting them off just in front of the eyes. Discard the head and separate the tentacles if they are large.

3 Squeeze out the beak-like mouth from the center of the tentacles and discard it.

4 If you want to retain the ink sac, look among the intestines for a very small, pearly white pouch with a slight blue tinge and carefully cut it away.

5 Reach into the body and pull out the clear, plastic-like quill.

6 Pull off the two fins from either side of the body pouch. Then pull away the brown, semi-transparent skin from both the body and the fins. Wash out the body pouch with water.

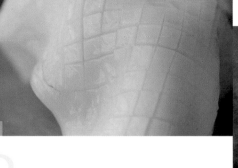

7 Insert the blade of a sharp, thin-bladed, flexible knife into the opening of the body pouch and slit it open along one side. Open it out flat and pull away any remaining intestines and membrane.

8 Score what was the inner side in a diamond pattern using the tip of a small, sharp knife, taking care not to cut too deeply. Then cut the squid into 2-inch (5-cm) pieces.

9 Heat a dry wok over a high heat until smoking. Add a little oil and a handful of the prepared squid. Constantly move the squid around the sides of the wok for 2 minutes, until it has taken on a light golden-brown color. Remove and repeat with the rest of the squid.

10 Add some of the toasted Sichuan pepper and salt mix, red chile, and green onions, and toss together briefly. Serve with the prepared dressed salad.

preparing octopus and tenderizing in the oven

OCTOPUS, PEA, AND RED WINE STEW (for full recipe see pages 217–8)

2 Pull away and discard the entrails. Remove the bone-like strips sticking to the sides of the body.

1 Turn the body of the octopus inside out.

3 Locate the stomach sac, which is about the size of an avocado pit, and cut it away.

7 For the stew, gently sauté some garlic and shallots in olive oil until soft and lightly colored.

9 Lower the heat and simmer until almost all the liquid has evaporated.

8 Add some red wine, sugar, and halved plum tomatoes, and bring to a boil.

10 Remove the octopus from the oven and lift it out of its cooking juices onto a chopping board. Reserve the juices.

4

4 Wash the octopus well inside and out, then turn the body right side out again. Press out the beak and soft surround from the center of the tentacles and cut it out with the tip of a small knife.

5 Put the prepared octopus into a shallow casserole.

6 Pour in some olive oil, then cover the casserole with a well-fitting lid and cook in a cool oven set at 300°F (150°C) for 2 hours, until very tender.

11 When it is cool enough to handle, cut it across into small, chunky pieces. Stir the octopus pieces, the reserved cooking juices, and a little extra water into the red wine and shallot reduction.

12 Simmer for 15 to 20 minutes, until the liquid has reduced once more. Add the peas and simmer for 5 minutes. Stir in some chopped parsley and seasoning, and serve drizzled with a little extra olive oil.

PREPARING
CUTTLEFISH
AND SEA
URCHINS

cleaning cuttlefish

SALAD OF RAW CUTTLEFISH

(for full recipe see page 219)

1 Cut off the tentacles, just in front of the eyes. Remove the beak-like mouth from the center of the tentacles and discard.

2 Separate the tentacles and pull the skin from each one.

3 Pull the tough skin away from the body section.

4 Run a sharp knife down the center of the back and lift out the cuttlebone.

5 Open up the body pouch. Locate the pearly white ink sac in among the entrails and remove it carefully. Remove and discard the rest of the entrails and the head.

6 Wash the body well, then cut it lengthwise in half. For serving raw, cut each piece across into very thin slices.

7 Arrange the tomatoes and cuttlefish strips on each plate. Squeeze a little lemon juice over them and sprinkle with sea salt flakes and coarsely ground black pepper. Drizzle with olive oil and garnish with a few arugula leaves.

4

preparing sea urchins

PASTA WITH SEA URCHIN ROE, LEMON, AND PARSLEY (for full recipe see page 218)

1 Wrap one hand in a towel and hold the sea urchin in it, with the mouth (the soft part in the center) facing uppermost. Push one blade of a pair of scissors into the mouth and cut around it to release a 2 to 3 inch (5 to 7.5 cm) disk of shell. Or, cut a 1-inch (2.5-cm) slice of the sea urchin with a large, serrated knife.

2 Lift away the disk of shell and pour away any liquid from inside the urchin.

3 Pull out all the black parts from inside the shell, leaving behind the small clusters of orange roe.

4 Scoop out the individual clusters of roe with a teaspoon, keeping them as whole as possible. Add them to the hot cooked pasta and turn over gently once or twice. The residual heat will be sufficient to lightly cook the roe.

chapters 5/12

2 recipes

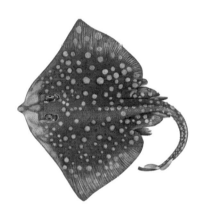

recipes

chapter 5

soups, stews, and mixed seafood

classic fish soup with rouille and croûtons

SERVES 4

2 lb (900 g) mixed fish such as gurnard or sea robin, conger eel, dogfish, cod, and gray or striped mullet

5 cups (1.2 liters) water

1/3 cup (85 ml) olive oil

1/2 cup (75 g) each roughly chopped onion, celery, leek, and fennel

3 garlic cloves, sliced

Juice of 1/2 orange, plus 2 pared strips of orange zest

1 cup (200 g) canned diced tomatoes

1 small, red bell pepper, seeded and sliced

1 bay leaf

1 sprig of thyme

Pinch of saffron strands

4 oz (100 g) small cold-water shrimp in shell

Pinch of cayenne pepper

Salt and freshly ground black pepper

CROÛTONS:

1 mini French baguette

Olive oil, for frying

1 garlic clove

1/4 cup (25 g) freshly grated Parmesan cheese

1/2 quantity Rouille (see pages 224–5)

1 Fillet the fish as described on pages 14 and 20, and use the bones with the water to make a fish stock (see page 222).

2 Heat the olive oil in a large pan, add the vegetables and garlic, and cook gently for 20 minutes until soft but not colored. Add the orange zest, tomatoes, red pepper, bay leaf, thyme, saffron, shrimp, and fish fillets. Cook briskly for 2 to 3 minutes, then add the stock and orange juice. Bring to a boil and simmer for 40 minutes. Meanwhile, for the croûtons, thinly slice the baguette and fry the slices in the olive oil until crisp and golden. Drain on paper towels, then rub one side of each piece with the garlic clove.

3 Blend the soup until smooth, then pass it through a conical sieve into a clean pan, pressing out as much liquid as possible with the back of a ladle. Return the soup to the heat and season to taste with the cayenne, salt, and pepper.

4 Ladle the soup into a warmed tureen. Put the croûtons, Parmesan cheese, and rouille into separate dishes. To serve, ladle the soup into warmed bowls, then let each person spread some rouille onto the croutons, float them on their soup, and sprinkle them with Parmesan.

brandade and haricot bean soup with truffle oil

SERVES 4

Scant 1 cup (175 g) dried white haricot beans, soaked in
   cold water overnight
900 ml (3¾ cups) water
1 lb (450 g) Fresh Salted Cod (see pages 67 and 227),
   soaked
2½ cups (600 ml) whole milk
6 garlic cloves, sliced
½ cup (120 ml) olive oil
1¼ cups (300 ml) heavy cream
1 tablespoon truffle oil
Chopped flat-leaf parsley, for garnish

1 Drain the beans and put them into a saucepan with the water. Bring
to a boil, then cover and simmer for 1 hour or until they are very soft
and just starting to break apart. Drain, reserving the cooking liquid.

2 Drain the salted cod and put it into a large saucepan with the milk.
Bring to a simmer and cook for 4 to 5 minutes or until just done. Lift
the cod out onto a plate. Reserve the milk. When the cod is cool enough
to handle, break it into flakes, discarding the skin and any bones.

3 Put the flaked fish into a blender with the garlic. Heat the oil and
cream together in a small pan until boiling, then add to the fish, along
with the beans, and blend together until smooth. With the machine still
running, gradually add the reserved milk.

4 Return the soup to the pan and reheat gently but do not let it boil.
Add a little of the bean cooking liquid, if necessary, to obtain a good
consistency. Ladle the soup into four warmed soup bowls, drizzle the
truffle oil over the surface, and garnish with a little chopped parsley.

shore crab bisque (see technique 57, page 86)

SERVES 4

2 lb (900 g) shore crabs or other small crabs, washed
¼ cup (50 g) butter
¼ cup (50 g) each minced onion, carrot, and celery
1 bay leaf
2 tablespoons Cognac
4 tomatoes
1 teaspoon tomato paste
5 tablespoons dry white wine
1 sprig of tarragon
7½ cups (1.75 liters) Fish Stock (see page 222)
4 tablespoons heavy cream
Pinch of cayenne pepper
2 teaspoons lemon juice
Salt and freshly ground black pepper

1 Bring a large pan of well-salted water to a boil. Add the crabs, bring
back to a boil, and cook for 2 minutes. Drain. Let them cool slightly, then
chop up roughly with a large knife.

2 Melt the butter in a large, heavy-based pan and add the minced
vegetables and the bay leaf. Cook for 3 to 4 minutes without letting
the vegetables brown.

3 Add the crabs and the Cognac, and cook until all the liquid
has evaporated.

4 Add the tomatoes, tomato paste, wine, tarragon, and stock. Bring to
a boil and simmer for 30 minutes.

5 Briefly blend the soup in batches until the shells have broken down
into pieces about the size of your fingernail.

6 Strain the soup through a conical strainer into a clean pan, pressing
out as much liquid as you can with the back of a ladle. Then pass it once
more through a very fine sieve.

7 Bring the soup back to a boil. Reduce a little to concentrate the
flavor, if necessary, then lower the heat. Add the cream, cayenne pepper,
and lemon juice, and season to taste with some salt and pepper.

BRANDADE AND HARICOT BEAN SOUP WITH TRUFFLE OIL

soups, stews, and mixed seafood

cacciucco (see technique 33, page 54)

SERVES 8–10

1 loaf of ciabatta bread

⅔ cup (150 ml) olive oil

5 garlic cloves, thinly sliced

1 lb (450 g) uncleaned, medium-sized squid

1 (2-lb/900-g) john dory, filleted (see page 30)

1 (3-lb/1.5-kg) gurnard or sea robin, filleted (see page 32)

1 (2-lb/900-g) thick, unskinned cod fillet

1 (1-lb/450-g) cooked lobster

1 large onion, chopped

1 large carrot, finely diced

2 celery stalks, finely diced

1¼ cups (300 ml) red wine

1 (14-oz/400-g) can diced tomatoes

2 bay leaves

2–3 medium-hot red chile peppers, slit open lengthwise

10 cups (2.4 liters) water

6 sage leaves

2 lb (900 g) mussels, cleaned (see page 88)

¼ cup dry white wine

Salt and freshly ground black pepper

1 Preheat the oven to 400°F (200°C). Cut the ciabatta into slices ½ inch (1 cm) thick. Spread out on a baking sheet and drizzle with about 2 tablespoons of the olive oil. Bake for 10 to 12 minutes or until crisp and golden. Remove and rub both sides of each piece with one of the peeled cloves of garlic. Set aside.

2 Clean the squid (see page 92), reserving one of the ink sacs. Slice the pouches across into rings and separate the tentacles. Cut the fish fillets into slices 1½ inches (4 cm) thick. Remove the meat from the lobster (see page 76) and reserve the shell. Season everything lightly.

3 Heat half of the remaining olive oil in a large pan. Add the onion, carrot, and celery, and fry for about 8 minutes until just beginning to brown. Add the red wine, the lobster shell, tomatoes, bay leaves, red chiles, and water. Mash the reserved ink sac with a little water and add to the pan. Bring to a boil, then let simmer for 45 minutes.

4 Strain the stock through a sieve into another large pan, pressing the debris against the sides of the sieve with a ladle to extract as much flavor and liquid as possible. You want to have about 5 cups (1.2 liters) of well-flavored stock. If there is more than this, bring it to a boil and boil rapidly for a few minutes until reduced to the required amount and well concentrated in flavor. Season to taste.

CACCIUCCO

5 Put the remaining olive oil and garlic and the sage leaves in a large, clean pan. Heat gently until beginning to sizzle. Add the squid and fry for 2 minutes, until lightly browned. Remove the squid and keep warm.

6 Put the mussels into a large saucepan with the white wine, cover, and cook over a high heat for about 3 minutes until the shells have opened. Tip into a colander set in a bowl; reserve the cooking liquid.

7 Add the prepared stock and pieces of fish to the pan in which you fried the squid. Bring to a boil and simmer for 2 minutes. Add the lobster meat, squid, mussels, and all but the last 2 tablespoons of the mussel cooking liquid, and simmer for 1 minute. Take the pan of Cacciucco to the table with the crisp olive-oil ciabatta slices and serve.

bouillabaisse

SERVES 8–10

CROÛTONS:

Olive oil, for frying

12 thin slices of French bread

2–3 whole garlic cloves

⅓ cup (85 ml) olive oil

2 onions, roughly chopped

White part of 2 leeks, cleaned and roughly chopped

4 celery stalk, thinly sliced

2 fennel bulbs, thinly sliced

10 garlic cloves, chopped

2 pared strips of orange zest

2 lb (900 g) plum tomatoes, skinned and chopped

½ medium-hot red chile pepper, seeded and chopped

1 teaspoon saffron strands

2 sprigs of thyme

4 bay leaves

15 cups (3.4 liters) Fish Stock (see page 222)

7 lb (3.5 kg) mixed fish, which traditionally includes weever fish, monkfish tail, conger eel, red gurnard or sea robin, and john dory, and may also include wrasse, grouper, conger eel, dogfish, bream or porgy, red mullet, bass, and gray or striped mullet

1½ lb (750 g) mussels, cleaned (see page 88)

1 teaspoon chopped herb fennel or bulb fennel tops

1 teaspoon chopped oregano

1 teaspoon thyme leaves

2 tablespoons Pernod

1½ lb (750 g) cooked lobster or spiny lobster pieces in the shell, cooked langoustines, or large shrimp

2 tablespoons extra virgin olive oil

Cayenne pepper (optional)

Salt and freshly ground black pepper

½ quantity Rouille (see pages 224–5), for serving

1 For the croûtons, heat the oil in a frying pan, add the slices of bread, and fry on both sides until golden brown. Drain briefly on paper towels, then rub one side of each piece with a garlic clove. Keep warm in a low oven.

2 Heat the oil for the bouillabaisse in a very large, deep pan. Add the onions, leeks, celery, fennel, and garlic. Cook for 4 to 5 minutes until soft. Season with some black pepper and add the strips of orange zest, tomatoes, chile pepper, saffron, thyme, bay leaves, and stock. Bring to a boil and boil for 10 minutes.

3 Add the firmer fish to the pan first, such as the conger eel, dogfish, and monkfish. Bring back to a boil and simmer for 3 minutes. Then add the softer fish, return to a boil, and simmer for 2 to 3 minutes longer. Add the mussels, herb fennel, oregano, thyme leaves, and Pernod, and boil for 1 minute. Finally, add the cooked shellfish and heat through.

4 Carefully lift the fish and shellfish out of the soup onto a large, warmed serving dish. Keep warm. Strain the soup, then return to the pan and add the extra virgin olive oil. Boil rapidly until concentrated and emulsified into a rich, well-flavored broth. Check the seasoning and add a little cayenne pepper, if desired.

5 To serve, scatter the croûtons over the soup and add a dollop of rouille.

mussel, cockle, and clam masala

SERVES 4

MASALA PASTE:

1 tablespoon coriander seeds

1 teaspoon whole cloves

2 tablespoons cumin seeds

2 onions, quartered

8 large garlic cloves

3-inch (7.5-cm) piece of fresh ginger, chopped

Walnut-sized piece of seedless tamarind pulp

1 teaspoon turmeric powder

3 medium-hot red chile peppers, chopped

2 tablespoons red wine vinegar

1¼-inch (3-cm) cube of creamed coconut

2 tablespoons canola oil

4 lb (1.75 kg) mixed mussels, cockles, and small hard-shell clams, cleaned (see pages 88–9)

2 tablespoons roughly chopped cilantro

1 For the masala paste, heat a heavy-based frying pan over a medium-high heat. Add the coriander seeds, cloves, and cumin seeds, and cook until they darken slightly and start to smell aromatic. Tip into a spice grinder and grind to a powder. Put this powder and all the other paste ingredients into a food processor and blend until smooth.

2 Heat the oil in a large pan, add the spice paste, and fry for a few minutes until it starts to separate from the oil.

3 Add the mussels, cockles, and clams. Cover and cook over a high heat for 3 to 4 minutes, shaking the pan now and then, until all the shells have opened.

4 Add a little water if there is not quite enough sauce and season with a little salt, if necessary, then add the chopped cilantro. Spoon into warmed bowls and serve.

seafood in a crab and ginger broth (see technique 58, page 87)

SERVES 4

1 (1-inch/2.5-cm) piece of fresh ginger
2 limes
7½ cups (1.7 liters) Chicken Stock (see page 222)
1 lemongrass stalk
1 bird chile pepper, cut in half lengthwise
1 tablespoon Thai fish sauce (nam pla)
1 tablespoon light soy sauce
8 raw large shrimp, in shell but headless
4 Asian blue swimming crabs or
    1 small cooked blue or other crab
½ oz (15 g) rice vermicelli noodles
4 oz (100 g) monkfish fillet, very thinly sliced
2 green onions, cut into 2-inch (5-cm) pieces and finely
    shredded lengthwise
25 g (1 oz) bok choy, cut into 1-inch (2.5-cm) pieces
¼ cup (25 g) beansprouts
Cilantro leaves, for garnish

FOR CLARIFYING THE STOCK:

4 oz (100 g) inexpensive white fish fillet, such as
    pollock, skinned and minced
1 small leek, thinly sliced
2 egg whites

FOR SERVING:

1 tablespoon each chopped mint and cilantro
2 bird chile peppers, thinly sliced
2 tablespoons rice wine vinegar or white wine vinegar

1 Peel the ginger, reserving the peel, and cut into very thin slices. Remove a strip of zest from one of the limes with a potato peeler, then squeeze the juice from both limes.

2 Pour the chicken stock into a large pan and add three-fourths of the sliced ginger, the ginger peel, the strip of lime zest, the lime juice, the outer leaves of the lemongrass, the bird chile, fish sauce, and soy sauce. Slowly bring to a boil.

3 Meanwhile, prepare the crabs as described on page 84. Peel and devein the shrimp, reserving the shells (see page 72).

4 Add the crab legs, body, and back shell, but not the claws, to the boiling stock, along with the shrimp shells. Bring back to a boil, cover, and simmer gently for 25 minutes, adding the claws after 20 minutes.

5 Pour the stock through a large sieve into another large pan, discarding all the solids except for the crab. Let the stock cool.

Meanwhile, remove the white meat from the claws, legs, and main body of the crab (see pages 80 to 81), in pieces as large as possible.

6 To clarify the stock, add the fish, leek, and egg whites to the pan and whisk steadily over a medium heat until the mixture boils. Stop whisking immediately, lower the heat, and let simmer very gently for 5 minutes.

7 Line a fine sieve or conical strainer with doubled cheesecloth and set it over a clean pan. Carefully pour the stock into the sieve and leave until all the liquid has dripped through. The stock is now ready to use.

8 Bring a pan of lightly salted water to a boil. Add the noodles, remove from the heat, and let soak for 2 minutes. Drain and set aside. Mince the remaining ginger and half the remaining lemongrass.

9 Bring the stock to a very gentle simmer, then add the shrimp, monkfish, ginger, and lemongrass, and cook gently for 1 minute. Add the noodles, crabmeat, green onions, bok choy, and beansprouts, and simmer for 30 seconds, then remove from the heat.

10 Mix the mint and cilantro together in one small bowl and the chiles and vinegar in another.

11 Divide the noodles among four large soup plates, then ladle the soup over them. Garnish with the cilantro leaves. Serve with the chopped herbs and chile vinegar, instructing your guests to season their soup to their own taste.

miso soup

SERVES 4

DASHI (STOCK):

5 cups (1.2 liters) water
1 (2-inch/5-cm) square of dried kombu seaweed
3 tablespoons bonito flakes

¼ oz (7 g) dried mixed seaweed (e.g. dulse, wakame,
    carrageen, and white moss)
1 (2-oz/50-g) piece of thick cod fillet, skinned
3 prepared bay scallops (see page 90)
1 tablespoon white miso paste
¼ oz (7 g) baby leaf spinach
¼ oz (7 g) mizuna leaves
2 green onions, thinly sliced on the diagonal
2 button mushrooms, thinly sliced

1 For the dashi, put the water and the dried kombu into a pan and slowly bring to a simmer. Strain immediately and return the liquid to the pan. Bring back to a simmer and add the bonito flakes. Bring to a boil, then remove the pan from the heat and let the flakes settle for

1 minute. Pour the dashi through a very fine or cheesecloth-lined sieve into a clean pan.

2 Drop the dried mixed seaweed into a large bowl of cold water and let soak for 8 to 10 minutes to rehydrate. Drain.

3 Cut the cod into 1-inch (2.5-cm) cubes and then into very thin slices. Slice the scallops horizontally into very thin slices. Drain the seaweed.

4 Bring the dashi back to a gentle simmer. Mix a ladleful of the hot liquid into the miso paste until smooth. Return the mixture to the pan, and add the scallops and cod. Cook for 30 seconds, then add the drained seaweed, spinach leaves, and mizuna, and simmer for a few seconds only.

5 Ladle the soup into bowls and garnish with the sliced green onions and mushrooms. Serve immediately.

sashimi of salmon trout, brill, and scallops

SERVES 4 AS A FIRST COURSE

4 oz (100 g) skinned salmon trout fillet, taken from a
   small fish
4 oz (100 g) skinned brill or flounder fillet, taken from
   a small fish
4 prepared bay scallops (see page 90), weighing about
   1 oz (25 g) each
1 tablespoon wasabi paste
Long chives, for garnish

SOY DIPPING SAUCE:

1 (½-inch/1-cm) piece of peeled fresh ginger, minced
2 green onions, minced
Finely grated zest and juice of ½ lime
3 tablespoons dark soy sauce
3 tablespoons water

1 Cut each piece of salmon trout and brill across into slices ¼ inch (5 mm) thick, angling the knife blade at 45 degrees as you do so and keeping the fish fillets in shape.

2 Remove the corals, if any, from the scallops, then slice each scallop horizontally into two or three disks. Divide the fish among four plates and place a small amount of wasabi paste alongside.

3 Mix all the ingredients for the soy dipping sauce together and pour into four small bowls or ramekins. Place on each plate next to the fish, garnish with the chives, and serve.

nigiri sushi (see technique 37, page 60)

SERVES 6 (MAKES APPROXIMATELY 30 PIECES)
STICKY RICE:

2 cups (375 g) Japanese sticky rice
2½ cups (600 ml) cold water
2 tablespoons sugar
6 tablespoons rice wine vinegar
1 teaspoon salt

6 small raw shrimp in shell
1 (1½–2 oz/40–50 g) piece of thick tuna loin
1 (1½–2 oz/40–50 g) piece of thick, skinned salmon fillet
1½–2 oz (40–50 g) skinned lemon sole, gray sole, or
   Petrale sole fillet
A little wasabi paste
6 teaspoons keta (salmon roe)

FOR SERVING:

¼ cup Japanese dark soy sauce
1 tablespoon mirin
1 oz (25 g) Japanese pickled ginger

1 For the sticky rice, put the rice into a large bowl, cover with cold water, and run the grains through your fingers, changing the water now and then, until the water remains relatively clear. Drain the rice and put it into a pan with the measured water. Bring to a boil and boil for 1 minute, then reduce the heat to low and simmer for 10 minutes. Remove from the heat, cover, and leave for 10 minutes. Meanwhile, put ¼ cup of the rice wine vinegar, the sugar, and the salt into a small pan and heat gently until the sugar has dissolved. Pour into a bowl and let cool.

2 Transfer the cooked rice to a large, shallow tray. Gradually add the vinegar mixture, gently lifting and folding over the rice so that as it cools it takes on a nice sheen from the vinegar. Transfer to a bowl and cover with plastic wrap, but do not refrigerate.

3 To stop the shrimp from curling during cooking, push a wooden toothpick or skewer just under the shell, from the head, along the under-belly, and down to the tail. Drop the shrimp into lightly salted, boiling water and simmer for 3 minutes. Drain, drop them into cold water, and let cool. Pull out the toothpicks, then peel the shrimp as described for raw shrimp on page 72, steps 1 to 3. Make a cut along the under-belly down to the tail, partway into the flesh, so that you can open them out flat.

4 Cut the tuna and salmon into thin slices, then cut all the fish into small rectangles, measuring about 2½ by 1¼ inches (6 by 3 cm).

5 Mix the remaining 2 tablespoons of rice wine vinegar with 1 cup (225 ml) cold water. Wet your hands with the vinegared water. Take about

3 tablespoons (20 g) of the rice and mold into a small block, slightly smaller than the piece of fish. Do not squash the rice together too firmly.

6 Smear one side of the tuna, lemon sole, and salmon slices and the cut face of the shrimp with a very small dot of wasabi paste. Lay each piece of fish and the shrimp, wasabi-side down, on top of each block of rice and press down lightly. Spread the top of the last remaining blocks of rice with wasabi and spoon 1 teaspoon of keta onto each.

7 To serve, mix the soy sauce and mirin together and divide among six dipping-sauce saucers. Arrange the sushi in the center of each plate. Put a little pile of pickled ginger and a saucer of sauce alongside.

laksa (malaysian seafood and noodle soup)

SERVES 4

LAKSA SPICE PASTE:

3 medium-hot, dried red chile peppers
1 oz (25 g) dried shrimp (optional)
2 lemongrass stalks, outer leaves removed and core
    minced
3 tablespoons cashew nuts
2 garlic cloves, chopped
1 (1-inch/2.5-cm) piece of fresh ginger, chopped
1 teaspoon turmeric powder
1 small onion, chopped
1 teaspoon ground coriander
3 tablespoons water

8 raw large shrimp, in shell but headless
5 tablespoons vegetable oil
3¾ cups (900 ml) Chicken Stock (see page 222)
4 oz (100 g) prepared small squid (see page 92)
6 oz (175 g) flat rice noodles
1 cup (100 g) beansprouts
1 (14-oz/400-g) can coconut milk
2 teaspoons palm sugar or light brown sugar
1–1½ teaspoons salt

FOR THE GARNISH:

1 (2-inch/5-cm) piece of hothouse cucumber, cut into
    fine matchsticks
1 tablespoon chopped cilantro
1 tablespoon chopped mint
4 green onions, thinly sliced
1 medium-hot red chile pepper, thinly sliced across
    into rings

1 For the laksa spice paste, put the dried red chiles and dried shrimp into a bowl, cover with warm water, and let soak for 15 minutes. Drain. Put into a food processor with the rest of the ingredients for the spice paste and blend until smooth. Set aside.

2 Peel the shrimp (see page 72) and devein if necessary.

3 Heat 1 tablespoon of the oil in a pan, add the shrimp shells, and fry for a few minutes until lightly browned. Add the chicken stock, bring to a boil, and simmer for 10 minutes.

4 Meanwhile, cut along one side of the squid pouch and open it out flat. Score the inner side into a diamond pattern using the tip of a small, short knife (see page 93), then cut into 1-inch (2.5-cm) squares and set aside.

5 Strain the stock and discard the shrimp shells. Heat the remaining oil in a clean pan, add the spice paste, and fry gently for 5 to 6 minutes, until it smells very fragrant and the spices are separating from the oil. Add the stock, bring to a boil, and cover. Simmer for 20 minutes.

6 Bring a pan of salted water to a boil. Add the rice noodles. Take the pan off the heat and let soak for 4 minutes. Add the beansprouts and let soak for 1 more minute, then drain well.

7 Add the coconut milk to the stock and simmer for 3 minutes. Add the shrimp, squid, sugar, and salt, and simmer for 4 minutes.

8 Divide the noodles among four large, warmed soup bowls. Spoon the hot soup over the noodles and garnish each bowl with some cucumber, cilantro, mint, green onions, and red chile pepper.

chickpea, parsley, and salt cod stew

SERVES 4

1¾ cups (350 g) dried chickpeas
1 (6-oz/75-g) potato, peeled
1½ lb (750 g) Fresh Salted Cod (see pages 67 and 227),
    soaked
⅓ cup (85 ml) olive oil
8 garlic cloves, minced
1 teaspoon dried red pepper flakes
4 plum tomatoes, roughly chopped
3–4 tablespoons chopped flat-leaf parsley
Salt and freshly ground black pepper

1 Cover the chickpeas in water and let them soak overnight.

2 The next day, drain the chickpeas and put them in a pan with enough fresh water to cover them by about 2 inches (5 cm). Bring to a

CHICKPEA, PARSLEY, AND SALT COD STEW

boil, add the peeled potato, and simmer until tender, adding hot water now and then if necessary to make sure the chickpeas stay just covered. Drain and set aside, saving the cooking liquid.

3 Drain the salted cod, drop it into a pan of boiling water, and simmer for 6 to 8 minutes or until just cooked. Drain and, when cool enough to handle, flake the flesh into large pieces, discarding the skin and any bones.

4 Heat the olive oil in a large pan, add the garlic and pepper flakes, and cook for 1 to 2 minutes without browning. Add the tomatoes, chickpeas, and potato, breaking it up into small pieces with the back of a wooden spoon. Add a little of the cooking liquid from the chickpeas and 1¼ cups (300 ml) of water. Simmer for 20 to 30 minutes, until the stew has reduced and thickened a little. Gently fold in the salt cod and parsley, and season liberally with freshly ground black pepper. Taste the stew for salt, although you probably won't need any.

ALTERNATIVE FISH

All fish from the cod family, such as haddock, hake, or pollock, are pleasant to eat when salted. I think the cheaper the fish, the more appropriate it is for salting.

seafood and white bean stew (cassoulet) with salt cod, garlic, and toulouse sausage

SERVES 6

¾ cup (175 ml) olive oil
1 (8-oz/225-g) Toulouse sausage, cut into 1-inch (2.5-cm) pieces
Pinch of dried red pepper flakes
3 cups (550 g) dried white haricot beans, soaked in cold water overnight
6 garlic cloves, minced
2 bay leaves
2 sprigs of thyme
3¾ cups (900 ml) Chicken Stock (see page 222)
8 oz (225 g) Fresh Salted Cod (see pages 67 and 227), soaked
12 oz (350 g) squid, cleaned (see page 92) and cut into thin slices
8 oz (225 g) monkfish fillet, cut into 1-inch (2.5-cm) pieces
2 cups (100 g) coarse, fresh white breadcrumbs
1 tablespoon chopped flat-leaf parsley
Salt and freshly ground black pepper

1 Preheat the oven to 300°F (150°C). Heat ½ cup (120 ml) of the olive oil in a large casserole. Add the sausage pieces and pepper flakes, and fry for 4 minutes, until the sausage is lightly browned.

2 Drain the beans and add them to the casserole with four of the minced garlic cloves, the bay leaves, thyme sprigs, 2½ cups (600 ml) of the chicken stock, and some freshly ground black pepper. Cover with foil or a well-fitting lid and bake for 1½ hours, until the beans are tender and most of the liquid has been absorbed.

3 Drain and skin the prepared salted cod and cut it into 1-inch (2.5-cm) pieces. Heat a little of the remaining oil in a frying pan over a high heat and sear the squid and monkfish, in batches if necessary, until nicely browned. Stir them into the cooked beans, along with the salted cod, the rest of the chicken stock, and a little more seasoning to taste. Increase the oven temperature to 400°F (200°C).

4 Put the breadcrumbs into a bowl and rub in the remaining oil. Stir in the remaining garlic, the chopped parsley, and a little salt and pepper. Spread this over the top of the beans. Return to the oven and bake, uncovered, for 30 minutes, until crisp and golden.

soups, stews, and mixed seafood

bourride of red mullet, brill, and fresh salted cod

SERVES 4

CROÛTONS:

2 tablespoons olive oil

4 slices of French bread, 1 inch (2.5 cm) thick, cut on the slant

1 medium-hot red chile pepper, seeded and minced

4 sun-dried tomatoes in oil, drained and chopped

BOURRIDE:

8 oz (225 g) unskinned red mullet fillet

8 oz (225 g) unskinned brill fillet

8 oz (225 g) Fresh Salted Cod (see pages 67 and 227), soaked

2 tablespoons olive oil

1 onion, chopped

1 small leek, chopped

½ fennel bulb, chopped

4 garlic cloves, chopped

2 pared strips of orange zest

2 tomatoes, sliced

1 bay leaf

1 sprig of thyme

5 cups (1.2 liters) Fish Stock (see page 222)

1 quantity Aïoli (see page 224)

½ teaspoon salt

Chopped flat-leaf parsley, for garnish

1 To make the croûtons, heat the oil in a frying pan and fry the bread slices on both sides until crisp and golden. Drain briefly on paper towels, and keep warm. Mix the chile and sun-dried tomatoes together in a bowl and stir in 1 tablespoon of the aïoli. Spread the mixture on the croûtons.

2 For the bourride, cut each of the fish into four pieces. Heat the oil in a large pan. Add the onion, leek, fennel, garlic, and orange zest, and fry gently, without coloring, for 5 minutes.

3 Add the tomatoes, bay leaf, thyme, fish stock, and salt. Bring to a boil and simmer for 30 minutes.

4 Add the fish pieces and simmer gently for 5 minutes. Then carefully lift them out onto a warmed serving dish and keep warm.

5 Strain the cooking liquid through a fine sieve into a clean pan, pressing out as much liquid as you can with the back of a ladle.

6 Put the aïoli into a bowl and whisk in a ladle of the cooking liquid. Stir the mixture back into the rest of the liquid and cook over a low heat until slightly thickened. Do not let it boil.

7 Pour the sauce over the fish and sprinkle with the chopped parsley. Serve with the croûtons and some plain boiled potatoes, if desired.

ALTERNATIVE FISH

A mixture of ocean perch, summer or winter flounder, and salted cod.

cotriade

SERVES 8

SORREL AND ANCHOVY BUTTER:

10 sorrel leaves

4 salted anchovy fillets in olive oil, drained

½ cup (100 g) unsalted butter, softened

COURT-BOUILLON:

2 carrots, chopped

1 leek, chopped

2 celery stalks, chopped

1 fennel bulb, chopped

½ onion, chopped

10 cups (2.4 liters) water

Pared zest and flesh of ½ lemon

2 garlic cloves, peeled

1 bay leaf

⅔ cup (150 ml) dry white wine

2 tablespoons Pernod

6 black peppercorns

1 tablespoon salt

½ cup (100 g) crème fraîche

1 cup (50 g) herb fennel (stems and leafy fronds)

3 lb (1.5 kg) mixed unskinned fish fillets, such as cod, hake, haddock, brill, john dory, gurnard or sea robin, sea bass, gray or striped mullet, mackerel, and herring (one type of fillet needs to be oily)

2 lb (900 g) new potatoes, halved

Unsalted butter, for brushing

1 lb (450 g) mussels, cleaned (see page 88)

Salt

1 For the sorrel and anchovy butter, put the ingredients into a food processor and blend until smooth. Spoon into the center of a large sheet of plastic wrap and shape into a roll 1½ inches (4 cm) thick. Wrap and chill until firm.

2 For the court-bouillon, put all ingredients but the crème fraîche and the leafy fronds of the herb fennel into a large pan. Bring to a boil and simmer for 30 minutes.

3 Cut each type of fish fillet into eight even-sized pieces.

4 Strain the court-bouillon into a clean pan, bring back to a boil, and boil rapidly until reduced by half. Add the crème fraîche and all but 1 sprig of the fennel fronds. Simmer for 5 minutes. Strain once more. Return the pan to the heat, add the potatoes, and bring back to a boil. Simmer for 15 minutes or until the potatoes are tender.

5 Preheat the broiler. Brush the oily fish fillet (such as the mackerel or herring) with the melted butter and season on both sides with some salt. Put skin-side up on a lightly buttered baking pan.

6 Put the mussels and a splash of the court-bouillon into a large pan, cover, and cook over a high heat for 3 to 4 minutes, until they have opened. Tip the mussels into a colander set over a bowl. Cover the mussels and keep warm. Pour all but the last tablespoon of the cooking liquid into the court-bouillon and bring it back to a boil.

7 Poach the remaining fish fillets in batches in the court-bouillon for 3 minutes, turning halfway through, until just firm; they will continue to cook after you have removed them. As each batch is cooked, lift out and keep warm. While cooking the last batch, broil the oily fish for 3 minutes.

8 To serve, divide the fish fillets attractively among eight warmed plates. Arrange the mussels and potatoes around the fish. Pour just enough of the court-bouillon over to half-cover the fillets.

9 Unwrap the butter and cut it into thin slices. Put two slices on each plate and serve.

a meurette of lemon sole with beaujolais

SERVES 4

SAUCE:

2 tablespoons (25 g) butter
¼ cup (50 g) each minced carrot, celery, leek, and
  onion
1 tablespoon brandy
5 cups (1.2 liters) Chicken Stock (see page 222)
½ bottle Beaujolais
1 bay leaf
1 sprig of thyme

FOR GARNISH:

2 tablespoons (25 g) butter
24 shallots, peeled
Large pinch of sugar
1 thick slice lean or Canadian bacon
8 oz (225 g) button mushrooms, quartered

CROÛTONS:

2 medium-thick slices white bread
2 tablespoons canola oil
1 tablespoon (15 g) butter

1½ lb (750 g) unskinned lemon sole, gray sole, or
  Petrale sole fillets
Butter, for brushing
2 tablespoons (25 g) Beurre Manié (see page 227)
1 quantity Persillade (see page 166)
Salt and freshly ground black pepper

1 For the sauce, melt the butter in a medium-sized saucepan, add the minced vegetables, and fry over a medium-high heat until they are lightly browned. Add the brandy and, as soon as it has evaporated, add 3¾ cups (900 ml) of the chicken stock, the wine, bay leaf, and thyme. Bring to a boil, then lower the heat and let simmer for 30 minutes. Strain the stock through a fine sieve into a wide sauté pan. Bring to a boil and boil rapidly until reduced to about 1½ cups (350 ml) and well concentrated in flavor.

2 Meanwhile, for the garnish, melt half the butter in a small pan. Add the shallots and the sugar, and cook until nicely browned. Add the rest of the chicken stock and simmer until the shallots are tender. Then turn up the heat and boil rapidly until the stock has reduced to a thick, sticky glaze, shaking the pan every now and then so that the shallots become coated in it. Cover and keep warm. Cut the bacon across into short, thin strips. Melt the rest of the butter in another pan, add the bacon, and fry gently until golden. Add the mushrooms and cook for 2 to 3 minutes until they are soft. Season to taste and keep warm.

3 For the croûtons, cut the bread into eight disks about 1 inch (2.5 cm) in diameter, using a pastry cutter. Heat the oil in a frying pan, add the butter and the disks of bread, and fry until golden on both sides. Lift out onto paper towels and keep warm.

4 Preheat the broiler. Brush the lemon sole fillets on both sides with melted butter, season with salt and pepper, and arrange on a lightly buttered baking pan or the rack of the broiler pan. Broil, 2 inches (5 cm) from the heat, for 2 to 3 minutes, until cooked through.

5 Meanwhile, whisk the beurre manié into the stock, a small piece at a time, and simmer for 2 to 3 minutes until the sauce has thickened. Adjust the seasoning if necessary, then whisk in the persillade.

6 To serve, put the sole fillets onto four warmed plates and garnish with the shallots, bacon, and mushrooms. Spoon the sauce over the fish and scatter on the croûtons.

soups, stews, and mixed seafood

a ragoût of seafood with lemon and saffron

SERVES 4

VEGETABLE NAGE:

½ **lemon**

1 **fennel bulb**

1 **large onion, peeled**

4 **celery stalks**

Handful of button mushrooms

½ **teaspoon salt**

1 **teaspoon black peppercorns**

2 **bay leaves**

3 **sprigs of thyme**

½ **teaspoon fennel seeds**

1¼ **cups (300 ml) white wine**

Large pinch of saffron strands

8 **raw large shrimp in shell**

2 (2–3 oz/50–75 g) **skinned lemon sole, gray sole, or Petrale sole fillets**

8 **baby carrots, scraped and trimmed**

8 **very small florets of broccoli**

8 **fine green beans, halved**

8 **mussels, cleaned (see page 88)**

4 **prepared bay scallops (see page 90)**

½ **cup (100 g) chilled unsalted butter, diced**

Salt and freshly ground black pepper

Maldon sea salt flakes, for garnish

A RAGOÛT OF SEAFOOD WITH LEMON AND SAFFRON

1 For the vegetable nage, pare the zest off the piece of lemon, then cut away and discard all the bitter white pith. Cut the flesh across into slices. Roughly chop all the vegetables and put them into a pan with the lemon zest and flesh, salt, peppercorns, herbs, fennel seeds, and enough water to cover. Bring to a boil and simmer for 20 minutes. Take the pan off the heat and add the wine. Cover and let cool for 2 hours.

2 Strain the nage and pour 5 cups (1.2 liters) into a wide-based pan. (Freeze the rest for later use.) Add the saffron, bring to a boil, and boil rapidly until it has reduced to ½ cup (120 ml). Transfer to a small pan and set aside.

3 Peel the shrimp, leaving the last tail segment in place (see page 72). Cut each lemon sole fillet diagonally across into four pieces.

4 Drop the vegetables into a pan of boiling salted water. Bring back to a boil, then drain and plunge into cold water to stop the cooking and set the color. Drain once more.

5 Prepare one stacked or two separate steamers (see pages 46 to 47). Put all the blanched vegetables onto one plate and the shrimp, lemon sole, mussels, and scallops on another plate. Steam the vegetables for 3 minutes and the fish for 3 to 4 minutes. Keep everything warm while you make the sauce.

6 Drain all the cooking juices from the plate of fish into the reduced stock. Bring back to a boil, then whisk in the butter, a few pieces at a time, until you have a smooth, emulsified sauce. Season to taste with salt and pepper.

7 To serve, arrange the seafood and vegetables on four warmed plates. Spoon the lemon and saffron sauce over the fish and sprinkle with some sea salt flakes.

ALTERNATIVE FISH

Lobster, oysters, langoustines, and freshwater crayfish.

5

gratin of seafood

SERVES 4

1 lb (450 g) cooked medium shrimp in shell
½ onion, roughly chopped
5 tablespoons (65 g) butter
1 tablespoon Cognac
2½ cups (600 ml) Fish Stock (see page 222)
¼ cup white wine
2 tomatoes, roughly chopped
2 lb (900 g) mussels, cleaned (see page 88)
2 shallots, minced
2 tablespoons all-purpose flour
⅔ cup (150 ml) heavy cream
1 tablespoon chopped flat-leaf parsley
Juice of ½ lemon
8 prepared bay scallops (see page 90)
6 oz (175 g) skinned haddock fillet, cut into small chunks
1½ cups (100 g) sliced button mushrooms
Scant 1 cup (100 g) fresh white crabmeat
Scant 1 cup (100 g) shredded Gruyère, Emmenthal, fontina, or Jarlsberg cheese
¾ teaspoon paprika
Pinch of cayenne pepper
Salt and freshly ground black pepper

1 Peel the shrimp, reserving the heads and shells (see page 72). Fry the onion in 1 tablespoon (15 g) of the butter until soft. Add the shrimp heads and shells and Cognac, and fry for 1 to 2 minutes. Add the fish stock, wine, and tomatoes, bring to a boil, and simmer for 20 minutes.

2 Add the mussels to the pan, cover, and cook over a high heat for 3 to 4 minutes. Tip into a large strainer set over a bowl. If there is less than 2½ cups (600 ml) of stock, add a little fish stock; if more than this you need to boil it once more until it is reduced to the required amount. Remove the mussels from their shells and set aside with the peeled shrimp. Discard everything else in the strainer.

3 Fry the shallots in 2 tablespoons (25 g) of the butter until soft. Add the flour and cook for 1 minute, stirring. Gradually stir in the stock and bring to a boil, then add the cream and simmer very gently for 10 minutes, until the sauce coats the back of a wooden spoon. Add the parsley and season to taste with some lemon juice, salt, and pepper.

4 Preheat the broiler. Melt the remaining butter. Scatter the scallops, haddock, and mushrooms into a large gratin dish, brush with the melted butter, season, and broil for 2 minutes.

5 Add the shrimp, mussels, and crabmeat to the dish, then spoon the sauce over the top. Sprinkle with the shredded cheese, dust with a little paprika and cayenne pepper, and broil, close to the heat, for 1 to 2 minutes, until golden and bubbling.

ALTERNATIVE FISH
A selection of cooked lobster, monkfish, cod, and queen or bay scallops.

hot shellfish with garlic and lemon juice

SERVES 4

8 cooked langoustines or large shrimp in shell
4 whelks
32 periwinkles
24 mussels, cleaned (see page 88)
¼ cup dry white wine
20 cockles, washed
16 small hard-shell clams, cleaned (see page 89)
8 Pacific oysters
⅓ cup (85 ml) extra virgin olive oil
2 garlic cloves, minced
Handful of flat-leaf parsley leaves, chopped
1 medium-hot red chile pepper, seeded and chopped
Juice of ½ lemon

1 Prepare a steamer as described on pages 46 to 47. Reheat the langoustines, and the periwinkles and whelks if they are already cooked, for 2 to 3 minutes.

2 If the periwinkles and whelks are raw, drop them into separate pans of boiling salted water; cook the periwinkles for 1 minute and the whelks for 4 minutes. Drain and keep warm.

3 Put the mussels into a pan with the white wine. Cover and cook over a high heat for 3 to 4 minutes until they have opened. Lift out with a slotted spoon, cover, and keep warm. Repeat with the cockles, small clams, and oysters, using the same cooking liquid. The oysters will not open fully, so finish opening them with a short, thick-bladed knife (see page 91).

4 Strain all but the last tablespoon of the cooking liquid into a pan and add the olive oil, garlic, parsley, chile, and lemon juice.

5 Arrange the warmed shellfish on a large, warmed serving platter. Bring the dressing to a boil, then pour it over the shellfish. Serve with plenty of French bread.

linguine ai frutti di mare
(linguine with mixed seafood)

SERVES 4

2¼ lb (1 kg) prepared mixed shellfish, such as small hard-shell or soft-shell clams, mussels, raw langoustines, and raw small or medium shrimp in shell

¼ cup dry white wine

1 lb (450 g) cherry tomatoes or small vine-ripened tomatoes

1 lb (450 g) linguine

½ cup (120 ml) olive oil

5 garlic cloves, thinly sliced

Pinch of dried red pepper flakes

3 tablespoons chopped flat-leaf parsley

Salt and freshly ground black pepper

1 Put the clams and mussels in a large pan with the wine, cover, and cook over a high heat for 3 to 4 minutes, until they have opened (discard any that remain closed). Tip into a colander placed over a bowl and set aside.

2 Squeeze the tomatoes to remove most of the seeds and juice, then coarsely chop them.

LINGUINE AI FRUTTI DI MARE

3 Bring a large pan of well-salted water (1 teaspoon salt to each 2½ cups/600 ml water) to a boil. Add the linguine and bring back to a boil, then cook for about 8 minutes or until al dente.

4 Meanwhile, put the olive oil and garlic into a large pan and heat slowly until the garlic begins to sizzle. Add the pepper flakes and tomatoes, and simmer for 5 minutes. Stir in all but the last 1 to 2 tablespoons of the cooking liquid from the clams and mussels. Bring back to a boil and simmer until reduced to a saucelike consistency.

5 Stir the langoustines into the sauce and turn them over until they turn pink. Add the shrimp and simmer for 2 to 3 minutes longer, until the langoustines and shrimp are both cooked. Stir in the cooked clams and mussels, along with the chopped parsley, and turn them over a few times until heated through. Season, if necessary, with a little salt and some pepper.

6 Drain the pasta well and tip it into a large, warmed serving dish. Pour the seafood sauce over the pasta and toss together well. Serve hot.

ALTERNATIVE FISH
Any mixture of shellfish, plus maybe some prepared and sliced bay scallops or squid.

seafood paella

SERVES 6

1 (1-lb/450-g) cooked lobster
5 cups (1.2 liters) Chicken Stock (see page 222)
2 bay leaves
1 large leek, sliced
12 mussels, cleaned (see page 88)
⅓ cup (85 ml) extra virgin olive oil
1 lb (450 g) monkfish fillet, cut into slices about ½ inch
  (1 cm) thick (see page 62, steps 1–5)
6 oz (175 g) skinless, boneless chicken breast, cut into
  thin strips
4 oz (100 g) small prepared squid (see page 92)
1 onion, minced
8 garlic cloves (4 minced and 4 cut into quarters)
1 red bell pepper, seeded and thinly sliced
2 cups (450 g) Arborio or Valencia rice
½ teaspoon saffron strands
6 cooked large shrimp in shell

1 Pull the claws and legs off the lobster, then detach the head from the tail (see page 77). Cut the tail through the shell into pieces at each section and the claws into three. Set aside.

2 Put the lobster head and legs into a pan with the chicken stock, bay leaves, and the green part of the leek. Bring to a boil, then let simmer for about 20 minutes. Strain through a sieve into a clean pan. You will need 3¾ cups (900 ml), so either boil to reduce or add water to make the required amount. Set aside.

3 Put the mussels into a pan with a splash of the stock. Cover and cook over a high heat for 3 to 4 minutes, until they have all opened. Tip into a colander set over a bowl to collect the liquid. Pour all but the last tablespoon of the liquid back into the stock. Cover the mussels and set aside.

4 Heat the oil in a large, deep, 12-inch (30-cm) frying pan. Add the monkfish and fry for 3 minutes, turning it over after 2 minutes. Transfer to a plate and set aside. Add the chicken (and a little more oil, if necessary) and fry for 2 to 3 minutes, until lightly browned. Set aside with the monkfish. Add the squid and stir-fry for 2 to 3 minutes, until lightly browned. Set aside with the monkfish and chicken.

5 Add the onion, all the garlic, the rest of the leek, and the bell pepper to the pan and fry for 4 to 5 minutes, until soft and lightly browned.

6 Add the rice to the pan and stir until all the grains are well coated with the oil. Add the saffron and stock, and bring to a boil. Lower the heat, cover, and simmer gently for 15 minutes.

7 Uncover the rice and lay the pieces of lobster, monkfish, chicken, squid, mussels, and shrimp on top. Cover and cook gently for 5 minutes longer. Remove from the heat and let rest for 5 minutes. Then uncover and gently fork the seafood and the rice together before serving.

rice-shaped pasta with seafood, arugula, and roasted vegetables

SERVES 4

1²/₃ cups (350 g) rice-shaped pasta, such as orzo or
    puntalette
1 small eggplant, cut into 1-inch (2.5-cm) cubes
1 red onion, cut into thin wedges
1 red bell pepper, seeded and cut into 1-inch (2.5-cm)
    pieces
1 plum tomato, cut into thin wedges
2 garlic cloves, minced
5 tablespoons extra virgin olive oil
½ teaspoon coarse sea salt
1 lb (450 g) mussels, cleaned (see page 88)
4 oz (100 g) prepared squid (see page 92), cut across
    into rings
4 oz (100 g) peeled, cooked small shrimp
3 sun-dried tomatoes in oil, drained and thinly sliced
1 medium-hot red chile pepper, seeded and minced
¼ cup (25 g) freshly grated Parmesan cheese
1 tablespoon white wine vinegar
5 tablespoons chopped flat-leaf parsley
2 oz (50 g) arugula
Salt and freshly ground black pepper

1 Preheat the oven to 425°F (220°C). Bring a large pan of well-salted water (1 teaspoon salt to each 2½ cups/600 ml water) to a boil in a large pan. Add the pasta and cook for 8 minutes, or until al dente, then drain and let cool.

2 Meanwhile, put the eggplant, onion, bell pepper, and tomato into a bowl with the garlic, 2 tablespoons of the oil, and the sea salt, and mix together well. Spread out in a small roasting pan, place in the oven, and roast for about 30 minutes or until well colored around the edges. Remove from the oven and let cool.

3 Put the mussels into a large pan with a splash of water, cover, and cook over a high heat for 3 to 4 minutes until they have opened. Tip into a colander and let cool slightly. Then remove the mussels from the shells and set aside.

4 Heat 1 tablespoon of the remaining oil in a frying pan. Add the squid and fry over a high heat for 2½ minutes, until lightly browned. Season with salt and pepper and let cool.

5 When the pasta, roasted vegetables, mussels, and squid are all cold, put them into a large bowl with the remaining olive oil, the shrimp, sun-dried tomatoes, chile, Parmesan cheese, vinegar, ¼ cup of the parsley, 1 teaspoon of salt, and 10 turns of the pepper mill. Toss together lightly, then fold in the arugula. Spoon the salad onto a large serving platter and sprinkle with the remaining chopped parsley.

le plateau de fruits de mer

SERVES 2

1 (1-lb/450-g) cooked lobster
1 (1½-lb/750-g) cooked crab
2 flat or belon oysters
2 Pacific oysters
12 mussels, cleaned (see page 88)
12 small hard-shell clams, washed
6 cooked langoustines in shell
4 large shrimp in shell
12 periwinkles, cooked (see page 111)
2 whelks, cooked (see page 111)
FOR SERVING:
¼ cup red wine
¼ cup red wine vinegar
1 shallot, minced
½ quantity Mayonnaise (see page 224), made with
    olive oil
Plenty of crushed ice
3 lb (1.5 kg) bladderwrack or other edible seaweed,
    washed
1 lemon, cut in half

1 Cut the lobster lengthwise in half (as described on page 76). Cut the crab in half right through the back shell, down between the eyes. Open the oysters as described on page 91, and open the raw mussels and clams as described on pages 88 and 89.

2 Mix together the red wine, red wine vinegar, and shallot, and pour into a small bowl. Spoon the mayonnaise into another bowl.

3 To assemble the dish, cover the bottom of a large serving platter with a thick layer of crushed ice and cover with the seaweed. Arrange the shellfish on top and garnish with the halved lemon. Serve with the shallot vinegar and mayonnaise.

ALTERNATIVE FISH

Raw cleaned bay scallops, prepared sea urchins, raw cockles (prepared as for clams), cooked small shrimp, cooked shore or other crabs, etc.

LE PLATEAU DE FRUITS DE MER

recipes

chapter 6

large meaty fish, skate, and eels

poached bonito with warm thyme-and-tomato potatoes

SERVES 4

WARM THYME-AND-TOMATO POTATOES:

1 lb (450 g) firm potatoes, peeled and cut into ¾–inch (2-cm) pieces

2 tablespoons (25 g) unsalted butter

1 large shallot, minced

Leaves from 1 sprig of thyme

1 plum tomato, skinned, seeded, and diced

1 tablespoon chopped flat-leaf parsley

4 (6-oz/175-g) pieces of thick bonito fillet

¼ cup Mayonnaise (see pages 224), made with olive oil

6 black olives, such as Kalamata, pitted and thinly sliced

Salt and freshly ground black pepper

4 flat-leaf parsley sprigs, for garnish

1 Cook the potatoes in boiling salted water for about 8 minutes or until just tender, then drain. Melt the butter in a medium-sized pan, add the shallot and the thyme leaves, and cook for about 4 minutes, until the shallot is soft but not browned. Add the potatoes and cook for 2 minutes, turning them over very gently every now and then so as not to break them up too much. Take the pan off the heat and stir in the tomato, parsley, and some seasoning.

2 While the potatoes are cooking, bring 2½ cups (600 ml) water and 1 tablespoon of salt to a boil in a large frying pan. Reduce to a simmer, then add the bonito fillets and poach for 3 minutes, turning them over after 1½ minutes. Lift them out with a slotted spoon and place on one side of a large, warmed serving plate. Cover and keep warm.

3 Stir 3 tablespoons of the poaching liquid into the mayonnaise, along with the black olives. Pour into a small, warmed serving bowl. Garnish the fish with the parsley sprigs and spoon the thyme-and-tomato potatoes alongside. Serve the sauce separately.

ALTERNATIVE FISH

This dish can be made equally well with those beautiful, plump, big mackerel you get in the winter. You'll need ones weighing about 12-14 oz (350–400 g). It would also work well with salmon trout, skipjack tuna, and salmon.

tuna carpaccio with arugula and parmesan cheese (see technique 39, page 63)

SERVES 4

1 (8-oz/225-g) piece of tuna loin fillet
¼ cup extra virgin olive oil
½ oz (15 g) Parmesan shavings
2 oz (50 g) arugula
Maldon sea salt flakes
Coarsely ground black pepper

1 Wrap the piece of tuna tightly in some plastic wrap so that it takes on a nice cylindrical shape. Place it in the freezer for about 3 hours until it is firm but not completely frozen.

2 Remove the tuna from the freezer, unwrap, and place on a chopping board. Cut across into very thin slices using a very sharp, long-bladed knife. They should be as thin as, if not thinner than, smoked salmon.

3 Arrange about four slices of tuna to cover four cold plates in a single layer, pressing them out slightly so that they butt up together. Drizzle the oil over the fish and sprinkle with a little black pepper and sea salt flakes.

4 Scatter the Parmesan shavings over the tuna and pile the arugula leaves in the center. Serve with a little crusty fresh bread.

VARIATION

carpaccio of monkfish with lemon olive oil

Replace the tuna with prepared monkfish fillets (see page 62). Wrap and freeze for just 1 hour. Serve drizzled with Lemon Olive Oil (see page 227) or extra virgin olive oil.

TUNA CARPACCIO WITH ARUGULA AND PARMESAN CHEESE

TUNA

pan-grilled tuna salad with guacamole

SERVES 4

1 (1-lb/450-g) piece of tuna loin fillet

Oil, for brushing

Sea salt and freshly ground black pepper

4 sprigs of cilantro, for garnish

GUACAMOLE:

1 large avocado

1 jalapeño pepper, seeded

Juice of 1 lime

2 green onions, chopped

1 tablespoon chopped cilantro

3 tablespoons canola oil

½ teaspoon salt

SOY DRESSING:

¼ cup water

1 tablespoon dark soy sauce

1 green onion, minced

¼ jalapeño pepper, seeded and chopped

Juice and zest of ½ lime

½ lemongrass stalk, outer leaves removed and core finely sliced

1 teaspoon minced fresh ginger

1 Heat a ridged cast-iron grill pan until it is very hot. Brush the piece of tuna with oil and sprinkle liberally with salt and freshly ground black pepper. Cook the tuna for 1 to 1½ minutes on each face, until colored all over. Remember the center of the tuna should remain raw. Remove from the pan and season again. Let cool completely.

2 Blend all the guacamole ingredients in a food processor until smooth. Mix all the soy dressing ingredients together.

3 Slice the tuna into ¼-inch (5-mm) slices and arrange on four cold plates. The slices should slightly overlap and be to the side of the plates. Put a spoonful of the guacamole on each plate, again slightly to the side (offsetting food on plates makes it look more natural). Add a generous pool of dressing and decorate the guacamole with a sprig of cilantro.

tonno con fagioli (tuna and cannellini beans)

SERVES 4

TUNA CONFIT:

1 (10-oz/275-g) thick tuna loin steak

About 1¼ cups (300 ml) inexpensive olive oil

1 onion, thinly sliced

2 garlic cloves, sliced

2 fresh or dried bay leaves

¼ small lemon, sliced

1 large sprig of thyme

1¼ cups (225 g) dried cannellini beans, soaked in cold water overnight

1 bay leaf

1 shallot, thinly sliced

2 sprigs of thyme

1 garlic clove, peeled but left whole, plus 1 small garlic clove, crushed

⅓ cup (85 ml) extra virgin olive oil, plus a little extra for serving

3 tablespoons lemon juice

1 small red onion, thinly sliced

3 tablespoons chopped flat-leaf parsley, plus extra for garnish

Salt and freshly ground black pepper

1 Make the tuna confit (if possible, make the confit the day before you plan to serve the dish, so you can leave it for 24 hours to allow all the flavors to permeate the fish): sprinkle a thin layer of salt in a shallow dish, lay the tuna on top, and cover it with another layer of salt. Set aside for 10 minutes. Now brush most of the salt off the fish and rinse it under cold water. Dry on paper towels, then cut it, if necessary, into pieces that will fit neatly in a single layer in a small saucepan.

2 Heat 3 tablespoons of the oil in the pan, add the onion and garlic, and fry gently for 5 minutes, until soft but not colored. Add the bay leaves, lemon slices, and thyme, put the tuna on top, and pour in the rest of the oil. If the oil does not cover the fish, add a little more. Place the pan over a low heat and slowly bring the temperature of the oil up to 212°F (100°C). Remove the pan from the heat and let the tuna cool.

3 Drain the beans, tip them into a large pan, and add enough fresh water to cover them by about 1 inch (2.5 cm). Bring to a boil, then add the bay leaf, shallot, thyme sprigs, and the whole garlic clove. Simmer for about 45 minutes or until tender, replenishing with boiling water, if necessary, to make sure that the beans stay just covered.

4 Just as the beans are ready, return the tuna to a low heat and bring back up to 212°F (100°C). Drain the beans. Discard the bay leaf, thyme, and garlic, and tip the beans into a bowl. Toss with the extra virgin olive oil, crushed garlic, lemon juice, some salt, and plenty of freshly ground black pepper. Let cool slightly.

5 As soon as the tuna is back up to temperature, lift it out of the pan and let the excess oil drain away. Break the fish into chunky pieces and season them with ½ teaspoon each of salt and pepper.

6 Toss the red onion and parsley into the beans, then carefully stir in the tuna so that you don't break up the flakes too much. Spoon into a large serving bowl, drizzle a little extra olive oil over the top, and sprinkle with chopped parsley. Serve with plenty of crusty fresh bread.

seared tuna with rice noodle and cilantro salad

SERVES 4

RICE NOODLE AND CILANTRO SALAD:

1 tablespoon sesame seeds
2 oz (50 g) cilantro (about 1 cup)
6 green onions, trimmed
Coarsely grated zest and juice of 1 lime
2 tablespoons Thai fish sauce (*nam pla*)
5 tablespoons water
2 teaspoons toasted sesame oil
2 tablespoons canola oil
3 oz (85 g) rice vermicelli noodles
3 medium-hot green chile peppers, seeded and minced
2 tablespoons Japanese pickled ginger, cut into shreds
1 small bunch garlic chives, chopped (optional)
1 bunch watercress, larger stems removed and
    broken into sprigs

4 (7-oz/200-g) tuna loin steaks
6 tablespoons dark soy sauce
¼ cup balsamic vinegar

1 For the salad, preheat the broiler. Spread the sesame seeds on a baking pan and toast under the broiler, shaking the pan now and then, until golden. Pick the leaves off the cilantro and discard the stems— if the leaves are quite large, very roughly chop them. You will need about 6 tablespoons in all. Very thinly slice the green onions on the diagonal. Mix together the lime juice, fish sauce, water, sesame oil, and canola oil.

2 Bring a pan of water to a boil. Drop in the noodles and take it off the heat. Let soak for 2 minutes, then drain well and tip the noodles back into the pan. Cover and keep warm. Heat a heavy-bottomed frying pan until very hot. Brush with a little oil, then add the tuna steaks and cook for 2 minutes on each side. Add the soy sauce and balsamic vinegar to the pan and boil vigorously, turning the steaks once, until they become coated in a rich brown glaze. Remove from the heat and keep warm.

3 Add the sesame seeds, cilantro, green onions, lime zest, chiles, pickled ginger, garlic chives, and watercress to the noodles. Add the dressing and toss everything together.

4 Pile some of the salad in the center of four warmed plates. Slice each tuna steak into three on the diagonal and place on top of the salad. Serve the rest of the salad separately.

pan-grilled white tuna on a warm salad of green beans, garlic, and tomatoes

SERVES 4

WARM SALAD OF GREEN BEANS:

12 oz (350 g) fine green beans, trimmed
2 tablespoons extra virgin olive oil
3 tomatoes, seeded and cut into small dice
1 large garlic clove, minced
½ teaspoon thyme leaves

4 (6–8 oz/175–225 g) pieces of white tuna loin (Albacore)
A little olive oil
Salt and freshly ground black pepper

1 For the salad, bring a pan of salted water to a boil. Drop in the beans and cook for 3 minutes or until al dente. Drain, refresh briefly under running cold water, and drain once more.

2 Return the beans to their pan and add the extra virgin olive oil, tomatoes, garlic, thyme leaves, and some salt and pepper to taste. Gently turn over until heated through, then keep warm.

3 Heat a ridged cast-iron grill pan until it is really hot. Brush the tuna generously on both sides with olive oil and season well with salt and pepper. Put on the pan and cook for just 2 minutes on each side.

4 To serve, spoon the beans into the center of four warmed plates and put the tuna on top. Drizzle a little virgin olive oil around the outside of the plate and sprinkle with some coarsely crushed black pepper.

shark vindaloo

SERVES 4

2 lb (900 g) small, skinned shark steaks
3–4 tablespoons peanut or canola oil
1 onion, chopped
2 tomatoes, roughly chopped
¼ cup Vindaloo Curry Paste (see pages 226)
1¼ cups (300 ml) water
8 small, hot green chile peppers
Coconut vinegar or white wine vinegar, to taste
Salt

1 Season the shark steaks with salt, then set aside. Heat the oil in a large, deep frying pan, add the onion, and fry until richly browned.

2 Add the tomatoes and cook until they form a deep golden paste.

3 Now stir in the vindaloo paste and fry gently for 5 minutes, stirring, until it has slightly caramelized. Pour in the water and let the sauce simmer for 10 minutes, giving it a stir every now and then.

4 Meanwhile, slit the green chiles open along their length and scrape out the seeds. Leave the chiles whole.

5 Add the shark steaks and chiles to the sauce and simmer for 10 minutes, carefully turning the steaks over halfway through.

6 Add vinegar and salt to taste, and serve with some pilau rice (see the recipe for Herring Recheado on page 160).

VARIATION

monkfish vindaloo

Replace the shark steaks with 1 (2-lb/900-g)) skinned monkfish tail (see page 62), sliced across into 1-inch (2.5-cm) steaks. Add to the sauce and simmer for 10 minutes. Then lift the steaks out onto a plate and boil the sauce rapidly until reduced to a good consistency (monkfish releases a lot more liquid during cooking than shark). Return the steaks to the sauce to reheat, and continue as for the main recipe.

ALTERNATIVE FISH
Swordfish, kingfish.

SHARK VINDALOO

pan-grilled swordfish kebabs with oregano, olive oil, and lemon juice

SERVES 4

1¼ lb (550 g) swordfish steaks, cut about
    1 inch (2.5 cm) thick
¼ cup olive oil
1 teaspoon chopped oregano
Juice of ½ lemon
1 teaspoon Maldon sea salt flakes
½ teaspoon cracked black peppercorns

1 Cut the swordfish steaks into 1-inch (2.5-cm) square pieces. Mix all the other ingredients together in a bowl. Add the swordfish pieces and mix together well, then set aside to marinate at room temperature for 20 minutes. Submerge eight bamboo skewers in water and let them soak.

2 Heat a ridged cast-iron grill pan, or a charcoal fire. Thread the pieces of swordfish onto the bamboo skewers and pan-grill or chargrill for 2 to 3 minutes, turning them as they brown. Serve, perhaps, with some pan-grilled potatoes (see page 146), or some potatoes deep-fried in olive oil, plus a mixed salad.

kingfish curry

SERVES 4

4 (6–8 oz/175–225 g) pieces of thick kingfish fillet,
    skinned
3 tablespoons peanut oil
½ teaspoon black mustard seeds
½ teaspoon cumin seeds
½ teaspoon fennel seeds
¼ teaspoon fenugreek seeds
1 onion, thinly sliced
1 quantity Goan Masala Paste (see page 226)
1 teaspoon turmeric powder
6 curry leaves
2 medium-hot red chile peppers, seeded and sliced
    across diagonally
12 small okra, ends trimmed
3 tomatoes, skinned and quartered
1¾ cups (400 ml) coconut milk
¼ cup Tamarind Water (see page 227)
⅔ cup (150 ml) water
Salt

1 Lightly salt the pieces of fish. Heat the oil in a pan that is just large enough to take the fish in one layer. Add the whole spices and fry them for about 30 seconds, then add the sliced onion and fry until golden.

2 Add the Goan masala paste and turmeric, and fry for 3 to 4 minutes. Add the curry leaves, chiles, okra, tomatoes, coconut milk, tamarind water, water, and salt to taste, and simmer for 5 minutes.

3 Add the pieces of fish and simmer for another 5 minutes. Serve with steamed basmati rice.

ALTERNATIVE FISH
This also works well with other big fish like shark, tuna, bonito, or some of the really big game fish like marlin or sailfish. But you could make it with pieces of the humble cod too, if desired.

gratin of skate cheeks with cheddar cheese and breadcrumbs

SERVES 4

2½ cups (600 ml) milk
1 small onion, halved
6 whole cloves
4 bay leaves
4 gratings of fresh nutmeg
2 small sprigs of thyme
1 teaspoon black peppercorns
6 tablespoons (75 g) unsalted butter
¼ cup all-purpose flour
½ cup (120 ml) heavy cream
1¼ lb (550 g) prepared skate cheeks (see page 35)
⅔ cup (75 g) shredded aged Cheddar cheese
½ cup (25 g) coarse white breadcrumbs, made from day-old bread
¼ teaspoon cayenne pepper
10 turns of the black pepper mill
Salt and freshly ground white pepper

1 Put the milk into a pan with the onion, cloves, bay leaves, nutmeg, thyme, and black peppercorns. Bring to a boil and simmer for 5 minutes. Remove from the heat and set aside for 1 hour to allow the flavors to infuse.

2 Bring the milk back to a boil, then strain through a sieve into a clean pan. Melt 4 tablespoons (50 g) of the butter in a pan, add the flour, and cook gently for 2 to 3 minutes without letting it color. Gradually stir in the hot milk, then bring to a boil. Simmer gently over a very low heat for 10 minutes, giving it an occasional stir, until slightly reduced and thickened. Stir in the cream and season with some salt and freshly ground white pepper to taste.

3 Heat the remaining butter in a large frying pan until foaming. Season the skate cheeks with salt and white pepper, then add to the pan and fry briskly for 4 minutes, turning them now and then, until lightly browned and just cooked through.

4 Divide the cheeks among four individual gratin dishes. Pour the sauce over them.

5 Preheat the broiler. Mix the shredded cheese with the breadcrumbs, cayenne pepper, and black pepper, and sprinkle this over each dish. Broil for 2 to 3 minutes, until crisp and golden. Serve with hot brown toast.

ALTERNATIVE FISH
Large chunks of skinned white fish such as cod, haddock, or monkfish.

skate with black butter

SERVES 4
COURT-BOUILLON:
1¼ cups (300 ml) dry white wine
5 cups (1.2 liters) water
⅓ cup (85 ml) white wine vinegar
2 bay leaves
12 black peppercorns
1 onion, roughly chopped
2 carrots, roughly chopped
2 celery stalks, roughly chopped
1 teaspoon salt

4 (8-oz/225-g) skinned skate wings (see page 34)
1½ tablespoons capers in brine, drained and rinsed
BLACK BUTTER:
¾ cup (175 g) butter
¼ cup red wine vinegar
1 tablespoon chopped flat-leaf parsley

1 For the court-bouillon, put all the ingredients into a large pan, bring to a boil, and simmer for 20 minutes. Set aside to cool, to allow the flavor to improve before using.

2 Put the skate wings into a large pan. Pour in the court-bouillon, bring to a boil, and simmer very gently for 15 minutes, until they are cooked through.

3 Carefully lift the skate wings out of the pan, letting the excess liquid drain off, and place them on four warmed plates. Sprinkle with the capers and keep warm.

4 For the black butter, melt the butter in a frying pan. As soon as it starts to foam, turn quite brown, and smell very nutty, add the vinegar and then the parsley. Let it boil down for a minute or so, until slightly reduced. Pour the butter over the skate and serve straight away.

ROASTED SKATE WINGS WITH CHILE BEANS

roasted skate wings with chile beans (see technique 17, page 34)

SERVES 4

CHILE BEANS:

2 cups (350 g) dried cannellini beans, soaked in cold
    water overnight

2 tablespoons extra virgin olive oil

1 garlic clove, minced

2 medium-hot red chile peppers, seeded and minced

1 small onion, minced

1½ cups (350 ml) Chicken Stock (see page 222)

2 beefsteak tomatoes, skinned, seeded, and diced

1 teaspoon chopped tarragon

4 (8-oz/225-g) prepared skate wings (see page 34)

1 teaspoon paprika

1 teaspoon coarsely crushed black pepper

¼ cup (50 g) butter

3 tablespoons sherry vinegar

Salt and freshly ground black pepper

1 Drain the cannellini beans and put them into a pan with plenty of fresh water to cover. Bring to a boil, skimming off any scum as it rises to the surface, then cover and let simmer for 1 hour or until just tender. Drain and set aside.

2 For the chile beans, put the extra virgin olive oil, garlic, and red chiles into a pan. As soon as the garlic and chiles start to sizzle, add the onion and cook for 5 minutes until soft. Add the drained cannellini beans and 1¼ cups (300 ml) of the chicken stock. Leave to simmer for 10 minutes.

3 Preheat the oven to 400°F (200°C). Dry the skate wings with paper towels, then sprinkle on both sides with some paprika and coarsely crushed black pepper.

4 To cook the skate wings, melt the butter in a roasting pan on top of the stove. Add the wings and lightly brown them for 1 minute on each side. Sprinkle with a little salt, transfer to the oven and roast for 10 minutes.

5 Meanwhile, stir the tomatoes into the beans and simmer for 10 more minutes. Stir in the chopped tarragon and season to taste with some salt and pepper.

6 To serve, spoon some of the beans into the center of four warmed plates and put a roasted skate wing on top. Place the roasting pan over a moderate heat, add the sherry vinegar and the rest of the chicken stock, and let boil for 1 to 2 minutes, scraping up all the crusty bits from the bottom of the pan. Strain the sauce through a fine sieve, season to taste, and spoon over the top of the skate.

a poêle of conger eel

SERVES 4

6 garlic cloves

1 (2¾-lb/1.25 kg) piece of skinned conger eel, cut from
    just behind the gut cavity

4 oz (100 g) caul fat or 4 slices of bacon

¼ cup (50 g) butter

1 carrot

1 large celery stalk

1 cup (100 g) pearl onions, peeled

Salt and freshly ground black pepper

1 Preheat the oven to 450°F (230°C). Thinly slice 2 of the garlic cloves. Make small, deep incisions all over the piece of conger eel and insert a slice of garlic into each. Then wrap it in the caul fat or bacon and tie in place with some fine string.

2 Cut the carrots and celery into 1½-inch (4-cm) pieces, then cut each piece lengthwise into ½-inch (1-cm) batons.

3 Melt the butter in a heavy casserole large enough to take the piece of eel. Add the carrots, celery, onions, and the remaining whole garlic cloves, cover, and cook gently for 5 minutes.

4 Add the eel and turn it once or twice until it is well coated in butter. Season with salt and pepper. Cover once more, transfer to the oven, and cook for 20 minutes, basting twice with the butter while it cooks.

5 Uncover the casserole, baste once more with the butter, and cook for 10 more minutes.

6 Lift the eel onto a warmed serving plate and spoon the vegetables and juices around it. Carve lengthwise into long slices to serve.

anguilles au vert

SERVES 4

1¼ cups (300 ml) Fish Stock (see page 222)
1 tablespoon (15 g) butter
2 large shallots, minced
½ garlic clove, crushed
1 small sprig of thyme
1 small bay leaf
¼ cup dry vermouth, such as Noilly Prat
¼ cup (25 g) shredded spinach leaves
¼ cup (25 g) watercress leaves (stems removed)
1 tablespoon each chopped tarragon, flat-leaf parsley, chervil, and chives, plus extra for garnish
¼ cup (25 g) shredded sorrel leaves
¼ loaf of French bread
¼ cup Clarified Butter (see page 226)
12 oz (350 g) skinned eel fillets (see page 36), cut into pieces about 4 inches (10 cm) long
¾ cup (175 ml) heavy cream
3 egg yolks
Lemon juice
Salt and freshly ground black pepper

1 For the sauce, boil the fish stock rapidly until reduced to about ¼ cup. Melt the butter in another pan, add the shallots, garlic, thyme, and bay leaf, and cook gently until soft but not colored. Add the reduced fish stock and the vermouth, and boil until reduced by about three-fourths. Discard the thyme and bay leaf. Add the spinach, watercress, and chopped herbs, and cook for 2 minutes. Add the sorrel and just let it wilt into the sauce. Tip into a blender and blend until smooth. Return the sauce to the pan and set aside.

2 Cut the bread on the diagonal into 4 long slices, no more than ½ inch (1 cm) thick. Fry the bread pieces in half the clarified butter for about 2 minutes on each side, until crisp and lightly golden. Keep warm in a low oven.

3 Preheat the broiler. Brush the pieces of eel with the rest of the clarified butter and season. Arrange on a greased baking pan and broil, about 2 inches (5 cm) from the heat, for 1 to 1½ minutes. Keep warm.

4 Mix the cream and egg yolks together until smooth, then stir them into the sauce. Cook over a low heat, stirring, until lightly thickened, but take care not to get it too hot and boil or it will scramble. Season with a little lemon juice, salt, and pepper to taste, and whisk to make the sauce slightly frothy.

5 To serve, put the slices of fried bread on four warmed plates and put some of the eel pieces on top. Spoon the sauce over the eel and garnish each plate with a small bunch of tarragon, parsley, chervil, and chives.

ALTERNATIVE FISH

This is a classic eel dish, so eel it's got to be … or does it? I have a feeling it would work well with thin fillets of flatfish such as plaice, lemon sole, gray sole, Petrale sole, or flounder, or with whiting.

jellied eels

SERVES 4–6

2 lb (900 g) skinned eels (see page 36)
Pared zest and juice of 1 lemon
3 bay leaves
4 whole cloves
8 black peppercorns
4 teaspoons salt
1 small bunch of curly parsley, chopped
Good malt vinegar
Freshly ground white pepper
Brown bread and butter, for serving

1 Cut out the spines from the top and bottom edges of the eels, then cut them across into 1½-inch (4-cm) pieces.

2 Put the pieces of eel into a large saucepan with the lemon zest, juice, bay leaves, cloves, peppercorns, and salt. Add enough cold water just to cover, then bring to a boil and simmer for 20 minutes.

3 Transfer the eels and their cooking liquid to a bowl and let cool.

4 Stir in the chopped parsley, then divide the mixture among four to six small pots. Cover and chill until the cooking liquid has set. Serve with the vinegar, pepper, and bread and butter.

stir-fried eel with black bean sauce (see technique 18, page 36)

SERVES 2

8–10 oz (225–275 g) skinned eel fillet (see page 36)

1½ teaspoons cornstarch

1½ tablespoons Chinese fermented salted black beans

½ teaspoon sugar

2 tablespoons toasted sesame oil

2 garlic cloves, cut into fine shreds

1-inch (2.5-cm) piece of peeled fresh ginger, cut into very thin shreds

1 medium-hot red chile pepper, thinly sliced

3 tablespoons Chinese rice wine or dry sherry

1 teaspoon dark soy sauce

4 green onions, cut on the diagonal into long, thin slices

Salt

1 Cut the eel fillet diagonally into pieces 1 inch (2.5 cm) wide. Toss with a little salt and then the cornstarch.

2 Put the black beans, sugar, and 2 tablespoons of cold water into a small bowl and crush to a coarse paste.

3 Heat a wok over a high heat until it is smoking hot. Add the sesame oil and garlic, quickly followed by the ginger, red chile, and black bean paste. Stir-fry for a few seconds, then add the eel pieces and stir-fry for 1 minute.

4 Add the rice wine or sherry, soy sauce, and 3 to 4 tablespoons of water, and cook for 2 minutes, until the eel is cooked through.

5 Add the green onions to the wok and stir-fry for about 1 minute. Serve immediately, with some steamed rice.

STIR-FRIED EEL WITH BLACK BEAN SAUCE

recipes
chapter 7

large
round fish

cod with
red wine sauce (see technique 4, page 20)

SERVES 4

LENTILS:

¼ cup (50 g) dried lentilles de Puy
1¼ cups (300 ml) Fish Stock (see page 222)
1 whole clove and 1 bay leaf
2 slices peeled onion
½ teaspoon salt

6 tablespoons (75 g) unsalted butter
4 (6-oz/175-g) pieces of thick, unskinned cod fillet
   (see page 20)
¼ cup (50 g) minced carrot
¼ cup (50 g) minced celery
¼ cup (50 g) minced onion
Small pinch of ground allspice
Small pinch of ground cloves
Small pinch of grated nutmeg
Large pinch of curry powder
2½ cups (600 ml) red wine
2½ cups (600 ml) Chicken Stock (see page 222)
1 teaspoon sugar
1 tablespoon all-purpose flour
Coarse sea salt and freshly ground black pepper

1 Put all the ingredients for the lentils into a pan and simmer until tender. Drain. Discard the clove and bay leaf, then cover and keep warm.

2 Melt 4 tablespoons (50 g) of the butter in a medium-sized pan and brush a little over the cod. Season the fish on both sides with sea salt and a little black pepper. Put it, skin-side up, in a greased baking pan.

3 For the sauce, add the carrot, celery, onion, and spices to the melted butter in the pan and fry over a high heat for about 10 minutes until the vegetables are well browned. Add the red wine, stock, sugar, and ¼ teaspoon of salt. Bring to a boil and boil until the sauce is reduced to ¾ cup (175 ml) and well concentrated in flavor. Strain the reduced sauce into a clean pan and keep warm.

4 Preheat the broiler. Broil the cod, about 4 inches (10 cm) from the heat, for 8 minutes, until the skin is well browned. Meanwhile, mix the remaining butter with the flour to make a smooth paste (beurre manié). Bring the sauce to a boil, then whisk in the paste, a little at a time. Simmer for 2 minutes until the sauce is smooth and thickened. Adjust the seasoning, if necessary.

5 To serve, spoon the lentils onto four warmed plates and place the cod on top. Spoon the sauce around the edge of the plate.

fish cakes

2 lb (900 g) baking or all-purpose potatoes, peeled and
  cut into chunks
2 lb (900 g) skinned cod fillet
2 tablespoons (25 g) butter, melted
1/4 cup (15 g) chopped flat-leaf parsley
Canola oil, for deep-frying
1/3 cup (50 g) flour seasoned with salt and pepper
2 eggs, beaten
3 cups (150 g) fresh white breadcrumbs
1 quantity of Tartar Sauce (see page 224)
Salt and freshly ground black pepper

1 Cook the potatoes in boiling salted water for 20 minutes until
tender. Drain well, then tip back into the pan and mash until smooth.
Let cool slightly.

2 Bring some water to a boil in a large, deep frying pan. Add the fish,
bring back to a boil, and simmer for 8 minutes. Lift the fish out onto a
plate and, when it is cool enough to handle, break it into large flakes,
discarding the skin and any bones.

3 Put the fish into a bowl with the mashed potatoes, melted butter,
parsley, and some salt and pepper, and mix together well. Shape the
mixture into eight rounds about 1 inch (2.5 cm) thick. Cover with plastic
wrap and chill for 20 minutes.

4 Heat some oil for deep-frying to 350°F (180°C). Put the seasoned
flour, beaten eggs, and breadcrumbs in three separate shallow bowls.
Dip the fish cakes into the flour, then into the egg, and, finally, in the
breadcrumbs, pressing them on well to give an even coating. Deep-fry
in batches for about 4 minutes until crisp and golden. Lift out with a
slotted spoon and drain briefly on paper towels, then keep warm in a
low oven while you cook the rest. Serve with the tartar sauce.

VARIATIONS

salmon fish cakes

Replace the white fish fillet with salmon fillet, and replace 1 tablespoon
of the chopped parsley with chopped dill.

mackerel fish cakes

Replace the white fish fillet with 2 lb (900 g) whole mackerel. Slash the
fish two or three times on both sides and broil, 4 inches (10 cm) from
the heat, for 5 minutes on each side. Let cool, then flake the flesh,
discarding the skin and bones. Replace the parsley with 2 tablespoons of
chopped herb fennel and beat in with 1 tablespoon of Pernod or Ricard.

pollock and smoked salmon fish cakes

Replace the white fish fillet with 1½ lb (750 g) pollock fillet and 5 oz
(150 g) finely diced smoked salmon. Replace the chopped parsley with
2 tablespoons of chopped fresh dill. Poach the pollock as in the main
recipe; mix into the potatoes along with the smoked salmon and dill.

fish and chips with tartar sauce

1¾ cups (240 g) all-purpose flour
3½ teaspoons baking powder
9 fl oz (270 ml) ice water
2 lb (900 g) baking or all-purpose potatoes
Canola oil, for deep-frying
4 (6-oz/175-g) pieces of thick cod fillet, cut from the
  head end, not the tail
1 quantity Tartar Sauce (see page 224)
Salt and freshly ground black pepper

1 To make the batter, mix the flour, 1 teaspoon of salt, and the baking
powder with the water. Keep cold and use within 20 minutes of making.

2 Preheat the oven to 300°F (150°C). Line a baking sheet with plenty
of paper towels and set aside.

3 Peel the potatoes and cut them lengthwise into fries ½ inch (1 cm)
thick. Pour some oil into a large, deep pan until it is about one-third full
and heat it to 260°F (130°C). Drop half the fries into a frying basket and
cook them for about 5 minutes, until tender when pierced with the tip
of a knife but not colored. Lift them out and drain off the excess oil.
Repeat with the rest of the fries, then set aside.

4 To fry the fish, heat the oil to 325°F (160°C). Season the cod fillets
with salt and pepper, then dip into the batter. Fry, two pieces at a time,
for 7 to 8 minutes, until crisp and golden brown. Lift out and drain on
the paper-lined baking sheet. Keep hot in the oven while you cook the
other two pieces of fish.

5 Raise the temperature of the oil to 375°F (190°C). Cook the fries in
small batches for about 2 minutes, until crisp and golden. Lift them out of
the pan and shake to remove the excess oil, then drain on paper towels.
Sprinkle with salt. Serve the cod and fries with the tartar sauce.

COD

broiled cod on green onion mash with a soy-butter sauce

SERVES 4

4 (6–8 oz/175–225 g) pieces of thick, unskinned cod fillet

Maldon sea salt flakes and freshly ground black pepper

A little melted butter, for brushing

GREEN ONION MASH:

2½ lb (1.25 kg) baking or all-purpose potatoes, peeled and cut into chunks

¼ cup (50 g) butter

1 bunch green onions, trimmed and thinly sliced

A little milk

Salt and freshly ground white pepper

SOY-BUTTER SAUCE:

2½ cups (600 ml) Chicken Stock (see page 222)

2 tablespoons dark soy sauce

6 tablespoons (75 g) unsalted butter

1 tomato, skinned, seeded, and diced

1 heaped teaspoon chopped cilantro

1 Put the fish, skin-side down, in a shallow dish and sprinkle with 1 teaspoon of salt. Set aside for 30 minutes.

2 Rinse the salt off the fish and dry well on paper towels. Brush each piece with melted butter and put them skin-side up on a greased baking pan or the rack of the broiler pan. Sprinkle the skin with a few sea salt flakes and some coarsely crushed black pepper.

3 For the green onion mash, cook the potatoes in boiling unsalted water for 20 minutes until tender.

4 Meanwhile, for the sauce, put the chicken stock and soy sauce into another pan and boil it rapidly until it has reduced by half.

5 Preheat the broiler. Broil the cod, about 4 inches (10 cm) from the heat, for 8 minutes on one side only.

6 Just before the fish is ready, add the butter to the sauce and whisk it in. Remove from the heat and add the tomato and chopped cilantro.

7 Drain the potatoes and, when the steam has died down, return them to the pan. Mash until smooth. Heat the butter in another pan, add the green onions, and turn them over in the butter for a few seconds. Beat them into the potato with a little milk and some salt and ground white pepper to taste.

8 To serve, spoon the green onion mash into the center of four warmed plates. Rest the the pieces of cod on top and spoon the sauce around the outside of the plate.

broiled cod with lettuce hearts and a rich chicken and tarragon dressing

SERVES 4

1 (1¼-lb/550-g) piece of thick, skinned cod fillet

5 cups (1.2 liters) Chicken Stock (see page 222)

A few tarragon stems

2 garlic cloves, peeled

2 tablespoons extra virgin olive oil

4 oz (100 g) asparagus tips

4 small heads of butter lettuce

12 very thin slices of pancetta

1 teaspoon chopped chives

1 teaspoon chopped tarragon

1½ teaspoons white wine vinegar

Salt and freshly ground black pepper

1 Put the cod into a shallow dish and sprinkle liberally with salt. Set aside for 20 minutes. Meanwhile, put the chicken stock, tarragon stems, and garlic cloves into a large pan and boil until reduced to about ⅓ cup (85 ml) and nicely concentrated in flavor. Strain into a small, clean pan and keep warm.

BROILED COD WITH LETTUCE HEARTS AND A RICH CHICKEN AND TARRAGON DRESSING

7

2 Rinse the salt off the fish and dry well on paper towels. Brush with a little of the olive oil, season with some pepper, and place on a lightly oiled baking pan.

3 Cook the asparagus tips in boiling salted water until just tender. Drain, refresh, and keep warm. Remove the outside leaves from each lettuce head until you reach the pale green hearts. Cut each heart into quarters.

4 Preheat the broiler, then broil the cod, about 4 inches (10 cm) from the heat, for 10 to 12 minutes. Put the slices of pancetta over the fish and broil for 1 to 2 minutes, until it is crisp and lightly golden.

5 Put the quartered lettuce hearts in the center of four warmed plates. Break the pancetta into small pieces and the cod into chunky flakes. Arrange the cod around the lettuce with the pancetta and asparagus. Sprinkle with the chopped chives and tarragon. Spoon the warm chicken stock over the lettuce and a little over the rest of the plates. Whisk the remaining olive oil, the vinegar, and some seasoning together, drizzle over the plates, and serve straight away.

ALTERNATIVE FISH

I particularly like thick fillets of flaky fish for this. Haddock would be a good alternative, of course, but salmon would work well, too.

FISH PIE

fish pie

SERVES 4

1 small onion, thickly sliced
2 whole cloves
1 bay leaf
2½ cups (600 ml) milk
1¼ cups (300 ml) heavy cream
1 lb (450 g) unskinned cod fillet
8 oz (225 g) smoked cod or haddock (finnan haddie) fillet
4 eggs
½ cup (100 g) butter
5 tablespoons all-purpose flour
5 tablespoons chopped flat-leaf parsley
Freshly grated nutmeg
2½ lb (1.25 kg) baking or all-purpose potatoes, peeled
1 egg yolk
Salt and freshly ground white pepper

1 Stud a couple of the onion slices with the cloves. Put the onion slices in a large pan with the bay leaf, 1¾ cups (450 ml) of the milk, the cream, cod, and smoked fish. Bring just to a boil and simmer for 8 minutes. Lift the fish out onto a plate and strain the cooking liquid into a measuring cup. When the fish is cool enough to handle, break it into large flakes, discarding the skin and any bones. Sprinkle it over the bottom of a shallow 8-cup (1.75-liter) baking dish.

2 Hard-boil the eggs for 8 minutes, then drain and let cool. Peel them, cut into chunky slices, and arrange on top of the fish.

3 Melt 4 tablespoons (50 g) of the butter in a pan, add the flour, and cook for 1 minute. Take the pan off the heat and gradually stir in the reserved cooking liquid. Return it to the heat and bring slowly to the boil, stirring all the time. Let it simmer gently for 10 minutes. Remove from the heat once more, stir in the parsley, and season with nutmeg, salt, and white pepper. Pour the sauce over the fish and let cool. Cover and chill for 1 hour.

4 Cook the potatoes in boiling salted water for 15 to 20 minutes. Drain, then mash and add the rest of the butter and the egg yolk. Season with salt and freshly ground white pepper. Beat in enough of the remaining milk to form a soft, spreadable mash.

5 Preheat the oven to 400°F (200°C). Spoon the potato over the fish filling and mark the surface with a fork. Bake for 35 to 40 minutes, until piping hot and golden brown.

ALTERNATIVE FISH

Try making this with haddock and smoked haddock, or, if you live in Australia, substitute flathead for the unsmoked fish.

taramasalata (see technique 45, page 69)

SERVES 4

4 oz (100 g) stale white bread (about 4 thin slices)
6 oz (175 g) prepared smoked cod's roe (see page 69)
1 garlic clove, crushed
1 thin slice onion
2 tablespoons lemon juice
6 tablespoons olive oil
Black olives and lemon wedges, for garnish
Lightly toasted pita bread or crusty bread, for serving

1 Remove the crusts from the white bread, then let it soak in cold water for 10 minutes.

2 Lift the bread out of the water and squeeze out the excess. Put it into a food processor with the smoked cod's roe, garlic, onion, and lemon juice. Blend for 2 minutes until smooth.

3 With the motor still running, gradually add the olive oil as you would if you were making mayonnaise. Transfer the mixture to a shallow serving dish, cover, and chill for 1 hour. Serve garnished with the olives and lemon wedges, with some lightly toasted pita bread or chunks of crusty bread.

COD,
HADDOCK

brandade de morue (see technique 42, page 67)

SERVES 4–6

12 thin slices of French bread
2/3 cup (150 ml) olive oil
1 lb (450 g) Fresh Salted Cod (see pages 67 and 227), soaked
3 garlic cloves, crushed
3/4 cup (175 ml) heavy cream
Lemon juice and freshly ground black pepper, to taste
Black olives and chopped flat-leaf parsley, for garnish

1 Fry the slices of French bread in 2 tablespoons of the olive oil for 1 to 2 minutes on each side until golden brown. Drain briefly on paper towels, then keep warm in a low oven.

2 Drain the soaked salted cod and remove the skin and any bones. Put it into a pan with enough fresh water to cover, bring to a boil, and simmer for 5 minutes. Lift out with a slotted spoon and drain away the excess water, then put into a food processor.

3 Put the garlic, remaining olive oil, and cream into a small pan and bring to a boil. Add to the fish and blend together until just smooth. Season to taste with lemon juice and plenty of black pepper, but only add salt if necessary.

4 Spoon the mixture into a warmed serving dish and arrange the fried bread slices around the outside of the dish. Garnish with the black olives and parsley and serve warm.

tortilla of salt cod with sweet onions and potatoes

SERVES 6

12 oz (350 g) Fresh Salted Cod (see pages 67 and 227), soaked
1/3 cup (85 ml) extra virgin olive oil
1 large onion, thinly sliced
1 lb (450 g) potatoes, peeled and cut into chunky matchsticks
8 eggs
3 tablespoons chopped flat-leaf parsley
Salt and freshly ground black pepper

TORTILLA OF SALT COD WITH SWEET ONIONS AND POTATOES

mild potato curry topped with smoked haddock and a poached egg

SERVES 4

POTATO CURRY:

12 oz (350 g) waxy boiling potatoes, peeled and cut into ¹/₂-inch (1-cm) dice

2 tablespoons canola oil

¹/₂ teaspoon yellow mustard seeds

¹/₄ teaspoon turmeric powder

¹/₂ cup (100 g) minced onions

2 tomatoes, skinned and chopped

1 teaspoon roughly chopped cilantro

Salt and freshly ground black pepper

4 (4-oz/100-g) pieces of smoked haddock (finnan haddie) fillet

2 teaspoons white wine vinegar

4 eggs

Sprigs of cilantro, for garnish

1 Drop the salted cod into a pan of boiling water and simmer for 6 to 8 minutes or until just cooked. Lift out and, when cool enough to handle, break it into large flakes, discarding the skin and any bones.

2 Heat the oil in a deep, 9-inch (23-cm), well-seasoned or nonstick frying pan. Add the onion and cook over a medium heat for 3 to 4 minutes. Add the potatoes and cook, stirring now and then, for 15 minutes or until just tender. Add the flaked fish and a little seasoning, and turn everything over once or twice to distribute the ingredients evenly. Beat the eggs with the parsley and a little salt and pepper. Pour them into the pan. Cook over a very low heat for about 15 minutes, until almost set.

3 Preheat the broiler. Put the pan under the broiler, close to the heat, for 2 to 3 minutes, until the tortilla is lightly browned on top. Cut it into wedges and serve warm.

1 For the potato curry, cook the potatoes in boiling salted water for 6 to 7 minutes until tender, then drain. Meanwhile, heat the oil in a pan, add the mustard seeds, and, when they begin to pop, add the turmeric and onions. Fry for 5 minutes or until the onions are soft and lightly browned. Add the potatoes and some salt and pepper, and fry for 1 to 2 minutes. Add the tomatoes and cook for 1 minute. Stir in the chopped cilantro. Set aside and keep warm.

2 Bring about 2 inches (5 cm) of water to a boil in a shallow pan. Add the pieces of smoked haddock, bring back to a simmer, and poach for 4 minutes. Lift out with a slotted spoon, cover, and keep warm.

3 Discard the fish poaching liquid. Pour another 2 inches (5 cm) of water into the pan and bring to a very gentle simmer; the water should be just trembling and there should be a few bubbles rising up from the bottom of the pan. Add the vinegar, then break in the eggs and poach for 3 minutes. Lift out with a slotted spoon and drain briefly on paper towels.

4 To serve, spoon the potato curry into the center of four warmed plates. Remove the skin from each piece of haddock and put it on top of the potatoes. Put a poached egg on top of the fish and garnish with the sprigs of cilantro.

smoked haddock kedgeree

SERVES 4

2 tablespoons (25 g) butter
1 small onion, chopped
2 green cardamom pods, split open
1/4 teaspoon turmeric powder
1-inch (2.5-cm) piece of cinnamon stick
1 bay leaf, very finely shredded
2 cups (350 g) basmati rice
2 1/2 cups (600 ml) Chicken Stock (see page 222)
2 eggs
1 lb (450 g) smoked haddock (finnan haddie) fillet
2 tablespoons chopped flat-leaf parsley, plus a few
    sprigs for garnish
Salt and freshly ground black pepper

1 Melt the butter in a large pan, add the onion, and cook over a medium heat for 5 minutes, until soft but not browned. Add the cardamom pods, turmeric, cinnamon stick, and shredded bay leaf, and cook, stirring, for 1 minute.

2 Add the rice and stir for about 1 minute, until it is well coated in the spicy butter. Add the stock and 1/2 teaspoon of salt, and bring to a boil. Cover the pan with a close-fitting lid, lower the heat, and let it cook very gently for 15 minutes.

3 Meanwhile, hard-boil the eggs for 8 minutes. Bring some water to a boil in a large, shallow pan, add the smoked haddock, and simmer for 4 minutes, until the fish is just cooked. Lift the fish out onto a plate and leave until cool enough to handle, then break it into flakes, discarding the skin and any bones (see page 39). Drain the eggs and cool slightly, then peel and cut into small pieces.

4 Uncover the rice and gently fork in the fish and the chopped eggs. Cover again and return to the heat for 5 minutes or until the fish has heated through. Then gently stir in the chopped parsley and season with a little more salt and black pepper to taste. Serve garnished with sprigs of parsley.

braised haddock with mussels, spinach, and chervil

SERVES 4

2/3 cup (150 g) butter
1 shallot, minced
1 lb (450 g) mussels, cleaned (see page 88)
4 (6-oz/175-g) pieces of unskinned haddock fillet
2 lb (900 g) fresh spinach, washed, large stems removed
1 tablespoon malt whisky
1 teaspoon lemon juice
1 teaspoon chopped chervil
Salt and freshly ground black pepper

1 Heat 2 tablespoons (25 g) of the butter in a medium pan, add the shallot, and cook gently for 3 minutes, until soft. Add the mussels and 2/3 cup (150 ml) of water, then cover and cook over a high heat for 3 to 4 minutes, until the mussels have opened. Tip them into a colander set over a bowl to collect the cooking liquid. When they are cool enough to handle, remove the mussels from all but eight of the nicest shells. Cover and set aside.

2 Pour the mussel liquid, except the last tablespoon or two (which might be gritty), into a 12-inch (30-cm) sauté pan. Bring to a simmer, then add the haddock, skin-side up. Cover and simmer gently for 3 minutes. Remove from the heat (leaving the lid in place) and set aside for about 4 minutes to continue cooking.

3 Meanwhile, melt another 2 tablespoons (25 g) of the butter in a large pan. Add the spinach and stir over a high heat until it has wilted. Cook, stirring briskly, until all the excess liquid has evaporated, then season to taste with some salt and pepper.

4 Divide the spinach among four warmed plates and put the haddock on top. Keep warm. Return the sauté pan to the heat, add the remaining butter, and boil rapidly for 3 to 4 minutes, until the liquid has reduced and emulsified into a sauce. Stir in the whisky and lemon juice, and boil for 30 seconds. Add the chervil and mussels, and stir for a few seconds, until they are heated through.

5 Spoon the mussels around the spinach and haddock, dividing the unshelled mussels equally among the plates, then pour the sauce over all and serve.

EGGS BENEDICT WITH SMOKED HADDOCCK

OMELET ARNOLD BENNETT

eggs benedict with smoked haddock

SERVES 4

¹/₂ quantity of Hollandaise Sauce (see page 223)
1¹/₄ cups (300 ml) milk
3 bay leaves
2 slices of onion
6 black peppercorns
4 (4-oz/100-g) pieces of thick smoked haddock (finnan
    haddie) fillet
1 tablespoon white wine vinegar
4 eggs
2 English muffins
**Coarsely crushed black peppercorns and a few chopped
    chives, for garnish**

1 Make the hollandaise sauce and keep it warm, off the heat, over a pan of warm water. Bring the milk and 1¹/₄ cups (300 ml) of water to a boil in a shallow pan. Add the bay leaves, onion, peppercorns, and smoked haddock pieces, bring back to a simmer, and poach for 4 minutes (see page 38). Lift the haddock out onto a plate, peel off the skin, and keep warm.

2 Bring about 2 inches (5 cm) of water to a boil in a medium-sized pan, add the vinegar, and reduce to a gentle simmer. Break the eggs into the pan one at a time and poach for 3 minutes. Meanwhile, slice the muffins in half and toast them until lightly browned. Lift the poached eggs out with a slotted spoon and drain briefly on paper towels.

3 To serve, place the muffin halves on four warmed plates and top with the haddock and poached eggs. Spoon the hollandaise sauce over the eggs and garnish with a sprinkling of black pepper and chives.

omelet arnold bennett

SERVES 2

1¹/₄ cups (300 ml) milk
3 bay leaves
2 slices of onion
6 black peppercorns
10 oz (275 g) smoked haddock (finnan haddie) fillet
6 eggs
1¹/₂ tablespoons (20 g) unsalted butter
2–3 tablespoons heavy cream
2 tablespoons freshly grated Parmesan cheese
Salt and freshly ground black pepper

1 Mix the milk with 1¹/₄ cups (300 ml) of water, pour it into a large shallow pan, and bring to a boil. Add the bay leaves, onion slices, and peppercorns, and bring to a boil. Add the smoked haddock, bring back to a gentle simmer, and poach for 3 to 4 minutes, until the fish is just cooked. Lift the fish out onto a plate and leave until cool enough to handle, then break it into flakes, discarding any skin and bones (see page 38).

2 Preheat the broiler. Whisk the eggs together with some seasoning. Heat a 9- to 10-inch (23- to 25-cm) nonstick frying pan over a medium heat, then add the butter and swirl it around to coat the bottom and sides of the pan. Pour in the eggs. As they start to set, drag the back of a fork over the bottom of the pan, lifting up little folds of egg to let the uncooked egg run underneath.

3 When the omelet is set underneath but still very moist on top, sprinkle with the flaked smoked haddock. Pour the cream on top, sprinkle with the Parmesan cheese, and put the omelet under the broiler, close to the heat. Broil until lightly golden brown. Slide it onto a warmed plate and serve with a crisp green salad, if desired.

HAKE

broiled hake with green onion mash and morel mushroom sauce

SERVES 4

MOREL MUSHROOM SAUCE:

6 tablespoons (75 g) unsalted butter

¼ cup (50 g) each minced onion, carrot, celery, and leek

1 tablespoon Laphroaig whisky

1 tablespoon balsamic vinegar

5 cups (1.2 liters) Fish Stock (see page 222)

½ oz (15 g) dried porcini mushrooms

¼ oz (7 g) dried morel mushrooms

1 teaspoon chopped herb celery or celery tops

GREEN ONION MASH:

2½ lb (1.25 kg) baking or all-purpose potatoes, peeled and cut into chunks

¼ cup (50 g) butter

1 bunch green onions, trimmed and thinly sliced

A little milk

Salt and freshly ground white pepper

4 (6–8 oz/175–225 g) pieces of thick, unskinned hake fillet

A little melted butter, for brushing

Maldon sea salt flakes and coarsely crushed black pepper

1 For the sauce, melt 3 tablespoons (40 g) of the unsalted butter in a shallow pan. Add the onion, carrot, celery, and leek, and cook over a high heat, stirring, until nicely colored. Take the pan off the heat and add the whisky and balsamic vinegar. Return to the heat and boil away to almost nothing. Add 4 cups (1 liter) of the fish stock and the dried porcini mushrooms, bring to a boil, and let simmer for 30 minutes.

2 Meanwhile, put the dried morel mushrooms and the remaining fish stock into a small pan. Bring to a boil, then take off the heat and let soak for 20 minutes, or until soft. Drain, reserving the soaking liquid, and slice the mushrooms into rounds.

3 Strain the stock through a fine sieve into a clean pan and add the reserved mushroom-soaking liquid. Bring to a boil and boil rapidly until reduced to about ¾ cup (175 ml) and well concentrated in flavor. Keep warm.

4 Meanwhile, for the green onion mash, cook the potatoes in boiling salted water for 20 minutes until tender.

5 Brush each piece of hake with melted butter and put them, skin-side up, on the rack of the broiler pan. Sprinkle the skin with a few sea salt flakes and some coarsely crushed black pepper. Preheat the broiler.

6 Broil the hake, 4 inches (10 cm) from the heat, for 8 minutes. Drain the potatoes and, when the steam has died down, return them to the pan. Mash until smooth. Heat the butter in another pan, add the green onions, and turn them over in the butter for a few seconds. Beat them into the potato with a little milk and some salt and white pepper to taste. Keep warm.

7 Whisk the remaining butter, the chopped herb celery or celery tops, and some seasoning to taste into the sauce, then stir in the sliced morel mushrooms.

8 Spoon the green onion mash into the center of four warmed plates and put the hake on top. Spoon the sauce around the outside of the plates and serve.

ALTERNATIVE FISH

Thick, unskinned fillets of cod or haddock.

hake en papillote with oven-roasted tomatoes and tapenade (see technique 32, page 53)

SERVES 4

OVEN-ROASTED TOMATOES:

1¹/₂ lb (750 g) ripe plum tomatoes
¹/₂ teaspoon Maldon sea salt flakes
1 teaspoon thyme leaves

Olive oil, for brushing
2 tablespoons finely shredded basil leaves
4 (6–8 oz/175–225 g) pieces of thick, unskinned
    hake fillet
¹/₄ cup Tapenade (see page 226)
Salt and freshly ground black pepper

1 For the oven-roasted tomatoes, preheat the oven to 475°F (240°C). Cut the tomatoes in half and place them, cut-side up, in a lightly oiled, shallow roasting pan. Sprinkle with the sea salt flakes, thyme leaves, and some pepper, and roast for 15 minutes. Lower the oven temperature to 300°F (150°C) and roast for 1½ hours more, until shriveled to about half their original size and concentrated in flavor. Remove and let cool. (The tomatoes can be roasted in advance, if desired.)

2 Raise the oven temperature to 475°F (240°C) again. Prepare the paper and foil squares as described on page 53. Put three pieces of tomato slightly off-center on each square and sprinkle with the basil. Season the pieces of hake on both sides with salt and pepper, then put them on top of the tomatoes. Seal the parcels (see page 53), place them on a baking sheet, and bake for 15 minutes.

3 Serve the papillotes on a large plate and slit them open at the table so that everyone can enjoy the aroma. Place the contents on four warmed plates and spoon some of the tapenade around.

ALTERNATIVE FISH
Any thick fillets of good-sized fish such as cod, haddock, salmon, and even large sea bass or other grouper-type fish, would work well cooked in this way.

simon hopkinson's warm hake with thinned mayonnaise and capers

SERVES 4

MAYONNAISE:

2 egg yolks
1 teaspoon Dijon mustard
A few dashes of hot pepper sauce
2 teaspoons dry white wine vinegar
²/₃ cup (150 ml) sunflower oil
²/₃ cup (150 ml) olive oil
Leaves from 4 sprigs of tarragon, minced

1 quantity Basic Court-bouillon (see page 223)
1 (4-lb/1.75-kg) piece of hake on the bone
1 small garlic clove, minced
1 (15-oz/425-g) can flageolet beans, drained and rinsed
2 large tomatoes, skinned, seeded, and finely diced
2 teaspoons tarragon vinegar
2 tablespoons olive oil
1 tablespoon small capers, rinsed
A few tarragon leaves, for garnish
Pinch of cayenne pepper
Salt and freshly ground black pepper

1 Make the mayonnaise as described on page 224. Stir in the tarragon and set aside.

2 Bring the court-bouillon to a boil in a large pan. Add the hake and bring back to a boil, then cover and remove from the heat. Let poach for 20 to 30 minutes.

3 Put the garlic, flageolet beans, tomatoes, vinegar, olive oil, and some seasoning together in a pan and warm through gently until hot. Do not let the mixture boil.

4 Pour the beans into a warmed, large, oval serving dish. Lift the hake onto a board or large plate and remove the skin. Carefully lift off the fillets and lay them on top of the beans. Stir 1 to 2 tablespoons of the warm court-bouillon into the mayonnaise to give it a good coating consistency. Spoon it over the fish, then sprinkle the capers and minced tarragon over the top. Dust with a little cayenne pepper and serve.

ALTERNATIVE FISH
Sea bass, cod.

large round fish

LING, POLLOCK

braised ling with lettuce, peas, and crisp smoked pancetta

SERVES 4

4 (6–8 oz/175–225 g) pieces of thick ling or cod fillet, skinned

7 tablespoons Chicken Stock (see page 222)

¹/₂ cup (100 g) butter

12 large green onions, trimmed and cut into 1-inch (2.5-cm) pieces

4 small romaine hearts, cut into quarters

2¹/₃ cups (350 g) freshly shelled or frozen green peas

8 very thin slices smoked pancetta or bacon

1 tablespoon chopped chervil or flat-leaf parsley

Salt and freshly ground white pepper

1 Season the pieces of ling with some salt. Bring the chicken stock to a boil in a small pan and keep hot.

2 Melt half the butter in a wide, shallow casserole that can be used for serving. Add the onions, and cook gently for 2 to 3 minutes, until tender but not browned. Add the quartered lettuce hearts and turn them over once or twice in the butter. Add the peas, hot chicken stock, and some salt and pepper, and simmer rapidly for 3 to 4 minutes, turning the lettuce hearts now and then, until the vegetables have started to soften and about three-fourths of the liquid has evaporated. Put the pieces of ling on top of the vegetables, then cover and simmer for 7 to 8 minutes, until the fish is cooked.

3 Shortly before the fish is done, heat a ridged cast-iron grill pan over a high heat. Pan-grill the pancetta or bacon for about 1 minute on each side, until crisp and golden. Keep warm.

4 Uncover the casserole, dot the remaining butter around the pan, and sprinkle the chopped chervil or parsley over the vegetables. Shake the pan over the heat until the butter has melted and amalgamated with the cooking juices to make a sauce. Garnish the fish with the pan-grilled pancetta, take the casserole to the table, and serve with some small new potatoes.

BRAISED LING WITH LETTUCE, PEAS, AND CRISP SMOKED PANCETTA

7

salt ling, tomato, and potato turnovers

MAKES 9

1¼ lb (550 g) commercially prepared salt ling or salt
    cod, or 1½ lb (750 g) Fresh Salted Cod (see
    pages 67 and 227), soaked
3 lb (1.5 kg) puff pastry, thawed if frozen
8 oz (225 g) plum tomatoes, roughly chopped
12 oz (350 g) potatoes, peeled and cut into small pieces
1 onion, cut into quarters and thinly sliced
4 oz (100 g) smoked chorizo sausage, finely diced
2 garlic cloves, minced
¼ cup (15 g) chopped flat-leaf parsley
Salt and freshly ground black pepper
2 tablespoons olive oil or melted butter
1 egg, beaten

1 Rinse the excess salt off the commercial salt ling or salt cod and place it in a large mixing bowl. Cover with plenty of cold water and let soak for 24 to 48 hours, changing the water now and then.

2 The next day, divide the pastry into nine pieces. Roll out each piece on a lightly floured surface and cut out a 7½-inch (9-cm) round, using a small plate as a guide. Keep cool while you prepare the filling.

3 Drain the soaked fish and remove the skin and any bones. Cut the fish into 1-inch (2.5-cm) pieces and mix in a bowl with the tomatoes, potatoes, onion, chorizo, garlic, parsley, a little salt, and plenty of black pepper. Gently stir in the olive oil or melted butter.

4 Divide the fish mixture among the pastry rounds, distributing the pieces of fish as evenly as you can. Brush one half of the edge on each pastry round with a little beaten egg, then fold over into a half-moon shape and pinch the edges together really well to seal. Crimp the edge decoratively between your fingers. Transfer the turnovers to a lightly greased baking sheet and chill for 20 minutes.

5 Preheat the oven to 400°F (200°C). Brush the turnovers with some of the remaining beaten egg and bake for about 50 minutes, or until crisp and richly golden.

VARIATION

crab turnovers with leek and saffron

MAKES 6

Soak ¼ teaspoon saffron strands in 2 teaspoons hot water for 5 minutes. Mix in a bowl with 1¼ lb (550 g) white crabmeat, 4 oz (100 g) brown crabmeat, if available (or additional white crabmeat), 3½ cups (350 g) thinly sliced leeks, 1½ cups (75 g) fresh white breadcrumbs, 1½ teaspoons salt, 15 turns of the white pepper mill, and 3 tablespoons (40 g) melted butter. Fill and bake as above.

thai fish cakes with green beans (*tod man pla*)

SERVES 4

SWEET-AND-SOUR CUCUMBER SAUCE:

¼ cup white wine vinegar
½ cup (100 g) sugar
1½ tablespoons water
2 teaspoons Thai fish sauce (*nam pla*)
⅓ cup (50 g) very finely diced hothouse cucumber
2 tablespoons very finely diced carrot
2 tablespoons minced onion
2 red bird chile peppers, thinly sliced

1 lb (450 g) pollock fillets, skinned and cut into chunks
1 tablespoon Thai fish sauce (*nam pla*)
1 tablespoon Thai Red Curry Paste (see page 226)
1 kaffir lime leaf or 1 strip of lime zest, very finely
    shredded
1 tablespoon chopped cilantro
1 egg
1 teaspoon palm sugar or raw brown sugar
½ teaspoon salt
⅓ cup (40 g) green beans, thinly sliced into rounds
⅔ cup (150 ml) peanut or canola oil

1 For the sauce, gently heat the vinegar, sugar, and water in a small pan until the sugar has dissolved. Bring to a boil and boil for 1 minute, then remove from the heat and let cool. Stir in the fish sauce, cucumber, carrot, onion, and chiles. Pour into four small dipping saucers or ramekins and set aside.

2 For the fish cakes, put the fish in a food processor with the fish sauce, curry paste, kaffir lime leaf or lime zest, chopped cilantro, egg, sugar, and salt. Process until smooth, then stir in the sliced green beans.

3 Divide the mixture into 16 pieces. Roll each one into a ball, then flatten into a 2½-inch (6-cm) patty. Heat the oil in a large frying pan and fry the fish cakes, in batches, for 1 minute on each side, until golden brown. Lift out and drain briefly on paper towels, then serve with the sweet-and-sour cucumber sauce.

MAHIMAHI,
WOLFFISH,
FLATHEAD,
RED EMPEROR

a feast of mahimahi, tortillas, and salsa de tomate verde

SERVES 4

SALSA DE TOMATE VERDE:

2 tomatillos or green tomatoes
2 jalapeño peppers
1 garlic clove, roughly chopped
1 small onion, roughly chopped
1 tablespoon chopped cilantro
A little freshly squeezed lime juice (if you are using
    green tomatoes)

1 romaine heart, thinly sliced crosswise
2 avocados, halved, peeled, and sliced
3 tomatoes, cut into small dice
1 red onion, halved and very thinly sliced
8 fresh corn tortillas
1¹/₂ lb (750 g) mahimahi fillets, skinned
A little canola oil
Salt and freshly ground black pepper

1 For the salsa, peel the papery husks off the tomatillos. Drop them (or the green tomatoes) and the jalapeños into a pan of boiling water. Simmer for 10 minutes, then drain and cool slightly. Tip them into a food processor and add the rest of the salsa ingredients (plus a little lime juice if you have used green tomatoes instead of tomatillos). Pulse the mixture for a few seconds until you have a fairly smooth sauce with a little bit of texture. Season with salt. Spoon into a serving bowl.

2 Put the shredded lettuce, avocados, tomatoes, and onion into five other small serving bowls.

3 To reheat the tortillas, stack them on a plate, cover with a dish towel, and microwave on high for about 30 seconds. Alternatively, heat a dry frying pan over a medium heat. Add a tortilla and leave it for a seconds, then turn it over and add a second tortilla on top of it. After a few seconds, turn them over together and add a third tortilla to the pan. Continue like this until all your tortillas are in the pan, then remove them and wrap them in a napkin. Keep them warm in a low oven while you cook the fish.

4 Preheat the broiler. Cut the mahimahi fillets into short, chunky strips. Toss them with a little oil and plenty of seasoning, spread them out on a baking pan, and broil them for about 2 minutes on one side only, until just cooked through.

5 Transfer the fish strips to a warmed serving plate and take it to the table with all the other bits and pieces. Let everyone fill their own tortillas with whatever they fancy.

ALTERNATIVE FISH
Sea bass, john dory.

steamed wolffish with mild greens, soy, and sesame oil

SERVES 4

4 (6-oz/175-g) pieces of thick wolffish fillet, skinned
2 thin slices of fresh ginger, peeled and cut into
    fine julienne
8 small heads of bok choy
4 teaspoons toasted sesame oil
6–8 teaspoons dark soy sauce
2 green onions, halved and very finely shredded
Salt

1 Season the fish on both sides with a little salt, then place the pieces side by side in a steamer over about ½ inch (1 cm) of water (see page 46). Sprinkle the ginger on top.

2 Cut the heads of bok choy lengthwise into quarters and put them in a second steamer. Cover and steam the fish for 2 to 3 minutes or until just cooked through, and the bok choy for 3 to 4 minutes until tender.

3 Put the bok choy on four warmed plates and sprinkle with the sesame oil and soy sauce. Set the fish on top. Spoon a tablespoon of the fish-steaming liquid over each piece of fish and garnish with the shredded green onion.

ALTERNATIVE FISH
Cod.

7

deep-fried flathead with mushrooms and walnuts

SERVES 4

1½ lb (750 g) skinned flathead fillet
¼ cup Mayonnaise (see page 224), made with olive oil
¼ cup warm water
6 good-quality green olives, pitted and thinly sliced
Canola oil, for deep-frying
2 cups (150 g) very finely diced crimini or button
   mushrooms
1 cup (100 g) minced, lightly toasted walnut pieces
All-purpose flour, for coating
2 eggs, beaten
1 tablespoon chopped flat-leaf parsley
Salt and freshly ground black pepper
Sprigs of flat-leaf parsley, for garnish

1 Cut the fish fillets across into slices about ½ inch (1 cm) thick. Season with a little salt and pepper. Put the mayonnaise, warm water, and sliced green olives into a small pan and set aside.

2 Heat some oil for deep-frying to 350°F (180°C). Mix the finely diced mushrooms and toasted walnuts together on a large plate. Put some flour on another plate and season it with salt and pepper. Whisk the eggs together in a shallow bowl.

3 Pat the pieces of flathead dry on paper towels. Dip four to six pieces at a time in the flour, then in beaten egg, and, finally, in the mushroom and walnut mixture, pressing it on well to give a thick, even coating. Lower the fish into the hot oil and cook for 3 minutes until crisp and golden. Lift onto a baking sheet lined with paper towels and keep hot in a low oven while you cook the rest.

4 Very gently heat the mayonnaise mixture in the pan until it feels warm to your little finger, but not hot. Do not let it boil or it will curdle. Stir in the parsley and season to taste with some salt and pepper.

5 Arrange the pieces of flathead in the center of four warmed plates. Spoon some of the sauce around the edge of the plates and garnish each with a sprig of fresh parsley.

ALTERNATIVE FISH
Cod, halibut, or monkfish.

braised red emperor fillet with olive oil, tomatoes, capers, and olives

SERVES 4

4 (6-oz/175-g) pieces of thick red emperor fillet,
   skinned
10 good-quality black olives in olive oil
¼ cup olive oil
⅔ cup (150 ml) water
Juice of ½ lemon
3 medium-sized vine-ripened tomatoes, seeded
   and roughly chopped
1 teaspoon small capers, drained and rinsed
2 tablespoons chopped flat-leaf parsley
Salt and freshly ground black pepper

1 Season the pieces of red emperor on each side with a little salt and pepper. Cut four slices from each black olive and discard the pits.

2 Heat the oil in a large, deep frying pan. Add the pieces of red emperor and sear for 2 minutes on each side until lightly colored. Lower the heat and add the water, lemon juice, and ½ teaspoon of salt. Bring up to a simmer.

3 Cover and cook over a gentle heat for 2 minutes until the fish is just cooked through.

4 Lift the pieces of fish out onto a plate, cover, and keep warm. Bring the juices in the pan to a vigorous boil. Throw in the olives, chopped tomatoes, capers, and chopped parsley, and boil for 30 seconds.

5 Put the pieces of fish on four warmed plates, spoon the sauce over them, and serve.

ALTERNATIVE FISH
Red emperor, one of Australia's best-flavored fish, could successfully be replaced with sea bass, john dory, or even turbot.

whole salmon baked in foil with tarragon (see technique 31, page 52)

SERVES 4

¼ cup (50 g) butter, melted

1 (3-lb/1.5-kg) salmon, cleaned and trimmed (see page 14)

1 small bunch of tarragon, roughly chopped

½ cup (120 ml) dry white wine

Juice of ½ lemon

Salt and freshly ground black pepper

1 quantity Beurre Blanc (see pages 223–4), for serving

1 Preheat the oven to 425°F (220°C). Brush the center of a large sheet of foil with some of the melted butter. Place the salmon on the buttered portion and bring the edges of the foil up around the fish slightly. Put the open parcel onto a large baking sheet.

2 Mix the tarragon with the rest of the melted butter, plus the wine, lemon juice, salt, and pepper. Spoon the mixture into the cavity of the fish and over the top. Bring the sides of the foil up over the fish and pinch together, folding over the edges a few times to make a loose, airtight parcel. Bake for 30 minutes.

3 Remove the fish from the oven and open up the parcel. If desired, remove the skin as follows: Cut through the skin just behind the head and above the tail, and lift it off. Carefully turn the fish over and repeat on the other side (see page 38).

4 Lift the salmon onto a warmed serving dish and serve with the beurre blanc and some boiled new potatoes.

ALTERNATIVE FISH

Large sea bass, snapper, salmon trout, or steelhead.

salmon en croûte with currants and ginger (see technique 29, page 50)

SERVES 6

2 (1¼-lb/550-g) pieces of skinned salmon fillet, taken from behind the gut cavity of a 7–9 lb (3–4 kg) fish (see page 28, steps 1 and 2)

½ cup (100 g) unsalted butter, softened

4 pieces of stem ginger in syrup, well drained and finely diced

3 tablespoons currants

½ teaspoon ground mace

1½ lb (750 g) puff pastry, thawed if frozen

1 egg, beaten, for glazing

Salt and freshly ground black pepper

1 Season the salmon fillets well on both sides with salt. Mix the softened butter with the stem ginger, currants, mace, ½ teaspoon of salt, and some black pepper. Spread the inner face of one salmon fillet evenly with the butter mixture, then lay the second fillet on top.

2 Cut the pastry in half and, on a lightly floured surface, roll out one piece into a rectangle about 1½ inches (4 cm) bigger than the salmon all the way around—approximately 7 by 13 inches (18 by 33 cm). Roll out the second piece into a rectangle 2 inches (5 cm) larger than the first one all the way around.

3 Lay the smaller rectangle of pastry on a well-floured baking sheet and place the salmon in the center. Brush a wide band of beaten egg around the salmon and lay the second piece of pastry on top, taking care not to stretch it. Press the pastry tightly around the outside of the salmon,

7

SALMON EN CROÛTE WITH CURRANTS AND GINGER

trying to ensure that you have not trapped in too much air, then press the edges together well to seal.

4 Trim the edges of the pastry neatly to leave a 1-inch (2.5-cm) band all the way around. Brush this once more with egg. Mark the edge with a fork and decorate the top with a fishscale effect by pressing an overturned teaspoon gently into the pastry, working in rows down the length of the parcel. Chill for at least 1 hour.

5 Preheat the oven to 400°F (200°C) and put in a large baking sheet to heat up. Remove the salmon en croûte from the refrigerator and brush it all over with beaten egg.

6 Take the hot baking sheet out of the oven and carefully transfer the salmon parcel onto it. Return to the oven and bake for 35 to 40 minutes.

7 Remove the salmon from the oven and let it rest for 5 minutes. Transfer it to a warmed serving plate and take it to the table whole. Cut it across into slices to serve.

escalopes of salmon with sorrel sauce (see technique 11, page 28)

SERVES 4

1½ lb (750 g) salmon fillet, taken from a good-sized
    salmon
2 tablespoons canola oil
Salt

SORREL SAUCE:

2½ cups (600 ml) Fish Stock (see page 222)
¾ cup (175 ml) heavy cream
¼ cup dry vermouth, such as Noilly Prat
¼ cup (25 g) sorrel leaves, washed and dried
6 tablespoons (75 g) unsalted butter
2 teaspoons lemon juice

1 Cut the salmon fillet into 12 escalopes (see page 28). Brush each one with oil, season with a little salt, and lay on a lightly oiled baking pan.

2 For the sauce, put the fish stock, half of the cream, and the vermouth into a large saucepan and boil vigorously until reduced to ¾ cup (175 ml). Meanwhile, remove the stems from the sorrel leaves and slice the leaves very thinly. When the sauce has reduced to the required amount, add the remaining cream, the butter, and lemon juice, and simmer until it has thickened slightly and reached a good saucelike consistency. In the meantime, preheat the broiler.

ESCALOPES OF SALMON WITH SORREL SAUCE

3 Stir all but a pinch of the sorrel into the sauce and season to taste. Keep warm. Broil the salmon escalopes, close to the heat, for about 30 seconds to 1 minute until only just firm.

4 To serve, spoon some of the sauce into the center of four warmed plates. Slightly overlap three escalopes on top of the sauce on each plate and sprinkle with the reserved shredded sorrel.

VARIATION

champagne and chive sauce

Melt 1½ teaspoons (7 g) of unsalted butter in a medium-sized saucepan. Add 1 minced shallot and cook gently, without coloring, until soft. Add ½ cup (100 ml) champagne and boil for 2 minutes. Add 2½ cups (600 ml) fish stock and ½ teaspoon of sugar, and boil rapidly until reduced by three-fourths to about ¾ cup (175 ml). Add ¼ cup heavy cream, bring back to a boil, and simmer until it has reached a good saucelike consistency. Keep warm. Whip together another ¼ cup heavy cream with 1 tablespoon of champagne and 2 teaspoons of chopped chives until it forms soft peaks. When you are ready to serve, bring the sauce back to a boil, then whisk in 1½ tablespoons (20 g) unsalted butter followed by the whipped cream mixture. Overlap the escalopes in the center of each warmed plate and pour the sauce around. Sprinkle with a few chopped chives and serve immediately, while the sauce is still foaming.

SALMON

salmon steaks with muscadet, watercress, and dill potatoes

SERVES 4

1½ lb (750 g) large new potatoes, scrubbed
1 small bunch of dill
4 (7-oz/200-g) salmon steaks
2 tablespoons Clarified Butter (see page 226)
¼ cup Muscadet or another dry white wine
½ cup (120 ml) Fish Stock or Chicken Stock (see page 222)
¼ cup (50 g) unsalted butter
1 tablespoon chopped flat-leaf parsley
1 cup (75 g) watercress, large stems removed
2 tablespoons extra virgin olive oil
1 teaspoon white wine vinegar
Salt and freshly ground black pepper

1 Cut each potato lengthwise into four or six pieces. Cook in a pan of boiling salted water with 2 sprigs of the dill for 10 minutes or until just tender.

2 Meanwhile, preheat the oven to 400°F (200°C). Season the salmon steaks on both sides with some salt and pepper. Heat the clarified butter in a frying pan that can be transferred to the oven. Add the salmon and cook for 1 to 2 minutes on each side until lightly browned.

3 Remove the pan from the heat and let cool for 30 seconds. Then pour in the wine. Place the pan in the oven and cook for 5 minutes.

4 Remove the salmon from the oven and lift the steaks onto a plate. Keep warm. For the sauce, pour the fish or chicken stock into the frying pan, bring to a boil, and add the unsalted butter. Boil rapidly until the liquid has reduced by half. Add the parsley and adjust the seasoning, if necessary.

5 To serve, arrange the salmon steaks, watercress, and potatoes on four warmed plates. Mix together the olive oil, vinegar, and ½ teaspoon of salt. Pour this dressing over the watercress and pour the sauce over the salmon, then serve.

pavés of salmon with roasted tomatoes and fennel (see technique 12, page 29)

SERVES 4

ROASTED TOMATOES AND FENNEL:
1 lb (450 g) small vine-ripened tomatoes
Olive oil, for brushing
Maldon sea salt flakes
Cracked black peppercorns
3 large fennel bulbs, trimmed

SAUCE VIERGE:
½ cup (120 ml) Cabernet Sauvignon vinegar
½ teaspoon fennel seeds, lightly crushed
½ teaspoon black peppercorns, coarsely crushed
⅔ cup (150 ml) extra virgin olive oil
Large pinch of Maldon sea salt flakes

4 (6-oz/175-g) prepared pavés of salmon (see page 29)
Olive oil, for brushing
A splash of white wine

1 For the roasted tomatoes and fennel, preheat the oven to 425°F (220°C). Cut the tomatoes in half horizontally and lay them, cut-side up, in a lightly oiled, shallow roasting pan. Sprinkle with some salt and pepper, then roast them for 10 minutes. Lower the oven temperature to 300°F (150°C) and roast for 1 hour longer, or until they have shriveled to about half their original size and are well concentrated in flavor. Cut the fennel down through the root into thin slices. Arrange in a single layer in a lightly oiled roasting pan and roast at 350°F (180°C) for 35 to 40 minutes, until softened and with a good color. When the tomatoes and fennel are ready, remove from the oven and keep warm.

2 For the sauce vierge, put the vinegar, fennel seeds, and black pepper into a small pan and boil until reduced to 2 tablespoons. Add the olive oil, season to taste with some Maldon salt, and set aside.

3 Brush the pieces of salmon on both sides with olive oil and season with salt and pepper. Heat a ridged cast-iron grill pan until smoking-hot. Add the salmon, skinned-side down, and sear until it has taken on a good golden color. Sprinkle with some wine and let sizzle for a few seconds, then turn and cook for 30 seconds. Remove from the heat and let the salmon continue cooking in the residual heat of the pan for 30 seconds or so.

4 To serve, arrange some of the fennel slices attractively in the center of each plate. Rest the pavés of salmon on top and arrange a few tomatoes around the fish. Spoon some of the dressing around the edge of the plates (make sure you take up some of the vinegar reduction with the oil in the dressing).

7

gravlax (dill-cured salmon) (see technique 41, page 66)

(see technique 41, page 66)

SERVES 6

2 (1½-lb/750-g) unskinned salmon fillets
1 large bunch of dill, roughly chopped
²/₃ cup (100 g) coarse sea salt
6 tablespoons (75 g) sugar
2 tablespoons crushed white peppercorns

HORSERADISH AND MUSTARD SAUCE:

2 teaspoons finely grated horseradish
   (fresh or from a jar)
2 teaspoons finely grated onion
1 teaspoon Dijon mustard
1 teaspoon sugar
2 tablespoons white wine vinegar
Large pinch of salt
³/₄ cup (175 ml) heavy cream

1 Put one of the salmon fillets, skin-side down, on a large sheet of plastic wrap. Mix the dill with the salt, sugar, and crushed peppercorns, and spread it over the cut face of the salmon. Place the other fillet on top, skin-side up.

2 Tightly wrap the fish in two or three layers of plastic wrap and lift it onto a large, shallow tray. Rest a slightly smaller tray or chopping board on top of the fish and weigh it down with cans of food. Refrigerate for 2 days, turning the fish every 12 hours so that the briny mixture, which will develop inside the parcel, bastes the outside of the fish.

3 For the horseradish and mustard sauce, stir together all the ingredients except for the cream. Whip the cream into soft peaks, then stir in the horseradish mixture. Cover and chill.

4 To serve, remove the fish from the briny mixture and slice it as you would smoked salmon (see page 66). Arrange a few slices of the gravlax on each plate and serve with the sauce.

GRAVLAX

tetsuya wakuda's confit of salmon (see technique 28, page 49)

SERVES 4

12 oz (350 g) skinned salmon fillet,
    taken from a large fish (see page 28,
    steps 1 and 2)
7 tablespoons grapeseed oil
5 tablespoons olive oil
1/2 tablespoon freshly ground coriander seeds
1/2 teaspoon freshly ground white pepper
10 whole basil leaves
3 sprigs of thyme
1/2 teaspoon minced garlic
2 tablespoons each minced carrot and celery
3 tablespoons chopped chives
1/4 cup minced dried kombu (Japanese kelp)
2 tablespoons keta (salmon roe)
Salt

FENNEL SALAD:

1/2 fennel bulb
1 teaspoon lemon juice
1/2 teaspoon Lemon Olive Oil (see page 227)
Salt and freshly ground black pepper

PARSLEY OIL:

Large handful of flat-leaf parsley leaves
7 tablespoons olive oil
1/2 teaspoon small salted capers, rinsed and
    drained

1 Cut the salmon fillet across into four pieces. Put the grapeseed oil, olive oil, coriander, pepper, basil leaves, thyme, and garlic into a small, shallow dish. Immerse the pieces of salmon in the mixture, cover, and let marinate in the refrigerator for a few hours.

2 To cook the fish, preheat the oven to 225°F (110°C). Take the fish out of the marinade and allow it to come back to room temperature. Spread the chopped vegetables in a small baking pan and put the pieces of salmon on top, ensuring that the salmon doesn't come into contact with the pan.

3 Cook the salmon in the oven for 8 to 10 minutes, brushing it occasionally with the flavored oil. The flesh should not change color at all, but remain a brilliant orange-red. It should be lukewarm to the touch, and when you press the end part, your finger should just go through the flesh.

4 Remove the fish from the oven and let it cool to room temperature. Meanwhile, for the parsley oil, put the parsley leaves into a blender and blend together. Add the capers and blend once more.

5 For the fennel salad, finely slice the fennel on a mandoline. Toss with the lemon juice, lemon oil, and some seasoning to taste.

6 To serve, sprinkle the top of the salmon with the chives, dried kombu, and a little salt. Put some of the fennel salad into the center of each plate and set the salmon on top. Drizzle a little parsley oil around the plate, then dot the keta at regular intervals around the salmon.

poached salmon with new potatoes, cucumber salad, and mayonnaise (see technique 19, page 38)

SERVES 4

1 quantity Basic Court-bouillon (see page 223)
1 (3–4 lb/1.5–1.75 kg) salmon, cleaned and trimmed
    (see page 14)
1 1/2 lb (750 g) new potatoes, scraped
3 sprigs of mint
1 hothouse cucumber
1 tablespoon white wine vinegar
1 quantity Mayonnaise (see pages 224), made with
    olive oil
Salt

1 Put the ingredients for the court-bouillon into a fish poacher, bring to a boil, and simmer for 20 minutes. Carefully lower the salmon into the court-bouillon, bring back to a gentle simmer, and poach gently for 16 to 18 minutes.

2 Meanwhile, cook the potatoes in boiling salted water with one of the mint sprigs until tender. Drain and keep warm.

3 Peel the cucumber and slice it as thinly as possible, preferably on a mandoline. Chop the leaves from the remaining mint sprigs and mix with the cucumber, the white wine vinegar, and a pinch of salt.

4 Lift the salmon, still sitting on the rack, out of the fish poacher and let any excess water drain away. Carefully lift it off the rack with two slotted spatulas and put it on a serving plate.

5 Remove the skin by making a shallow cut through the skin along the backbone and around the back of the head, and carefully peeling it back. Carefully turn the fish over and repeat on the other side.

6 To serve, run a knife down the length of the fish between the two fillets and gently ease them apart and away from the bones. Lift portion-sized pieces of the salmon onto each plate, then turn the fish over and repeat. Serve with the new potatoes, mayonnaise, and cucumber salad.

broiled fillet of hapuku with roasted wild mushrooms and a cider vinegar-butter sauce

SERVES 4
ROASTED WILD MUSHROOMS:
5 slices dried porcini mushroom
3 tablespoons warm water
12 oz (350 g) mixed fresh wild mushrooms
Leaves from 1 sprig of thyme
3 tablespoons olive oil
Salt and freshly ground black pepper

4 (6–8 oz/175–225 g) pieces of unskinned hapuku fillet
1 tablespoon (15 g) butter, melted
CIDER VINEGAR-BUTTER SAUCE:
1/4 cup good-quality cider vinegar
3/4 cup (175 g) chilled unsalted butter,
    cut into small pieces

1 For the roasted mushrooms, preheat the oven to 400°F (200°C). Put the dried porcini mushroom slices into a small bowl, cover with the warm water, and let soak for 10 minutes. Meanwhile, brush any dirt off the fresh wild mushrooms and trim away the base of the stems. Thickly slice the mushrooms and put them in a small roasting pan. Lift the porcini mushrooms out of their soaking liquid and thinly slice them. Add them to the wild mushrooms, along with the thyme leaves, olive oil, salt, pepper, and 3 tablespoons of the soaking liquid. Toss together well. Spread out in the pan and roast for 15 minutes. Meanwhile, preheat the broiler (if it is not separate from the oven, you will have to wait for the mushrooms to finish roasting before you can cook the fish).

2 Brush the pieces of hapuku with melted butter and season on both sides with some salt and pepper. Put, skin-side up, on a lightly buttered baking pan or the rack of the broiler pan.

3 After the mushrooms have been cooking for 7 minutes, broil the hapuku, about 4 inches (10 cm) from the heat, for 6 to 7 minutes. Meanwhile, for the sauce, bring the vinegar to a boil in a small pan. Whisk in the butter, a few pieces at a time, until you have a smooth, emulsified sauce. Season to taste with salt and pepper.

4 Spoon the roasted wild mushrooms into the center of four warmed plates and put the hapuku on top. Spoon a little of the sauce over the fish and the rest around the outside edge of the plates. Serve with some boiled new potatoes.

ALTERNATIVE FISH
Unskinned sea bass or gray or striped mullet fillet.

broiled mulloway with asparagus and a cream and caviar sauce (see technique 43, page 68)

SERVES 4
4 (6-oz/175-g) pieces of thick, unskinned mulloway
    fillet
1 tablespoon (15 g) butter, melted
8–12 oz (225–350 g) asparagus
Salt and freshly ground black pepper
CREAM AND CAVIAR SAUCE:
2 1/2 cups (600 ml) Fish Stock (see page 222)
1/4 cup dry vermouth, such as Noilly Prat
1/3 cup (85 ml) heavy cream
1 teaspoon lemon juice
1 heaped teaspoon caviar

1 For the sauce, put the stock, vermouth, and cream into a wide-based pan. Boil rapidly until it has reduced by three-fourths to about 3/4 cup (175 ml). Keep warm.

2 Preheat the broiler. Brush the mulloway fillets on both sides with melted butter and season with some salt and pepper. Put, skin-side up, on a lightly greased baking pan or the rack of the broiler pan.

3 Bring about 1 inch (2.5 cm) of water to a boil in a large, deep frying pan. Trim off and discard the woody ends of the asparagus, then place on a petal steamer.

4 Broil the fish for 7 to 8 minutes or until just cooked through. Halfway through this time, put the petal steamer into the shallow pan, cover, and steam the asparagus for 3 to 4 minutes until just tender.

5 To serve, put the asparagus in the center of four warmed plates and put the fish on top. Whisk the lemon juice, caviar, and some seasoning to taste into the sauce and spoon a little around the edge of each plate.

ALTERNATIVE FISH
Thick, unskinned hake or sea bass fillet.

pan-grilled king snapper with lemon, thyme, and charmoula

SERVES 4

PAN-GRILLED POTATOES:

2 lb (900 g) baking or all-purpose potatoes

2 tablespoons olive oil, plus extra for cooking

2 large garlic cloves, minced

Leaves from 2 sprigs of thyme

Salt and freshly ground black pepper

4 (6-oz/175-g) pieces of king snapper fillet

2 tablespoons extra virgin olive oil

Pared zest of 1 lemon, minced

3 bay leaves, finely shredded

Leaves from 3 sprigs of thyme

1 teaspoon dried red pepper flakes

$^1/_2$ teaspoon Maldon sea salt flakes

CHARMOULA:

2 tablespoons roughly chopped cilantro

3 garlic cloves, chopped

$1^1/_2$ teaspoons ground cumin

$^1/_2$ medium-hot red chile pepper, seeded and chopped

$^1/_2$ teaspoon saffron strands

$^1/_4$ cup extra virgin olive oil

Juice of 1 lemon

$1^1/_2$ teaspoons paprika

1 teaspoon salt

SNAPPER

1 For the pan-grilled potatoes, cut the potatoes lengthwise into chunky wedges. Drop them into a pan of boiling salted water, bring back to a boil, and drain. Let cool slightly, then toss in a bowl with the olive oil, garlic, thyme leaves, and some seasoning.

2 For the snapper, mix the olive oil, lemon zest, bay leaves, thyme leaves, pepper flakes, and Maldon salt together in a shallow dish. Add the pieces of snapper and turn them over once or twice to coat them well with the mixture.

3 Meanwhile, put all the ingredients for the charmoula into a food processor and blend until smooth. Transfer to a bowl and stir in some seasoning to taste.

4 Heat a ridged cast-iron grill pan over a high heat until smoking hot. Drizzle with a little oil, then lay a batch of the potato wedges diagonally across the pan. Lower the heat and cook for 4 to 5 minutes on each side, until crisp and golden brown. Transfer to a serving dish and keep hot in a low oven while you cook the rest of the potatoes.

5 Lift the pieces of snapper out of the marinade and place skin-side down on the grill pan. Cook for 3 to 4 minutes, then turn over and cook for 1 to 2 minutes, or until cooked through.

6 Lift the snapper onto warmed serving plates and spoon some of the charmoula over the top. Pile the potatoes alongside and serve.

ALTERNATIVE FISH

Red snapper or large john dory fillet.

7

grilled snapper with a mango, shrimp, and chile salsa

SERVES 4

4 (6-oz/175-g) pieces of unskinned snapper fillet
Extra virgin olive oil
Salt and freshly ground black pepper
Cilantro sprigs, for garnish

SALSA:

2 large, medium–hot red chile peppers
4 oz (100 g) peeled, cooked tiger shrimp, thickly sliced
4 green onions, thinly sliced
1 small garlic clove, minced
1 ripe but firm avocado, peeled and cut into small dice
1/2 ripe but firm mango, peeled and cut into small dice
Juice of 1 lime
Pinch of salt

1 If you are using a charcoal grill, prepare and light it 30 to 40 minutes before you want to cook the fish.

2 For the salsa, cut the chiles in half lengthwise and scrape out the seeds with the tip of a small knife; leave the ribs behind to give the salsa a little more heat. Cut the chiles across into thin slices. Then simply mix all the salsa ingredients together.

3 If you are not cooking the fish over charcoal, put a ridged cast-iron grill pan over a high heat (or preheat the broiler). Brush the snapper fillets on both sides with olive oil and season well with salt and pepper. Cut each one into three, slightly on the diagonal.

4 Cook the pieces of snapper, either skin-side down on the grill or grill pan, or skin-side up under the broiler, for 3 to 4 minutes.

5 To serve, spoon the salsa onto four plates and arrange the grilled strips of fish on top. Drizzle a little oil around the edge of the plates and garnish with cilantro sprigs.

ALTERNATIVE FISH
Red mullet, sea bass, bream or porgy, john dory, or gray or striped mullet.

GRILLED SNAPPER WITH A MANGO, SHRIMP, AND CHILE SALSA

baked sea bass with roasted red peppers, tomatoes, anchovies, and potatoes

(see technique 27, page 48)

SEA BASS,
SALMON
TROUT

SERVES 4
Large pinch of saffron strands
2 lb (900 g) potatoes, peeled and cut into $^1/_2$-inch
    (1-cm) slices
4 plum tomatoes, skinned and cut lengthwise into
    quarters
2 oz (50 g) anchovy fillets in oil, drained
$^2/_3$ cup (150 ml) Chicken Stock (see page 222)
4 red bell peppers, each one seeded and cut into
    8 chunks
8 garlic cloves, each sliced into 3 lengthwise
8 small sprigs of oregano
$^1/_3$ cup (85 ml) olive oil
1 (3–4 lb/1.5–1.75 g) sea bass, cleaned and trimmed
    (see page 14)
Salt and freshly ground black pepper

1 Preheat the oven to 400°F (200°C). Place the saffron in a tea cup, pour in 2 tablespoons of hot water, and let soak.

2 Put the potatoes in a pan of boiling salted water and parboil for 7 minutes. Drain well, then arrange them in a narrow strip on the bottom of a baking dish large enough to hold the sea bass either lengthwise or diagonally. The potatoes should form a bed for the fish, leaving plenty of room on either side for the red peppers.

3 Scatter the tomatoes and anchovy fillets over the potatoes, then pour the saffron water and stock on top. Scatter the pieces of red pepper down either side of the potatoes and sprinkle with the garlic, oregano sprigs, and olive oil. Season everything well with salt and pepper. Bake for 30 minutes.

4 Slash the fish five or six times down each side, then slash it in the opposite direction on just one side to give an attractive criss-cross pattern. Rub it generously with some olive oil and season well with salt and pepper. Lay it on top of the potatoes.

5 Return the dish to the oven and bake for 35 minutes, until the fish is cooked through. Serve with the roasted vegetables.

ALTERNATIVE FISH
Striped bass or kingfish.

BAKED SEA BASS WITH ROASTED RED PEPPERS,
TOMATOES, ANCHOVIES, AND POTATOES

7

braised salmon trout fillets with white wine and basil (see technique 24, page 44)

6 tablespoons (75 g) butter
$^1/_2$ cup (75 g) very thinly sliced carrots
$^1/_2$ cup (75 g) very thinly sliced celery
$^3/_4$ cup (75 g) very thinly sliced leeks
$^1/_3$ cup (85 ml) dry white wine
$2^1/_2$ cups (600 ml) Chicken Stock (see page 222)
4 (5-oz/150-g) pieces of skinned salmon trout fillet
Handful of very finely shredded basil leaves, plus sprigs
of basil for garnish
1 teaspoon lemon juice
Salt and freshly ground black pepper

1 Melt 4 tablespoons (50 g) of the butter in a shallow pan large enough to hold the fish in one layer. Stir in the carrots, celery, and leeks, cover, and cook gently over a medium heat for about 3 minutes.

2 Add the wine and stock to the pan and simmer, uncovered, until almost all the liquid has evaporated but the vegetables are still moist.

3 Lay the salmon trout fillets on top, season with some salt and pepper, and sprinkle with half the basil. Cover and simmer very gently for 8 to 10 minutes, or until the fish is just cooked through.

4 Put the fish onto four warmed plates and keep warm. If there is a little too much liquid left in the pan, boil rapidly until reduced and the sauce is glistening. Stir in the rest of the butter, the lemon juice, and the rest of the basil, and adjust the seasoning, if necessary. Spoon the sauce over the fish and garnish with basil sprigs.

ALTERNATIVE FISH
Salmon, steelhead, or king trout fillets.

marinated salmon trout with lime and pink peppercorns

1 (8-oz/225-g) piece of unskinned sushi-quality salmon
trout fillet
$^1/_2$ cup (120 ml) canola oil
2 teaspoons minced fresh ginger
1 teaspoon pink peppercorns in brine, drained and
rinsed
Finely grated zest and juice of 1 lime
$^1/_2$ teaspoon salt

1 Put the salmon trout fillet, skin-side down, on a chopping board and slice it as you would gravlax or smoked salmon (see page 66).

2 Flatten the slices slightly and arrange them over four dinner plates, overlapping them very slightly.

3 Mix together the rest of the ingredients. About 5 minutes before serving, drizzle the dressing over the fish and spread it out with the back of a teaspoon. Serve immediately.

large round fish

sea bass baked in a salt crust with lemon sauce and a potato, tomato, and basil confit (see technique 30, page 51)

SERVES 4

LEMON SAUCE:

2¹/₂ cups (600 ml) Fish Stock (see page 222)

1 tablespoon fennel seeds

1 small lemon, sliced

¹/₂ cup (120 ml) dry white wine

1 egg

1 egg yolk

1¹/₄ cups (300 ml) olive oil

Salt and freshly ground black pepper

POTATO, TOMATO, AND BASIL CONFIT:

¹/₄ cup olive oil

1 small onion, minced

1 garlic clove, minced

1 lb (450 g) waxy new potatoes, peeled and cut into quarters

1 beefsteak tomato or 2 large plum tomatoes, skinned and chopped

2 tablespoons finely shredded basil

2 (1¹/₂-lb/750-g) sea bass, gutted but not scaled or trimmed (see page 14)

4 lb (1.75 kg) cooking salt

2 egg whites

SEA BASS,
ARCTIC CHAR

1 Preheat the oven to 400°F (200°C). For the sauce, put the fish stock, fennel seeds, sliced lemon, and white wine into a pan and boil rapidly until the liquid has reduced to about ¼ cup. Strain into a small bowl and let cool. Put the whole egg, egg yolk, reduced stock mixture, and some salt and pepper into a blender. With the motor running, gradually pour in the oil to make a thick, mayonnaiselike mixture. Transfer to a bowl and season to taste.

SEA BASS BAKED IN A SALT CRUST WITH LEMON SAUCE AND A
POTATO, TOMATO, AND BASIL CONFIT

2 For the potato confit, heat the olive oil in a pan, add the onion and garlic, and cook for 5 minutes until soft and lightly browned. Add the potatoes, tomato, and basil, and cook gently for 25 minutes or until the potatoes are tender.

3 While the potatoes are cooking, mix the salt with the egg whites. Spread a thick layer of the mixture in the bottom of a small roasting pan. Put the sea bass on top, then cover completely with the remaining salt mixture, making sure that there are no gaps (but don't worry if the tail is still exposed). Bake for 20 minutes.

4 Remove the fish from the oven and crack the top of the salt crust with the back of a large knife. Lift the crust away from the top of the fish, then carefully transfer the fish to a serving plate, leaving behind the rest of the salt crust.

5 Pull the skin away from the top of the fish and gently lift the fillets off the bones (see pages 38 to 9) onto four warmed serving plates. Season the potato, tomato, and basil confit with some salt and pepper, then spoon alongside the fish with some of the lemon sauce.

3 Lift the char fillet out of the brine and dry it on paper towels. Rest a sushi mat (or something else that is flat and permeable, to let the smoke through) on top of the chopsticks and lay the fish on top. Cover the wok or pan with a lid and smoke the fish for 3 to 4 minutes.

4 Remove the mat with the fish on top from the pan and, with a metal spatula, carefully lift the fish off the mat onto a board. Cut into four even-sized pieces.

5 For the chive dressing, set aside 4 of the chives for a garnish; mince the remainder. Mix them with the shallot, olive oil, vinegar, and salt.

6 Heat a ridged cast-iron grill pan until smoking-hot. Brush the pieces of smoked char with a little oil, place diagonally on the grill pan, and cook for 30 seconds on each side until the surface is lightly marked by the ridges and the center of the fish is just warm.

7 Spoon some of the dressing into the center of four plates and put the pieces of arctic char on top. Garnish with the reserved whole chives and serve immediately.

ALTERNATIVE FISH
Salmon trout.

pan-grilled lightly smoked arctic char with chive dressing (see technique 40, page 64)

SERVES 4
LIGHT BRINE:
3 tablespoons salt
2¹/₂ cups (600 ml) water

1 (12 oz–1 lb/350–450 g) arctic char fillet, skinned
1 small bunch of chives
1 small shallot, minced
¹/₃ cup (85 ml) extra virgin olive oil
1 tablespoon white wine vinegar
¹/₂ teaspoon salt
Hardwood sawdust, for smoking

1 Make the brine by dissolving the salt in the water. Pour it into a shallow dish, add the arctic char fillet, cover, and leave for 20 minutes.

2 To smoke the arctic char, put a 1-inch (2.5-cm) layer of hardwood sawdust into the bottom of a wok or chef's pan. Rest six wooden chopsticks over the top of the sawdust, to act as a platform. Place the pan over a high heat until the sawdust starts to smoke, then reduce the heat to low.

MONKFISH

roast stuffed monkfish with saffron, lemon, tomato, and capers

SERVES 6

1 (3–lb/1.5–kg) monkfish tail, skinned
   (see page 62)
1 tablespoon black peppercorns, coarsely crushed
1 tablespoon roughly chopped thyme
1 tablespoon Maldon sea salt flakes
Salt and freshly ground black pepper

STUFFING:

Large pinch of saffron strands
2 oz (50 g) can anchovy fillets in oil, drained
$^1/_2$ Preserved Lemon (see page 227), cut into thin slices
1 Roasted Red Pepper (see page 227), seeded and torn
   into wide strips
4–5 sun-dried tomatoes in oil, drained and thinly sliced
2 tablespoons olive oil

SAUCE:

$^3/_4$ cup (175 ml) Fish Stock (see page 222)
2 tablespoons extra virgin olive oil
1 tablespoon (15 g) butter
1 tablespoon lemon juice
1 tablespoon chopped flat-leaf parsley
1 tablespoon capers in brine, drained and rinsed

1 Preheat the oven to 400°F (200°C). Mix the saffron for the stuffing with 2 teaspoons of warm water and set to one side.

2 To remove the bone from the monkfish tail, but still keeping the fillets attached, put the fish on a board, with the side with the bone sticking out more facing upward. Carefully cut along either side of the bone, keeping the fillets attached where you can on the underside. Trim away the membrane from the outside of the fillets as described on page 62.

3 Season the cavity of the fish from which the bone was removed with a little salt and pepper. Lay the anchovy fillets at regular intervals along the cut face of each fillet, followed by the slices of preserved lemon, pieces of roasted red pepper, and, finally, the sun-dried tomatoes. Sprinkle with the saffron water and a little of the olive oil, then bring the sides up together so that you trap all the stuffing in place. Tie the fish at 1-inch (2.5-cm) intervals along its length with fine string.

4 Sprinkle the crushed black peppercorns, thyme, and sea salt over the bottom of a small roasting pan. Add the monkfish and turn it over in

the mixture so that it takes on an even coating. Now turn it right-side up again and sprinkle with the rest of the olive oil.

5 Roast the monkfish for 25 minutes, then remove from the oven and transfer to a serving plate. Cut it across, between the pieces of string, into slices 1 inch (2.5 cm) thick. Keep warm while you make the sauce.

6 Place the roasting pan over a medium heat and add the fish stock. Bring to a boil, scraping up all the bits and pieces from the bottom of the pan as you do so. Strain the juices into a small pan and add any juices from the serving plate, plus the extra virgin olive oil, butter, and lemon juice. Bring to a boil and let boil vigorously for about 4 minutes, until it has reduced slightly and emulsified. Remove from the heat and stir in the parsley, capers, and $^1/_2$ teaspoon of salt. Spoon the sauce around the fish and serve.

ALTERNATIVE FISH

Substitute 2 thick loin fillets from a large cod. Stuff them in the same way, then tie them together gently with plenty of fine string, as you would a boned and rolled roast of meat. Cod will not be as firm as the monkfish but will taste just as good. You will probably be able to break it apart with a fork to serve.

roast monkfish with crushed potatoes, olive oil, and watercress

SERVES 4

2 (12–oz/350–g) pieces of prepared thick monkfish fillet
   (see page 62)
$1^1/_2$ lb (750 g) new potatoes, scraped clean
2 tablespoons olive oil
$^1/_3$ cup (85 ml) extra virgin olive oil, plus extra for
   serving
$^1/_2$ cup (50 g) watercress sprigs, very roughly chopped
Balsamic vinegar, Maldon sea salt flakes, and coarsely
   crushed black pepper, for serving

1 Preheat the oven to 400°F (200°C). Season the monkfish with some salt, then set it aside for 15 minutes.

2 Cook the potatoes in well-salted boiling water until tender. While the potatoes are cooking, heat the 2 tablespoons of olive oil in a large frying pan that can be transferred to the oven. Pat the monkfish dry on paper

7

ROAST MONKFISH WITH CRUSHED POTATOES, OLIVE OIL, AND WATERCRESS

towels, add to the pan, and sear for 3 to 4 minutes, turning it three or four times, until nicely browned on all sides. Transfer the pan to the oven and roast for 10 to 12 minutes, until the fish is cooked through but still moist and juicy in the center. Remove from the oven, cover with foil, and set aside for 5 minutes.

3 When the potatoes are done, drain them well and return them to the pan with the extra virgin olive oil. Gently crush each potato against the side of the pan with the back of a fork until it just bursts open.

4 Season the potatoes and add any juices from the fish. Add the watercress and turn over gently until the watercress is well mixed in.

5 To serve, cut the monkfish across into thick slices. Spoon the crushed potatoes onto four warmed plates and put the monkfish on top. Put your thumb over the top of the bottle of extra virgin olive oil and drizzle a little of it around the outside edge of each plate. Do the same with the balsamic vinegar, then sprinkle around a few sea salt flakes and coarsely crushed black pepper.

MONKFISH

pan-fried fillet of monkfish with the new season's garlic and fennel

SERVES 4

$^2/_3$ cup (100 g) semolina

16 large, new season's garlic cloves

$^1/_3$ cup (15 g) sprigs of herb fennel

$^1/_2$ cup (100 g) unsalted butter

1 lb (450 g) fennel bulb, thinly sliced

$2^1/_2$ cups (600 ml) Fish Stock (see page 222)

4 (8-oz/225-g) pieces prepared monkfish fillet
   (see page 62)

$^1/_4$ cup canola oil

2 teaspoons lemon juice

A splash of Pernod or Ricard

Salt and freshly ground black pepper

1 Put the semolina, 2 sliced cloves of garlic, and all but 1 sprig of fennel into a food processor and blend until you have an aromatic, pale-green powder.

2 Cut the rest of the garlic cloves lengthwise into long, thin pieces. Melt half the butter in a pan, add the garlic and sliced fennel, and fry over a medium heat until lightly browned. Add the fish stock and some seasoning, and simmer for 15 minutes until the fennel is tender.

3 Preheat the oven to 400°F (200°C). Coat the pieces of monkfish with the semolina mixture. Heat the oil in a frying pan that can be transferred to the oven, add a small bit of butter and the monkfish pieces, and fry over a moderate heat, turning now and then, until they are golden brown all over. Transfer the pan to the oven and cook the monkfish for 10 minutes.

4 Remove the pan from the oven and lift the fillets onto a chopping board. Slice diagonally into thick slices, keeping each piece in shape. Transfer to a plate and keep warm.

5 Add the sautéed fennel mixture, lemon juice, Pernod, and remaining herb fennel, minced, to the pan in which the monkfish was cooked. Simmer rapidly until slightly reduced, then add the remaining butter and simmer until it has blended in to make a rich sauce. Adjust the seasoning, if necessary. Lift the fish onto four warmed plates and spoon some of the sauce around each piece.

grilled monkfish with saffron and roasted red pepper dressing

SERVES 4

ROASTED RED PEPPER DRESSING:

$2^1/_2$ cups (600 ml) Fish Stock (see page 222)

$^1/_3$ cup (85 ml) dry vermouth, such as Noilly Prat

Large pinch of saffron strands

2 Roasted Red Peppers (see page 227)

$^1/_3$ cup (85 ml) extra virgin olive oil

1 tablespoon balsamic vinegar or sherry vinegar

1 teaspoon unsalted butter

2 tablespoons olive oil

1 tablespoon chopped thyme

$^1/_2$ teaspoon salt

Freshly ground black pepper

4 (7-oz/200-g) pieces of prepared monkfish fillet
   (see page 62)

SALAD:

2 oz (50 g) mixed salad leaves

1 tablespoon Lemon Olive Oil (see page 227)

Large pinch of Maldon sea salt flakes

Salt and freshly ground black pepper

1 For the roasted red pepper dressing, put the fish stock, vermouth, and saffron into a small pan and simmer until reduced to ¾ cup (175 ml). Meanwhile, break the roasted red peppers in half and remove the stems, seeds, and skin. Mince the flesh. Mix together the extra virgin olive oil, vinegar, and some salt and pepper to taste.

2 Prepare and light a charcoal fire, or preheat a ridged cast-iron grill pan. Mix together the olive oil, thyme, salt, and some black pepper. Brush the fillets of monkfish with the mixture, place them on the grill or grill pan, and cook for 10 minutes, turning them every now and then.

3 While the monkfish fillets are cooking, return the pan of reduced fish stock to the heat and add the red peppers and olive oil dressing. Bring to a brisk boil and check the seasoning. Whisk in the butter and remove from the heat.

4 Mix the salad leaves with the lemon oil and Maldon salt. Pile them into the center of four plates. Lift the monkfish fillets onto a board and cut each diagonally into four slices. Set a sliced fillet on top of each pile of salad and pour some of the dressing around the edge of the plate. Serve immediately.

ceviche of monkfish
with avocado (see technique 38, page 62)

SERVES 6

1 lb 2 oz (500 g) prepared monkfish fillets (see page 62)
Juice of 3 limes
1 medium-hot red chile pepper, halved and seeded
1 small red onion
6 vine-ripened tomatoes, skinned
3 tablespoons extra virgin olive oil
2 tablespoons chopped cilantro
Salt
1 large, ripe but firm avocado

1 Cut the monkfish fillets across into thin slices and put them into a shallow dish. Pour the lime juice over the fish, making sure that all the slices are completely covered in juice. Cover with plastic wrap and refrigerate for 40 minutes, during which time the fish will turn white and opaque.

2 Meanwhile, slice across each chile half so that you get very thin, slightly curled slices. Cut the onion into quarters and then each wedge lengthwise into thin, arc-shaped slices. Cut each tomato into quarters and remove the seeds. Cut each piece of flesh lengthwise into thin, arc-shaped slices.

3 Just before you are ready to serve, lift the monkfish out of the lime juice with a slotted spoon and put it into a large bowl with the chile, onion, tomato, olive oil, most of the cilantro, and a little salt to taste. Toss together lightly.

4 Halve the avocado, remove the pit, and peel. Slice each half lengthwise into thin slices.

5 Arrange three or four slices of avocado on one side of each plate. Pile the ceviche onto the other side and sprinkle with the rest of the cilantro. Serve at once.

CEVICHE OF MONKFISH WITH AVOCADO

recipes
chapter 8

small round fish

salted pilchard bruschetta

SERVES 4

4 salted pilchards, scales removed (see page 16)
1 loaf of ciabatta or other rustic white bread, cut into
    slices ½ inch (1 cm) thick
3 garlic cloves, peeled
⅓ cup (85 ml) extra virgin olive oil
6 vine-ripened tomatoes, thinly sliced
1 small red onion, halved and very thinly sliced
3 tablespoons coarsely chopped flat-leaf parsley or basil
Freshly ground black pepper

1 Preheat the broiler. Broil the pilchards, 2 inches (5 cm) from the heat, for about 3 minutes on each side, until cooked through. Let cool, then break the fish into small flakes, discarding the skin and bones.

2 Toast the bread on both sides under the broiler until golden brown. Rub one side of each piece with the peeled garlic cloves, then drizzle on some of the olive oil. Put the flaked pilchards, tomatoes, onion, and parsley on top of the bread, then drizzle with the remaining oil and season well with black pepper. Serve straight away, before the bread has time to soften.

deviled mackerel with mint and tomato salad

SERVES 4

4 (12-oz/350-g) mackerel, cleaned and trimmed
    (see page 14)
3 tablespoons (40 g) butter
1 teaspoon sugar
1 teaspoon English mustard powder
1 teaspoon cayenne pepper
1 teaspoon paprika
1 teaspoon ground coriander
2 tablespoons red wine vinegar
1 teaspoon freshly ground black pepper
2 teaspoons salt

DEVILED MACKEREL WITH MINT AND TOMATO SALAD

hot potato salad with smoked mackerel and dandelions

SERVES 4

10 oz (300 g) new potatoes, scrubbed

1 oz (25 g) dandelion leaves

3 oz (75 g) smoked mackerel fillet

2 tablespoons red wine vinegar

$^2/_3$ cup (150 ml) canola oil

$1^1/_2$ tablespoons minced onion

$^1/_2$ teaspoon salt

Freshly ground black pepper

1 Cook the potatoes in boiling salted water for 15 minutes or until tender.

2 Meanwhile, wash the dandelion leaves and discard the stems. Blanch them in boiling water for a few seconds, then drain and refresh under cold running water.

3 Remove the skin and bones from the smoked mackerel, then cut it across into thin slices. Whisk together the vinegar, oil, salt, and some pepper.

4 Drain the potatoes and thinly slice them. Put them into a large pan with the dandelion leaves, mackerel, onion, and dressing, and turn together over a low heat until warmed through. Divide the mixture among four plates, grind a little more black pepper on top, and serve.

MINT AND TOMATO SALAD:

8 oz (225 g) small vine-ripened tomatoes, sliced

1 small onion, halved and very thinly sliced

1 tablespoon chopped mint

1 tablespoon lemon juice

1 Preheat the broiler. Slash the skin of the mackerel at $^1/_2$-inch (1-cm) intervals on both sides, from the head all the way down to the tail, taking care not to cut too deeply into the flesh.

2 Melt the butter in a small roasting pan. Remove from the heat and stir in the sugar, mustard, spices, vinegar, pepper, and salt, mixing together well. Add the mackerel to the butter and turn them over once or twice until well coated, spreading some butter into the cavity of each fish as well. Transfer them to a lightly oiled baking sheet or the rack of the broiler pan and broil, 4 inches (10 cm) from the heat, for 4 minutes on each side, until cooked through.

3 Meanwhile, for the salad, layer the sliced tomatoes, onion, and mint on four serving plates, sprinkling the layers with the lemon juice and seasoning. Put the cooked mackerel alongside and serve.

poached mackerel fillets with a warm mint, sherry vinegar, and butter sauce (see technique 5, page 22)

SERVES 4

SAUCE:

2 tablespoons sherry vinegar
1 shallot, minced
2 tablespoons cold water
2 egg yolks
1 cup (225 g) Clarified Butter (see page 226)
1 teaspoon lemon juice
Large pinch of cayenne pepper
1 tablespoon chopped mint
Salt and freshly ground black pepper

8 (3-oz/75-g) mackerel fillets (see page 22)
Mint sprigs, for garnish

1 First make the sauce: Put the sherry vinegar and shallot in a small pan and bring to a boil. Boil until reduced to about 1 teaspoon. Half-fill a pan with water and bring to a boil, then reduce to a simmer and rest a glass or stainless-steel bowl on top. Put the water, egg yolks, and sherry vinegar reduction into the bowl and whisk vigorously until voluminous and fluffy.

2 Remove the bowl from the heat and gradually whisk in the clarified butter, building up an emulsion as if making mayonnaise. Add the lemon juice, cayenne pepper, chopped mint, ½ teaspoon of salt, and some black pepper. Set aside and keep warm in a bowl of warm water.

3 Bring 5 cups (1.2 liters) of water and 2 tablespoons of salt to a boil in a large, clean frying pan. Reduce to a simmer, then add the mackerel fillets and poach for 3 minutes, turning them over halfway through cooking. Lift out, draining away the excess water, and put two mackerel fillets on each warmed plate. Spoon a little of the sauce over the fish and the rest around, and garnish with sprigs of fresh mint.

POACHED MACKEREL FILLETS WITH A WARM MINT,
SHERRY VINEGAR, AND BUTTER SAUCE

split herring with a caper and fresh tomato salsa (see technique 2, page 16)

SERVES 4

4 (8-oz/225-g) herring, fins trimmed (see page 14, step 2)
8 oz (225 g) vine-ripened tomatoes, roughly diced
1 garlic clove, minced
2½ tablespoons capers in brine, drained and rinsed
1 tablespoon coarsely chopped flat-leaf parsley
Salt and freshly ground black pepper

1 Preheat the broiler. Remove the bones from the herring as described on page 16.

2 Sprinkle the fish with a little salt and pepper on both sides, then lift them off the board and push them gently back into shape. Place them on a lightly oiled baking pan and broil, 4 inches (10 cm) from the heat, for 2 minutes on each side.

3 For the salsa, mix together the diced tomatoes, chopped garlic, capers, parsley, and some seasoning. Serve the herring with the salsa.

8

herring in an oat coating with bacon

SERVES 4

4 (8-oz/225-g) herring, cleaned and filleted
(see page 22, steps 1–3)
1 cup (100 g) rolled oats, ground in a food processor
to a coarse meal
1 tablespoon canola oil
4 thick bacon slices, cut into lardons (short strips)
Salt and freshly ground black pepper
1 lemon, cut into wedges, for serving

1 Season the herring fillets on both sides with salt and pepper. Spread the oat meal over a plate and coat the herring fillets in it, pressing it well onto both sides.

2 Heat the oil in a large frying pan. Add the bacon lardons and fry until crisp and golden. Remove from the pan with a slotted spoon and keep warm.

3 Add the herring fillets to the pan, flesh side down, and fry for 1 minute. Turn over and fry for another 1 to 2 minutes, until the skin is golden brown. Put the fillets on four warmed plates and sprinkle with the bacon. Serve with the lemon wedges, and some boiled potatoes that have been tossed with a little chopped parsley.

marinated herring and potato salad

SERVES 4 AS A FIRST COURSE

1 tablespoon salt
1¹/₂ teaspoons sugar
³/₄ teaspoon crushed white peppercorns
8 oz (225 g) prepared herring fillets (see page 22)
Olive oil, to cover
1 lb (450 g) new potatoes, scraped
3 tablespoons chopped chives
Freshly ground black pepper

1 At least 2 days before you want to serve this, mix together the salt, sugar, and crushed white pepper to make a dry cure. Layer the herring fillets in a shallow dish, sprinkling each layer generously with the dry cure mix. Cover with plastic wrap and leave in the refrigerator for 24 hours, turning the fish once, after 12 hours.

2 The next day, cut the herring fillets slightly on the diagonal into long, thin strips. Pack them into a large, airtight glass container (a canning jar is ideal) and pour in enough olive oil to cover. Refrigerate for at least another 24 hours before serving.

3 To serve, cook the potatoes in well-salted boiling water (1 teaspoon of salt to every 2¹/₂ cups/600 ml of water) for 15 minutes, until tender. Drain and cut lengthwise into quarters.

4 Put the warm potatoes into a bowl with the herring strips, chives, and 3 tablespoons of olive oil. Toss together.

5 Pile the salad into the center of four large plates and grind a little black pepper over the top. Serve while the potatoes are still warm.

pan-fried herring roe on toasted brioche with beurre noisette and capers (see technique 44, page 69)

SERVES 4

2 tablespoons extra virgin olive oil
¹/₂ teaspoon white wine vinegar
2 oz (50 g) mixed baby salad leaves
1 small bunch of chervil sprigs, large stems removed
4 slices of brioche or white bread, ¹/₂ inch (1 cm) thick
6 tablespoons (75 g) unsalted butter
12 oz (350 g) soft herring roe
3 tablespoons flour seasoned with salt and pepper
Juice of ¹/₂ lemon
1 tablespoon chopped flat-leaf parsley
1 tablespoon capers in brine, drained and rinsed
Salt

1 Whisk together the olive oil, vinegar, and a pinch of salt. Toss with the salad leaves, then divide them among four slightly warmed plates. Sprinkle with the chervil. Toast the brioche and put beside the salad.

2 Melt 2 tablespoons (25 g) of the butter in a frying pan. Dust the roe in the seasoned flour, then fry for 2 minutes, turning once, until lightly browned. Put them on top of the brioche.

3 Wipe the pan clean, then add the rest of the butter and cook over a medium heat until it foams and starts to smell nutty. Add the lemon juice, parsley, and a pinch of salt. Spoon the butter over the roe and scatter on the capers. Serve immediately.

herring recheado with katchumber salad and pilau rice (see technique 6, page 23)

SERVES 4 AS A FIRST COURSE
4 (8-oz/225-g) herring
1 quantity Goan Masala Paste (see page 226)
RICE:
Canola oil, for frying
6 large shallots, thinly sliced
3 whole cloves
3 green cardamom pods
2-inch (5-cm) piece of cinnamon stick
1 bay leaf
1²/₃ cups (275 g) basmati rice
¹/₂ teaspoon salt
2¹/₂ cups (600 ml) boiling water
KATCHUMBER SALAD:
1 lb (450 g) vine-ripened tomatoes, thinly sliced
1 red onion, quartered and thinly sliced
2 tablespoons roughly chopped cilantro
¹/₄ teaspoon ground cumin
Pinch of cayenne pepper
1 tablespoon white wine vinegar
¹/₄ teaspoon salt

1 If you are going to grill the herring, prepare and light the charcoal fire about 40 minutes before cooking.

2 Prepare the herring as described on page 23. Spread the cut face of one fillet with 1 teaspoon of the masala paste. Put the fish back into shape and tie in two places with string.

3 For the rice, heat ½ inch (1 cm) of oil in a large frying pan. Add the sliced shallots and fry them, stirring now and then, until they are crisp and golden. Lift out with a slotted spoon onto plenty of paper towels and let drain.

4 Heat 2 tablespoons of oil in a large pan, add the whole spices and the bay leaf, and cook for a few seconds until they start to smell aromatic. Stir in the rice, salt, and water and bring to a boil, then cover and cook over a low heat for 10 minutes. If you are cooking the herring under the broiler, preheat it.

5 For the katchumber salad, layer all the ingredients together in a shallow dish.

6 Remove the rice from the heat and leave for 5 minutes. Meanwhile, grill the herring, or broil 4 inches (10 cm) from the heat, for 3 minutes on each side, until crisp and lightly golden. Lift them onto four warmed plates. Toss the fried shallots with a little salt, then stir them into the cooked rice. Serve with the herring and the katchumber salad.

VARIATION

mackerel recheado

Replace the herring with 4 (8-oz/225-g) mackerel and spread each one with 1 tablespoon of masala pasta. Cook for 3 to 4 minutes on each side.

broiled smelts with coarsely chopped green herbs (see technique 35, page 57)

SERVES 4
2 strips of pared lemon zest
¹/₂ tablespoon minced rosemary
1 tablespoon minced flat-leaf parsley
1 garlic clove, minced
¹/₂ tablespoon minced pitted green olives
¹/₂ tablespoon chopped capers
¹/₂ teaspoon Maldon sea salt flakes
¹/₄ teaspoon freshly ground black pepper
16–20 smelts, cleaned and trimmed (see page 14)
Extra virgin olive oil, for brushing and serving
Lemon wedges and crusty fresh bread, for serving

1 Soak four bamboo skewers in cold water for 30 minutes. Cut the strips of lemon zest across into very thin shreds, then mince them. Mix with the rosemary, parsley, garlic, olives, capers, salt, and pepper. Set to one side.

2 Preheat the broiler. Thread the smelts onto the skewers by piercing them through the head. Lay them on a lightly oiled baking pan and sprinkle them with some extra virgin olive oil, salt, and pepper. Broil, 2 inches (5 cm) from the heat, for 2 minutes on one side only.

3 To serve, lift the skewered smelts into the center of four warmed plates and scatter some of the herb mixture over them. Pour a little more oil around the edge of the plates and serve, with lemon wedges and plenty of crusty bread.

8

jansson's temptation

SERVES 4

2 oz (50 g) good-quality anchovies canned in olive oil
2 onions, thinly sliced
³/₄ cup (175 ml) milk
2 lb (900 g) baking or all-purpose potatoes, peeled
³/₄ cup (175 ml) heavy cream
Butter, for greasing
Salt and freshly ground black pepper

1 Preheat the oven to 375°F (190°C). Tip the anchovies and their oil into a frying pan. Add the onions and fry over a medium-high heat for 5 minutes, until soft and lightly browned.

2 Meanwhile, cut the potatoes into slices about ¼ inch (5 mm) thick. Stack the slices up a few at a time and cut them lengthwise into ¼-inch (5-mm) matchsticks.

3 Add the milk and cream to the onions and bring to a boil. Season to taste with salt (depending on the saltiness of the anchovies) and pepper, then stir in the potatoes, mixing well so that the ingredients are evenly distributed.

4 Pour the mixture into a lightly buttered, shallow baking dish. Bake for 45 minutes, until the potatoes are tender and the top is lightly browned. Serve with a crisp green salad.

marinated anchovies (see technique, page 57)

SERVES 4

1 lb (450 g) fresh anchovies
Juice of 1 lemon
1 teaspoon minced medium-hot red chile pepper
1 garlic clove, minced
1 tablespoon chopped flat-leaf parsley
¼ cup extra virgin olive oil
Salt and freshly ground black pepper

1 To prepare the anchovies, pinch off the heads and pull them away; the guts should come out with them. Then pinch along the top edge of each fish and pull out the spine—it should come away quite easily because the fish is soft. You will then be left with lots of little double fillets.

2 Lay them skin-side down in a large, shallow dish and pour the lemon juice over them. Leave for 20 minutes, during which time the flesh will become slightly opaque and firm.

3 Drain off the excess lemon juice, then sprinkle with the chile, garlic, parsley, and some salt and pepper. Pour the oil on top. Cover and leave for 24 hours in the refrigerator to allow all the flavors to permeate the fish.

ALTERNATIVE FISH
Sprats, sardines, or small mackerel.

SARDINES,
BASS

linguine with tomato and anchovy sauce and flaked fresh sardines

SERVES 4

8 sardines, cleaned (see page 14)

1/4 cup extra virgin olive oil

3 garlic cloves, minced

4 sage leaves, finely shredded

1 medium-hot red chile pepper, seeded and minced

1 lb (450 g) vine-ripened tomatoes, skinned and chopped

1/3 cup (50 g) capers, drained

2/3 cup (100 g) chopped well-flavored black olives

4 oz (100 g) anchovy fillets canned in oil, drained and minced

1 tablespoon chopped oregano

1 lb (450 g) dried linguine or spaghetti

3 tablespoons chopped flat-leaf parsley

Salt and freshly ground black pepper

1 Brush the sardines on both sides with olive oil, season with plenty of salt and pepper, and put them onto a lightly oiled baking pan or the rack of the broiler pan.

2 Heat the extra virgin olive oil in a pan, add the garlic and sage, and cook until the garlic begins to take on a little color. Add the red chile and fry for a few seconds. Add the tomatoes, capers, olives, anchovies, oregano, and some freshly ground black pepper, and let simmer for 10 minutes.

3 Cook the pasta in well-salted boiling water for about 8 minutes or until al dente. Meanwhile, preheat the broiler. Broil the sardines, 4 inches (10 cm) from the heat, for 2 minutes on each side. Let cool slightly, then flake the fish away from the bones in largish pieces.

4 Drain the pasta and tip it into a large serving bowl. Stir the chopped parsley into the sauce, pour it over the pasta, and toss together well. Add the flaked sardines and turn over gently to mix.

ALTERNATIVE FISH

Mackerel, pilchards, or herring.

sardine and potato curry puffs

MAKES 12

2/3 cup (100 g) peeled potato cut into 1/2-inch (1-cm) cubes

1 tablespoon peanut or canola oil, plus extra for deep-frying

2 garlic cloves, crushed

1/2-inch (1-cm) piece of fresh ginger, finely grated

1/2 onion, thinly sliced

1 tablespoon Goan Masala Paste (see page 226) or good-quality garam masala paste

8 oz (225 g) sardines, cleaned, filleted (see page 22), and cut across into strips 1 inch (2.5 cm) wide

1 medium-hot red chile pepper, seeded and minced

1 tablespoon lemon juice

1/4 teaspoon salt

2–3 green onions, sliced

2 tablespoons chopped cilantro

1 lb (450 g) puff pastry, thawed if frozen

Lemon wedges and cilantro sprigs, for garnish

1 Boil the potato in salted water until just tender, then drain. Heat the oil in a large frying pan and fry the garlic, ginger, and onion for 1 minute. Add the masala paste and fry for 1 minute, then add the pieces of sardine and fry for another minute. Finally, add the potato, chile, lemon juice, and salt, and cook for 1 minute. Take the pan off the heat, stir in the green onions and cilantro, and let cool.

2 Roll out the puff pastry on a lightly floured surface and cut out 12 rounds 4 inches (10 cm) in diameter. Spoon a heaped teaspoon of the filling mixture onto each round. Brush half of the edge of one round with a little water, then fold it over the filling to make a half-moon shape and press together well to seal the edge. Mark along the edge with a fork to make an even tighter seal.

3 Heat some oil for deep frying to 375°F (190°C). Deep-fry the puffs three or four at a time for 7 to 8 minutes, turning them over every now and then, until they are golden brown. Drain on paper towels. Keep warm in a low oven while you cook the rest. Pile them on a plate and serve warm, garnished with some lemon wedges and cilantro.

ALTERNATIVE FISH

Mackerel, pilchards, sprats, herring, or any other oily fish with lots of flavor.

8

escabèche of sardines

SERVES 4

12 sardines, cleaned (see page 16)
1/3 cup (50 g) flour seasoned with salt and pepper
2/3 cup (150 ml) olive oil
1/3 cup (85 ml) red wine vinegar
1 onion, thinly sliced
2-inch (5-cm) strip of pared orange zest
1 sprig of thyme
1 sprig of rosemary
1 bay leaf
4 garlic cloves, crushed
2 dried, hot red chile peppers
1 small bunch of flat-leaf parsley, roughly chopped
Salt and freshly ground black pepper

1 Remove the heads from the sardines (see page 16), then dust them in the seasoned flour. Fry them in half the olive oil for 1 minute on each side, then transfer to a shallow dish.

2 Add the vinegar, onion, orange zest, thyme, rosemary, bay leaf, garlic, chiles, and 1 teaspoon salt to the pan, bring to a boil, and simmer for about 15 minutes.

3 Add the rest of the olive oil and the parsley, then pour the hot marinade over the sardines and leave until cold.

fillets of bass with vanilla butter vinaigrette

SERVES 4

4 (4-oz/100-g) skinned sea bass fillets
1/2 cup (100 g) Clarified Butter (see page 226)
VANILLA BUTTER VINAIGRETTE:
1/2 vanilla bean
1/4 cup dry vermouth, such as Noilly Prat
2 teaspoons white wine vinegar
1 shallot, halved
2/3 cup (150 ml) Fish Stock (see page 222)
2 tablespoons skinned, seeded, and finely diced tomato
1 tablespoon coarsely chopped chervil
Salt and freshly ground black pepper

1 Brush both sides of each sea bass fillet with a little of the clarified butter and season with salt and pepper.

2 For the vanilla butter vinaigrette, split the vanilla bean open lengthwise and scrape out the seeds with a small teaspoon, then mince the bean. Put the seeds and bean into a small pan with the vermouth, vinegar, and shallot. Bring to a boil and boil for a few minutes until reduced to about 1 tablespoon. Add the fish stock and boil once more until reduced to about 3 tablespoons. Remove the shallot halves and add the remaining clarified butter, the diced tomato, chervil, 1/4 teaspoon of salt, and 6 turns of the black pepper mill. Keep warm over a very low heat.

3 Heat a ridged cast-iron grill pan until very hot. Add the sea bass fillets, skin-side down, and cook for 1 minute, pressing down on each fillet in turn with the back of a spatula to help mark them with the lines from the pan. Turn over and cook for 30 seconds on the other side.

4 To serve, put the fish fillets on four warmed plates and spoon some of the vanilla butter vinaigrette to one side.

grilled whole sea bass with pernod and fennel

(see technique 1, page 14)

SERVES 4

4 (1–1 1/4 lb/450–550 g) sea bass, cleaned and trimmed
   (see page 14)
2 tablespoons olive oil
1 large bunch of herb fennel
3 tablespoons Pernod
1 quantity Fennel Mayonnaise (see page 224)
Salt and freshly ground black pepper

1 Light the charcoal fire 40 minutes before you are going to cook.

2 Slash each fish four or five times down each side. Rub them with the oil and season well with salt and pepper, both outside and inside the gut cavities. Push some of the fennel into the gut cavity of each fish.

3 If you prefer to broil the fish, preheat the broiler.

4 Grill the fish, or broil 6 inches (15 cm) from the heat, for 6 to 8 minutes. Sprinkle each fish with about 1 teaspoon of Pernod, carefully turn over the wire clamp (or turn the fish, if broiling them), and cook for another 6 to 8 minutes, until they are cooked right through to the backbone. Sprinkle with the rest of the Pernod.

5 Lift the fish onto a warmed serving plate and serve with the fennel mayonnaise and some boiled new potatoes.

deep-fried sea bass with chile sauce

SERVES 4

CHILE SAUCE:

2 tablespoons minced garlic

2 medium-hot red chile peppers, minced

2 tablespoons canola oil

2 tablespoons palm sugar or light, raw brown sugar

3 tablespoons Thai fish sauce (*nam pla*)

1 tablespoon Tamarind Water (see page 227)

GARNISHES:

4 shallots, thinly sliced

2 garlic cloves, thinly sliced

$^1/_3$ cup (50 g) cashew nuts, halved

2 kaffir lime leaves, finely shredded (optional)

$^1/_2$ cup (25 g) basil leaves

4 (12-oz/350-g) sea bass, cleaned and trimmed
   (see page 14)

$^1/_3$ cup (50 g) flour seasoned with salt and pepper

Canola oil, for deep-frying

1 For the sauce, pound together the garlic and chiles in a mortar until they form a coarse paste. Heat the oil in a small saucepan, add the garlic and chile paste, and fry for 1 minute. Stir in the sugar, fish sauce, and tamarind water and bring to a simmer. Keep warm.

2 Next, prepare the garnishes. Fill a pan large enough to accommodate the fish about one-third full with canola oil. Heat to 375°F (190°C). Add the sliced shallots, garlic, and cashew nuts, and fry for 2 minutes. Lift out with a slotted spoon and drain on paper towels. Add the shredded lime leaves and the basil leaves and fry for about 30 seconds. Drain and set aside.

3 Rinse the fish and pat dry. Coat in the seasoned flour and deep-fry, one at a time, for 5 to 6 minutes, until crisp and golden. Lift out, drain briefly on paper towels, and keep warm while you cook the remaining fish.

4 Put the fish on four warmed plates and spoon the sauce over them. Scatter with the garnishes and serve.

ALTERNATIVE FISH
Black bream.

black bream steamed over seaweed with a fennel-butter sauce (see technique 26, page 47)

SERVES 4

4 (8-oz/225-g) black bream, cleaned and trimmed
   (see page 14)

$1^1/_2$ lb (750 g) fresh edible seaweed

Salt and freshly ground black pepper

FENNEL-BUTTER SAUCE:

14 tablespoons (200 g) unsalted butter

$^1/_2$ fennel bulb, trimmed and thinly sliced

$^1/_3$ cup (40 g) thinly sliced onion

$^1/_2$ small garlic clove, chopped

$^2/_3$ cup (150 ml) Fish Stock or Chicken Stock
   (see page 222)

1 tablespoon white wine

2 tablespoons Pernod

2 teaspoons lemon juice

2 egg yolks

3 tablespoons chopped herb fennel

1 Season the fish inside and out with a little salt and pepper. Wash the seaweed and spread it over the bottom of a sauté pan large enough to hold the fish in a single layer (if you don't have a pan large enough, use two). Add 1¼ cups (300 ml) of water, put the fish on top, and cover with a tight-fitting lid. Set to one side.

BLACK BREAM STEAMED OVER SEAWEED WITH
A FENNEL-BUTTER SAUCE

8

2 For the sauce, melt 2 tablespoons (25 g) of the butter in a pan. Add the fennel, onion, and garlic, and cook for 5 minutes until soft but not browned. Add the stock, white wine, and some salt and pepper, and simmer for 15 minutes until the vegetables are very soft and most of the liquid has evaporated.

3 Spoon the mixture into a blender and let cool slightly. Then add the Pernod, lemon juice, and egg yolks. Melt the rest of the butter in a clean pan. As soon as it begins to bubble, turn on the blender and blend the contents for 1 minute. Then slowly pour in the hot melted butter to make a hollandaiselike mixture. Pour the sauce into a bowl and stir in the chopped herb fennel and some seasoning to taste. Keep warm.

4 Place the pan of fish and seaweed over a high heat. As soon as some steam starts to leak from underneath the lid, turn the heat down and steam for 5 minutes until the fish are cooked through. Without lifting the lid, take the pan of fish to the table, together with the fennel butter sauce. Remove the lid so your guests can appreciate the aroma and serve with some plain boiled potatoes.

ALTERNATIVE FISH
Red porgy or scup.

baked red bream with fennel, orange, and provençal herbs

SERVES 4

1 orange
3 fennel bulbs
1 teaspoon dried herbes de Provence or 1 tablespoon chopped mixed thyme, rosemary, and oregano
1¹/₂ teaspoons chopped herb fennel
2 tablespoons Pernod
1 large onion, chopped
2 bay leaves, finely shredded
3 garlic cloves, thinly sliced
2 tablespoons white wine vinegar
¹/₃ cup (85 ml) olive oil
1 teaspoon sugar
4 (1¹/₄-lb/550-g) red sea bream or porgy, trimmed and scaled (see page 14)
Salt and freshly ground black pepper

1 Pare the zest from half the orange with a potato peeler, then cut each strip across into fine shreds like pine needles. Squeeze the juice from the whole orange. Remove the outer leaves from the fennel bulbs and chop the remainder.

2 Put the herbs, orange zest and juice, chopped fennel, herb fennel, Pernod, onion, bay leaves, garlic, white wine vinegar, olive oil, and sugar into a heavy-based saucepan. Cover and cook for 15 minutes until the fennel is soft.

3 Preheat the oven to 400°F (200°C). Spoon half of the fennel mixture over the bottom of a shallow baking dish. Put the fish on top and spoon the rest of the fennel mixture over it. Cover with foil and bake for about 20 minutes.

4 Remove the foil and bake for 5 minutes more. Drizzle with a little extra oil before serving.

patricia wells's porgy with red peppers, capers, and cumin

SERVES 4

5–6 tablespoons extra virgin olive oil
2 large red bell peppers, halved, seeded, and diced
2 tablespoons capers in brine, drained and rinsed
2 teaspoons cumin seeds
4 (10-oz/300-g) porgy, red bream, or black bream, cleaned and trimmed (see page 14)
Salt and freshly ground black pepper

1 Heat 1 tablespoon of the oil in a medium-sized frying pan. Add the red peppers and fry for 4 to 5 minutes until tender. Remove the pan from the heat and stir in the capers and cumin seeds. Set aside.

2 Season the cavities of each fish with some salt and pepper, then generously brush with oil. Heat another 2 tablespoons of the oil in a frying pan, add two of the fish, and cook for 4 to 5 minutes on each side. Keep warm while you cook the remaining two fish.

3 Reheat the red pepper sauce. Lift the fish onto warmed plates and spoon some of the red pepper sauce alongside. Drizzle a little more oil around the outside of the plate and serve.

WHITEBAIT,

WHITING,

GARFISH

DEEP-FRIED WHITEBAIT WITH LEMON AND PERSILLADE

deep-fried whitebait with lemon and persillade (see technique 34, page 56)

SERVES 4

1¼ lb (550 g) whitebait
Canola oil, for deep-frying
½ cup (75 g) all-purpose flour
½ teaspoon cayenne pepper
1 teaspoon salt
1 lemon, cut into wedges, for serving

PERSILLADE:

2 garlic cloves
1 small bunch of flat-leaf parsley, large stems removed

1 Rinse the whitebait in plenty of cold water, then drain and shake vigorously in a colander.

2 Heat some oil for deep-frying to 375°F (190°C). For the persillade, mince the garlic on a chopping board. Then add the parsley and continue to chop them together until you have a very fine mixture.

3 Put the flour, cayenne pepper, and salt into a large bowl and mix together. Add the whitebait and toss until they are all well coated, then lift them out and shake off the excess flour.

4 Deep-fry the fish in batches for about 3 minutes, until crisp. Drain briefly on paper towels, then tip into a large serving bowl and sprinkle with the persillade. Serve with the lemon wedges.

merlan frit en colère (deep-fried whiting) (see technique 16, page 32)

SERVES 4

TOMATO TARTAR SAUCE:

3 tablespoons white wine vinegar
6 black peppercorns, coarsely crushed
½ shallot, minced
A few tarragon stems, broken into small pieces
2 plum tomatoes, skinned, seeded, and minced
2 tablespoons each minced green olives, gherkins, and capers
2 teaspoons each chopped tarragon, flat-leaf parsley, and chives
½ cup (100 ml) Mustard Mayonnaise (see page 224)

4 (12-oz/350-g) whiting, cleaned and trimmed (see page 14)
Canola oil, for deep-frying
½ cup (75 g) all-purpose flour
2 eggs, beaten
3½ cups (175 g) fresh white breadcrumbs, made from day-old bread
Salt and freshly ground black pepper

1 For the tomato tartar sauce, put the vinegar, peppercorns, shallot, and tarragon stems into a small pan and boil until the vinegar is reduced to 1 teaspoon. Cool slightly, then strain into a bowl. Mix in the rest of the sauce ingredients with some salt and pepper to taste.

2 Prepare the whiting for cooking as described on page 32. Heat some oil for deep-frying to 325°F (160°C). Season the flour with ½ teaspoon of salt and some pepper. Season each fish with a little salt, then coat them one at a time in the flour, followed by the beaten egg and then the breadcrumbs.

3 Deep-fry the fish, in batches, for 5 minutes, or until crisp and golden and cooked through. Transfer to a baking sheet lined with paper towels and keep warm in a low oven while you coat and cook the rest of the fish in the same way. Serve with the tomato tartar sauce and some chunky fries.

ALTERNATIVE FISH
Small hake or cod (scrod).

8

salad of pan-grilled garfish with sun-dried tomatoes and fennel seeds (see technique 14, page 31)

SERVES 4

3 tablespoons olive oil

2 teaspoons lemon juice

1 teaspoon chopped thyme

1 teaspoon fennel seeds, lightly crushed

Pinch of dried red pepper flakes

4 (10–12 oz/275–350 g) garfish, filleted (see page 31)

1 oz (25 g) arugula

1 oz (25 g) prepared curly endive

$^{1}/_{3}$ cup (15 g) flat-leaf parsley leaves

$^{1}/_{3}$ cup (15 g) chervil sprigs

4–6 sun-dried tomatoes in oil, drained and thinly sliced

1 tablespoon sherry vinegar

Salt and freshly ground black pepper

1 Mix together the olive oil, lemon juice, thyme, fennel seeds, red pepper flakes, ½ teaspoon of salt, and a few twists of freshly ground black pepper. Brush a little of this mixture over both sides of the garfish fillets and set aside for 5 minutes.

2 Toss the arugula, curly endive, parsley, and chervil together, then divide among four plates.

3 Heat a flat griddle or ridged cast-iron grill pan over a high heat until smoking-hot. Add the garfish fillets, skin-side down, and cook for 1 to 1½ minutes, turning them over halfway through. Transfer them to a plate. Break them into 3-inch (7.5-cm) pieces.

4 Arrange the pieces of fish and the strips of sun-dried tomato among the salad leaves, taking care not to flatten the leaves too much.

5 Add the remaining marinade and the sherry vinegar to the pan and swirl it around briefly. Spoon a little over the salad and the rest around the outside of the plate, then serve straight away.

ALTERNATIVE FISH

Mackerel or gurnard or sea robin.

SALAD OF PAN-GRILLED GARFISH WITH
SUN-DRIED TOMATOES AND FENNEL SEEDS

broiled pompano fillet with a noilly prat and thyme butter sauce

SERVES 4

NOILLY PRAT AND THYME BUTTER SAUCE:

2¹/₂ cups (600 ml) Fish Stock (see page 222)

¹/₄ cup heavy cream

¹/₄ cup dry vermouth, such as Noilly Prat

6 tablespoons (75 g) chilled unsalted butter, cut into small pieces

1 teaspoon thyme leaves

4 (6-oz/175-g) pompano fillets, skinned

2 tablespoons (25 g) butter, melted

Salt and freshly ground black pepper

POMPANO,
JOHN DORY

1 For the sauce, put the fish stock, cream, and Noilly Prat into a medium-sized pan and boil rapidly until reduced by three-fourths to about ¾ cup (175 ml). Keep warm.

2 Preheat the broiler. Brush the pompano fillets on both sides with melted butter and season. Place on a lightly buttered baking pan and broil, about 4 inches (10 cm) from the heat, for 8 minutes until just cooked through.

3 Bring the sauce reduction back to a simmer, then whisk in the chilled butter a piece at a time. Stir in the thyme leaves and season to taste.

4 Lift the pieces of pompano into the center of four warmed plates. Spoon some of the sauce over the fish and the rest around the edge of the plates.

ALTERNATIVE FISH

Pieces of salmon fillet.

fillets of john dory with warm potatoes, olives, capers, and rosemary

SERVES 4

1 lb (450 g) unskinned john dory fillets

¹/₄ cup extra virgin olive oil, plus extra for brushing

4 small, waxy new potatoes

2 anchovy fillets canned in olive oil, drained

2 vine-ripened tomatoes, skinned and seeded

3 sun-dried tomatoes in oil, drained and cut into thin strips

4 black olives, pitted and sliced

12 small capers in brine, drained and rinsed

10 "needles" of rosemary

Small handful of roughly chopped flat-leaf parsley

Salt and freshly ground black pepper

1 Cut small john dory fillets in half lengthwise, and larger ones lengthwise into three. Brush them with the oil and put them skin-side up in a lightly oiled baking pan. Season with salt and pepper.

2 Cut each potato lengthwise into quarters and cook in boiling salted water for about 10 minutes or until tender. Drain and keep warm.

3 Cut the anchovy fillets lengthwise into long, thin slivers. Cut each wedge-shaped piece of tomato flesh into thin, arc-shaped pieces.

4 Preheat the broiler. Broil the john dory, 4 inches (10 cm) from the heat, for 2 to 3 minutes until just cooked through. Meanwhile, put the rest of the olive oil into a shallow pan with the potatoes, anchovies, tomato pieces, sun-dried tomato strips, olives, capers, and rosemary. Warm through over a gentle heat. Add the parsley and season to taste.

5 Arrange the pieces of fish and the warmed vegetables attractively on four warmed plates. Serve immediately.

8

john dory with soft-boiled eggs, leeks, and mustard vinaigrette (see technique 13, page 30)

(see technique 13, page 30)

SERVES 4

16–20 baby leeks, trimmed and cleaned
2 eggs
A thick piece of Parmesan cheese
2 (12 oz–1 lb/350–450 g) john dory, filleted
   (see page 30)
2 tablespoons (25 g) butter, melted
Maldon sea salt flakes and freshly ground black pepper
Coarsely crushed black pepper, for serving

MUSTARD VINAIGRETTE:

1½ teaspoons Dijon mustard
1½ teaspoons white wine vinegar
8 teaspoons extra virgin olive oil

1 Preheat the broiler. Cook the leeks in boiling salted water for 2 to 3 minutes, until just tender but still al dente. Drain and refresh under cold water, then dry on paper towels.

2 Cook the eggs in boiling water for just 7 minutes so that the yolks remain slightly soft. Cool, peel, and cut in half. Shave some thin slices off the piece of Parmesan cheese with a sharp potato peeler and set aside.

3 For the mustard vinaigrette, mix the mustard and vinegar together in a small bowl, then gradually whisk in the olive oil. Season to taste with some salt and pepper.

4 Heat a ridged cast-iron grill pan over a high heat. Brush with a little oil, then place the leeks diagonally across it and cook them for slightly less than 1 minute on each side, so that they get nicely marked with diagonal lines. Remove the leeks from the pan and arrange in the center of four large, warmed plates.

5 Cut each john dory fillet diagonally across into two similar-sized pieces. Brush on both sides with the melted butter and season well with salt and pepper. Lay the fillets, skin-side up, on a lightly greased baking pan or the rack of the broiler pan. Broil, 4 inches (10 cm) from the heat, for 4 minutes. Remove and place on top of the leeks. Put one egg half on each plate. Stir 1½ teaspoons of warm water into the mustard vinaigrette, then drizzle this over the leeks. Scatter the Parmesan shavings on top, sprinkle with a little coarsely crushed black pepper and some sea salt flakes, and serve.

JOHN DORY WITH SOFT-BOILED EGGS, LEEKS, AND MUSTARD VINAIGRETTE

hard-fried fish in red curry

SERVES 4

**2 tablespoons peanut or canola oil, plus extra for
deep-frying**

3 tablespoons Thai Red Curry Paste (see page 226)

7 fl oz (200 ml) coconut milk

1 tablespoon Thai fish sauce (*nam pla*)

1 teaspoon palm sugar or light, raw brown sugar

4 (8-oz/225-g) john dory steaks

Juice of ¹/₂ lime

Salt and freshly ground black pepper

1 Heat the 2 tablespoons of oil in a large, deep frying pan. Add the red
curry paste and fry for about 2 minutes, until the paste starts to
separate from the oil. Add the coconut milk, fish sauce, and sugar, and
simmer very gently for 10 minutes, until thickened.

2 Meanwhile, heat some oil for deep-frying to 375°F (190°C). Deep-fry
the john dory steaks, two at a time, for 2 minutes, until crisp, golden,
and cooked through. Lift onto a baking sheet lined with paper towels
and keep warm in a low oven while you cook the remaining steaks.

3 Once the excess oil has drained off the fish, place the steaks on four
warmed serving plates. Stir the lime juice into the sauce, along with
some seasoning to taste. Spoon it over the fish and serve with some
steamed rice.

ALTERNATIVE FISH

Steaks of haddock, hake, or salmon, or even steaks of monkfish, skinned
and cut across the bone, would be a great idea. You could also try shark
and swordfish steaks.

JOHN DORY,
RED MULLET,
GRAY MULLET

8

HARD-FRIED FISH IN RED CURRY

moroccan fish tagine

SERVES 4 AS A FIRST COURSE

2 tablespoons olive oil, plus extra for brushing

2 celery stalks, chopped

1 carrot, chopped

1 small onion, chopped

1/4 Preserved Lemon (see page 227), minced

1 quantity Charmoula (see page 146)

4 plum tomatoes, sliced

2 1/2 cups (600 ml) Fish Stock (see page 222)

8 small new potatoes, cut lengthwise into quarters

2 (1-lb/450-g) red mullet, filleted (see page 22)

8 black olives, halved

1 teaspoon chopped cilantro

1 teaspoon chopped mint

Salt and freshly ground black pepper

1 Heat the oil in a large pan. Add the celery, carrot, and onion, and fry gently for 5 minutes, until softened but not browned. Add half the minced preserved lemon, 2 tablespoons of the charmoula, the tomatoes, and the stock. Bring to a boil and simmer for 30 minutes. Add the potatoes and simmer for 6 to 8 minutes until tender.

2 Preheat the broiler. Brush the red mullet fillets with olive oil and season with salt and pepper, then cut each one diagonally in half. Put skin-side up on an oiled baking pan or the rack of the broiler pan. Broil, 4 inches (10 cm) from the heat, for 6 minutes or until cooked through.

3 Stir the olives, the rest of the charmoula, and the remaining preserved lemon into the sauce and check the seasoning. Put the fish in four warmed soup bowls, spoon the sauce over, and sprinkle with the chopped cilantro and mint.

ALTERNATIVE FISH
Gray or striped mullet, ocean perch.

steamed gray mullet with garlic, ginger, and green onions (see technique 25, page 46)

SERVES 2

2 (1-lb/450-g) gray or striped mullet, cleaned and trimmed (see page 14, steps 1 to 4)

1-inch (2.5-cm) piece of fresh ginger, peeled and cut into fine julienne

4 green onions, trimmed and thinly sliced

2 tablespoons dark soy sauce

2 tablespoons toasted sesame oil

4 garlic cloves, minced

1 Put the fish into a steamer (see page 46) and sprinkle with the ginger. Cover and steam for 10 to 12 minutes until cooked through. Lift the fish onto two warmed serving plates and scatter the green onions on top. Keep warm.

2 Pour 1/4 cup of the cooking juices into a small pan and add the soy sauce. Bring to a boil, then pour this over the fish.

3 Heat the sesame oil in a small pan. Add the garlic and fry for a few seconds, then pour this over the fish and serve.

small round fish

red mullet en papillote with thyme

SERVES 4

4 (8–10 oz/225–275 g) red mullet, cleaned and trimmed (see page 14)
1 small bunch of thyme
¹/₂ cup (120 ml) extra virgin olive oil
¹/₄ cup dry white wine
Juice of 1 lemon (about 8 teaspoons)
Sea salt and freshly ground black pepper

TOMATO, BLACK OLIVE, AND CHILE SALAD:

1 lb (450 g) small vine-ripened tomatoes, cut into wedges
¹/₂ medium-hot red chile pepper, seeded and minced
1 garlic clove, minced
¹/₄ cup (50 g) good-quality black olives, pitted
¹/₄ cup extra virgin olive oil
1 tablespoon chopped flat-leaf parsley

1 Preheat the oven to 425°F (220°C). Season the whole fish inside and out with salt and pepper and put 2 sprigs of thyme in the cavity of each one.

2 Brush four 12-inch (30-cm) squares of foil with a little of the olive oil and put a fish diagonally across the center of each piece. Bring the sides of the foil up around the fish and crimp it together tightly at each end, leaving the top open.

3 Mix the wine with ¼ cup of water. Pour 2 tablespoons of the wine and water mixture, 2 tablespoons of olive oil, and 2 teaspoons of lemon juice into each parcel. Add the remaining sprigs of thyme and season with a little more salt and pepper. Seal the parcels well and place on a large baking sheet. Bake the fish for 10 minutes.

4 Meanwhile, for the salad, scatter the tomato wedges, red chile, garlic, and olives on four small plates. Drizzle the olive oil over the salad. Season with some salt and pepper and sprinkle with the parsley.

5 To serve, put the unopened parcels of fish on four warmed plates. Take them to the table with a bowl of fries cooked in olive oil and the plates of tomato salad. Let each person open up their own parcel.

RED MULLET

RED MULLET EN PAPILLOTE WITH THYME

broiled red mullet with sauce vierge and toasted fennel seeds

SERVES 4

4 (6-oz/175-g) red mullet, cleaned and trimmed
(see page 14)

A little melted butter, for brushing

Salt and freshly ground black pepper

SAUCE VIERGE:

1/4 cup extra virgin olive oil

1 teaspoon lemon juice

1/4 teaspoon Pernod

1/4 teaspoon dark soy sauce

1 small garlic clove, minced

4 vine-ripened cherry tomatoes, skinned, seeded, and
cut into small dice

Maldon sea salt flakes

Coarsely crushed black pepper

4 small, dried heads of fennel seeds or a small
pinch of ordinary fennel seeds

10 whole tarragon leaves

1 Brush the red mullet on both sides with melted butter and season inside and out with salt and pepper.

2 For the sauce, put the extra virgin olive oil, lemon juice, Pernod, soy sauce, garlic, and tomatoes in a small pan with some Maldon salt to taste and a pinch of pepper. Set aside.

3 Preheat the broiler. If you have some fennel seed heads, put them, seed-side up, on a baking sheet and broil for a few seconds until they are starting to smoke and have darkened slightly in color. Remove and add about 10 seeds to the pan of sauce. Set aside the rest for garnishing. Alternatively, lightly toast the pinch of dried fennel seeds in a hot, dry frying pan for a few seconds until they start to smell aromatic, then add these to the pan of sauce.

4 Brush another baking pan really well with ordinary olive oil and put under the broiler to get hot. Remove, add the red mullet, and broil, 4 inches (10 cm) from the heat, on one side only for about 5 minutes, until cooked through. Just before the fish is cooked, warm through the sauce over a very low heat, then add the whole tarragon leaves.

5 Lift the red mullet onto four warmed plates and garnish with toasted fennel seed heads, if using. Spoon a tablespoon of the sauce alongside the fish and serve with some fries cooked in olive oil.

sautéed red mullet with parsley, garlic, and spaghettini

SERVES 4

4 (5-oz/150-g) red mullet, filleted (see page 22)

1 lb (450 g) dried spaghettini

1/4 cup olive oil

2 garlic cloves, minced

1 medium-hot red chile pepper, seeded and minced

4 plum tomatoes, skinned, seeded, and chopped

1/2 cup (20 g) flat-leaf parsley, minced

Salt and freshly ground black pepper

Extra virgin olive oil, for serving

1 Cut the red mullet fillets across into strips 3/4 inch (2 cm) wide.

2 Bring 15 cups (3.4 liters) of water to a boil in a large pan with 2 tablespoons of salt. Add the spaghettini, bring back to a boil, and cook for 5 minutes or until al dente.

3 Meanwhile, heat the olive oil in a large frying pan. Fry the strips of red mullet, skin-side down, for 3 minutes. Turn them over and fry for 1 minute, then season with some salt and pepper.

4 Drain the pasta well and tip it into a large, warmed serving bowl.

5 Add the garlic and red chile to the frying pan with the red mullet and fry for 30 seconds. Add the tomatoes and fry for another 30 seconds.

6 Tip everything into the bowl with the pasta, scraping up all the little bits that may have stuck to the bottom of the pan. Add 3 tablespoons of the parsley and gently toss everything together so that the fish just begins to break up. Serve immediately, drizzled with extra virgin olive oil and sprinkled with the remaining parsley.

gurnard fillets with a potato, garlic, and saffron broth

SERVES 4

¹/₄ cup extra virgin olive oil

4–6 sprigs of oregano, plus 1¹/₂ teaspoons chopped oregano

1 small head of garlic, broken into cloves

¹/₄ cup dry white wine

1 leek, cleaned and sliced

1¹/₄ lb (550 g) potatoes, peeled and thickly sliced

2¹/₂ cups (600 ml) Fish Stock or Chicken Stock (see page 222)

Pinch of saffron strands

4 (1-lb/450-g) gurnard or sea robins, cleaned and filleted (see pages 14 and 22)

2 tablespoons Rouille (see pages 224–5)

1 teaspoon capers in brine, drained and rinsed

Salt and freshly ground black pepper

GURNARD

1 Heat 2 tablespoons of the oil in a medium saucepan. Add the oregano sprigs and unpeeled garlic cloves and cook for 2 minutes, until the garlic is lightly browned. Remove the pan from the heat and let cool a little, then add the wine. Return to the heat and boil rapidly until it has almost completely evaporated. Add the leek to the pan and cook, stirring, for 1 minute. Add the sliced potatoes with the stock, saffron, and some seasoning, then cover and let simmer for 15 to 20 minutes, until the potatoes are tender.

2 Shortly before the potatoes are ready, heat the rest of the olive oil in a large frying pan. Add the gurnard fillets, skin-side down, and fry for 2 minutes, until lightly browned. Turn over and fry for another minute or until they are cooked through and lightly browned on both sides.

3 Put the rouille into a small bowl and whisk in ¼ cup of slightly cooled cooking liquid from the pan of potatoes. Stir this back into the pan and cook over a gentle heat for about 1 minute; take care not to let it boil or it will curdle. Divide the potatoes and their liquid among four warmed soup plates and place the gurnard fillets on top. Sprinkle with the capers and chopped oregano, and serve.

quenelles of gurnard with shrimp sauce (see technique 36, page 58)

SERVES 4

2 tablespoons (25 g) butter

²/₃ cup (150 ml) milk

1 heaped cup (50 g) fresh white breadcrumbs

12 oz (350 g) gurnard or sea robin fillets, skinned and boned (see page 32)

Pinch of freshly grated nutmeg

2 teaspoons lemon juice

1 egg

¹/₂ cup (120 ml) heavy cream

Salt and freshly ground white pepper

SHRIMP SAUCE:

1 quantity Shellfish Reduction (see page 222), made with shrimp

¹/₃ cup (85 ml) heavy cream

1 teaspoon Beurre Manié (see page 227)

1 egg yolk

1 To make the quenelles, melt the butter and mix with the milk and breadcrumbs to form a coarse paste. Cover and chill for 30 minutes. Make sure all the other ingredients are cold, too.

2 Cut the gurnard fillets into small pieces and put into a food processor with the breadcrumb paste, nutmeg, lemon juice, egg, and seasoning. Blend for at least 1 minute to a very smooth paste.

3 Transfer the mixture to a large bowl sitting in a bowl of ice water. Add the cream a little at a time, beating between each addition, so that the mixture becomes light and thickens. Cover and chill for 30 minutes.

4 For the sauce, heat the shellfish reduction in a small pan. Add half of the cream and the beurre manié and whisk over a medium heat for a few minutes until smooth and thickened. Keep warm.

5 Bring a wide, shallow pan of lightly salted water to a boil, then reduce the heat to a slow simmer. Mold the fish mixture into quenelles (see page 59) and drop them into the simmering water. Poach for 3 to 4 minutes, turning them over halfway through, then remove with a slotted spoon to a clean dish towel and let drain briefly.

6 Divide the quenelles among four individual gratin dishes or one large gratin dish. Preheat the broiler.

7 Whisk together the egg yolk and remaining cream, and stir into the sauce. Stir over a low heat until thickened, but not boiling. Pour the sauce over the quenelles and broil, close to the heat, for about 1 minute until lightly browned. Serve.

pan-fried gurnard with sage and garlic butter (see technique 15, page 32)

SERVES 4

4 (12 oz–1 lb/350–450 g) gurnard or sea robins
4 teaspoons canola oil
6 tablespoons (75 g) unsalted butter
2 garlic cloves, minced
2 tablespoons small sage leaves
2 tablespoons lemon juice
Salt and freshly ground black pepper

1 Skin the whole gurnard as described on page 32, then season them on both sides with some salt and pepper.

2 Heat the oil in a large frying pan. Add the fish and 1 tablespoon (15 g) of the butter to the pan, and fry over a medium-high heat for about 4 minutes on each side until golden brown. Lift into the center of four warmed serving plates and keep warm.

3 Pour away any remaining oil from the pan and wipe it out with a paper towel. Add the rest of the butter to the pan and, as it starts to melt, add the garlic and whole sage leaves. Return the pan to the heat and leave the butter to cook gently for about 30 seconds. Quickly add the lemon juice and some seasoning, then immediately spoon this sauce over the fish, trying to divide the bits of garlic and sage leaves equally among each plate. Serve straight away.

PAN-FRIED GURNARD WITH SAGE AND GARLIC BUTTER

recipes

chapter 9

flatfish

steamed fillet of brill with poached oysters

SERVES 4

1¼ cups (300 ml) Fish Stock (see page 222)
¼ cup (50 g) butter
1 shallot, minced
¼ cup dry white wine
16 oysters
4 (8-oz/225-g) brill fillets (see page 25)
2 tablespoons heavy cream
1 tablespoon chopped chives
Salt and freshly ground black pepper

1 Put the fish stock into a small pan and boil it rapidly until reduced to about ½ cup (120 ml).

2 Melt ½ tablespoon (7 g) of the butter in a medium-sized pan. Cut the rest into small pieces. Add the shallot to the pan and cook gently for 5 minutes, until soft. Add the wine and simmer until reduced to about 2 tablespoons. Add the reduced fish stock and keep warm.

3 Shuck the oysters as described on page 91. Clean four of the deeper shells for serving.

4 Season the fish fillets on both sides with a little salt and lay them on a heatproof plate. Place a rack or an upturned plate in a large pan and pour in about 1 inch (2.5 cm) of water. Bring to a vigorous simmer, then put the plate on the rack, cover the pan, and steam for 4 minutes. Lift the fish out of the steamer and pour the juices from the plate into the sauce. Cover the fish and keep it warm.

5 Bring the sauce to a gentle simmer, add the oysters and their juice, and poach for 2 minutes. Lift them out with a slotted spoon and keep them warm with the brill.

6 Add the cream to the sauce and simmer vigorously for 3 minutes. Then whisk in the remaining butter, a few pieces at a time, to form an emulsified sauce. Stir in the chives and season with black pepper and a little salt, if necessary.

7 To serve, place the fish fillets skin-side down on four warmed plates. Rest an oyster shell alongside the fish on each plate. Put a poached oyster in each shell and arrange the rest over and around the fish. Pour the sauce over the top and serve.

ALTERNATIVE FISH
This is a dish where only a few fish will do—turbot, lemon sole, gray sole, Petrale sole, winter or summer flounder, or john dory.

a casserole of brill with shallots and wild mushrooms

SERVES 4

1/2 oz (15 g) dried porcini mushrooms
7 tablespoons (90 g) unsalted butter
12 small shallots
1/2 teaspoon sugar
8 garlic cloves
3 3/4 cups (900 ml) Chicken Stock (see page 222)
1 thick slice of cooked ham, cut into small dice
1 carrot, chopped
1 leek, cleaned and chopped
1 celery stalk, chopped
1/2 onion, chopped
2 teaspoons balsamic vinegar
2 sprigs of thyme
1/4 cup red wine
4 (6-oz/175-g) unskinned brill fillets
4 oz (100 g) fresh wild mushrooms, cleaned and sliced
Salt and freshly ground black pepper

1 Soak the dried porcini in 2/3 cup (150 ml) warm water for 30 minutes.

2 Melt 2 tablespoons (25 g) of the butter in a shallow pan large enough to take the fillets of brill side by side. Add the shallots, sugar, and garlic, and cook until lightly browned. Barely cover with some of the chicken stock, and add the ham, 1/4 teaspoon salt, and some pepper. Simmer gently until both the shallots and garlic are tender. Then turn up the heat and boil rapidly until the stock has reduced to a thick, sticky glaze, shaking the pan now and then so that the onions and garlic become well coated. Remove them from the pan to a plate and keep warm. Set the pan to one side, unwashed.

3 Melt another 2 tablespoons (25 g) of the butter in a medium-sized saucepan. Add the carrot, leek, celery, and onion, and fry until nicely colored. Add the remaining chicken stock, the balsamic vinegar, 1 thyme sprig, the red wine, and the soaking liquid from the dried mushrooms and simmer for 20 to 30 minutes. Then strain through a fine sieve and discard all the vegetables.

4 Heat 1/2 tablespoon (7 g) of butter in a frying pan. Add the brill fillets, skin-side down, and cook for about 1 minute until lightly browned. Season with salt and pepper, then put side by side in the pan used for glazing the shallots. Pour in the stock, add the second thyme sprig, cover, and simmer for 5 minutes until the brill is cooked.

5 Meanwhile, melt 1 tablespoon (15 g) of the butter in the frying pan, add the soaked porcini and fresh wild mushrooms, and fry briskly for 2 to 3 minutes. Season with a little salt and pepper.

6 Remove the brill from the pan and keep warm. Boil the remaining liquid until reduced and well-flavored, then whisk in the remaining butter. Stir in the mushrooms.

7 Put the brill on four warmed plates. Add the glazed shallots and garlic, spoon the sauce over the top, and serve.

ALTERNATIVE FISH
Unskinned flounder or sole fillets.

PLAICE,
FLOUNDER

broiled scored plaice with roasted red pepper, garlic, and oregano (see technique 7, page 24)

SERVES 4

4 (1–lb/450–g) plaice
1 Roasted Red Pepper (see page 227)
$^1\!/_2$ medium-hot red chile pepper, seeded and minced
$^1\!/_4$ cup extra virgin olive oil
1 large garlic clove, minced
1 teaspoon chopped oregano
2 teaspoons lemon juice
Salt and freshly ground black pepper

1 Trim the fins from the plaice, then cut away the frills as described on page 24. Put the fish dark-side up on a board. Make a deep cut down the center of each fish from head to tail. Then make a series of smaller cuts out from the first one toward the sides so that they look like the veins of a leaf. Turn the fish over and repeat on the other side.

2 Remove the skin and seeds from the roasted red pepper, then mince the flesh. Mix with the chile, oil, garlic, oregano, lemon juice, 1 teaspoon of salt, and some pepper to make the marinade.

3 About 1 hour before cooking, put the fish into a shallow dish and pour the marinade over them, making sure it goes right into the slashes. Set aside.

4 Preheat the broiler. Transfer the fish to baking pans, dark-side up. Depending on the size of your broiler, cook them one or two at a time, 4 to 6 inches (10 to 15 cm) from the heat, for 7 to 8 minutes or until the flesh is firm and white at the thickest part, just behind the head. Spoon the remaining marinade over the fish 4 minutes before the end of cooking. Serve with some fries and a salad of soft green leaves.

ALTERNATIVE FISH

Flounder or sole.

plaice with leeks, mint, and beaujolais

SERVES 4 AS A FIRST COURSE

1 (4–oz/100–g) leek, cleaned
$^1\!/_2$ cup (100 g) butter
1 thick slice Canadian bacon, cut into thin strips
1 teaspoon chopped mint
$^3\!/_4$ cup (175 ml) Beaujolais
$^1\!/_4$ cup port
1$^1\!/_4$ cups (300 ml) Fish Stock (see page 222)
$^1\!/_4$ teaspoon sugar
4 (3–oz/75–g) skinned plaice fillets
Sprigs of mint, for garnish
Salt and freshly ground white pepper

1 Cut the leek in half lengthwise and once more into quarters if it is quite large. Cut across these strips into $^1\!/_2$-inch (1-cm) pieces. Bring a small pan of salted water to a boil, add the leek, and simmer for a few minutes, until tender but still al dente. Drain well.

2 Melt 1 tablespoon (15 g) of the butter in a small pan, add the bacon and leeks, and cook gently until all the excess water has evaporated. Stir in the mint and season with some salt and pepper. Set aside and keep warm.

3 Preheat the broiler. Put the Beaujolais, port, fish stock, and sugar into a large pan and boil rapidly until reduced by three-fourths.

4 Melt another 1 tablespoon (15 g) of the butter and brush over both sides of each plaice fillet. Season with salt and pepper and lay them on the lightly oiled rack of the broiler pan. Broil, 2 to 4 inches (5 to 10 cm) from the heat, for 2 minutes.

5 Dice the remaining butter. Bring the reduced wine and stock back up to a boil, then whisk in the butter, a few small pieces at a time. Adjust the seasoning, if necessary.

6 To serve, spoon the leeks onto four warmed plates. Put the plaice fillets on top and pour the sauce around. Garnish with sprigs of mint.

ALTERNATIVE FISH

Thin flounder or sole fillets.

9

deep-fried flounder with green onion and chile seasoning

SERVES 4

GREEN ONION AND CHILI SEASONING:

Canola oil, for frying

1 small onion, minced

2 garlic cloves, minced

1 medium-hot red chile pepper, thinly sliced

2 green onions, thinly sliced

1 teaspoon Maldon sea salt flakes

$1/2$ teaspoon Sichuan peppercorns, crushed

BATTER:

$1/3$ cup (50 g) all-purpose flour

$1/2$ cup (50 g) cornstarch

Pinch of salt

$3/4$ cup (175 ml) ice-cold soda water from a new bottle

$1 1/2$ lb (750 g) skinned, thick flounder fillets (see page 25)

Canola oil, for deep-frying

Salt

1 small bunch of cilantro sprigs, for garnish

Lime wedges, for serving

1 For the green onion and chile seasoning, pour about ½ inch (1 cm) of canola oil into a frying pan and let it get hot. Add the minced onion and fry for 3 to 4 minutes, until it is beginning to brown. Then add the garlic and cook for 1 minute. Add the chile and fry until the onion and garlic are crisp and golden brown.

2 Lift the mixture out with a slotted spoon onto lots of paper towels and let cool completely. Then transfer to a bowl and mix in the green onions, salt, and Sichuan pepper.

3 For the batter, sift the flour, cornstarch, and salt into a bowl. Stir in the ice-cold soda water until only just mixed; it should be a bit lumpy.

4 Heat some oil for deep-frying to 375°F (190°C). Meanwhile, season the flounder fillets with salt on both sides and cut them into strips about 1 inch (2.5 cm) wide.

5 Dip the strips of flounder into the batter a few at a time, then drop them into the hot oil and fry for 2 minutes, until golden. Drain briefly on paper towels and keep hot while you cook the rest.

6 Pile the fried flounder on a serving platter and sprinkle with the green onion and chile seasoning. Scatter the fresh cilantro sprigs all over and serve straight away, with the lime wedges.

spiced fillets of flounder in warm tortillas with a fresh cilantro and tomato salsa

SERVES 4

MARINADE:

1 teaspoon ground cumin

1 teaspoon hot paprika

2 garlic cloves, crushed

Juice of 1 lemon (about 3 tablespoons)

Maldon sea salt flakes and freshly ground black pepper

FRESH CILANTRO AND TOMATO SALSA:

4 vine-ripened tomatoes, seeded and diced

1 small red onion, minced

2 tablespoons chopped cilantro

2 medium-hot red chile peppers, seeded and minced

1 lb (450 g) skinned flounder fillets (see page 25)

8 flour tortillas

$1/2$ cup (120 ml) Mayonnaise (see page 224)

1 For the marinade, mix together the ground cumin, paprika, garlic, 2 tablespoons of the lemon juice, and some salt and pepper in a shallow dish. Add the flounder fillets and turn them over once or twice, then let them marinate at room temperature for 20 minutes.

2 Mix all the ingredients for the salsa together in a small bowl with the rest of the lemon juice and ½ teaspoon salt. Spoon the mayonnaise into another bowl.

3 Preheat the broiler. Lift the flounder fillets out of the marinade and put them onto a lightly oiled baking pan or the rack of the broiler pan.

4 Broil the flounder fillets, about 4 inches (10 cm) from the heat, for 3 to 4 minutes on one side only. Meanwhile, lightly toast the tortillas, one at a time, in a dry, hot frying pan for about 15 seconds on each side. Wrap in a napkin and keep warm.

5 When the fish is cooked, break it into large flakes and pile it into a warmed serving bowl. Take the broiled fish, salsa, tortillas, and mayonnaise to the table and let everyone fill their own tortillas.

LEMON SOLE,
DOVER SOLE

goujons of lemon sole with parmesan breadcrumbs (see technique 8, page 25)

SERVES 4

1 lb (450 g) skinned lemon sole fillets (see page 25)
2 heaped cups (100 g) fresh white breadcrumbs
$1/4$ cup (25 g) freshly grated Parmesan cheese
$1/2$ teaspoon cayenne pepper
Canola oil, for deep-frying
$1/3$ cup (50 g) all-purpose flour
3 eggs, beaten
Salt
Lemon wedges, for serving

1 Cut each lemon sole fillet diagonally across into strips about the thickness of your little finger. Mix the breadcrumbs with the grated Parmesan and cayenne pepper, and set aside.

2 Heat some oil for deep-frying to 375°F (190°C) and line a baking sheet with plenty of paper towels.

3 Coat the goujons a few at a time in the flour, then in beaten egg, and, finally, in the breadcrumb mixture, making sure that they all take on an even coating and remain separate.

4 Drop a handful of goujons into the oil and deep-fry for about 1 minute, until crisp and golden. Lift out with a slotted spoon onto the paper-lined tray to drain. Repeat with the remainder of the goujons, making sure the oil comes back to temperature between each batch.

5 Pile the goujons on four warmed plates and garnish with the lemon wedges. Serve, if desired, with a mixed whole-leaf or herb salad, dressed with a little extra virgin olive oil and some seasoning.

ALTERNATIVE FISH

Gray or Petrale sole fillets.

deep-fried fillets of lemon sole with salsa verde mayonnaise

SERVES 4

SALSA VERDE MAYONNAISE:

3 heaped tablespoons flat-leaf parsley leaves
1 heaped tablespoon mint leaves
3 tablespoons capers, drained and rinsed
6 anchovy fillets in oil, drained
1 garlic clove
6 tablespoons Mayonnaise (see page 224),
   made with olive oil
1 teaspoon Dijon mustard
1 tablespoon lemon juice
$1/2$ teaspoon salt

Canola oil, for deep-frying
1 loaf of black olive ciabatta bread
12 ($2^{1}/2$-oz/65-g) skinned lemon sole fillets
   (see page 25)
$1/3$ cup (50 g) all-purpose flour
2 extra large eggs, beaten
Salt and freshly ground black pepper
Lemon wedges, for serving

1 For the salsa verde mayonnaise, coarsely chop the parsley, mint, capers, anchovy fillets, and garlic all together, then mix with the mayonnaise, mustard, lemon juice, and salt.

2 Heat some oil for deep-frying to 375°F (190°C). Work the ciabatta in a food processor into fine breadcrumbs. Season the fish fillets with a little salt and pepper, then coat each one with flour, then beaten egg, and then breadcrumbs.

3 Deep-fry the fish, two pieces at a time, for about 2 minutes, until crisp and golden. Drain on paper towels and keep warm while you fry the remaining fish. Serve straight away, with the salsa verde mayonnaise and some lemon wedges.

ALTERNATIVE FISH

Sole, cod, haddock, or Australian flathead fillets.

sole veronique

SERVES 4

8 (3-oz/75-g) skinned Dover sole fillets (see page 25)
A little butter, for greasing
2¹/₂ cups (600 ml) Fish Stock (see page 222)
5 tablespoons dry vermouth, such as Noilly Prat
1¹/₄ cups (300 ml) heavy cream
25–30 seedless green grapes, halved
Lemon juice, salt, and freshly ground white pepper

1 Preheat the oven to 350°F (180°C). Season the sole fillets lightly on both sides. Fold them in half, skinned-side innermost, and lay side by side in a buttered shallow baking dish. Pour in the fish stock, cover with foil, and bake for 20 minutes.

2 Remove the fish from the dish and put on a warmed serving plate. Cover once again with the foil and keep warm. Pour the cooking liquid into a saucepan, add the vermouth, and bring to a boil. Boil vigorously until reduced to about 6 tablespoons. Add the cream and a squeeze of lemon juice, and simmer until it has thickened to a good saucelike consistency.

3 Add the grapes to the sauce and warm through gently. Season the sauce to taste, then pour it over the fish and serve immediately.

dover sole à la
meunière (see technique 3, page 18)

SERVES 2

3 tablespoons all-purpose flour
2 (14 oz–1 lb/400–450 g) Dover sole, trimmed and
   skinned (see page 18)
2 tablespoons canola oil
¹/₄ cup (50 g) unsalted butter
2 teaspoons lemon juice
1 tablespoon chopped flat-leaf parsley
Salt and freshly ground white pepper
1 lemon, cut into 6 wedges, for serving

1 Season the flour with ½ teaspoon of salt and 10 turns of the pepper mill. Coat the Dover sole on both sides with the flour, then gently pat off the excess.

DOVER SOLE À LA MEUNIÈRE

2 Heat half of the oil in a large, well-seasoned or nonstick frying pan. Add one of the sole, lower the heat slightly, and add ½ tablespoon (7 g) of the butter. Fry over a moderate heat for 4 to 5 minutes, without moving the fish, until it is richly golden.

3 Carefully turn the fish over and cook for 4 to 5 minutes, until golden brown and cooked through. Lift onto a serving plate and keep warm. Repeat with the second fish. Prepare the fish for serving as described on page 19, if desired.

4 Discard the frying oil and wipe the pan clean. Add the remaining butter and let it melt over a moderate heat. When the butter starts to smell nutty and turn light brown, add the lemon juice, parsley, and some seasoning. Pour some of this beurre noisette over each fish and serve straight away.

TURBOT,

HALIBUT

roasted tronçons of turbot with a sauce vierge (see technique 9, page 26)

SERVES 4

⅓ cup (85 ml) extra virgin olive oil,
  plus extra for brushing
1 teaspoon chopped rosemary
1 teaspoon chopped thyme
1 bay leaf, minced
½ teaspoon crushed fennel seeds
1 teaspoon coarsely crushed black peppercorns
Maldon sea salt flakes
4 (6–8 oz/175–225 g) tronçons of turbot (see page 26)

SAUCE VIERGE:

⅓ cup (85 ml) extra virgin olive oil
2 tablespoons lemon juice
1 plum tomato, seeded and cut into small dice
8 black olives, pitted and cut into fine strips
2 small anchovy fillets in oil, drained and diced
1 garlic clove, minced
1 heaped teaspoon coarsely chopped flat-leaf parsley
Salt and coarsely ground black pepper

1 Preheat the oven to 450°F (230°C). Mix together the olive oil, chopped herbs, fennel seeds, crushed peppercorns, and 1 teaspoon of sea salt in a small roasting pan. Add the pieces of turbot and turn them over in the mixture so that they are well coated.

2 For the sauce, put everything except the chopped parsley and seasoning into a small pan, ready to warm through just before serving.

3 Heat a heavy-based frying pan that can be transferred to the oven over a high heat until smoking-hot. Add the tronçons of turbot, dark-side down, to the pan and sear for about 1 minute until the skin has taken on a good color. Turn them over and transfer the pan to the oven. Roast for 8 to 10 minutes. Just as the fish is ready, place the sauce over a very low heat to warm through.

4 To serve, lift the pieces of fish onto the center of four warmed plates. Stir the parsley and seasoning into the sauce, then spoon it around the fish. Brush the top of each piece of fish with a little more oil and sprinkle with a few sea salt flakes.

ALTERNATIVE FISH

Thick fillets of brill, john dory, or sea bass, or fillets of flaky fish such as cod, haddock, or hake.

myrtle's turbot (see technique 23, page 42)

SERVES 4

1 (3-lb/1.5-kg) turbot
1 small bunch of thyme
1 small bunch of flat-leaf parsley
1 small bunch of chives
6 tablespoons (75 g) butter
Salt and freshly ground black pepper

1 Preheat the oven to 400°F (200°C). With a sharp knife, cut through the skin on the top (dark) side only, all the way around the fish close to the frill-like fins. Season on top with some salt and pepper.

2 Pour 2½ cups (600 ml) water into a roasting pan large enough to hold the turbot. Put the fish in the pan and bake for 30 minutes. Meanwhile, mince half the herbs. Gently melt the butter in a small pan, stir in the minced herbs, and set aside.

3 Remove the fish from the oven and carefully peel away the top skin. Transfer it to a warmed serving dish. Reduce the remaining cooking juices to a few tablespoons and add to the pan of herb butter.

4 Pour the sauce over the white flesh of the turbot. Shape the rest of the herbs into a bouquet and lay them near the head as a garnish. Serve, as described on page 43, with plenty of boiled new potatoes.

ROASTED TRONÇONS OF TURBOT WITH A SAUCE VIERGE

9

braised fillet of turbot with slivers of potato, mushrooms, and truffle oil

SERVES 4

2¹/₂ cups (600 ml) Chicken Stock (see page 222)

6 oz (175 g) waxy boiling potatoes

¹/₂ cup (100 g) unsalted butter

1 thin slice of cooked ham, weighing about 1 oz (25 g), cut into very fine dice

2 tablespoons minced shallots

¹/₃ cup (85 ml) dry vermouth, such as Noilly Prat

1¹/₂ cups (100 g) thinly sliced button mushrooms

2 teaspoons lemon juice

1 tablespoon truffle oil

1 (1¹/₂-lb/750-g) piece of unskinned turbot fillet, cut into 8 pieces

1 tablespoon chopped flat-leaf parsley

Salt and freshly ground black pepper

1 Put the chicken stock into a wide-based pan and boil rapidly until reduced by half.

2 Peel the potatoes and slice as thinly as you can, then cut them across into thin matchsticks.

3 Melt half the butter in a frying pan that is large enough to hold all the pieces of fish in one layer. Add the potatoes, ham, and shallots, and cook gently for 4 to 5 minutes.

4 Add the vermouth and chicken stock, and simmer for about 8 minutes, until the potatoes are almost, but not quite, cooked. You can prepare the dish to this stage some time in advance, if desired.

5 Stir the mushrooms, lemon juice, truffle oil, and some salt and pepper into the potatoes, then rest the pieces of turbot on top, skin-side up. Cover and simmer for about 6 minutes, or until the fish is cooked through.

6 Lift the fish onto a plate and keep warm. Add the remaining butter to the pan and boil rapidly for 10 minutes or until the sauce has thickened and the potatoes are just beginning to break up.

7 To serve, peel the skin off the turbot and divide the pieces among four warmed plates. Stir the parsley into the sauce and spoon it on top of the fish.

HALIBUT POACHED IN OLIVE OIL WITH CUCUMBER AND DILL

halibut poached in olive oil with cucumber and dill (see technique 22, page 41)

SERVES 4

2¹/₂ cups (600 ml) inexpensive olive oil

4 (6-oz/175-g) pieces of thick halibut fillet, skinned

1 tablespoon extra virgin olive oil

1 large hothouse cucumber, peeled and thinly sliced

1 tablespoon chopped dill, plus a few sprigs for garnish

2 teaspoons white wine vinegar

Sea salt

1 Pour a thin layer of the olive oil into a pan just large enough to hold the pieces of halibut side by side. Season the fish on both sides with a little salt, put them in the pan, and pour the rest of the oil over them—it should just cover the fish. Very slowly heat the oil to 130–140°F (55–60°C), agitating it with a spatula now and then so that it heats evenly. If you don't have a thermometer, you can test with your little finger: the oil should just feel unpleasantly hot.

2 Take the pan off the heat and leave it somewhere warm on top of the stove for 15 minutes so the fish can poach gently in the oil. The temperature should remain at 130–140°F (55–60°C); if necessary, keep taking the pan on and off a low heat to maintain this temperature.

3 Shortly before the fish is ready, heat the extra virgin olive oil in a large frying pan. Add the cucumber slices and toss over a medium heat for 1 minute. Add the dill, vinegar, and a little salt.

4 To serve, divide the cucumber among four serving plates. Carefully lift the fish out of the oil, letting the excess drain off, and set it on top of the cucumber. Pour the oil into a cup, leaving behind the juices from the fish, which will have settled to the bottom of the pan. Spoon these juices around the edge of each plate, sprinkle the fish with a few sea salt flakes, and garnish with a sprig of fresh dill.

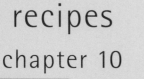

recipes
chapter 10

crustaceans

steamed crab with lemongrass dressing (see technique 56, page 84)

SERVES 4

8–12 Asian swimming crabs or 2 (2-lb/900-g) blue crabs, live or cooked

LEMONGRASS DRESSING:

1 lemongrass stalk, outer leaves removed and the core minced
Finely grated zest and juice of 1 lime
2 tablespoons Thai fish sauce (*nam pla*)
$^2/_3$ cup (150 ml) water
1 medium-hot green chile pepper, seeded and minced
$^1/_2$ teaspoon sugar
1 tablespoon roughly chopped cilantro

1 Prepare the crabs as described on pages 80 and 84. Mix all the ingredients for the lemongrass dressing together and set aside.

2 Bring about 1 inch (2.5 cm) of water to a boil in a wide, shallow pan. Either put some sort of rack in the bottom on which you can rest a plate —a couple of pastry cutters or another upturned plate will do—or use a petal steamer. Pour in some water so that it doesn't quite cover the rack and bring to a boil.

3 Pile the pieces of crab on the petal steamer or a heatproof plate and lower it into the pan. Cover and steam for 8 minutes, by which time the crab should be cooked. If you are using cooked crabs, just give them 3 to 4 minutes to heat through.

4 Arrange the pieces of crab on a large, warmed serving plate. Spoon on the lemongrass dressing and serve straight away.

ALTERNATIVE FISH

Lobster, steamed and served with this dressing, is a bit of a work of art. If you throw all the dressing ingredients in a large pot of mussels and steam them open, you'll be amazed too.

singapore chile crab

SERVES 4

2 (2-lb/900-g) live or cooked crabs

¼ cup peanut or canola oil

4 fat garlic cloves, minced

1-inch (2.5-cm) piece fresh ginger, peeled and minced

¼ cup ketchup

3 medium-hot red chile peppers, minced

2 tablespoons dark soy sauce

⅔ cup (150 ml) water

A few turns of the black pepper mill

2 green onions, cut into 2-inch (5-cm) pieces and finely shredded lengthwise

1 If using live crabs, kill them as described on page 80 and prepare them for stir-frying (see page 84).

2 Heat the oil in a large wok. Add the crab pieces and stir-fry for 3 minutes, adding the garlic and the ginger after 1 minute.

3 Add the juices from the back shell, the ketchup, red chiles, soy sauce, water, and black pepper. Cover and simmer over a medium heat for 5 minutes if the crab is fresh, or 2 to 3 minutes if using cooked crab.

4 Spoon the crab onto a large plate or into four soup plates, sprinkle with the shredded green onions, and serve straight away.

ALTERNATIVE FISH

Large raw shrimp or uncooked lobster.

crab and gruyère tartlets

SERVES 4

1 quantity Short Pastry (see page 227)

1 egg white

1½ cups (225 g) fresh white crabmeat

2 oz (50 g) fresh brown crabmeat, if available

2 egg yolks

⅓ cup (85 ml) heavy cream

Pinch of cayenne pepper

½ cup (50 g) finely grated Gruyère cheese

Salt and freshly ground black pepper

1 Preheat the oven to 425°F (220°C). Briefly knead the pastry on a lightly floured surface until smooth. Roll out and use to line four shallow, 4½-inch (11-cm) tartlet pans with removable bottoms. Chill for 20 minutes.

2 Line the pastry shells with crumpled parchment paper, cover the bottom with a generous layer of baking beans, and bake "blind" for 15 minutes. Remove the paper and beans and brush the inside of each pastry shell with a little unbeaten egg white. Return to the oven to bake for 2 minutes. Remove from the oven and lower the temperature to 400°F (200°C).

3 Mix the crabmeat with the egg yolks, cream, cayenne, and some salt and pepper. Spoon the mixture into the tartlet shells and sprinkle with the grated Gruyère cheese. Bake at the top of the oven for 15 to 20 minutes, until lightly golden. Serve warm.

SINGAPORE CHILE CRAB

185

ravioli of fresh crab with warm parsley and lemon butter

SERVES 4

1 heaped cup (175 g) fresh white crabmeat
1 tablespoon melted butter
Pinch of cayenne pepper
Salt and freshly ground black pepper
1 quantity Fresh Egg Pasta (see page 227)
PARSLEY AND LEMON BUTTER:
½ cup (100 g) butter
2 tablespoons chopped flat-leaf parsley
½ teaspoon finely grated lemon zest
2 teaspoons lemon juice
2 garlic cloves, minced

1 For the filling, mix the crabmeat with the melted butter, cayenne pepper, and a little salt to taste.

2 Cut the pasta dough in half and set one piece aside, wrapped in plastic wrap so that it doesn't dry out. Roll out the other piece on a floured work surface into a 15-inch (38-cm) square, making sure it doesn't stick.

3 With your fingertips, make small marks at 3-inch (7.5-cm) intervals in three evenly spaced rows (i.e. three rows of five indentations) over one half of the square.

4 Place 1 teaspoon of the crab mixture on each mark, then brush lines of water between the piles of mixture.

5 Fold over the other half of the square so that the edges meet. Working from the center of the folded edge, moving outward and toward you, press firmly around each pile of mixture with your fingers to remove any trapped air and seal in the filling.

6 Trim off the edges of the dough and cut between the rows with a sharp knife. Lift the ravioli onto a lightly floured tray. Repeat with the second piece of pasta dough to make 30 ravioli in all.

7 Bring 15 cups (3.5 liters) of water to a boil in a large pan with 2 tablespoons of salt. Drop the ravioli into the pan of boiling water and cook for 4 minutes.

8 For the parsley and lemon butter, gently melt the butter with the parsley, lemon zest, lemon juice, and garlic. Season to taste with a little salt and pepper.

9 Drain the ravioli well and divide them among four warmed pasta plates. Spoon the warm parsley and lemon butter over, and serve.

NOTE

If you want to make the ravioli in advance, drop them into the pan of boiling water and cook for just 30 seconds. Drain well, then place in a single layer on a plastic tray and cover with plastic wrap. Keep chilled. Before serving, cook for 3½ minutes, then finish as above.

betsy apple's crab salad with basil, parsley, and chives in a lemon vinaigrette

SERVES 4

1 lb (450 g) fresh white crabmeat (about 3 cups)
2 tablespoons finely shredded basil
2 tablespoons each minced flat-leaf parsley and chives
A few whole chives, with blossoms attached if possible
LEMON VINAIGRETTE:
1½ tablespoons lemon juice
1 teaspoon Dijon mustard
4–5 tablespoons extra virgin olive oil
Salt and freshly ground black pepper

BETSY APPLE'S CRAB SALAD WITH BASIL, PARSLEY, AND CHIVES IN A LEMON VINAIGRETTE

1 Pick over the crabmeat for any tiny pieces of shell, then put it into a serving bowl.

2 For the vinaigrette, mix together the lemon juice and mustard, then gradually whisk in the oil, ½ teaspoon of salt, and plenty of freshly ground black pepper.

3 Just before serving, stir the vinaigrette into the crab, along with the chopped herbs. Check the salad for seasoning and garnish with a few whole chives. Serve with crusty French bread and chilled white wine.

maryland crab cakes with a tarragon and butter sauce (see technique 54, page 82)

SERVES 4

1 lb (450 g) fresh white crabmeat (about 3 cups)

½ cup (40 g) finely crushed Saltine crackers

1 egg, beaten

2 tablespoons Mayonnaise (see pages 224), made with sunflower oil

1 tablespoon English mustard powder

1 tablespoon lemon juice

Dash of Worcestershire sauce

2 tablespoons chopped flat-leaf parsley

¼ cup Clarified Butter (see page 226)

Salt and freshly ground white pepper

TARRAGON AND BUTTER SAUCE:

¼ cup white wine vinegar

¼ cup Clarified Butter (see page 226)

1 plum tomato, skinned, seeded, and diced

1 teaspoon chopped tarragon

1 Put the crabmeat into a bowl and add just enough of the cracker crumbs to absorb any moisture from the crab. (You may not need to add them all.)

2 Break the egg into a small bowl and whisk in the mayonnaise, mustard, lemon juice, Worcestershire sauce, and some seasoning. Fold this mixture into the crabmeat, taking care not to break up the lumps of crab too much. Stir in the parsley. Shape the mixture into eight 3-inch (7.5-cm) patties. Put them on a plate, cover with plastic wrap, and chill for at least 1 hour.

MARYLAND CRAB CAKES WITH A
TARRAGON AND BUTTER SAUCE

3 Heat the clarified butter in a large frying pan. Add the crab cakes (in two batches, if necessary) and cook over a medium heat for 2 to 3 minutes on each side, until crisp and richly golden. Keep the first batch warm if you need to, while you cook the second batch.

4 Meanwhile, for the sauce, boil the vinegar in a small pan until reduced to about 2 tablespoons. Add the clarified butter, diced tomato, chopped tarragon, and some salt and pepper to taste, and gently warm through. Serve with the crab cakes.

sautéed soft-shell crabs with garlic butter (see technique 55, page 83)

SERVES 4

SHRIMP BOIL SEASONING:

2 tablespoons yellow mustard seeds

1 tablespoon black peppercorns

1 tablespoon dried red pepper flakes

3 dried bay leaves

1/2 tablespoon celery seeds

1/2 tablespoon coriander seeds

1/2 tablespoon ground ginger

2 pieces of blade mace

1/4 cup salt

8–12 soft-shell crabs

2/3 cup (100 g) all-purpose flour

1 tablespoon shrimp boil seasoning (see the recipe below) or "Old Bay" seasoning mix

3 tablespoons Clarified Butter (see page 226)

1/2 cup (100 g) butter, at room temperature

3 garlic cloves, crushed

1 tablespoon lemon juice

2 tablespoons chopped flat-leaf parsley

Salt and freshly ground black pepper

CRAB

1 To make the shrimp boil seasoning, put everything except the salt into a spice grinder and grind to a fine powder. Add the salt and blend for 2 to 3 seconds.

2 Prepare the crabs as described on page 83. Sift the flour, shrimp boil seasoning, 1 teaspoon of salt, and some pepper onto a plate. Dredge the crabs well in the flour, then pat off the excess.

3 Heat the clarified butter in a large frying pan. Fry the crabs in batches over a moderate heat for 2 minutes on each side, until lightly browned. Shake off any excess butter as you transfer them from the pan to warmed plates. Keep warm while you fry the rest.

4 Add the rest of the butter and the crushed garlic to the pan, and let it sizzle for a few seconds. Add the lemon juice, then throw in the parsley and some seasoning. Spoon the garlic butter over the crabs and serve immediately.

BAKED CRABS IN SHELL WITH BERKSWELL CHEESE

baked crabs in shell with berkswell cheese

SERVES 4

4 "dressed" small crabs (see page 80)

2 tablespoons (25 g) butter

Juice of 1/2 lemon

1 teaspoon prepared English mustard

4 gratings of fresh nutmeg

Large pinch of cayenne pepper

Lemon wedges for serving

TOPPING:

1/3 cup (15 g) fresh white breadcrumbs

1 tablespoon melted butter

1/4 cup (25 g) finely grated Berkswell or Parmesan cheese

1 Preheat the oven to 400°F (200°C). Remove all the crabmeat from the shells and put it in a large bowl. Melt the butter, then mix in the lemon juice, mustard, nutmeg, and cayenne. Gently fold this mixture through the crabmeat, taking care not to break up the large chunks.

2 Spoon the crab mixture back into the crab shells and lightly level the tops.

3 For the topping, mix the breadcrumbs with the melted butter, then stir in the grated cheese. Sprinkle the mixture evenly over the crab.

4 Place the crabs on a baking sheet and bake for 10 to 12 minutes, until they are golden brown and the filling is heated through. Serve hot, with the lemon wedges.

spider crab with pasta, parsley, and chile

SERVES 4

1 lb (450 g) dried linguine or spaghetti
3 medium vine-ripened tomatoes, skinned, seeded, and chopped
2 cups (275 g) fresh white spider crabmeat
1 tablespoon chopped flat-leaf parsley
1½ tablespoons lemon juice
¼ cup extra virgin olive oil
Pinch of dried red pepper flakes
1 garlic clove, minced

1 Cook the pasta in a large pan of boiling well-salted water (i.e. 1 teaspoon salt to each 2½ cups/600 ml water) for 8 minutes or until al dente.

2 Meanwhile, put the tomatoes, crabmeat, parsley, lemon juice, olive oil, red pepper flakes, and garlic into another pan and warm over a gentle heat.

3 Drain the pasta, return to the pan with the sauce, and briefly toss together. Divide among four warmed plates and serve immediately.

ALTERNATIVE FISH
Other white crabmeat.

warm salad of salicornia, asparagus, and crab

SERVES 4 AS A FIRST COURSE

1 (2½–3 lb/1.25–1.35 kg) cooked crab (see page 80)
12 oz (350 g) thin asparagus
8 oz (225 g) salicornia, picked over and washed
¼ garlic clove, minced
2 tablespoons extra virgin olive oil, plus extra for serving
2 teaspoons lemon juice
1 tablespoon chopped flat-leaf parsley
Salt and freshly ground black pepper
Maldon sea salt flakes
A few Parmesan shavings, for garnish

1 Remove the meat from the crab (see page 80).

2 Snap off the woody ends from the asparagus where they break naturally and discard them. Cut the asparagus spears in half. Break off and discard the woody ends of the salicornia and break the rest into 1-inch (2.5-cm) pieces.

3 Bring a pan of water to a boil. Add the salicornia and asparagus, and cook for 1 minute. Drain and refresh under cold water to stop them cooking and help set the color. Drain well once more, then tip into a bowl. Add the garlic, olive oil, and lemon juice, toss together lightly, and season to taste, if necessary.

4 Divide the asparagus and salicornia among four plates and arrange the crabmeat over the top. Sprinkle with the chopped parsley, drizzle on a little more olive oil, and season with a few sea salt flakes. Scatter on some Parmesan shavings and serve.

shangurro
(basque-style stuffed crab)

SERVES 4

2 large cooked crabs, or 1¹/₄ lb (550 g) fresh crabmeat
(about 3¹/₂ cups), including 4 oz (100 g) brown
crabmeat, if available

3 tablespoons olive oil

2 onions, minced

9 small garlic cloves, minced

8 oz (225 g) plum tomatoes, skinned, seeded, and
chopped

¹/₄ cup dry white wine

1 teaspoon sugar

¹/₄ teaspoon dried red pepper flakes

3 tablespoons chopped flat-leaf parsley

1 heaped cup (50 g) fresh white breadcrumbs

1 tablespoon (15 g) butter, melted

Salt and freshly ground black pepper

1 Preheat the oven to 400°F (200°C). If using cooked crabs, remove
the meat from the shell (see page 80). Wash out the back shells, then
break away the edge along the visible natural line to give a flat, open
shell. Set aside.

2 Heat the oil in a heavy-based frying pan, then add the onions and all
except 1 minced garlic clove. Fry over a gentle heat for 2 minutes, until
softened.

3 Increase the heat and add the tomatoes, wine, sugar, red pepper
flakes, and some salt and pepper. Simmer for about 4 minutes, until the
mixture has reduced to a thick sauce.

4 Stir in 2 tablespoons of the parsley and the flaked crabmeat, and
spoon the mixture into the crab shells, or into individual gratin dishes. If
using crab shells, rest them in a shallow baking dish.

5 Mix the breadcrumbs with the melted butter and the rest of the
parsley and garlic. Sprinkle this mixture over the crab and bake for
10 minutes, or until the topping is crisp and golden.

broiled langoustines with a
pernod and olive oil dressing

(see technique 49, page 74)

SERVES 4

16 large or 24 smaller cooked langoustines
(see page 74)

2 small shallots, minced

¹/₂ tablespoon roughly chopped tarragon

¹/₂ tablespoon roughly chopped flat-leaf parsley

1 teaspoon Dijon mustard

1 teaspoon dark soy sauce

¹/₃ cup (85 ml) extra virgin olive oil

1¹/₂ tablespoons lemon juice

1 teaspoon Pernod

¹/₄ cup (50 g) butter, melted

Salt and freshly ground black pepper

1 Preheat the broiler. Cut the langoustines open lengthwise and scoop
out the creamy contents of the heads and any red roe using a teaspoon.
Put this into a small bowl and stir in the shallots, tarragon, parsley,
mustard, soy sauce, oil, lemon juice, Pernod, and a little salt and pepper
to taste.

2 Place the halved langoustines cut-side up on a baking pan or the
rack of the broiler pan and brush with the melted butter. Season lightly
and broil, about 4 inches (10 cm) from the heat, for 1 to 2 minutes, until
the shells as well as the meat are heated through.

3 Put the langoustines on four serving plates and spoon a little of the
dressing over them. Divide the rest of the dressing among four dipping
saucers or small ramekins and serve alongside.

ALTERNATIVE FISH

Two 1-lb (450-g) cooked lobsters, halved.

10

goan lobster with cucumber and lime salad

SERVES 4

CUCUMBER AND LIME SALAD:

1 hothouse cucumber

2 limes

Salt

2 (1½–2 lb/750–900 g) cooked lobsters

2 tablespoons peanut oil

1 onion, chopped

3 garlic cloves, crushed

1-inch (2.5-cm) piece fresh ginger, finely grated

2 hot green chile peppers, seeded and chopped

**3 tablespoons Goan Masala Paste (see page 226) or
a good-quality bought curry paste**

1 For the salad, peel the cucumber and cut it into thick slices. Overlap the cucumber slices on a plate and sprinkle with the juice of one of the limes and some salt. Slice the other lime into wedges to serve with the lobster.

2 Preheat the oven to 300°F (150°C). Remove the meat from the cooked lobsters as described on page 76. Place the shells on a baking sheet and warm them through in the oven.

3 Heat the oil in a large, deep frying pan. Add the onion, garlic, ginger, and chiles, and fry for about 5 minutes, until soft. Add the masala paste and fry for 2 to 3 minutes. Fold in the lobster meat and cook gently until it is heated through.

4 Spoon the mixture back into the lobster shells and serve with the cucumber and lime salad, the lime wedges, and, if desired, some warm naan bread.

ALTERNATIVE FISH

Any spiny or rock lobster is ideal for this dish, such as the native lobsters of the west coasts of the United States, Australia, New Zealand, South Africa, and, for that matter, India.

GOAN LOBSTER WITH CUCUMBER AND LIME SALAD

lobster tourte

SERVES 6

1 (4-lb/1.75-kg) cooked lobster

MOUSSELINE:

6 oz (175 g) skinned whiting or pollock fillets

1 egg

1 small shallot, minced

1/2 cup (120 ml) heavy cream

1 lb (450 g) puff pastry, thawed if frozen

1 egg, beaten

Salt and freshly ground black pepper

SAUCE:

5 tablespoons Shellfish Reduction (see page 222),
    made with the lobster shell

2/3 cup (150 ml) heavy cream

6 tablespoons (75 g) chilled unsalted butter, cut into
    small pieces

2 teaspoons lemon juice

1 Remove the meat from the lobster (see page 76). Make the shellfish reduction with the shell as described on page 222. Let cool.

2 For the mousseline, cut the fish fillets into small pieces and put them into a food processor with 3 tablespoons of the shellfish reduction, the egg, shallot, and 3/4 teaspoon of salt. Process until smooth, then, with the motor still running, add the cream in a steady stream. Take care not to process for more than 10 seconds or the mixture may curdle. Scrape into a bowl, cover, and chill for 1 hour.

3 Preheat the oven to 425°F (220°C). Cut the pastry in half and roll out one piece into a 10-inch (25-cm) disk. Roll out the second piece into an 11-inch (28-cm) disk.

4 Put the smaller disk of pastry on a lightly greased baking sheet and spread half the mousseline over it to within 1 1/2 inches (4 cm) of the edge. Arrange the lobster meat over the mousseline and season with salt and pepper, then carefully spread the remaining mousseline over the top.

5 Brush the edge of the pastry with a little water, cover with the larger disk of pastry, and press the edges together to seal. Crimp the edges decoratively, then brush the top with the beaten egg. Using the tip of a small, sharp knife, score either a diamond pattern over the top, or mark with curves radiating from the center. Make a hole in the center, then bake for 25 minutes.

6 Shortly before the tourte is ready, make the sauce: Put the rest of the shellfish reduction and the cream into a pan, bring to a boil, and simmer for 5 minutes. Whisk in the butter, a piece at a time, followed by the lemon juice.

7 Take the tourte out of the oven and pour about 2 tablespoons of the sauce into it through the hole in the top. Return it to the oven for 5 minutes. Then remove once more and transfer to a warmed serving plate. Serve the rest of the sauce separately.

VARIATION

Replace the lobster meat with 20 cooked and shucked mussels, 6 prepared bay scallops, sliced in half horizontally, and 2/3 cup (100 g) fresh white crabmeat.

ALTERNATIVE FISH

Spiny or rock lobster.

broiled lobster with fines herbes (see technique 52, page 79)

SERVES 4

2 (1 1/2–1 3/4 lb/750–800 g) live lobsters

1 tablespoon (15 g) butter, melted

3/4 cup (175 ml) Fish Stock (see page 222)

1/2 teaspoon Thai fish sauce (nam pla)

2 teaspoons lemon juice

1/4 cup (50 g) unsalted butter, cut into small pieces

1 teaspoon each chopped flat-leaf parsley, chervil,
    chives, and tarragon

Salt and freshly ground black pepper

1 Preheat the broiler. Prepare the lobster for broiling as described on page 79.

2 Put the lobster halves onto a baking pan or the rack of the broiler pan. Brush the meat with melted butter and season with a little salt and pepper. Broil, about 6 inches (15 cm) from the heat, for 8 to 10 minutes until cooked through.

3 Just before the lobster is ready, bring the fish stock, fish sauce, and lemon juice to a boil in a small pan and boil for 1 minute. Whisk in the butter, a piece at a time, to build up an emulsified sauce. Stir in the chopped herbs and adjust the seasoning, if necessary.

4 Lift the lobster halves onto four warmed plates and spoon the sauce over them.

lobster with ginger, green onions, and soft egg noodles (see technique 51, page 78)

SERVES 2–3

1 (1½-lb/750-g) live lobster or spiny or rock lobster

Canola oil, for deep-frying, plus 1 tablespoon

1 teaspoon salt

½ teaspoon sugar

1 tablespoon dark soy sauce

1 tablespoon oyster sauce

Pinch of freshly ground white pepper

1 teaspoon toasted sesame oil

2 tablespoons Chinese rice wine or dry sherry

2 tablespoons cornstarch

2 garlic cloves, crushed

1 (4½-oz/120-g) piece fresh ginger, peeled and thinly sliced on a mandoline

¾ cup (90 g) green onions cut into 1-inch (2.5-cm) pieces

1 cup (250 ml) Chicken Stock (see page 222)

6 oz (175 g) fresh, fine Chinese egg noodles

1 Prepare the lobster for stir-frying as described on page 78.

2 Heat some oil for deep-frying to 375°F (190°C). Mix the salt, sugar, dark soy sauce, oyster sauce, white pepper, sesame oil, and Chinese rice wine or sherry together in a small bowl. Set aside. Bring a large pan of water to a boil for the noodles.

3 Sprinkle the lobster pieces with 1½ tablespoons of the cornstarch, then deep-fry, in batches if necessary, for 2 minutes. The larger claw might take longer—about 3 minutes. Lift out and drain on paper towels.

4 Heat the tablespoon of canola oil in a wok. Add the garlic, ginger, and green onions and stir-fry for a few seconds. Add the lobster to the wok along with the soy sauce mixture and stir-fry for 1 minute. Add the chicken stock, then cover and cook over a medium heat for 2 minutes.

5 Meanwhile, drop the noodles into the pan of boiling water, cover, and remove from the heat. Let soak for 2 minutes, loosening them now and then with some chopsticks or a fork.

6 Mix the rest of the cornstarch with 2 tablespoons of cold water, add to the wok, and stir for 1 minute, until the sauce thickens.

7 Drain the noodles and put them on a large, oval serving plate. Spoon the lobster mixture on top and serve straight away.

LOBSTER WITH GINGER, GREEN ONIONS, AND SOFT EGG NOODLES

193

LOBSTER

open ravioli of lobster with tomato and basil sauce

SERVES 4 AS A FIRST COURSE

TOMATO AND BASIL SAUCE:

2 vine-ripened tomatoes, skinned, seeded, and diced

6 basil leaves, finely sliced

$^{1}/_{4}$ cup extra virgin olive oil

Salt and freshly ground black pepper

CREAM SAUCE:

$^{2}/_{3}$ cup (150 ml) Fish Stock (see page 222)

2 tablespoons heavy cream

2 tablespoons white wine

$^{1}/_{4}$ cup Mayonnaise (see pages 224), made with olive oil

$^{1}/_{2}$ quantity of Fresh Egg Pasta (see page 227)

6 oz (175 g) cooked lobster meat, thinly sliced (see page 77)

Sprigs of basil, for garnish

1 For the tomato and basil sauce, put all the ingredients into a small pan and place over a very low heat to warm through.

2 For the cream sauce, bring the fish stock, cream, and white wine to a boil and boil until reduced by half to about 5 tablespoons. Put the mayonnaise into a bowl and gradually whisk in the reduced fish stock. Season to taste with salt. Keep warm, but take care not to get it too hot or it will curdle.

3 Bring a large pan of well-salted water to a boil. Roll out the pasta dough on a lightly floured surface into a 6- by 12-inch (15- by 30-cm) rectangle. Cut into eight 3-inch (7.5-cm) squares.

4 Put the slices of lobster meat onto a plate and warm through in a steamer for 2 to 3 minutes. Meanwhile, drop the pasta squares into the boiling water and cook for 3 to 4 minutes or until al dente, then drain and lay out on a sheet of plastic wrap.

5 To serve, put a square of pasta in the center of each of four warmed plates. Spoon a little of the cream sauce on each one. Divide the lobster meat among them, then spoon on half the tomato and basil sauce. Cover with the remaining pasta squares and pour the remaining cream sauce over and around each ravioli. Spoon on the rest of the tomato and basil sauce and serve immediately, garnished with sprigs of basil.

lobster thermidor (see technique 50, page 76)

SERVES 2

1 (1$^{1}/_{2}$-lb/750-g) cooked lobster

2 tablespoons (25 g) butter

2 large shallots, minced

2$^{1}/_{2}$ cups (600 ml) Fish Stock (see page 222)

$^{1}/_{4}$ cup Noilly Prat

5 tablespoons heavy cream

$^{1}/_{2}$ teaspoon prepared English mustard

1 teaspoon chopped fines herbes (chervil, tarragon, flat-leaf parsley, and chives)

1 teaspoon lemon juice

2 tablespoons freshly grated Parmesan cheese

Salt and freshly ground black pepper

1 Remove the meat and any roe from the lobster as described on page 76. Scoop out the head matter and set it aside for the sauce. Cut the meat into small chunky pieces and return it to the cleaned half-shells along with any roe. Cover and set aside.

2 For the sauce, melt the butter in a small pan. Add the shallots and cook gently for 3 to 4 minutes until soft but not browned. Add the fish stock, Noilly Prat, and half the cream, and boil until reduced by three-fourths to about $^{3}/_{4}$ cup (175 ml). Add the rest of the cream and simmer until reduced to a good coating-sauce consistency. Whisk in the reserved lobster head matter, the mustard, fines herbes, and lemon juice. Season to taste with salt and pepper.

3 Preheat the broiler. Carefully spoon the sauce over the lobster meat and sprinkle lightly with Parmesan cheese. Broil, close to the heat, for 2 to 3 minutes, until lightly golden and bubbling.

10

spiny lobster salad with a tomato, tarragon, and chervil dressing

SERVES 4

1 (4–5 lb/1.75–2.3 kg) spiny or rock lobster

DRESSING:

1¼ cups (300 ml) Fish Stock (see page 222)

¼ cup olive oil

1 tablespoon Clarified Butter (see page 226)

1 plum tomato, skinned, seeded, and diced

1 small garlic clove, minced

1 teaspoon each chopped tarragon and chervil

¼ small, medium-hot red chile pepper, seeded and minced

1 tablespoon white wine vinegar

Small pinch of saffron strands

½ teaspoon minced anchovy fillets

2 tablespoons Lemon Olive Oil (see page 227)

½ teaspoon white wine vinegar

Salt and freshly ground black pepper

2 oz (50 g) prepared salad leaves, such as curly endive, watercress, escarole, and Belgian endive

1 Cook the spiny lobster as described on page 76. Meanwhile, for the dressing, put the fish stock into a pan and boil rapidly until it has reduced to about 2 tablespoons. Remove from the heat.

2 Remove the spiny lobster from the water and leave it until it is cool enough to handle. Then remove the meat from the tail as described on page 77. Cut it across into slices, put onto a plate, and keep warm while you remove the rest of the meat from the claws and legs (see page 76).

3 Add all the other dressing ingredients to the pan containing the reduced fish stock and let warm through over a low heat—but don't let it come anywhere near boiling.

4 Whisk together the lemon olive oil, vinegar, salt, and pepper to make a light salad dressing. Toss with the salad leaves and divide among four plates. Arrange the lobster meat to the side of the leaves, spoon the warm dressing over the lobster, and serve immediately.

potted squat lobsters with ginger and basil

SERVES 4 AS A FIRST COURSE

60 cooked squat lobsters, about 4½ lb (2 kg), or 6–8 oz (175–225 g) cooked squat lobster meat

½ cup (100 g) unsalted butter

½ teaspoon finely grated fresh ginger

½ teaspoon salt

½ teaspoon finely grated lemon zest

1 tablespoon finely shredded basil

1 If using whole squat lobsters, remove the meat from the shells as you would for raw shrimp (see page 72); take care because the shells are quite sharp.

2 Melt the butter in a pan and add the ginger, salt, and lemon zest, followed by the squat lobster meat. Stir together over a low heat for 2 to 3 minutes, until the lobster meat is heated through.

3 Take the pan off the heat and stir in the basil. Divide the lobster meat among four 2½-inch (6-cm) ramekins; try to arrange it neatly in the ramekins so that they will look attractive when you unmold them. Pour any remaining butter into the ramekins, then leave them somewhere cool to set for at least 2 hours—if you can avoid doing this in the refrigerator, they will have a softer, smoother texture.

4 To serve, dip the ramekins briefly into hot water and unmold them onto four plates. Accompany with plenty of hot brown toast.

NOTE

An alternative way to serve this is to divide 2 oz (50 g) mixed baby salad leaves among the plates. Spoon the warmed lobster mixture onto the leaves, sprinkle with a little extra salt, and serve.

ALTERNATIVE FISH

Cooked peeled shrimp, diced cooked lobster meat.

moreton bay bug and fennel risotto with lemon oil

SERVES 4

10 raw Moreton Bay bug tails or 2 (1-lb/450-g) raw lobsters

5–5¹/₂ cups (1.2–1.25 liters) Chicken Stock (see page 222)

1 teaspoon fennel seeds

2 tablespoons olive oil

¹/₂ fennel bulb, thinly sliced

¹/₄ teaspoon dried red pepper flakes

2 shallots, minced

1 garlic clove, crushed

1¹/₂ cups (350 g) risotto rice, such as arborio

¹/₂ cup (50 g) freshly grated Parmesan cheese

1 tablespoon (15 g) butter

1 tablespoon lemon juice

2 tablespoons chopped herb fennel (or the frondy tops from the fennel bulb)

Salt and freshly ground black pepper

FOR GARNISH:

Sprigs of herb fennel

Parmesan shavings

Lemon Olive Oil (see page 227)

1 If you are using Moreton Bay bugs, break open the shell along the underside of each one and lift out the meat. Cut the bug meats across into slices ³/₄ inch (2 cm) thick. If you are using lobsters, kill them (see page 76), then drop them into a large pan of rapidly boiling water. Bring back to a boil and simmer for 5 minutes. They will still be partly raw, but this will make it easier for you to get the meat out of the shell. Lift out of the pan and, when cool enough to handle, crack open the shells and remove the meat as described on page 76. Cut the meat into chunks.

2 Bring the chicken stock to a boil in a pan and leave over a low heat. Heat a dry, heavy-bottomed frying pan over a high heat, add the fennel seeds, and toss them around for a few seconds until they start to darken slightly and smell nicely aromatic. Tip into a mortar or spice grinder and grind to a fine powder.

3 Heat the olive oil in a pan, add the fennel, ground fennel seeds, red pepper flakes, shallots, and garlic and cook until the shallots are soft and translucent, about 7 minutes. Season with a little salt and pepper. Add the rice and stir until it is well coated with the oil. Increase the heat, add a ladleful of the hot chicken stock, and bring to a boil. Reduce the heat to very low and let simmer, adding another ladleful of stock as each one is absorbed and stirring frequently, until the rice is almost cooked, approximately 20 to 25 minutes.

4 Add the sliced bug meats or lobster meat and stir. Let simmer for 2 to 3 minutes or until just cooked through.

5 Fold in the Parmesan, butter, lemon juice, and some seasoning to taste. Stir in the herb fennel. The risotto should not be not too wet—if it is, increase the heat and cook to evaporate the excess liquid.

6 Spoon the risotto into warmed bowls. Garnish each with fennel sprigs, Parmesan shavings, black pepper, and a drizzle of lemon oil.

ALTERNATIVE FISH

Moreton Bay bugs (also called shovel-nosed lobster and locust lobster) are from the same family as lobster, spiny or rock lobster, and crayfish, and all would be suitable for this dish. Peeled, raw large shrimp would also work very well, but leave them whole—don't cut them up. You'll need to use about 12 to 16. You could also use cooked lobster meat, folded in at the end of cooking just to heat through.

pad thai noodles with shrimp

SERVES 2

6 oz (175 g) Asian flat rice noodles

¹/₄ cup peanut oil

2 garlic cloves, minced

¹/₂ teaspoon dried red pepper flakes

10 peeled, raw large shrimp (see page 72)

2 eggs, beaten

2–3 tablespoons Thai fish sauce (*nam pla*)

2–3 tablespoons Tamarind Water (see page 227)

1 tablespoon palm sugar or light, raw brown sugar

1 tablespoon dried shrimp, coarsely chopped

¹/₄ cup roasted peanuts, coarsely chopped

4 green onions, cut into 2-inch (5-cm) pieces and finely shredded lengthwise

¹/₂ cup (50 g) fresh beansprouts

2 tablespoons roughly chopped cilantro

1 Soak the noodles in cold water for 1 hour, then drain and set to one side.

2 Heat the oil in a wok over a high heat. Add the garlic, pepper flakes, and shrimp. Stir-fry for 2 to 3 minutes, until the shrimp are just cooked.

3 Pour in the beaten eggs and stir-fry for a few seconds, until they just start to look scrambled. Lower the heat, then add the noodles, fish sauce, tamarind water, and sugar. Toss together for 1 to 2 minutes until the noodles are tender.

4 Add the dried shrimp, half the peanuts, half the green onions, half the beansprouts, and all the cilantro and toss for another minute. Serve sprinkled with the rest of the peanuts, green onions, and beansprouts.

ALTERNATIVE FISH
Thinly sliced squid, sliced bay scallops, or mussels.

shrimp caldine (see technique 48, page 72)

SERVES 4

1¼ lb (550 g) raw medium shrimp, in shell but headless
2 tablespoons coconut vinegar or white wine vinegar
1 teaspoon turmeric powder
1 teaspoon black peppercorns
1 tablespoon coriander seeds
1 teaspoon cumin seeds
2 tablespoons white poppy seeds or ground almonds
¼ cup peanut oil
1 onion, thinly sliced
3 garlic cloves, cut into slivers
1-inch (2.5-cm) piece fresh ginger, minced
1¾ cups (400 ml) coconut milk
¼ cup Tamarind Water (see page 227)
⅔ cup (150 ml) water
5 mild green chile peppers, halved, seeded, and cut
    into long, thin shreds
2 tablespoons chopped cilantro
Salt

1 Peel the shrimp, leaving the last tail segment in place (see page 72). Mix the shrimp with the vinegar and ½ teaspoon of salt. Set aside for 5 minutes.

2 Meanwhile, put the turmeric powder, black peppercorns, coriander seeds, cumin seeds, and white poppy seeds into a spice grinder and grind to a fine powder.

SHRIMP CALDINE

3 Heat the oil in a medium-sized pan. Add the onion, garlic, and ginger and fry gently for 5 minutes. Stir in the ground spices and fry for 2 minutes. Add the ground almonds if you aren't using poppy seeds, along with the coconut milk, tamarind water, water, three-fourths of the sliced chiles, and ½ teaspoon of salt. Bring to a simmer and cook for 5 minutes.

4 Add the shrimp and simmer for just 3 to 4 minutes so they don't overcook. Stir in the rest of the sliced chiles and the cilantro, and serve with some steamed rice.

ALTERNATIVE FISH
Any type of raw shrimp, or goujons of fish such as brill, flounder, or john dory.

crustaceans

shrimp in marie rose sauce with avocado and romaine salad

SERVES 4

MARIE ROSE SAUCE:

**1 quantity Mayonnaise (see page 224), made with
  1 cup (225 ml) sunflower oil**
5 tablespoons ketchup
1/4 cup thick, plain yogurt
Salt and freshly ground white pepper

12 oz (350 g) peeled, large cooked shrimp
ROMAINE SALAD:
1 romaine heart
2 ripe, but firm avocados

1 For the Marie Rose sauce, put the mayonnaise into a bowl and stir in the ketchup and yogurt. Season to taste with a little white pepper.

2 Dry the shrimp on paper towels, then stir them into the sauce. Spoon this into a serving bowl and set to one side.

3 For the salad, cut the lettuce across into strips 1 inch (2.5 cm) wide. Toss with a little salt and pepper, then divide among four serving plates.

4 Cut each avocado in half and remove the pit. Peel off the skin, then cut the halves across into semi-circular slices. Arrange these among the strips of lettuce.

5 To serve, take the plates of salad and the bowl of shrimp to the table separately and let everyone help themselves to the shrimp.

ALTERNATIVE FISH
This salad would also taste great made with cooked and peeled small or medium shrimp.

gremolata shrimp

SERVES 4

1 large lemon
2 tablespoons olive oil
20 raw large shrimp in shell
Cayenne pepper (optional)
3 garlic cloves, minced
1/4 cup chopped flat-leaf parsley
Coarse sea salt and freshly ground black pepper

1 Peel the zest off the lemon with a potato peeler. Pile the pieces up a few at a time and cut them across into short, thin strips.

2 Heat the oil in a large frying pan. Add the shrimp and toss them over a high heat for 4 to 5 minutes, seasoning them with some cayenne pepper or black pepper and sea salt as you do so.

3 Cut the lemon in half and squeeze the juice from one half over the shrimp. Continue to cook until the juice has almost evaporated—the

10

shrimp should be quite dry. Take the pan off the heat and let the shrimp cool for about 1 minute.

4 Sprinkle with the lemon zest, chopped garlic, parsley and ¼ teaspoon of salt and toss together well. Pile the shrimp into a large serving dish and serve with some finger bowls and plenty of napkins.

ALTERNATIVE FISH
Any raw shrimp in the shell—jumbo or tiger shrimp, if desired.

shrimp po' boys

MAKES 6

2 French baguettes
Canola oil, for deep-frying
12 oz (350 g) peeled, raw large shrimp (see page 72)
¾ cup (175 ml) Mayonnaise (see page 224), made with
    sunflower oil, plus extra Mayonnaise for serving
2½ tablespoons milk
3 tablespoons all-purpose flour
4 cups (175 g) fresh white breadcrumbs
1 small head of crisp green lettuce
Salt and cayenne pepper

1 Preheat the broiler. Cut each baguette into three, then cut each piece in half lengthwise. Pull out a little of the soft white crumb to make a very shallow hollow in each half. Lay them on a baking sheet, cut-side up, and toast very lightly under the broiler. Remove and set aside.

2 Heat some oil for deep-frying to 375°F (190°C). Season the shrimp well with salt and cayenne pepper. Whisk the mayonnaise and milk together in a bowl, put the flour into a second bowl, and spread the breadcrumbs over a large plate.

3 Dip the shrimp into the flour, then mayonnaise, and then breadcrumbs so that they take on an even coating. Treat them gently once they are done because the coating is quite delicate. Pick them up by the tip of their tails, drop them into the hot oil, about six at a time, and fry for 1 minute, until crisp and golden. Transfer to a baking sheet lined with paper towels and keep warm in a low oven while you cook the rest.

4 To serve, spread the bottom half of each piece of bread with a little mayonnaise, then put some lettuce leaves on top. Pile on a few of the fried shrimp, cover with the tops, and eat straight away.

ALTERNATIVE FISH
Oysters, small goujons of flatfish such as lemon or gray sole and flounder, or soft-shell clams.

SHRIMP PO' BOYS

tandoori shrimp (see technique 47, page 70)

SERVES 4

LEMON-CHILE MARINADE:

1 teaspoon cayenne pepper

1 teaspoon salt

Juice of 1 lemon

32 raw large shrimp in shell

TANDOORI MASALA PASTE:

1½ tablespoons fennel seeds

1 tablespoon coriander seeds

1 tablespoon cumin seeds

1 oz (25 g) fresh ginger, roughly chopped

6 garlic cloves, chopped

4 medium-hot red chile peppers, seeded and roughly chopped

2 teaspoons paprika

1 teaspoon turmeric powder

Juice of 1 lemon

1–2 tablespoons cold water

¾ cup (175 g) thick, plain yogurt

KATCHUMBER SALAD:

3 tomatoes, halved and thinly sliced

1 medium red onion, halved and thinly sliced

2 tablespoons roughly chopped cilantro

¼ teaspoon ground cumin

Large pinch of cayenne pepper

1 tablespoon white wine vinegar

½ teaspoon salt

1 If you are grilling the shrimp, prepare and light the charcoal fire now. Mix together the ingredients for the lemon-chile marinade. Make three small slits in either side of each shrimp, between the shell segments, to allow the marinade to penetrate (see page 70). Put the shrimp and marinade into a bowl, toss together well, and set aside for 20 minutes.

2 For the tandoori masala paste, put the fennel seeds, coriander seeds, and cumin seeds together in a spice grinder or mortar and grind to a fine powder. Tip the spices into a food processor, add the rest of the masala paste ingredients, and blend until smooth. Stir the paste into the yogurt, then stir this into the shrimp. Leave for another 20 minutes.

3 If you are broiling the shrimp, preheat the broiler. Thread the shrimp onto metal or soaked bamboo skewers, piercing them just behind the head and through the tail (see page 71). Cook them on the grill or under the broiler, about 4 inches (10 cm) from heat, for about 2 minutes on each side.

4 While the shrimp are cooking, layer the ingredients for the salad in a shallow dish. Serve the shrimp with the salad and some warm naan bread.

TANDOORI SHRIMP

deep-fried shrimp wontons with chile jam

SERVES 4

20 raw large shrimp, in shell but headless

20 Chinese wonton wrappers

Canola oil, for deep-frying

CHILE JAM:

¼ cup canola oil

2 tablespoons minced garlic

4 teaspoons minced fresh ginger

1 cup (225 g) minced onions

5 medium-hot red chile peppers, seeded and minced

½ cup (120 ml) red wine vinegar

2 tablespoons dark soy sauce

½ teaspoon ground star anise

1½ tablespoons palm sugar or light, raw brown sugar

Salt

1 Peel the shrimp, leaving the last tail segment in place (see page 72), and reserve the shells.

2 For the chile jam, heat the canola oil in a medium-sized pan. Add the shrimp shells and fry over a high heat for 1 to 2 minutes, until they are quite crisp. Tip into a strainer resting over a small pan and press well to remove all the oil that will now be pleasantly flavored with shrimp.

3 Reheat the oil, then add the garlic and ginger and fry quickly until they are lightly browned. Add the onions and chiles and fry for 3 to 4 minutes. Stir in the vinegar, soy sauce, star anise, sugar, and some salt to taste. Bring to a boil and simmer gently for 20 to 30 minutes, until the onions are very soft and the jam is well reduced and thick. Let cool, then spoon into four small dipping bowls or small ramekins.

4 Wrap each shrimp in one of the wonton wrappers, leaving the tail end uncovered, and seal with a little water.

5 Heat some oil for deep-frying to 375°F (190°C). Fry the shrimp, in batches, for 1 to 1½ minutes, until crisp and golden. Lift out and drain briefly on paper towels. Serve hot with the chile jam.

shrimp jambalaya

SERVES 6

¼ cup canola oil

4 oz (100 g) smoked chorizo or spicy sausage, sliced

2 teaspoons paprika

8 garlic cloves, chopped

1 onion, chopped

2 green bell peppers, seeded and chopped

4 celery stalks, sliced

2 medium-hot red chile peppers, seeded and minced

1 lb (450 g) skinned boneless chicken, cut into
    1-inch (2.5-cm) pieces

1 lb (450 g) peeled, raw medium shrimp (see page 72)

2 bay leaves

Leaves from 1 sprig of thyme

1 teaspoon chopped oregano

2⅔ cups (450 g) long-grain rice

5 cups (1.2 liters) Chicken Stock (see page 222)

3 green onions, trimmed and thinly sliced

Salt and cayenne pepper

1 Heat the oil in a large, deep frying pan. Add the sliced sausage and fry until lightly browned. Add the paprika and stir to color the oil.

2 Add the garlic and cook for 30 seconds, then add the onion, green bell peppers, celery, and red chiles. Cook over a medium heat until lightly browned.

3 Add the chicken, shrimp, bay leaves, thyme, and oregano, and fry over a medium heat for 5 minutes.

4 Add the rice and stir for 2 minutes. Add the chicken stock and 1 teaspoon of salt and bring to a boil, then cover and simmer for about 15 minutes, until the rice has absorbed all the liquid and is tender.

5 Stir in the green onions and some cayenne pepper to taste. Serve with a green salad.

potted shrimp

SERVES 6

1/2 cup (100 g) butter

2 pieces of blade mace

Large pinch of cayenne pepper

Freshly grated nutmeg

2 1/2 cups (600 ml) peeled, cooked, tiny cocktail or bay
  shrimp

6 tablespoons Clarified Butter (see page 226)

1 Put the butter, mace, cayenne pepper, and a little grated nutmeg
into a pan and let melt very slowly over a gentle heat, so that the butter
becomes infused by the spices.

2 Add the peeled shrimp and stir for a couple of minutes until they
have heated through, but don't let the mixture boil.

3 Remove the mace, then divide the shrimp and butter among six small
ramekins. Level the tops. Cover and leave them to set in the refrigerator.

4 Spoon a thin layer of clarified butter over the surface, then let set
once more. Serve with plenty of brown toast or crusty brown bread.

cream of shrimp soup

SERVES 4

1/2 cup (100 g) butter

1 carrot, finely diced

1 onion, minced

1 1/2 lb (750 g) raw or cooked small shrimp in shell

3 3/4 cups (900 ml) Fish Stock (see page 222)

1 bay leaf

2/3 cup (150 ml) dry white wine

3 tablespoons all-purpose flour

1 1/4 cups (300 ml) milk

2/3 cup (150 ml) heavy cream

Pinch of cayenne pepper

Salt and freshly ground black pepper

1 Melt 2 tablespoons (25 g) of the butter in a medium-sized pan. Add
the carrot and onion and cook over a medium heat for 3 to 4 minutes.
If you are using raw shrimp, add them to the pan and turn them
over for 5 minutes, until they are just cooked and have all turned pink.

2 Remove one-third of the shrimp from the pan and, when they are
cool enough to handle, peel them. Return the shells to the pan. If you
are using cooked shrimp, just peel one-third of them and put the shells
and the rest of the shrimp into the pan. Add the fish stock, bay leaf, and
white wine, bring to a boil, and simmer for 20 minutes.

3 Blend the soup, in batches if necessary, for a few seconds until
coarsely blended but not completely smooth. Pour into a conical sieve
set over a clean pan and press out all the liquid with the back of a ladle
(see page 86).

4 Melt 3 tablespoons (40 g) of the remaining butter in another pan,
stir in the flour, and cook for 30 seconds. Gradually stir in the milk and
then the strained soup. Simmer over a low heat for 15 minutes, stirring
occasionally. Whisk in the rest of the butter, along with the cream and
cayenne pepper. Season with a little more black pepper and some salt.

5 Pour the soup into a warmed tureen and serve with a bowl of the
peeled shrimp. Place a few of the shrimp into each bowl before ladling
in the soup.

10

shrimp and salicornia risotto

SERVES 4

1½ lb (750 g) cooked medium or small shrimp in shell,
    preferably cold-water pink shrimp
4 oz (100 g) salicornia, picked over and washed
6 tablespoons (75 g) unsalted butter
½ onion, chopped
5 cups (1.2 liters) Fish Stock (see page 222)
1 piece of blade mace
2 shallots, minced
1 garlic clove, minced
1½ cups (350 g) risotto rice
½ cup (120 ml) dry white wine
¼ cup (25 g) freshly grated Parmesan cheese
Salt and freshly ground black pepper

1 Peel the shrimp and set them aside, reserving the shells. Break off and discard the woody ends of the salicornia and break the rest into 1-inch (2.5-cm) pieces.

2 Melt 2 tablespoons (25 g) of the butter in a large saucepan, add the onion, and fry for 5 minutes, until soft and lightly browned. Add the shrimp shells and fry for 3 to 4 minutes, then add the stock and mace and bring to a boil. Cover and simmer for 20 minutes. Strain the stock through a conical sieve into a clean pan, pressing out as much liquid as you can with the back of a ladle. Bring back to a simmer, then keep hot over a low heat.

3 Melt the rest of the butter in a large saucepan. Add the shallots and garlic, and cook gently for 2 minutes. Add the rice and turn it over until all the grains are coated with the butter. Pour in the wine and simmer, stirring constantly, until it has been absorbed. Then add a ladleful of the hot stock and stir until it has all been taken up before adding another. Continue like this for about 20 minutes, stirring constantly, until all the stock has been added and the rice is tender but still a little al dente.

4 Shortly before the risotto is ready, drop the salicornia into a pan of boiling water and cook for 1 minute, then drain well. Stir the shrimp, Parmesan, and some seasoning into the risotto. Heat for 1 minute, then stir in all but a handful of the salicornia. Divide the risotto among four warmed bowls and serve, garnished with the rest of the salicornia.

SHRIMP AND SALICORNIA RISOTTO

recipes
chapter 11

mollusks and other seafood

new england clam chowder (see technique 60, page 89)

SERVES 4

16 large hard-shell clams (chowder clams), washed and steamed open (see page 89)
1 tablespoon (15 g) butter
2 thick slices (50 g) unsmoked bacon, pancetta, or salt pork, cut into small dice
1 small onion, minced
1¼ cups (300 ml) milk
½ cup (100 ml) heavy cream
1⅔ cups (225 g) peeled potatoes cut into small dice
1 bay leaf, very finely shredded
1 tablespoon chopped flat-leaf parsley
Salt and freshly ground white pepper

1 Remove the clams from their shells and cut into small pieces. Reserve all the liquid.

2 Melt the butter in the pan, add the bacon, and fry over a medium heat until golden. Add the onion and cook gently until softened.

3 Add the milk, cream, potatoes, bay leaf, and reserved clam liquid. Bring to a boil, then simmer for 5 minutes or until the potatoes are tender.

4 Return the clams to the pan along with the chopped parsley and season to taste with some salt and pepper. Reheat gently and serve.

clams with sauce mignonette (see technique 61, page 89)

SERVES 4

2½ cups (600 ml) littlenecks or other small hard-shell clams, washed
A little bladderrack or other edible seaweed, for serving

SAUCE MIGNONETTE:

3 tablespoons good-quality white or red wine vinegar
1 teaspoon sunflower oil
¼ teaspoon coarsely crushed black peppercorns
1 tablespoon thinly sliced green onion tops

1 Prepare the clams as described on page 89.

2 Mix together the ingredients for the sauce just before serving. Arrange the clams on a plate with a little seaweed, spoon a little of the sauce into each one, and serve.

linguine alle vongole (clams with linguine, garlic, parsley, and white wine)

SERVES 4

12 oz (350 g) dried linguine

¼ cup extra virgin olive oil

4 garlic cloves, thinly sliced

½ medium-hot red chile pepper, seeded and minced

3 tablespoons chopped flat-leaf parsley

2 lb (900 g) littlenecks or other small hard-shell clams, washed

2 tablespoons dry white wine

1 Cook the linguine pasta in a large pan of well-salted boiling water (i.e. 1 teaspoon salt to every 2½ cups/600 ml water) for just 5 minutes.

2 Meanwhile, put the olive oil, garlic, and chile into a small pan and heat until the garlic begins to sizzle. Lower the heat and cook gently for 1 to 2 minutes until the garlic is soft. Add the parsley and remove from the heat.

3 Drain the pasta. Return the empty pan to a high heat and add the clams, the white wine, and the par-cooked linguine. Cover and cook over a high heat, shaking the pan now and then, for 3 to 4 minutes until all the clams have opened.

4 Uncover the pan and add the olive oil mixture. Simmer for a further 2 minutes or until the linguine is tender, then serve.

RAZOR CLAMS A LA PLANCHA

razor clams a la plancha

SERVES 4

Good olive oil

24 razor clams, washed

Lemon wedges, for serving (optional)

1 Heat your largest heavy-based frying pan or a flat griddle over a high heat until very hot. Add a little olive oil and then the clams, hinge-side down, arranging them in a single layer (you may have to cook the clams in batches).

2 As soon as they have opened up, turn the clams over so that their meat comes into contact with the pan. Cook for about 1 minute, until lightly browned.

3 Turn the clams back over again and drizzle with a little more olive oil. Transfer them to a warmed serving plate. Serve with a lemon wedge or two, if desired, and any juices from the pan. Repeat the process with any remaining clams.

ALTERNATIVE FISH

Medium or large hard-shell clams.

stir-fried clams with garlic and ginger

SERVES 4

12 large hard-shelled clams, or 36 small hard-shell
   clams, washed
3 tablespoons canola oil
3 garlic cloves, minced
2-inch (5-cm) piece of peeled fresh ginger,
   very finely shredded
4 oz (100 g) shiitake mushrooms, sliced
1 head bok choy, sliced into 1-inch (2.5-cm) strips
Large pinch of dried red pepper flakes
1 tablespoon dark soy sauce
1 tablespoon oyster sauce
Freshly ground Sichuan pepper or black pepper
4–6 green onions, sliced on the diagonal

1 If using large clams, arrange them in a single layer in a large, shallow pan with a little water. Cover and cook over a high heat for 2 to 3 minutes, until only just opened—this is so that you can remove the clams from the shells, but not cook them completely (see page 89).

2 Slide a small knife into each shell and cut through the two muscles that hold the shells together. Break off the top shells, then remove the clams from the bottom shells and slice them thinly (see page 89).

3 If using small clams, put them into a pan with ¼ cup water. Cover and cook over a high heat for 2 to 3 minutes until just opened. Drain in a colander. When cool enough to handle, remove the clams from the shells; leave them whole.

4 Heat a wok over a high heat. Add the oil, followed by the garlic and ginger, and stir-fry for 30 seconds. Add the clams and stir-fry for 30 seconds to 1 minute, then add the mushrooms and stir-fry for 30 seconds. Add the bok choy and pepper flakes and stir-fry for 30 seconds, then add the soy sauce, oyster sauce, Sichuan or black pepper, and, finally, the green onions. Toss together briefly and serve.

steamed clams with toasted almonds, garlic, and parsley

SERVES 4

½ cup (100 g) unsalted butter
2 fat garlic cloves, minced
6 lb (2.75 kg) littleneck or other small hard-shell clams,
   washed
¼ cup dry white wine
Juice of ½ lemon
2 tablespoons finely chopped, lightly toasted almonds
3–4 tablespoons chopped flat-leaf parsley

1 Melt the butter in a very large saucepan. Add the garlic and cook very gently for 3 to 4 minutes. Add the clams, white wine, lemon juice, and chopped almonds. Cover and cook over a high heat, giving the pan a good shake every now and then, until all the clams have opened. Add half the chopped parsley and stir well.

2 Using a large slotted spoon, divide the clams among four large, warmed bowls, discarding any that have remained closed. Spoon the cooking juices over the clams, leaving behind the last tablespoon or so because it might be a bit gritty. Sprinkle with the remaining parsley and serve with plenty of crusty sourdough bread.

11

salad of abalone with noodles, shiitake mushrooms, ginger, and truffle oil

SERVES 4

4 (2-oz/50-g) prepared abalone
1/2 cup (120 ml) olive oil
2-inch (5-cm) piece of cinnamon stick
2 star anise
1 oz (25 g) dried rice stick noodles
4 oz (100 g) mixed enoki and shiitake mushrooms
4 thin slices of peeled fresh ginger, cut into fine julienne
2 green onions, halved and very finely shredded
2 teaspoons dark soy sauce
4 teaspoons truffle oil

1 Preheat the oven to 225°F (110°C). Put the abalone into a small casserole with the olive oil, cinnamon, and star anise. Cover and bake for 4 to 5 hours, until tender.

2 Remove the casserole from the oven. Lift the fish out of the oil and let cool. Then cut it into the thinnest possible slices and set to one side.

3 Drop the noodles into a pan of boiling water, then remove from the heat and let soak for 2 minutes. Drain and refresh under cold water. Drain well again.

4 Slice the enoki mushrooms away from their matted base and break into separate stems, leaving them as long as possible. Trim the stems of the shiitake mushrooms and cut the caps into thin slices.

5 Build up the salad in layers on four plates, using the noodles, mushrooms, ginger, green onions, and sliced abalone, shaping each salad into a small mound about the size of a cricket ball. Drizzle with the soy sauce and truffle oil, and serve.

ALTERNATIVE FISH
Instead of abalone, you can use a 4-oz (100-g) piece of cleaned cuttlefish. Bake for only 1 hour.

cockle and spinach vol-au-vents with hollandaise sauce

MAKES 12

12 oz (350 g) puff pastry, thawed if frozen
1 egg, beaten, for glazing
1/2 cup (100 g) Clarified Butter (see page 226)
2 lb (900 g) cockles, washed
1 egg yolk
1 teaspoon lemon juice
1 tablespoon water
4 teaspoons finely chopped cooked spinach
  (see page 244)
Salt

1 Preheat the oven to 400°F (200°C). Roll out the pastry on a lightly floured surface until it is 1/4 inch (5 mm) thick. Cut out twelve 2 1/2-inch (6.5-cm) disks using a plain pastry cutter. Press a 2-inch (5-cm) plain cutter into the center of each one, only halfway down into the pastry. Take care not to cut all the way through.

2 Put the cut-out pastries on a lightly buttered baking sheet and brush the tops with a little beaten egg. Bake for about 10 to 12 minutes, until crisp and richly golden, then remove from the oven. While they are still warm, carefully remove the centers with a teaspoon, making sure you scoop out all the partly cooked pastry from inside. Cover and keep warm in a low oven.

3 Pour the clarified butter into a small pan and leave it over a low heat. Put the cockles into a large pan with 1/2 cup (120 ml) of water. Cover and cook over a high heat for 4 to 5 minutes, shaking the pan well every now and then, until all the cockles have opened. Tip them into a colander to drain. When they are cool enough to handle, remove them from their shells. Transfer to a bowl and keep warm.

4 Put the egg yolk, lemon juice, and water into a blender. Heat the clarified butter until it begins to bubble. Turn on the blender and slowly pour in the butter through the hole in the lid, to make a smooth, creamy hollandaise sauce.

5 Scrape the sauce into a bowl and stir in the spinach and a little salt to taste. Fold in the cooked cockles, leaving behind any liquid that might have collected at the bottom of the bowl. Spoon the mixture into the warm vol-au-vent pastries and serve immediately.

cockle cream with bacon, tomatoes, and potatoes

SERVES 4

5 pints (2.4 liters) cockles, washed
3³/₄ cups (900 ml) water
2 tablespoons (25 g) butter
2 thick slices (50 g) Canadian bacon, cut into small dice
1 leek, thinly sliced
1 celery stalk, thinly chopped
2 plum tomatoes, skinned and thinly sliced
2 potatoes (about 12 oz/350 g), peeled and diced
Juice of 1 small lemon
2 eggs
2 tablespoons chopped flat-leaf parsley
Salt and freshly ground black pepper

1 Put the cockles into a large pan with ²/₃ cup (150 ml) of the water. Cover and cook over a high heat for 4 to 5 minutes, occasionally shaking the pan, until they have all opened. Tip them into a colander set over a bowl to collect the liquid and let them cool a little.

2 Melt the butter in a large pan, add the bacon, and cook until it is just beginning to brown. Add the leek, celery, and tomatoes and cook until the mixture begins to "flop." Meanwhile, remove the cockles from their shells.

3 Pour all but the last 1 to 2 tablespoons of the cockle liquid into the pan and add the rest of the water and the potatoes. Let the soup simmer until the potatoes are soft, about 10 minutes.

4 Add the cockles to the soup and season to taste with some salt and pepper. Whisk the lemon juice with the eggs in a bowl. Pour on a ladleful of the hot soup and whisk together, then stir this liaison into the soup in the pan. Stir it over a low heat until thickened slightly, but don't let it boil. Stir in the parsley and serve.

mussels with romesco sauce

MAKES APPROXIMATELY 60
ROMESCO SAUCE:

1 dried choricero or other large, mild chile pepper
8 oz (225 g) vine-ripened tomatoes
4 garlic cloves, peeled
2 tablespoons blanched hazelnuts
1 thin slice (15 g) day-old white bread, crusts removed
¹/₂ cup (120 ml) olive oil
Pinch of dried red pepper flakes
1 tablespoon sherry vinegar
2 tablespoons chopped oregano
Salt and freshly ground black pepper

2 lb (900 g) mussels, cleaned (see page 88)
¹/₄ cup dry white wine

1 For the romesco sauce, pull out the stem of the dried chile pepper. Cover the pepper with warm water and let it soak overnight. The next day, drain it, slit it open, and remove the seeds. Chop the flesh roughly.

2 Preheat the oven to 400°F (200°C). Put the tomatoes and 3 garlic cloves into a small roasting pan and roast for 10 minutes. Sprinkle with the hazelnuts and roast for 15 minutes more, until they are golden. Remove the pan from the oven and let cool.

3 Rub the slice of bread with the remaining garlic clove. Heat a little of the olive oil in a frying pan, add the bread, and fry until richly golden on both sides. Let cool, then break it into pieces and put it into a blender with the contents of the roasting pan, the soaked chile pepper, red pepper flakes, sherry vinegar, ¹/₂ teaspoon of salt, and some freshly ground black pepper. Blend until smooth. Then, with the motor still running, very gradually add the rest of the olive oil to make a thick, mayonnaiselike sauce. Scrape into a bowl and set aside.

4 Put the mussels into a large pan with the wine. Cover and cook over a high heat, shaking the pan now and then, for 3 to 4 minutes until they have opened. Tip into a colander set over a bowl and leave until cool enough to handle. Meanwhile, return all but the last 2 tablespoons of the mussel liquid to a sauté pan and boil vigorously until reduced to about 1 tablespoon. Let cool, then stir into the romesco sauce.

5 Preheat the broiler. Break the empty half-shell off each mussel, Loosen the mussels in their other shell and arrange them on a baking sheet in one layer. Dot each mussel with about 1 teaspoon of the romesco sauce and sprinkle with a little of the chopped oregano. Put under the broiler, close to the heat, and cook for about 1 minute until bubbling and hot. Serve straight away.

11

cozze con fagioli (mussels with cannellini beans)

SERVES 4

1¼ cups (225 g) dried cannellini beans, soaked
   overnight
1 bay leaf
1 sprig of thyme
4 garlic cloves, peeled
2½ lb (1 kg) mussels, cleaned (see page 88)
¼ cup dry white wine
½ cup (120 ml) extra virgin olive oil
2 large plum tomatoes, roughly chopped
2 tablespoons chopped flat-leaf parsley
Salt and freshly ground black pepper

1 Drain the beans and tip them into a pan. Pour in enough fresh water to cover them by about 2 inches (5 cm), then add the bay leaf, thyme, and 2 of the peeled garlic cloves. Bring to a boil, skimming any scum from the surface as it appears, then lower the heat and simmer for about 1 hour or until the beans are very soft.

2 Now increase the heat and boil rapidly until most of the liquid has disappeared. Discard the thyme and bay leaf.

3 Put the mussels into a pan with the wine. Cover and cook over a high heat for 3 to 4 minutes, until they have opened. Drain them in a colander set over a bowl to catch the cooking liquid. When they are cool enough to handle, remove about three-fourths of the mussels from their shells.

4 Slice the rest of the garlic into a large pan and add the olive oil. Slowly heat the oil, then, as soon as the garlic begins to sizzle, add the tomatoes and simmer for 2 to 3 minutes. Add the cooked beans and ⅔ cup (150 ml) of the mussel cooking liquid. Simmer for 5 minutes, until the liquid has reduced to a rich, creamy sauce. Season with pepper and a little salt, if necessary (you probably won't need any because mussels are quite salty).

5 Add the mussels and simmer for 1 to 2 minutes, until they are heated through. Stir in the chopped parsley and spoon into four warmed soup plates to serve.

la mouclade

SERVES 4

Large pinch of saffron strands
4 lb (1.75 kg) mussels, cleaned (see page 88)
½ cup (120 ml) dry white wine
2 tablespoons (25 g) butter
1 small onion, minced
2 garlic cloves, minced
½ teaspoon good-quality medium curry powder
2 tablespoons Cognac
2 teaspoons all-purpose flour
7 fl oz (200 ml) crème fraîche
3 tablespoons chopped flat-leaf parsley
Salt and freshly ground black pepper

1 Put the saffron into a small bowl and moisten it with 1 tablespoon of warm water.

2 Place the mussels and wine in a large pan, cover, and cook over a high heat for 3 to 4 minutes, shaking the pan now and then, until the mussels have opened. Tip them into a colander set over a bowl to catch all the cooking liquid. Transfer the mussels to a large serving bowl and keep warm.

3 Melt the butter in a pan, add the onion, garlic, and curry powder, and cook gently without browning for 2 to 3 minutes.

4 Add the Cognac and cook until it has almost all evaporated, then stir in the flour and cook for 1 minute. Gradually stir in the saffron liquid and all except the last 1 to 2 tablespoons of the mussel cooking liquid (which might contain some grit).

5 Bring the sauce to a simmer and cook for 2 to 3 minutes. Add the crème fraîche and simmer for 3 minutes more, until slightly reduced. Season to taste and stir in the parsley, then pour the sauce over the mussels. Stir them together gently and serve with plenty of French bread.

mollusks and other seafood

mussels en croustade with leeks and white wine

SERVES 4

4 large, round, crusty bread rolls
³/₄ cup (175 g) butter
2 lb (900 g) mussels, cleaned (see page 88)
¹/₄ cup dry white wine
2 large or 4 small leeks, minced
2 tablespoons heavy cream
1 teaspoon Beurre Manié (see page 227)
1 tablespoon chopped chives
Salt and freshly ground white pepper

1 Preheat the oven to 400°F (200°C). Cut a thin slice off the top of each bread roll and set aside. With a teaspoon, scoop out all the soft bread from inside each roll, leaving a wall about ¼ inch (5 mm) thick. Melt ¼ cup (50 g) of the butter and use to brush the inside of each roll and the lids. Place them on a baking sheet and bake for 5 to 7 minutes, until crisp and golden. Keep warm.

2 Put the mussels into a large pan with the wine, then cover and cook over a high heat for about 3 minutes, shaking the pan now and then, until they have just opened. Tip them into a colander set over a bowl to collect all the cooking liquid. Remove the mussels from their shells, cover, and set aside.

3 Melt 2 tablespoons (25 g) of the remaining butter in a pan. Add the leeks, cover, and cook for 4 to 5 minutes, until soft. Add the mussel cooking liquid except the last 1 to 2 tablespoons (which might contain some grit), then bring to a boil and simmer until reduced by half. Stir in the rest of the butter, the heavy cream, and the beurre manié. Simmer for 1 minute until slightly thickened.

4 Stir the mussels, chives, and some seasoning into the sauce. Spoon the mixture into the warm rolls, partly cover with the lids, and serve.

MUSSELS EN CROUSTADE WITH LEEKS AND WHITE WINE

11

tarte aux moules

SERVES 8

1 quantity Short Pastry (see page 227)

1 egg white

2 lb (900 g) mussels, cleaned (see page 88)

¼ cup dry white wine

3 tablespoons chopped flat-leaf parsley, stems reserved

2 tablespoons (25 g) butter

5–6 shallots, minced

5 garlic cloves, minced

3 eggs, beaten

1¼ cups (300 ml) heavy cream

Salt and freshly ground black pepper

1 Preheat the oven to 400°F (200°C). Briefly knead the pastry on a lightly floured work surface until smooth. Roll out and use to line a 10-inch (25-cm) tart pan, with a removable bottom, that is 1½ inches (4 cm) deep. Prick the bottom here and there with a fork, then chill for 20 minutes.

2 Line the pastry shell with a crumpled sheet of parchment paper, fill with baking beans, and bake "blind" for 15 minutes. Remove the paper and beans, and return the pastry shell to the oven to bake for 5 minutes.

3 Remove the pastry shell once more and brush the bottom with the unbeaten egg white. Return to the oven for 1 minute. Remove, and lower the oven temperature to 375°F (190°C).

4 Put the mussels into a large pan with the wine and parsley stems. Cover and cook over a high heat for 3 to 4 minutes, shaking the pan every now and then, until the mussels have opened. Tip them into a colander set over a bowl to collect all the cooking liquid. Let cool slightly, then remove the mussels from their shells.

5 Melt the butter in a pan and add the shallots and garlic. Cook gently for about 7 minutes, until very soft. Add all but the last 1 to 2 tablespoons of the mussel cooking liquid and simmer rapidly until it has evaporated. Scrape the mixture into a bowl and let cool. Then stir in the eggs, cream, and chopped parsley, and season to taste with pepper and a little salt, if necessary.

6 Scatter the mussels over the bottom of the pastry shell and pour in the egg mixture. Bake for 25 to 30 minutes, until just set and lightly browned. Remove and let cool slightly before serving.

mussel, leek, and saffron soup

SERVES 4

3 lb (1.5 kg) mussels, cleaned (see page 88)

¼ cup dry white wine

1 lb (450 g) leeks, cleaned

6 tablespoons (75 g) unsalted butter

1 small onion, minced

2 tablespoons all-purpose flour

Scant 2 cups (450 ml) Fish Stock (see page 222)

Large pinch of saffron strands

¼ cup heavy cream

Salt and freshly ground black pepper

1 Put the mussels and 2 tablespoons of the wine into a large pan. Cover and cook over a high heat, shaking the pan every now and then, until they have opened. Tip them into a colander set over a bowl to collect the liquid and let cool slightly. Then remove the mussels from all but 12 of the nicest-looking shells.

2 Cut a 2-inch (5-cm) piece of leek into matchsticks. Mince the rest. Melt the butter in a pan, add the minced leeks and the onion, and cook gently for 3 to 4 minutes, until soft but not browned.

3 Stir in the flour and cook gently for 1 minute. Gradually stir in the mussel liquid, the remaining wine, and the fish stock, and bring to a boil, stirring. Add the saffron and let simmer for 25 minutes.

4 Meanwhile, drop the leek matchsticks into a pan of boiling salted water. Bring back to a boil, then drain and refresh under running cold water.

5 Blend the soup, in batches if necessary, until smooth. Return to a clean pan and stir in the cream. Bring back to a simmer, then stir in the mussels and leek matchsticks. Adjust the seasoning, if necessary, and serve.

mollusks and other seafood

moules farcies
(stuffed broiled mussels)

SERVES 4 AS A FIRST COURSE

48 large mussels, cleaned (see page 88)
1/4 cup water
1 large garlic clove, halved
1 large shallot, halved
Handful of flat-leaf parsley leaves
Pared zest of 1/4 lemon
1/2 cup (100 g) unsalted butter, softened
1 2/3 cups (75 g) fresh white breadcrumbs
Salt and freshly ground black pepper

1 Put the mussels and water into a large pan, cover, and place over a high heat for 3 to 4 minutes, shaking the pan now and then, until the mussels have just opened.

2 Drain the mussels in a colander, then break off and discard the empty half-shells, leaving the mussels in the other shell.

3 Preheat the broiler. Mince the garlic, shallot, parsley, and lemon zest together—if you have one of those mini food processors, it will do the job beautifully and easily. Mix with the softened butter in a bowl and season to taste.

4 Dot each mussel with some of the garlic and parsley butter, then sprinkle with some of the breadcrumbs. Arrange them in one layer on a baking pan and broil, close to the heat, for 2 to 3 minutes, or until they are crisp and golden brown. Serve immediately.

broiled mussels with pesto

SERVES 4 AS A FIRST COURSE

60 large mussels, cleaned (see page 88)
A splash of dry white wine or water
2 slices white bread, made into breadcrumbs
PESTO:
1/3 cup (15 g) basil leaves
2 large garlic cloves
3/4 cup (175 ml) olive oil
2 tablespoons freshly grated Parmesan cheese
2 tablespoons pine nuts

1 Put the mussels and wine into a large pan, cover, and place over a high heat for 3 to 4 minutes, shaking the pan now and then, until the mussels have just opened. Remove from the heat straight away and discard one side of each open shell.

2 Tip the mussels into a colander set over a bowl to collect the cooking liquid.

3 Pour all but the last 1 to 2 tablespoons of the cooking liquid into a small pan and boil rapidly until reduced to about 1 tablespoon.

4 Put the pesto ingredients and the reduced mussel cooking liquid into a food processor and blend to a coarse paste.

5 Preheat the broiler. Arrange the mussels on their half shells in one layer on a baking pan and spoon a little pesto onto each one. Sprinkle with the breadcrumbs and broil, close to the heat, for 2 to 3 minutes until the breadcrumbs are beginning to brown.

11

MOULES MARINIÈRE

warm oysters with black beans, ginger and cilantro (see technique 63, page 91)

SERVES 4

20 Pacific oysters
1-inch (2.5-cm) piece of fresh ginger, peeled and minced
3-inch (7.5-cm) piece of hothouse cucumber
1 tablespoon chopped cilantro
1 teaspoon chopped chives
1 tablespoon Chinese fermented salted black beans
1 garlic clove, minced
1 tablespoon dark soy sauce
2 tablespoons dry sherry
¼ cup toasted sesame oil
Salt

1 Preheat the broiler. Open the oysters as described on page 91 and pour away half of the juices surrounding the meats. Make a thick layer of salt on a heatproof platter or the broiler pan and nestle in the oysters in their half shells (the salt will prevent them from rolling over during cooking). Sprinkle each one with the minced ginger and set aside.

2 Cut the cucumber into 1-inch (2.5-cm) pieces, then thinly slice each piece and cut lengthwise into matchsticks. Mix with the cilantro and chives, and set aside.

3 Rinse the black beans, then chop them up a little. Put them into a small pan with the garlic, soy sauce, sherry, and sesame oil. Leave over a very low heat to warm through.

4 Broil the oysters, about 4 inches (10 cm) from the heat, for 3 minutes. Sprinkle a little of the cucumber mixture over each one, spoon on a little of the sauce, and serve immediately.

moules marinière (see technique 59, page 88)

SERVES 4

4 lb (1.75 kg) mussels, cleaned (see page 88)
¼ cup (50 g) unsalted butter
1 onion, minced
¼ cup dry white wine
1 tablespoon coarsely chopped flat-leaf parsley

1 Put the mussels, butter, onion, and white wine into a very large pan. Cover and cook over a high heat for 3 to 4 minutes, shaking the pan every now and then, until the mussels have opened.

2 Spoon the mussels into one large or four individual warmed bowls. Add the parsley to the cooking juices, then pour all but the last 1 to 2 tablespoons, which might contain some grit, over the mussels. Serve with plenty of crusty white bread.

mollusks and other seafood

oysters charentais

SERVES 4

SAUSAGES:

12 oz (350 g) fresh pork belly, roughly chopped
1/2 teaspoon salt
1/2 teaspoon paprika
1/2 teaspoon freshly ground black pepper
1/2 teaspoon thyme leaves
1/2 teaspoon cayenne pepper
3 oz (75 g) smoked chorizo sausage, chopped
4 oz (100 g) caul fat

20 Pacific oysters

1 Put all the sausage ingredients (except for the caul fat) into a food processor and process into a coarse paste. Scrape the mixture into a bowl. Cut the caul into 4-inch (10-cm) squares.

2 Divide the sausage mixture into 12 pieces about the size of a golf ball and shape them into small sausages. Wrap each one in a piece of the caul fat.

3 About 20 minutes before serving, carefully open the oysters (see page 91), taking care not to lose too much of their juices. Divide them, on their half shells, among four plates.

4 Preheat the broiler. Broil the sausages, 4 to 6 inches (10 to 15 cm) from the heat, turning them now and then, until lightly browned and cooked through. Put three of the sausages onto each plate and serve.

broiled oysters with parmesan cheese

SERVES 4

24 Pacific oysters
3/4 cup (175 ml) heavy cream
1/4 cup (25 g) freshly grated Parmesan cheese
1/4 cup (50 g) butter, melted
Freshly ground black pepper

1 Preheat the broiler. Open the oysters (see page 91) and release them from the deeper bottom shells, then pour off most of their juices. Put them, on their half shells, on a baking pan or the rack of the broiler pan.

OYSTERS IN TEMPURA BATTER WITH SESAME SEEDS AND LIME

2 Spoon about 1 1/2 teaspoons of the cream over each oyster and season with a little black pepper. Sprinkle with the Parmesan cheese, then drizzle with the melted butter.

3 Broil the oysters, about 4 inches (10 cm) from the heat, for 1 minute, until the cheese is golden brown. Serve straight away.

11

oysters in tempura batter
with sesame seeds and lime

SERVES 4

DIPPING SAUCE:

¹/₄ cup dark soy sauce

¹/₄ cup water

Juice of 1 lime

20 Pacific oysters

Canola oil, for deep-frying

TEMPURA BATTER:

¹/₃ cup (50 g) all-purpose flour

¹/₂ cup (50 g) cornstarch

Small pinch of salt

4 teaspoons toasted sesame seeds

³/₄ cup (175 ml) ice-cold soda water from a new bottle

Lime wedges, for serving

1 Mix together the ingredients for the dipping sauce and pour into four small dipping saucers or bowls.

2 Shuck the oysters (see page 91) and discard all the juices. Keep the deeper bottom shells for serving.

3 Heat some oil for deep-frying to 375°F (190°C). Make the batter by sifting the flour, cornstarch, and salt into a bowl. Stir in the sesame seeds, then stir in the ice-cold soda water (it must be very, very cold and from a new bottle for this batter to be successful). Stir until only just mixed in; the batter should still be a little lumpy. If it seems a bit thick, add a drop more soda water. You want the batter to be very thin and almost transparent.

4 Dip the oysters, one at a time, into the batter, then drop them into the hot oil and fry for 1 minute, until crisp and golden. Lift out and drain very briefly on paper towels.

5 Put the oysters back in their bottom shells and arrange on four plates. Serve with the lime wedges and dipping sauce.

SEARED SCALLOPS WITH SERRANO HAM

seared scallops with
serrano ham (see technique 61, page 90)

SERVES 4

8 thin slices of serrano ham or a similar cured ham

Leaves from 1 curly endive heart and a handful of other bitter salad leaves

¹/₄ cup (50 g) chilled unsalted butter

12 prepared bay scallops (see page 90)

3 tablespoons sherry vinegar

1 tablespoon chopped flat-leaf parsley

Salt and freshly ground black pepper

1 Arrange the ham and a pile of salad leaves on each of four plates. Generously rub the bottom of a large, nonstick frying pan with the butter; cut the remainder into small pieces.

2 Set the pan over a high heat and, as soon as the butter starts to smoke, add the scallops. Sear for 2 minutes on each side, seasoning them with a little salt and pepper as they cook. Arrange the scallops on top of the ham.

3 For the dressing, remove the pan from the heat, add the sherry vinegar, and stir to scrape up any residue from the bottom of the pan. Return the pan to the heat and whisk in the pieces of butter, a few at a time, then add the parsley and season with a little salt and pepper. Spoon the dressing over the leaves and serve at once.

SCALLOPS,
OCTOPUS

steamed scallops in the shell with ginger, soy, sesame oil, and green onions

SERVES 4

16 prepared bay scallops in the shell (see page 90)

1 teaspoon minced fresh ginger

1 tablespoon toasted sesame oil

2 tablespoons dark soy sauce

1 tablespoon roughly chopped cilantro

3 green onions, thinly sliced

1 Pour 1 inch (2.5 cm) of water into the bottom of a wide, shallow pan and bring it to a boil. Loosen the scallops from their shells, but leave them in place. Sprinkle each one with some of the ginger.

2 Arrange the scallops, in batches if necessary, on a petal steamer. Lower them into the pan, reduce the heat to medium, cover, and steam for about 4 minutes until just set. Remove and keep warm while you cook the rest.

3 Meanwhile, put the sesame oil and soy sauce into a small pan and warm through.

4 Lift the scallops onto four warmed plates and pour some of the warm soy sauce and sesame oil over them. Sprinkle with the cilantro and green onions, and serve immediately.

BROILED SCALLOPS IN THE SHELL WITH
TOASTED HAZELNUT AND CILANTRO BUTTER

broiled scallops in the shell with toasted hazelnut and cilantro butter

SERVES 4

TOASTED HAZELNUT AND CILANTRO BUTTER:

2 heaped tablespoons unblanched hazelnuts

6 tablespoons (75 g) unsalted butter, softened

2 heaped tablespoons cilantro leaves

2 tablespoons flat-leaf parsley leaves

1 tablespoon roughly chopped shallot

1 teaspoon lemon juice

16 prepared bay scallops in the shell (see page 90)

2 tablespoons (25 g) unsalted butter, melted

Salt and freshly ground black pepper

1 Preheat the broiler. For the toasted hazelnut and cilantro butter, spread the hazelnuts in a baking pan and toast under the broiler for 4 to 5 minutes, shaking the pan now and then, until they are golden brown. Tip them into a clean dish towel and rub off the skins. Let cool, then chop them roughly and tip them into a food processor. Add the softened butter, the cilantro, parsley, shallot, lemon juice, a large pinch of salt, and some pepper. Blend together until well mixed.

2 Put the scallops on a large baking pan (cook them in batches, if necessary) and brush them with the melted butter. Season with a little salt and pepper, then broil, about 4 inches (10 cm) from the heat, for 1½ minutes.

3 Drop a generous teaspoonful of the hazelnut and cilantro butter onto each scallop and return to the broiler for 1½ minutes, until they are cooked through. Serve immediately.

11

scallops with duck livers and spaghettini

SERVES 4

12 prepared large bay scallops or small sea scallops (see page 90)
4 oz (100 g) duck livers
1¼ cups (300 ml) Fish Stock (see page 222)
½ cup (120 ml) heavy cream
½ cup (120 ml) Muscat de Beaumes de Venise or a similar sweet white wine
6 oz (175 g) dried spaghettini
2 tablespoons (25 g) unsalted butter
Salt and freshly ground black pepper
Sprigs of flat-leaf parsley, for garnish

1 Bring a large pan of well-salted water (1 teaspoon salt to each 2½ cups/600 ml water) to a boil. Meanwhile, slice the scallops horizontally in half; cut the duck livers into similar-sized pieces, being sure to remove any traces of the greeny-yellow gall bladder.

2 Put the fish stock, ⅓ cup (85 ml) of the cream, and the wine into a wide-based pan and boil rapidly until reduced to ⅔ cup (150 ml).

3 Add the pasta to the pan of boiling water and cook for 4 minutes or until al dente. Drain, then cover and keep warm.

4 Melt ½ tablespoon of the butter in a frying pan over a high heat. Add the scallop slices and fry them for 30 seconds on each side. Transfer them to a plate and keep warm.

5 Add the rest of the butter to the pan along with the duck livers and fry for just 1 minute, turning them over as they color. Set aside with the scallops.

6 Add the reduced stock and wine mixture to the pan and bring to a boil, scraping up all the bits from the bottom of the pan. Strain through a sieve into a small pan. Stir in the rest of the cream and check the seasoning, then heat through.

7 To serve, pile the pasta onto four warmed plates and arrange the scallops and duck livers on top. Pour the sauce around the pasta and serve garnished with flat-leaf parsley.

OCTOPUS, PEA, AND RED WINE STEW FROM LA VELA IN NAPLES

octopus, pea, and red wine stew from la vela in naples (see technique 64, page 94)

SERVES 4

1 (1½-lb/750-g) octopus, cleaned (see pages 94–5)
½ cup (120 ml) extra virgin olive oil
2 garlic cloves, thinly sliced
4 shallots, sliced
2½ cups (600 ml) Italian red wine
1 teaspoon sugar
2 plum tomatoes, halved
⅔ cup (100 g) shelled fresh or frozen green peas
1 tablespoon minced flat-leaf parsley
Salt and freshly ground black pepper

1 Preheat the oven to 300°F (150°C). Put the octopus into a small casserole with ⅓ cup (85 ml) of the olive oil. Cover and cook in the oven for 2 hours, until very tender.

2 Heat the rest of the olive oil in a large, shallow pan with the garlic until it begins to sizzle. Add the shallots and cook gently until they are

soft and lightly colored. Add the red wine, sugar, and tomatoes. Bring to a boil, then let simmer until almost all the wine has evaporated. Lift out the tomato skins and discard them.

3 Lift the octopus out of its cooking juices and cut it across into smaller pieces. Add to the red wine reduction along with the cooking juices and ½ cup (120 ml) of water. Bring to a simmer and cook for 15 to 20 minutes, until the liquid has reduced by about three-fourths.

4 Add the peas and simmer for 5 minutes. Season to taste and stir in the parsley. Serve hot or cold in large soup plates, with plenty of crusty Italian bread.

pulpo a la feria (fairground octopus)

SERVES 4

1 octopus, weighing about 1½ lb (750 g)
1 onion, peeled
4 bay leaves
½ teaspoon paprika
Large pinch of cayenne pepper
¼ cup good olive oil
½–1 teaspoon Maldon sea salt flakes

1 You will need to start the preparation for this dish well in advance. Seal the octopus in a plastic bag and leave it in the freezer for 2 weeks (this helps to tenderize it). Transfer it to the refrigerator the day before you want to cook it, to let it thaw slowly over 24 hours.

2 The next day, clean the octopus as described on page 94. Bring a large pan of water to a boil with the onion and bay leaves.

3 Add the octopus and simmer for at least 1 hour. Test after 30 minutes; if it is still a bit tough, cook for another 30 minutes. Don't cook any longer than this because the octopus loses its fresh taste with long cooking.

4 Lift the octopus out of the pan and drain away all the excess water. Put it on a board. Cut off the tentacles and slice each one on the diagonal into pieces about ¼ inch (5 mm) thick. Cut the body into similar-sized pieces.

5 Divide the octopus among four small pine boards or one large warmed serving plate and sprinkle with the paprika and the cayenne pepper. Heat the olive oil in a small pan until it is sizzling. Drizzle it over the octopus, then sprinkle with the sea salt. Serve with plenty of crusty fresh bread.

pasta with sea urchin roe, lemon, and flat-leaf parsley (see technique 67, page 97)

SERVES 4

1 lb (450 g) dried spaghetti
¼ cup extra virgin olive oil
1 garlic clove, minced
Very small pinch of dried red pepper flakes
2 oz (50 g) fresh sea urchin roe (see page 97)
2 tablespoons chopped flat-leaf parsley
2 teaspoons lemon juice
Salt and freshly ground black pepper

1 Cook the spaghetti in boiling well-salted water (1 teaspoon of salt for every 2½ cups/600 ml of water) for 8 minutes or until al dente.

2 Just before you drain the pasta, put the olive oil, garlic, and pepper flakes into another large pan and set it over a medium heat. Cook gently for 1 minute without letting the garlic color.

3 Drain the spaghetti and add to the garlic oil along with the sea urchin roe and parsley. Turn together over a low heat for 1 minute. You simply want the residual heat in the pasta to lightly cook the roe. Season with the lemon juice, a pinch of salt, and a little pepper, and serve straight away.

risotto nero

SERVES 4

1 lb (450 g) small, uncleaned cuttlefish
5 cups (1.2 liters) Fish Stock (see page 222)
2 tablespoons (25 g) butter
3 tablespoons olive oil
2 large shallots, minced
3 garlic cloves, minced
1½ cups (350 g) risotto rice, such as Carnaroli or
   Arborio
⅔ cup (150 ml) dry white wine
3 tablespoons chopped flat-leaf parsley
1 tablespoon freshly grated Parmesan cheese
Salt and freshly ground black pepper

1 Prepare the cuttlefish as described on page 96, carefully removing the little pearly-white ink sacs without bursting them. Squeeze out the ink into the fish stock, then slit open the sacs and rinse them out in the stock to remove as much of the ink as you can. Bring the stock to a boil in a pan and keep it hot over a low heat. Cut the cuttlefish bodies into very thin strips; slice the tentacles into 1½-inch (4-cm) pieces.

2 Heat the butter and 1 tablespoon of the oil in a heavy-based saucepan. Add the shallots and garlic, and cook gently until soft but not browned.

3 Stir in the rice so that all the grains become well coated with the oil and butter. Add the wine and simmer over a low heat for a few minutes until it has almost disappeared.

4 Add a ladleful of stock and simmer, stirring frequently, until it has all been absorbed. Continue to add the stock a ladleful at a time, stirring, until it has all been used and the rice is creamy and tender but still with a little bit of a bite—al dente. This should take 20 to 25 minutes.

5 Heat the rest of the oil in a large frying pan. Add the cuttlefish and fry it over a high heat for 1½ minutes. Remove from the heat, stir in the chopped parsley, and season with some salt and pepper. Stir the Parmesan cheese into the risotto. Season with salt and pepper.

6 Spoon the risotto into four warmed bowls and pile some of the cuttlefish into the center of each bowl. Serve straight away.

ALTERNATIVE FISH

Squid would be a good substitute, but there's not enough ink in squid to make this satisfactorily. However, you can buy little sachets of ink from your fishmonger. You'll need about 4 sachets for this dish.

a salad of raw cuttlefish with vine tomatoes and arugula (see technique 66, page 96)

SERVES 4

1 small, uncleaned cuttlefish
6 vine-ripened tomatoes
Juice of ¼ lemon
Extra virgin olive oil
1½ oz (40 g) arugula leaves
Maldon sea salt flakes and coarsely ground black pepper

1 Clean the cuttlefish as described on page 96; reserve the tentacles for another dish. Cut the cleaned body in half lengthwise, then cut each piece across, slightly on the diagonal, into very thin slices.

2 Slice each of the tomatoes across into very thin slices.

3 To serve, arrange 6 tomato slices in one layer over each plate. Arrange one-fourth of the cuttlefish slices loosely over the top of the tomatoes. Squeeze on a few drops of lemon juice, sprinkle with some sea salt flakes and a little coarsely ground black pepper, and drizzle on a little oil. Scatter a few arugula leaves on top and serve straight away.

deep-fried squid and aïoli

SERVES 4

12 oz (350 g) cleaned squid (see page 92)
1 quantity Aïoli (see page 224)
⅓ cup (50 g) flour seasoned with salt and pepper
Canola oil, for deep-frying
Thin lemon wedges, for serving
TOMATO AND DILL SALAD:
2 vine-ripened tomatoes, thinly sliced
1 sprig of dill, broken into small pieces
Maldon sea salt flakes and coarsely ground black pepper

1 Cut the squid pouches across into rings. Heat oil for deep-frying to 375°F (190°C).

2 Season the squid with a little salt and toss in the seasoned flour, then deep-fry, in batches, for 1 minute until crisp and golden. Drain briefly on paper towels.

3 For the salad, layer 3 or 4 thin slices of tomato on each plate with the dill and some seasoning. Put the squid and 1 heaped tablespoon of aïoli alongside. Garnish with the lemon wedges and serve.

steamed stuffed squid with sweet chile sauce

SERVES 4

4 small squid, with pouches no longer than
    6 inches (15 cm), cleaned (see page 92)
1 oz (25 g) peeled, raw small shrimp
4 oz (100 g) ground pork (about ½ cup)
½-inch (1-cm) piece of fresh ginger, peeled and finely
    grated
2 garlic cloves, crushed
1 tablespoon light soy sauce
1 tablespoon chopped cilantro
¼ teaspoon sugar
1½ teaspoons toasted sesame oil
½ teaspoon salt
Freshly ground Sichuan pepper
2 green onions, chopped, plus 1 green onion,
    finely shredded, for garnish

SWEET CHILE SAUCE:

2 tablespoons dark soy sauce
2 tablespoons sweet chile sauce
2 teaspoons rice wine vinegar or white wine vinegar
1 teaspoon toasted sesame oil

1 Rinse out the squid pouches. Roughly chop the tentacles and fins and put them in a food processor with the shrimp and ground pork. Blend to a coarse mixture. Scrape the mixture into a bowl. Add the rest of the ingredients (except for the shredded green onion and the sauce ingredients) and mix together well.

2 Spoon the pork mixture into the squid pouches and secure the open ends with wooden toothpicks.

3 Pour about 1 inch (2.5 cm) of water into a shallow, wide-based pan and bring to a boil. Arrange the squid on a petal steamer, lower it into the pan, cover, and steam for 20 to 25 minutes, until the squid are cooked through.

4 Meanwhile, put the ingredients for the sauce into a small pan. Just before the squid are ready, warm the sauce through. Lift the squid onto a board and cut each one across into about six thin slices. Arrange them on four warmed plates, spoon some of the sauce over them, and garnish with the green onion shreds.

squid, mint, and cilantro salad with roasted rice

SERVES 4

DRESSING:

1 medium-hot red chile pepper, thinly sliced into rings
¼ cup white wine vinegar
Juice of 1 lime
2 tablespoons Thai fish sauce (*nam pla*)
2 tablespoons water
½ teaspoon sugar
1 lemongrass stalk, outer leaves removed and core
    minced

8 oz (225 g) prepared small squid (see page 92)
2 tablespoons peanut oil
Large pinch of cayenne pepper
2 teaspoons long-grain rice
1 romaine heart, cut across into wide strips
4 green onions, halved and finely shredded
Handful of mint leaves
Handful of cilantro sprigs
Salt and freshly ground black pepper

1 For the dressing, cover the chile slices with vinegar and let steep for 30 minutes. Combine the rest of the dressing ingredients in a separate bowl and set aside.

2 Cut along one side of each squid pouch and open it out flat. Score the inner side into a diamond pattern with the tip of a small, sharp knife, then cut into 2-inch (5-cm) squares. Separate the tentacles if large (see page 93). Season with a little salt and pepper.

3 Heat the peanut oil in a wok. Add the squid and stir-fry for about 2 minutes. Transfer to a plate, sprinkle with the cayenne, and let cool, but don't refrigerate.

4 Meanwhile, heat a small, heavy-based frying pan over a high heat. Add the rice and toss for a few minutes until it is richly browned and smells nutty. Tip into a mortar and pound it with a pestle or the end of a rolling pin to break it up; don't grind it into fine powder.

5 To serve, toss together the lettuce, green onions, mint, and cilantro, and spread on a large, oval platter. Scatter the squid on top along with any oil left in the pan. Lift the chile slices out of the vinegar and mix with the rest of the dressing ingredients. Spoon this over the squid and sprinkle with the roasted rice. Serve straight away.

11

STIR-FRIED SALT-AND-PEPPER SQUID WITH RED CHILE AND GREEN ONION

stir-fried salt-and-pepper squid with red chile and green onion (see technique 64, page 92)

SERVES 4 AS A FIRST COURSE

SALAD:

¼ **hothouse cucumber, peeled, halved, and seeded**
½ **cup (50 g) beansprouts**
½ **cup (25 g) watercress, large stems removed**
2 **teaspoons dark soy sauce**
2 **teaspoons toasted sesame oil**
¼ **teaspoon sugar**
Pinch of salt

1½ **lb (750 g) squid**
½ **teaspoon black peppercorns**
½ **teaspoon Sichuan peppercorns**
1 **teaspoon Maldon sea salt flakes**
1–2 **tablespoons canola oil**
1 **medium-hot red chile pepper, thinly sliced (seeds removed, if you prefer)**
3 **green onions, sliced**

1 For the salad, cut the cucumber lengthwise into short strips. Toss with the beansprouts and watercress, then keep in the refrigerator until needed. Whisk together the soy sauce, sesame oil, sugar, and salt.

2 Prepare the squid as described on pages 92 to 93.

3 Heat a small, heavy-based frying pan over a high heat. Add the black peppercorns and Sichuan peppercorns and toast them for a few seconds, shaking the pan now and then, until they darken slightly and become aromatic. Tip into a mortar and crush coarsely with the pestle, then stir in the sea salt flakes.

4 Heat a wok over a high heat until smoking. Add half the oil and half the squid and stir-fry it for 2 minutes, until lightly colored. Tip onto a plate, then cook the remaining squid in the same way.

5 Return the first batch of squid to the wok and add 1 teaspoon of the salt-and-pepper mixture (the rest can be used in other stir-fries). Toss together for about 10 seconds, then add the red chile and green onions and toss together very briefly.

6 Divide the squid among four serving plates. Toss the salad with the dressing and pile alongside the squid. Serve immediately.

recipes
chapter 12

stocks, sauces, and basic recipes

fish stock

MAKES 5 CUPS (1.2 LITERS)

2¹/₄ lb (1 kg) bones from flatfish, such as sole and flounder
10 cups (2.4 liters) water
1 onion, chopped
1 fennel bulb, chopped
1 cup (100 g) sliced celery
1 cup (100 g) chopped carrot
¹/₃ cup (25 g) sliced button mushrooms
1 sprig of thyme

1 Put the fish bones and water into a large pan, bring just to a boil, and simmer very gently for 20 minutes.

2 Strain through a cheesecloth-lined sieve into a clean pan. Add the vegetables and thyme, and bring back to a boil. Simmer for 35 minutes or until reduced to about 5 cups (1.2 liters).

3 Strain once more, and use or store as required.

shellfish stock and shellfish reduction

MAKES 3³/₄ CUPS (900 ML) STOCK OR ²/₃ CUP (150 ML) REDUCTION

1 tablespoon (15 g) unsalted butter
¹/₂ cup (50 g) chopped carrot
¹/₂ cup (50 g) chopped onion
¹/₂ cup (50 g) chopped celery
12 oz (350 g) small shrimp in shell or small crabs
1 tablespoon Cognac
2 tablespoons white wine
1 teaspoon chopped tarragon
¹/₂ cup (75 g) roughly chopped tomato
5 cups (1.2 liters) Fish Stock (see above)
Pinch of cayenne pepper

TO MAKE THE STOCK:

1 Melt the butter in a large saucepan. Add the carrot, onion, and celery, and fry over a medium-high heat for 3 to 4 minutes.

2 Add the shrimp or crabs and the Cognac, and fry for 2 minutes more.

3 Add the remaining ingredients, lower the heat, cover, and let simmer for 40 minutes.

4 Strain the stock through a fine sieve, pressing out as much liquid as you can with the back of a ladle. It is now ready to use.

TO MAKE THE REDUCTION:

1 Blend the stock, in batches if necessary, before straining. Press the pulpy mixture through a cheesecloth-lined sieve into a clean pan, pressing out as much liquid as you can.

2 Bring the stock to a boil and boil rapidly until it has reduced to about ²/₃ cup (150 ml). It is now ready to use.

chicken stock

MAKES 7¹/₂ CUPS (1.7 LITERS)

Bones from 1 (3–lb/1.5–kg) uncooked chicken, or 1 lb (450 g) chicken wings
1 large carrot, chopped
2 celery stalks, sliced
2 leeks, sliced
2 fresh or dried bay leaves
2 sprigs of thyme
10 cups (2.4 liters) water

1 Put all the ingredients into a large pan and bring just to a boil, skimming off any scum from the surface as it appears. Let it simmer very gently for 2 hours—it is important not to let the liquid boil because this will force the fat from even the leanest chicken and the resulting stock will be cloudy.

2 Strain the stock through a cheesecloth-lined sieve. If not using immediately, let the stock cool, then keep it in the refrigerator or freezer.

basic court-bouillon

6 fresh bay leaves
1 teaspoon black peppercorns
1 carrot, sliced
1 small onion, sliced
2 tablespoons salt
1/4 cup white wine vinegar
15 cups (3.4 liters) water

Put all the ingredients into a saucepan or fish poacher, bring to a boil, and simmer for 20 minutes. Use immediately, or set aside, or chill until needed. Bring back to a boil before using.

shellfish bouillon

MAKES 10 CUPS (2.4 LITERS)
1 fennel bulb
1 large onion
4 celery stalks
Handful of button mushrooms
1/2 teaspoon salt
1 teaspoon black peppercorns
2 bay leaves
3 sprigs of thyme
1/2 teaspoon fennel seeds
1 1/4 cups (300 ml) dry white wine

1 Roughly chop all the vegetables and put them into a large pan with the salt, peppercorns, herbs, fennel seeds, and enough water to cover.

2 Bring to a boil and simmer for 20 minutes. Take the pan off the heat and add the wine. Cover and let cool for 2 hours.

3 Strain the stock, then use as required or keep in the refrigerator or freezer.

hollandaise sauce

SERVES 4
2 tablespoons water
2 egg yolks
1 cup (225 g) Clarified Butter
   (see page 226), warmed
Juice of 1/2 lemon

Large pinch of cayenne pepper
3/4 teaspoon salt

1 Put the water and egg yolks into a stainless-steel or glass bowl set over a pan of simmering water, making sure that the base of the bowl is not touching the water. Whisk until voluminous and creamy.

2 Remove the bowl from the pan and gradually whisk in the clarified butter until thick. Then whisk in the lemon juice, cayenne, and salt.

NOTE

This sauce is best used as soon as it is made, but will hold for up to 2 hours if kept, covered, in a warm place, such as over a pan of warm water.

VARIATIONS

béarnaise sauce

Put 1 tablespoon chopped tarragon, 2 minced shallots, 20 turns of the black pepper mill, and 1/4 cup white wine vinegar into a small pan. Boil rapidly until reduced to 1 tablespoon. Stir into 1 quantity of Hollandaise Sauce.

maltaise sauce

Stir the finely grated zest of 1 blood orange and the juice of 2 blood oranges into 1 quantity of Hollandaise Sauce.

vanilla hollandaise

Slit open 1 vanilla bean and scrape out the seeds. Put 1 1/4 cups (300 ml) Fish Stock (see page 222), 2 tablespoons Noilly Prat, and the vanilla bean and seeds into a small pan and boil rapidly until reduced to 1 1/2 to 2 tablespoons. Strain and stir into 1 quantity of Hollandaise Sauce.

mussel sauce

Put 1 lb (450 g) small mussels, 2 tablespoons white wine, 1 minced shallot, and 1 teaspoon chopped parsley into a pan. Cover and cook over a high heat for 3 to 4 minutes, until the mussels have opened. Tip into a colander set over a bowl to collect the cooking liquid. When they are cool enough to handle, remove the mussels from their shells and put to one side. Boil the cooking liquid until reduced to 1 to 2 tablespoons. Stir the reduced liquid and mussels into 1 quantity of Hollandaise Sauce.

seafood sauce

Stir 1 quantity of Shellfish Reduction (see page 222) into 1 quantity of Hollandaise Sauce.

sauce messine

Bring 1 teaspoon Dijon mustard, 2 minced shallots, and 1/4 cup heavy cream to a boil in a small pan. Stir into 1 quantity of Hollandaise Sauce with 1 teaspoon each of chopped chervil, tarragon, and chives.

quick hollandaise sauce

Using the same quantities as for Hollandaise Sauce, (see left, below) put the water, egg yolks, and lemon juice into a blender. Turn on the machine, then slowly pour in the warm clarified butter through the hole in the lid. Season with cayenne pepper and salt.

beurre blanc

SERVES 4
1/4 cup (50 g) minced shallots or onion
2 tablespoons white wine vinegar

stocks, sauces, and basic recipes

¹/₄ cup dry white wine

6 tablespoons water or Fish Stock
  (see page 222)

2 tablespoons heavy cream

³/₄ cup (175 g) unsalted butter, cut into
  small pieces

Salt and freshly ground white pepper

1 Put the shallots, vinegar, wine, and water into a small pan and simmer until nearly all the liquid has evaporated. Add the cream and boil until reduced a little more.

2 Lower the heat, then gradually whisk in the butter, a few pieces at a time, until the sauce has amalgamated. Season to taste with salt and white pepper.

mayonnaise

This recipe includes instructions for making mayonnaise in the blender or by hand. It is lighter when made mechanically because the process uses a whole egg and is very quick. You can use either sunflower oil or olive oil, or a mixture of the two if you prefer. It will keep in the refrigerator for up to 1 week.

MAKES 1¹/₄ CUPS (300 ML)

1 egg or 2 egg yolks

2 teaspoons white wine vinegar

¹/₂ teaspoon salt

1¹/₄ cups (300 ml) sunflower oil or
  olive oil

TO MAKE THE MAYONNAISE BY HAND:

1 Make sure all the ingredients are at room temperature before you start. Put the egg yolks, vinegar, and salt into a mixing bowl that is set on a cloth to prevent it from slipping.

2 Using a wire whisk, lightly whisk to break up the yolks. Gradually whisk the oil into the egg mixture, starting with a few drops at a time. Once you have added the same volume of oil as the original mixture of egg yolks and vinegar, you can add the oil a little more quickly. Keep whisking until all the oil is incorporated.

TO MAKE THE MAYONNAISE IN A
MACHINE:

Put the whole egg, vinegar, and salt into a blender or food processor. Turn on the machine, then slowly add the oil through the hole in the lid until you have a thick emulsion.

VARIATIONS

fennel mayonnaise

Stir 1 tablespoon Pernod, 1 teaspoon chopped chives, and 1 tablespoon minced fennel bulb into 1 quantity of Mayonnaise made with olive oil.

sauce verte

Blanch 1 oz (25 g) each of spinach and arugula leaves in boiling water for 1 minute. Drain and refresh under cold water. Squeeze dry, then put into a food processor with ¹/₂ cup (25 g) of mixed parsley, chervil, tarragon, and chives and 1 quantity of Mayonnaise made with olive oil. Blend until smooth.

marie rose sauce

Stir 5 tablespoons ketchup, ¹/₄ cup thick, plain yogurt, and some salt and freshly ground white pepper into 1 quantity of Mayonnaise made with sunflower oil.

lemon mayonnaise

Make the mayonnaise in a machine, using 1 tablespoon lemon juice in place of the vinegar, adding the finely grated zest of 1 small lemon,

and using a mixture of half sunflower oil and half olive oil.

mustard mayonnaise

Make the mayonnaise in a blender using a whole egg, 1 tablespoon white wine vinegar, 1 tablespoons prepared English mustard, ³/₄ teaspoon salt, a little white pepper, and sunflower oil.

tartar sauce

Stir 1 teaspoon each of minced green olives, gherkins, and capers and 2 teaspoons each of chopped chives and chopped parsley into ¹/₂ quantity of Mustard Mayonnaise (see above).

aïoli

MAKES ³/₄ CUP (175 ML)

4 garlic cloves, peeled

¹/₂ teaspoon salt

1 large egg yolk

2 teaspoons lemon juice

³/₄ cup (175 ml) extra virgin olive oil

1 Put the garlic cloves on a chopping board and crush them under the blade of a large knife. Sprinkle them with the salt, then work them with the knife blade into a smooth paste.

2 Scrape the garlic paste into a bowl and add the egg yolk and the lemon juice. Using a hand-held electric mixer, beat everything together. Very gradually beat in the olive oil to make a thick, mayonnaiselike mixture.

rouille

MAKES 1¹/₄ CUPS (300 ML)

1 thin slice day-old, crustless white bread

A little Fish Stock (see page 222) or water

3 fat garlic cloves, peeled

1 egg yolk

1 cup (250 ml) olive oil

HARISSA:

1 quantity Roasted Red Peppers
  (see page 227)

12

1 teaspoon tomato paste
1 teaspoon ground coriander
Pinch of saffron strands
2 medium-hot red chile peppers, stems
    removed and roughly chopped
1/4 teaspoon cayenne pepper
1/2 teaspoon salt

1 For the harissa, put the roasted red pepper
flesh, tomato paste, ground coriander, saffron,
chiles, cayenne pepper, and 1/4 teaspoon of the
salt into a food processor and blend until
smooth.

2 Cover the slice of bread with the fish stock or
water and let soften. Squeeze out the excess
liquid, then put the bread into the food processor
with 2 tablespoons of the harissa paste, the
garlic, egg yolk, and the remaining salt. Blend
until smooth.

3 With the machine still running, gradually add
the olive oil until you have a smooth, thick,
mayonnaiselike mixture. This can be kept in the
refrigerator for up to 1 week.

italian salsa verde

SERVES 6–8

1/2 cup (20 g) flat-leaf parsley leaves,
    very roughly chopped
2 tablespoons very roughly chopped mint
    leaves
3 tablespoons capers in brine, drained
    and rinsed
6 anchovy fillets in olive oil, drained
1 garlic clove
1 teaspoon Dijon mustard
1 1/2 tablespoons lemon juice
1/2 cup (120 ml) extra virgin olive oil
1/2 teaspoon salt

1 Pile the parsley, mint, capers, anchovies, and
garlic on a chopping board and chop together
into a coarse paste.

2 Transfer the mixture to a bowl and stir in the
mustard, lemon juice, olive oil, and salt.

parsley butter

1 small bunch of flat-leaf parsley, large
    stems removed
5 anchovy fillets in olive oil, drained
1/2 cup (100 g) unsalted butter, softened
2 teaspoons lemon juice
5 turns of the black pepper mill
1/2 teaspoon salt

1 Chop the parsley and anchovy fillets together
on a board into a coarse paste.

2 Mix into the butter with the lemon juice,
pepper, and salt.

3 Spoon into the center of a large sheet of
plastic wrap and shape into a roll 1 1/2 inches
(4 cm) thick. Wrap and chill until firm.

garlic butter

2 large garlic cloves
1/2 cup (100 g) unsalted butter, softened
1 teaspoon lemon juice
1 teaspoon brandy
1/2 cup (25 g) chopped flat-leaf parsley
Salt and freshly ground black pepper

1 Crush the garlic cloves on a board with the
blade of a large knife. Add a large pinch of salt
and work into a smooth paste.

2 Beat into the butter with the lemon juice,
brandy, parsley, and some freshly ground black
pepper. Shape, wrap, and chill as for Parsley
Butter (above).

shrimp butter

3 oz (75 g) cooked small shrimp in shell,
    preferably cold-water shrimp
1/2 cup (100 g) unsalted butter,
    softened
1 teaspoon lemon juice
1/4 teaspoon salt
Pinch of cayenne pepper

1 Put all the ingredients into a food processor
and blend until smooth, then press through a
chinois or very fine sieve with the back of a
wooden spoon.

2 Adjust the salt if necessary, then shape, wrap,
and chill as for Parsley Butter (left).

lemongrass butter

1 lemongrass stalk, outer leaves removed
    and core minced
Finely grated zest of 1/2 lime
2 teaspoons lime juice
1/2-inch (1-cm) piece of fresh ginger,
    minced
2 tablespoons chopped flat-leaf parsley
1/2 cup (100 g) slightly salted butter,
    softened
1 tablespoon Thai fish sauce (nam pla)
Freshly ground black pepper

Put all the ingredients into a food processor and
season well with freshly ground black pepper.
Blend until smooth, then shape, wrap, and chill
as for Parsley Butter (above left).

roasted red pepper
and chile butter

1 quantity Roasted Red Peppers
    (see page 227)
2 sun-dried tomatoes in oil, drained and
    minced
1 medium-hot red chile pepper, seeded
    and minced
2 tablespoons chopped flat-leaf parsley

½ cup (100 g) slightly salted butter, softened

½ teaspoon salt

1 Mince the flesh of the roasted red peppers. Mix into the butter along with the rest of the ingredients, then shape, wrap, and chill as for Parsley Butter (see page 225).

pesto butter

⅓ cup (15 g) basil leaves

2 large garlic cloves, roughly chopped

2 heaped tablespoons freshly grated Parmesan cheese

2 tablespoon pine nuts

3 tablespoons olive oil

½ teaspoon salt

½ cup (100 g) butter, softened

1 Put the basil, garlic, Parmesan, pine nuts, olive oil, and salt into a food processor and blend until smooth. Add the butter and blend again until smooth. Shape, wrap, and chill as for Parsley Butter (see page 225).

vindaloo curry paste

MAKES 1 CUP (225 ML)

1½ oz (40 g) dried red Kashmir chile peppers

1 small onion

1 teaspoon black peppercorns

1½ teaspoons whole cloves

3-inch (7.5-cm) piece of cinnamon stick

1 teaspoon cumin seeds

1-inch (2.5-cm) piece of fresh ginger

¼ cup chopped garlic

Walnut-sized piece of tamarind pulp, without seeds

1 teaspoon light brown sugar

2 tablespoons white wine vinegar

1 Cover the dried chiles with plenty of hot water and keep them submerged under a small plate. Let soak overnight.

2 The next day, preheat the oven to 450°F (230°C). Place the unpeeled onion on the middle rack of the oven and roast for 1 hour, until the center is soft and nicely caramelized. Let cool, then peel off the skin.

3 Drain the chiles and squeeze out the excess water. Put the peppercorns, cloves, cinnamon, and cumin seeds in a spice grinder and grind to a fine powder.

4 Put the chiles, roasted onion, ground spice mixture, ginger, garlic, tamarind pulp, sugar, and vinegar into a food processor and blend to a smooth paste.

goan masala paste

1 teaspoon cumin seeds

1 teaspoon coriander seeds

1 teaspoon black peppercorns

½ teaspoon fennel seeds

½ teaspoon whole cloves

½ teaspoon turmeric powder

⅓ cup (50 g) roughly chopped medium-hot red chile peppers

½ teaspoon salt

3 garlic cloves, chopped

1 teaspoon light, raw brown sugar

1½ teaspoons Tamarind Water (see page 227)

1-inch (2.5-cm) piece of fresh ginger, roughly chopped

1 tablespoon red wine vinegar

Grind the cumin, coriander, peppercorns, fennel, and cloves to a fine powder in a spice grinder. Put into a food processor with the remaining ingredients and blend to a smooth paste.

thai red curry paste

SERVES 4

5 large, medium-hot red chile peppers, stems removed, then roughly chopped

1-inch (2.5-cm) piece of fresh ginger, chopped

2 lemongrass stalks, outer leaves removed and core roughly chopped

6 garlic cloves

3 shallots, roughly chopped

1 teaspoon ground coriander

1 teaspoon ground cumin

¼ teaspoon blachan (Thai shrimp paste)

2 teaspoons paprika

½ teaspoon turmeric powder

1 teaspoon salt

1 tablespoon sunflower oil

Put everything into a food processor and blend to a smooth paste.

tapenade

MAKES 1 SMALL JAR

½ cup (75 g) pitted black olives, drained and rinsed

4 anchovy fillets in olive oil, drained

2 heaped tablespoons capers, drained and rinsed

3 garlic cloves

6 tablespoons olive oil

Freshly ground black pepper

1 Put the olives, anchovies, capers, and garlic into a food processor and pulse three or four times. Then turn the processor on and add the oil in a thin steady stream through the lid.

2 Stir in black pepper to taste. Spoon the mixture into a sterilized glass jar and seal. This will keep in the refrigerator for up to 3 months.

beurre manié

Blend equal quantities of softened butter and flour together into a smooth paste. Cover and keep in the refrigerator until needed. It will keep for the same period of time as butter.

clarified butter

Place the butter in a small pan and leave it over a very low heat until it has melted. Skim off any scum from the surface, then pour off the clear (clarified) butter into a bowl, leaving behind the milky white solids that will have settled to the bottom of the pan.

tamarind water

Take a piece of tamarind pulp about the size of a tangerine and put it in a bowl with ⅔ cup (150 ml) warm water. Work the paste into the water with your fingers until it has broken down and all the seeds have been released. Strain the slightly syrupy mixture through a fine sieve into another bowl and discard the fibrous material left in the sieve. The tamarind water is now ready to use. It can be kept in the refrigerator for up to 24 hours.

lemon olive oil

Pare the zest from 1 lemon with a potato peeler. Cut the zest into thin strips and mix with 2½ cups (600 ml) of extra virgin olive oil. Let infuse for 24 hours before using.

preserved lemons

NOTE
The lemons must be small ones or they won't fit or fill the jar.

3–4 small lemons for each 1-pint (500-ml) canning jar
¼ cup (75 g) salt for each jar
Fresh lemon juice

1 Cut the lemons almost into quarters, leaving them attached at the stem end.

2 Sprinkle as much salt as you can into the cuts, then press the lemons back into shape. Push them into the jar, stem-end down, packing them in tightly—they will fit with a little persuasion.

3 Sprinkle in the rest of the salt. Seal and leave for 4 to 5 days, giving the jar a shake every now and then, until the lemons have produced quite a lot of juice.

4 Add enough lemon juice to the jar so that the lemons are completely covered. Seal again and leave for a couple of weeks before using.

fresh egg pasta

MAKES 8 OZ (225 G)
1²⁄₃ cups (225 g) all-purpose flour
¼ teaspoon salt
½ teaspoon olive oil
2 medium eggs
4 medium egg yolks

1 Put all the ingredients into a food processor and blend until they come together into a dough.

2 Tip out onto a work surface and knead for about 10 minutes until smooth and elastic. Wrap in plastic wrap and let rest for 10 to 15 minutes before using.

roasted red peppers

EITHER: Spear the stem end of a red bell pepper on a long-handled fork and turn the pepper in the flame of a gas burner or blowtorch until the skin has blistered and blackened all over.

OR: Roast the pepper in the oven preheated to 425°F (220°C) for 20 to 25 minutes, turning once, until the skin is black.

Whichever roasting method you use, remove the pepper from the heat and let cool. Break it in half and remove the stem and seeds, then peel off the blackened skin. The flesh is now ready to use as required.

fresh salted cod

Sprinkle a ½-inch (1-cm) layer of salt over the bottom of a plastic container. Put a thick piece of unskinned cod fillet on top, then completely cover it with another thick layer of salt. Cover and refrigerate overnight. By the next day, the salt will have turned to brine. Remove the cod from the brine and rinse it under cold water. Cover with fresh water and let soak for 1 hour. It is now ready to use.

short pastry

1²⁄₃ cups (225 g) all-purpose flour
½ teaspoon salt
5 tablespoons (65 g) chilled butter, cut into pieces
5 tablespoons (2½ oz/65 g) chilled lard, cut into pieces
1½–2 tablespoons cold water

1 Sift the flour and salt into a food processor or a mixing bowl. Add the pieces of chilled butter and lard and work together until the mixture looks like fine breadcrumbs. Stir in the water with a round-bladed knife until the mixture comes together into a ball.

2 Turn out onto a lightly floured work surface and knead briefly until smooth. Roll out on a floured surface and use as required.

chapter 13

information

information
chapter 13

seafood families

introduction

In a practical book like this one it seems sensible to classify fish by "families" for cooking purposes. First, however, you'll need to refer to Classifying Seafood on page 256 to see what family the fish you're interested in belongs to. Then go to the relevant family section of this chapter (arranged in alphabetical order of family name or category), for more information about the fish and how to cook it. The majority of species in each family are anatomically similar. Occasionally, however, I've included an odd fish, which, though not related, has a similar shape or similar fillet make-up and can be cooked in the same way. I've also been wildly inconsistent on occasions and grouped fish not by their biological connection but by their shape and size. It's much more significant, for example, to know that a garfish and needlefish, though not related, are so similar in looks and taste that they ought to be considered together.

The standard classification of fish throughout the world is in Latin. Paradoxically, the reason I felt resentful about learning Latin at school—namely that it's a dead language and therefore seemed impractical—is precisely why it's such a perfect language for science: it doesn't change. The problem with the colloquial naming of fish is that you end up with dozens of different names for the same fish, or dozens of different fish with the same name. Using Latin nails them down. Now I find myself trading Latin fish names with the sort of authority that I've only heard before from the lips of botanists.

It's a common misconception to think that fish on the other side of the world are different. A few are though, and I've grouped these in more detail under the headings "Australian Catchall" and "US Catchall." While the morwong, loved by spear fishermen, belongs to a family that only exists in Australia and New Zealand, most fish belong to families that can be found all over the world and, broadly speaking, can all be cooked in the same way.

I've had to be selective in my choice of fish to write about in this chapter—after all, there are more than 25,000 species. For example, do you need to know about all the hagfishes, which are saltwater lampreys, or do you just need to know about lampreys in general, which, though not common, are quite a colorful part of European cooking? A book that described the cooking and eating qualities of every fish would take years to write—and probably to read—so I have highlighted the most common fish in each country, in the hope that you'll find just the information you are looking for.

australian catchall

This section includes all those fish from Australia and New Zealand that don't appear anywhere else in the world. The MORWONG, known as the TERAHIKI in New Zealand, is a pan-sized fish with firm, white, mildly flavored flesh, normally caught by anglers and spear fishermen. As a testimony to the plentifulness of the morwong off the coast of New South Wales, I once went spear-fishing with a couple of friends and their father near Sydney. I stayed in the boat with the old man. When one of the sons appeared with a 4½-lb (2-kg) red morwong, he was promptly told by his dad to go and get another one as there wouldn't be enough for the barbecue that afternoon. He was soon back and quite excellent they were, too.

There's another family of fish called TREVALLAS that is unique to Australasia. The most well-known are the WAREHOU, RUDDERFISH, and the BLUE-EYE, often called the BLUE-EYE COD. The off-white flesh is firm, moist, and delicately flavored, and they're very highly regarded in the southern states of Australia and New Zealand. There are plans to farm these fish, as they are so popular.

Also in Australia, the STRIPED TRUMPETER and the TASSIE TRUMPETER (which is called the BLUE MOKI in New Zealand) are very good eating, with firm, white, tasty, and fatty flesh. It's suitable for cooking in any way you like, but I like to broil the fillets and serve them with a sauce of mayonnaise thinned with a little hot water, to which I add green olives, sliced into shards, and a touch of garlic. This and a chopped tomato and red onion salsa, seasoned with hot green chile pepper, salt, olive oil, and lime juice, work a treat.

Finally, there's the Australian SAND WHITING and KING GEORGE WHITING. These fish are excellent broiled whole or in fillets and require little addition. The best way I've ever had a whiting was at a restaurant called the Claireville Kiosk on Pittwater in New South Wales. It was pan-fried with noisette butter and capers, and served with a salad of warm sliced potatoes and crisp romaine. Sand whiting are a much better flavored fish than European whiting and would make the Merlan Frit en Colère, on page 166, something quite special.

billfish

swordfish

I think swordfish is the perfect fish for grilling. The idea of cooking fish outdoors so often proves disappointing in the execution, but you really can't go wrong with a steak of swordfish. Of course, it's much better undercooked, but it seems quite forgiving in that even when the flesh is over-cooked and dry, it's quite interesting to eat. It is also the perfect flesh for marinating and is firm enough for cutting up and skewering to make kebabs. It's immensely popular in Europe and the US, less so in Australia: I recall a visit to the Sydney fish market once when one of the traders said that he couldn't give these fish away. There is a popular misconception among the concerned public that all swordfish come from unsustainable sources. The same thing is happening with cod—a feeling that it's inevitable that all the cod will soon be gone. Not all swordfish fisheries are non-sustainable, so don't necessarily feel guilty when you enjoy this excellent fish.

marlin and sailfish

The other main members of the billfish family, marlin and sailfish, have similar qualities to swordfish. However, neither quite hit the spot with me, although WHITE MARLIN is better than BLUE MARLIN and is widely used in Japan to make fish sausages. These fish should probably be reserved for some rich, game-fishing acquaintances of mine, who spend "shed loads" of money pulling them out of the sea, only to put them back in again.

bony-cheeked fish

This is a group of fish distinguished by having a noticably hard head. It includes the Australian flathead, which when viewed from this perspective, do look similar to the gurnard, though their flatness is rather more obvious than their hard-headedness.

In the Atlantic, the most common species are the REDFISH, *Sebastes marinus*, sold in the US as OCEAN PERCH and marketed at 2¼ to 4½ lb (1 to 2 kg). There is also a slightly smaller species known as NORWAY HADDOCK, *Sebastes vivipurus*. Neither fish bears any relation to the cod family, but because they have a soft, flaky texture, they can be cooked in the same way. I would suggest broiling the fillets and serving on some mashed potatoes with a soy, butter, and cilantro sauce (see the recipe using cod on page 128). In the north Pacific, there are also a number of the same species of fish, i.e. *Sebastes*, which are rather better eating than the redfish of the Atlantic, and they are called ROCKFISH. The best tasting of these are the BOLINA and the GOLDEN EYE ROCKFISH. In the southern Pacific, there is an entirely different group of redfish, which includes the ALFONSINO, the BIGHT REDFISH, the IMPERADOR, the REDFISH (also known as the red snapper, just to be totally confusing), the SWALLOWTAIL, and the YELLOWEYE REDFISH. All of these are sold at about 2¼-lb (1-kg) weights and produce soft fillets of fish with a delicate flavor. They are oilier than the northern redfish and as such suit pan-frying or pan-grilling very well. I would suggest serving them as for snapper with shrimp and mango, on page 147.

flatheads

The AUSTRALIAN FLATHEAD provides thick, white fillets of moderately well-flavored fish. It is actually the mainstay of the fish and chip industry in Australia. It can be cooked in any of the ways that you might cook cod. Those of good eating are the DEEPWATER, DUSKY, SOUTHERN TIGER, SAND FLATHEAD, and, best of all, the ROCK FLATHEAD.

gurnard and scorpion fish

Gurnard are underrated everywhere, because they're regarded as bony. But they grow quite large, up to 5½ lb (2.5 kg), and a fillet cut from a large gurnard is firm and sweet. I always think of gurnard as being a Mediterranean-type of fish, it being one of the most common of three or four species such as RACASSE (SCORPION FISH) and the WEEVER FISH (see page 240) that go into a good bouillabaisse or soupe de poisson. I like to cook my gurnard in a quite robust, southern European sort of way, like the recipe on page 174. Gurnards come in two common types, RED or GRAY. I've never been able to find any difference in flavor, but the red ones are much more attractive, leading perhaps to the Dutch name for them, "*engelese soldaat*" (English soldiers), presumably a reference to the red coats. In Cornwall, the very largest gurnard are known as "tubs" and can reach as much as 5½ lb (2.5 kg). This species has the most beautiful, translucent, blue-green pectoral fins. A couple of oddities of this fish are, first, the name, derived from the French word "grondin," meaning grunt, which apparently these rather porky-looking fish do underwater. Secondly, its three pectoral spines look like little legs on which the fish "walk" along the sea bed, feeling for food. Gurnard fillets are very good lightly dusted with flour, fried in a little oil and butter, and served with lightly broiled pancetta or very thin slices of bacon and some beurre noisette. The red gurnard also appears as the SEA ROBIN in the US and the LATCHET in Australia and New Zealand, where they are also alternatively known as gurnards.

cephalopods

In many parts of the world, SQUID (also called INKFISH and sometimes CALAMARI in the US and Australia), CUTTLEFISH, and OCTOPUS have only recently become popular. The Southeast Asians, Japanese, Chinese, and people of the Mediterranean regions have always revered the lobster-like taste and slightly chewy texture of cephalopods. Unlike fish, each of the cephalopod groups is similar in taste and shape wherever you go in the world. However, no octopus are found on the Eastern Seaboard of North America, north of the Carolinas.

seafood families

The general rule of thumb is: the smaller the species, the more tender it will be. With the exception of octopus, they need to be cooked quickly so that they remain so—no more than 1 minute in a hot pan—after which time they tend to toughen, and then you should slow-cook them in the same way as octopus to render them tender again.

squid

To me, the taste of squid is of pure seafood. Nothing is more exciting than the smell of fresh squid cooking quickly in hot olive oil, or in a wok with the attendant aromas of garlic and ginger, in somewhere like the Seafood Restaurant in Bangkok. Squid is popular everywhere now. It should be cooked for the briefest time, in the hottest oil, or broiled, baked, or stuffed and steamed (see page 220). I don't enjoy the taste of boiled squid so, for a fish stew, I add it fried at the last minute.

There is a theory that frozen squid are as good as fresh, but I don't find this to be so. Freezing seems to make them tougher and remove most of their taste, but, like all frozen seafood, the quality depends more on the length of time they have been frozen rather than any deterioration caused by the rapid drop in temperature. Cuttlefish is also becoming more popular, though it tends to be a little tougher than squid.

octopus

Actually, octopus is always tough and needs tenderizing, either by slow-cooking in the oven with oil and spices, by bashing it against a rock in the Greek-style, or by freezing the cleaned bodies for 2 weeks before slow simmering them in salted water for 1 to 1½ hours. This is the treatment for the classic Spanish dish, Pulpo a la Feria (see recipe, page 218), where it is sliced and finished with paprika, cayenne, sea salt, and olive oil.

cod and cod-like fish

cod

In one of my earlier books I included a recipe for Crab Newburg by Marjorie Kinnan Rawlings, which ends: "I sit alone and weep for the misery of a world that does not have blue crabs and a Jersey cow," to which list I would add cod.

The world cries out for a thick, white, flaky fillet of fish, not assertive in flavor and not filled with bones, and cod is that fish. The fact that it is fished-out on the Grand Banks of the US Eastern Seaboard and virtually fished-out in the North Sea has, more than anything, drawn attention to the alarming reduction in fish stocks everywhere. I recall people saying that cod was bland and boring, but it only takes a shortage to concentrate the mind on appreciating one of the best fish in the sea.

Anyone with even a passing interest in fish should read Mark Kurlansky's book *Cod*. In it you will discover that the cod along the Grand Banks in the US were once so plentiful that they could be gathered simply by dropping weighted baskets over the sides of the boats and lifting them, brimming with fish, back up through the shoals. As a colorful illustration of the fecundity of cod, and the appalling cack-handedness of our failure to preserve the species through greed and political expediency, I enjoy this quote by Alexander Dumas in *Le Grand Dictionaire*, 1873: "It has been calculated that if no accident prevented the hatching of the eggs, and each egg reached maturity, it would take only 3 years to fill the sea, so that you could walk across the Atlantic dry shod on the backs of cod."

There are still stocks of the smaller but similar PACIFIC COD, which is marketed as TRUE COD on the West Coast to distinguish it from various other unrelated fish that are sold as cod. This problem is prevalent in Australia and New Zealand too—testimony perhaps to the worldwide demand for the characteristic clean taste of this prized fish.

Fortunately, the Norwegians and Icelanders have long practiced sensible conservation of cod stocks off their coasts, and much of the world's cod come from these cold waters. Though the records of enormous cod weighing 120 lb (50 kg) or more are now mere historical facts, you can still buy 11- to 13-lb (5- to 6-kg) fish, which are fantastic eating. Fish of this size are normally sold in fillets and a portion brushed with butter, sprinkled with sea salt and cracked black pepper, and broiled is as good as cod gets. Whenever possible, therefore, go for thick fillets.

Small cod up to 2¼ lb (1 kg), known as CODLING in Europe and SCROD in America, are nice to eat if fresh, but don't have the superb falling-away flaky texture of the bigger fish. Cod when it's just caught is quite tough, and while I love this chewiness, some prefer to leave it a day or two until the flesh goes through the same enzymatic change as meat and becomes more tender.

preserved cod

Historically, far more cod was consumed salted because of lack of refrigeration, but even today the demand for SALT COD, BACALAO, and dried cod (STOCKFISH) is enormous. Properly soaked—over a couple of days—and then poached and served with some sympathetic flavors such as garlic, tomato, and olive oil, it is real comfort food for the Spanish, Portuguese, Italians, and French. I recently had a carpaccio of salt cod where the salt cod had been soaked for sufficiently long to remove any trace of salt and was then served raw and thinly sliced with sliced San Marzano tomatoes, arugula,

and extra virgin olive oil. Accompanied by a glass of Greco di Tufo, the versatility of this ancient way of curing cod was brought alive to me.

haddock

This, the next most popular member of the cod family, has also suffered from serious over-fishing. It's just as good as cod and, while it lacks the whiteness and beautiful flakes of that fish, it has a slightly sweeter flavor. Again, it is best in thick fillets, but it's not as big a fish as cod, weighing on average 4½ to 6½ lb (2 to 3 kg). In Britain, a great deal of rather small fish is landed, especially owing to the preference for haddock over cod in the fish-and-chip shops of the North. But I think they are rather unsuited to being coated in batter and deep-fried because they dry out.

smoked haddock

Of all the cod family, haddock is best for smoking due to its slightly sweet flavor. All haddock-fishing countries have a range of smoked haddock specialties. In Britain, FINNAN HADDOCK is traditionally smoked over peat, and ARBROATH SMOKIES are small, whole haddock, hot-smoked over pits of smoldering oak. In Europe, Denmark produces some good-quality smoked haddock, as does France, where it is called "haddock" to distinguish it from the fresh fish or *eglefin*.

In the US, smoked haddock (called FINNAN HADDIE) comes from New England and other eastern coastal states. The smoked haddock on sale in Australia and New Zealand will have come from either northern Europe or North America.

hake

Of the rest of the cod family, hake is the most far-flung species, appearing not only in the North Atlantic, Mediterranean, and North Pacific, but also as far south as New Zealand as the SOUTHERN HAKE, and *Merluccius australis*. A very similar species, *Merluccius capensis*, is currently the prime target of a massive European fishery off the coast of South Africa. In Europe, the Spanish are by far and away the biggest consumers of hake. Like them, I find it hard to see why it's not more popular in North America and Australasia. It has a beguiling soft texture and good flavor and, I think, takes to butter or cream better than any other fish, except for turbot or brill. It is also rather good served cold with mayonnaise or sauce verte, an olive-oil mayonnaise with spinach, arugula, and herbs.

whiting

Whiting is extensively fished worldwide. It's not the best flavored of the cod family, but small fish cooked whole—particularly deep-fried "en colère" (see page 166)—are a delight.

13

ling, forkbeard, white hake, and pollack

I would describe all the rest of the cod family as lesser species as they don't have the same commercial appeal. All LING are firm textured with a mild, delicate flavor. I've had some success cooking fillets of our British ling on a charcoal grill. I wrote the recipe for SALT LING turnovers (see page 137) after a visit to the English Market in Cork, Ireland, where they specialize in dry-salting really thick fillets. It's a first-class product.

There is a species similar to ling in the Mediterranean—it's called the FORKBEARD and is usually cooked in the same way as hake—and also a couple in North America, the WHITE HAKE (also called the BOSTON LING) and the SQUIRREL HAKE.

Like hake, ling appears not just in the North Atlantic but also in the South Pacific as PINK LING and ROCK LING. POLLACK, not to be confused with the North American pollock, which is a different fish, is quite a good substitute for cod. Pollack doesn't grow as big as cod, its average size being 4½ to 6½ lb (2 to 3 kg), but a fillet taken from a larger fish and broiled is almost as good as the real thing.

pollock, cusk, and pouting

Also known as COLEY, SAITHE, or COALFISH, POLLOCK has quite a good flavor but is let down by its dull gray color on the slab, some of which remains after cooking. It can be substituted for either cod or haddock in any recipe and makes very good fish cakes (see page 127). The flesh of TUSK, or CUSK, as it is more commonly known in North America, is rather oilier than most *Gadidae* (members of the cod family) and is therefore best broiled or baked. POUTING or POUT is a cheap member of the cod family that doesn't keep well. Rather a dull, light brown in color, with a very fragile fillet, it is best used in fish cakes or fish pies and is most similar to whiting. It has bulbous eyes that seem to expand when it is trawled up from any great depth—testimony to the fact that fish brought up from the deep suffer, as we do, from the "bends."

crustaceans

crabs

The meat of all crabs is fairly similar in taste all over the world, with each region asserting that theirs is the best. So I have simply organized them by size—small, medium, and large.

small crabs

The very smallest of crabs are called OYSTER or PEA CRABS. Some weeks ago, I received a letter from a woman who had watched me prepare mussels on one of my television programs. In it she warned me of the need to clean mussels on the inside, as well as the outside, because of the poisonous little crabs that live inside the shell of mussels and oysters. I've heard of this anxiety before, but actually these crabs are perfectly edible, and some oyster-shucking houses in the US used to sell them as a valuable by-product, for deep-frying or adding to soups.

The GREEN CRAB or SHORE CRAB weighs no more than ⅓ oz (10 g), but it has a ready market in Europe for such soups as the Shore Crab Bisque, on page 101. We have had success gathering them when soft-shelled, dipping them in tempura batter and serving them with a dipping sauce of chile, lime, and *nam pla* (Thai fish sauce). The SWIMMING CRAB or VELVET CRAB, called the ETRILLE by the French, is surprisingly full of sweet, fibrous meat. I once ate a plate of them in Spain, and noted that there was a distinction made between the local velvet crabs (called NECORA) and those described as "foreign," which presumably come from Cornwall, and fetch a lower price. I must say I couldn't tell the difference.

Of all the small crabs, the one that grabs the biggest peon of praise is the BLUE CRAB from the Eastern Seaboard of the US, which reaches weights of up to 7 oz (200 g). Whether in its hard shell or in its all-edible soft-shell form, it seems to have a higher ratio of lumpy, exquisite meat than any other crab. Would that in the UK we could buy tubs of fresh white crabmeat as you can in the Chesapeake Bay area.

medium crabs

The crab most similar to the blue crab, but of medium size, is the ASIAN BLUE SWIMMER, *Portunus pelagicus*, of Australia. It is ideal for stir-frying in the shell, as it's easy to pick out the chunky, fibrous meat, and it's the best choice for Singapore Chile Crab (see recipe, page 185). The other major crab from Australia and New Zealand is the MUD CRAB (MANGROVE CRAB), which has a much thicker shell and incredibly powerful claws. It much more resembles the European BROWN CRAB and the DUNGENESS CRAB of the northern Pacific, but is also very closely related to the excellent-flavored SAND CRAB of the Carolinas and Florida in the US. Another excellent-flavored American crab, with pink-tinged meat, is the RED CRAB. It lives on the outer continental shelf at depths of between 1,200 and 6,000 feet (369 and 1,846 meters).

Naturally, I consider the brown crab to be second to none for flavor, but possibly the European SPIDER CRAB has the most scented flavor of all crabs. The similar-looking SNOW CRAB in North America has rather coarser, yellowish meat.

large crabs

One of the two most spectacular large crabs is the ALASKAN KING CRAB, which can weigh up to 22½ lb (10 kg). These are sold as crabmeat, rarely as whole crabs, because their enormous size and the fact that they are fished for off Alaska would make bringing the whole crab to market uneconomical.

The largest crab in the world is the KING CRAB from Southern Australia and Tasmania. It can weigh up to 38 lb (17 kg), though the normal market size is about half that. These are favored by the Chinese communities of Australian cities, where they are often kept spectacularly on show in tanks at the front of the restaurant.

lobster

A trip to New England last year and the pleasure of eating lobster rolls at Bob's Clam House showed me that in some favored parts of the world, lobster need not be the frighteningly expensive luxury that it is where I come from. Lobster rolls are simply lobster meat in a slightly sweet finger bun with mayonnaise—now that's fast food I approve of!

Lobster is the world's most sought-after seafood. Its firm, sweet, white meat is satisfyingly full of flavor and the flavor of all lobsters is remarkably similar the world over. The question of which country's lobsters are the best is easily answered for me. Wherever you can get one straight from the sea and cooked on the spot, that's the place where the best one will be. Lobsters deteriorate very quickly after death, so they have to be kept alive in a re-circulation tank called a vivarium. But they can't be fed in them because this would contaminate the water and they would die. Unfortunately, the relatively small amount of water in which they live while in these tanks can affect their flavor. This explains why a lobster at the Seafood Restaurant in Padstow, straight out of the Atlantic and broiled with a little butter and chopped fines herbes, or cooked and served just with mayonnaise, will always taste better than one eaten in London.

The only lobsters with significant claws, the EUROPEAN and AMERICAN LOBSTERS, come from the North Atlantic. The American lobster is slightly larger than the European and is dark green when alive, whereas the European one is blue. The claws of the American lobster are more rounded and, when cooked, it has a more orange hue than the European one. But in both cases the best sizes are 1 lb 2 oz to 3 lb 5 oz (500 to 1 kg).

Lobsters with claws tend to prefer cold water, though they can be found as far south as the

seafood families

Mediterranean and South Carolina. SPINY LOBSTERS (or ROCK LOBSTERS), on the other hand, occur both in the Southern Hemisphere and Northern Hemisphere, as far north as Norway. They grow a lot bigger than true lobsters, but I still think that the best size is 1 lb 2 oz to 4½ lb (500 g to 2 kg). The most obvious difference between them and true lobster is the absence of any claws, but they are cooked in the same way and make just as good eating. My current preference is for the WESTERN ROCK LOBSTER from western Australia.

Similar to spiny lobsters are various FLAT or SLIPPER LOBSTERS of Europe, called *cigales*. This is the French word for cicada, and refers to the cricket-like noises that they make underwater. With typical Australian bluntness, these slipper lobsters are known there as bugs, notably the BALMAIN BUG and MORETON BAY BUG. In the US, the similar species are known as SHOVEL-NOSED or SPANISH LOBSTERS, or, echoing the French name, LOCUST LOBSTER. All these species are good eating though, due to a tendency to dryness, I find them far better if slightly undercooked. Incidentally, there is no danger in eating raw or undercooked lobster, as the splendor of thinly sliced lobster sashimi will testify. As with spiny lobsters, the meat of slipper lobsters is all in the tail.

If you find you have bought a lobster with soft, wooly flesh, it will be because it has been cooked after it has died. On death, the flesh of both lobsters and crabs goes through a rapid enzyme change, which reduces it almost to pulp within a couple of hours. The only ways to prevent this with lobster are either to remove the tail and claws from the head on death, or rapidly freeze it.

Although I have classed LANGOUSTINES as large shrimp, they are more closely related to lobsters, and in the US are often called LOBSTERETTES. They also suffer from this rapid deterioration on death, which is why cooked langoustines can so often be disappointing.

shrimp and prawns

Until it became easy in Britain to buy shrimp from North America, Asia, and Australia, cooked shrimp dishes were relatively rare, simply because our native shrimp are small and don't suit broiling or grilling, pan-frying, or deep-frying. We do have great shrimp dishes, but generally a pile of cooked shrimp was something to peel at leisure and eat with a bowl of mayonnaise and some brown bread and butter.

There are really only three main types of shrimp native to Britain—the smallest we call a shrimp, whereas everything else is a prawn to us, the same usage as in Australia. The BROWN SHRIMP, caught off the coast of East Anglia and in Morecombe Bay in Lancashire, has a beautiful, ephemeral flavor and should be eaten immediately after being boiled in seawater. I like to think of them as the seafood equivalent of violets in spring. They are also the *sine qua non* of potted shrimp, the superb delicacy that is thankfully still alive and well in Morecambe. (See the recipe on page 202.) The COMMON PRAWN is excellent, but difficult to get hold of unless you live near the coast in the UK. I like to eat the larger ones just with mayonnaise, but the smaller ones are great in a seafood risotto, where the shells can be used in the stock to add a good seafood flavor.

The other common shrimp available on sale everywhere in Britain is the MEDITERRANEAN PRAWN or CREVETTE, which I think is best served whole with mayonnaise or aïoli, the garlic mayonnaise from Provence. I really like to squeeze the roe out of the heads of these shrimp—it's delicious and a treat missed by most people.

Now that it's easy for us to get large shrimp, we can make dishes like Jambalaya (page 201), Tandoori Shrimp (page 200), and Shrimp Caldine (page 197). But imported shrimp are still rather unhelpfully labeled just as small, medium, or large, raw or cooked. Sometimes they're called by their correct name, such as BLACK TIGER SHRIMP, but we look forward to a time when we can enjoy the subtle differences of shrimp and prawns as found in Australia.

In Australia, the BANANA PRAWN is known for its sweet, moist, and medium-firm texture, while the KING PRAWN can reach up to 12 inches (30 cm) in length. The BAY PRAWN is only ever sold locally where it's caught and, though fetching less money than other shrimp, is much sought after because of its seasonality.

In the US, you'll find the ROYAL RED SHRIMP from the Gulf of Mexico, with a deep red color even when raw, and the CARIBBEAN (GULF) WHITE SHRIMP, which is the best-eating shrimp in the country, found from North Carolina down to the Gulf of Mexico and Texas. On the Pacific coast are the SIDE-STRIPE SHRIMP, the PINK SHRIMP, and the COON-STRIPE SHRIMP. When sold, though, shrimp are usually just identified by size, like imported shrimp in the UK. In some parts of the US, British usage applies: all shrimp other than tiny ones are called prawns; in other parts of the country only very large shrimp are called prawns.

langoustine, lobsterette

With their rather important-sounding name of *Nephrops norvegicus*, LANGOUSTINES, also known as LOBSTERETTES, DUBLIN BAY PRAWNS, and SCAMPI, are the crowning glory of the large shrimp (although they are, in fact, a member of the lobster family). They can grow to 9 oz (250 g) in weight, at which size they do look like small lobsters. Generally I prefer to eat them as they are, served in their shell. But a very simple way to serve cooked langoustines hot is to cut them in half, brush them with melted butter, and broil them briefly. Serve them with hot melted butter and lemon juice. You can add some minced fines herbes (chives, tarragon, chervil, and parsley) to the butter, if desired. A similar species, found on the same sort of ground off the coast of Scotland, is the SQUAT LOBSTER.

deep-sea fish

This is, of course, not a family of fish, but rather a group in which all the species have a sort of similarity, conditioned by the dark depths in which they live. For the most part this means they have enormous eyes with which to catch what little light there is and generally, possibly due to the decompression when raising them to the surface, they always look wan and flabby.

The PATAGONIAN TOOTHFISH, also known as the CHILEAN SEA BASS or ANTARCTIC SEA BASS, comes from the southern oceans of the world, around South Georgia in the Falklands and off the bottom of South America. It always comes in skinned fillets and, though not related to bass at all, it can be cooked in much the same way. There is considerable concern, though, about the long-term stability of stocks of this fish. Like all deep-water fish, there are no restrictions on the fishing of them as they are outside territorial waters.

Other prize fish from these depths are the ORANGE ROUGHY and HOKI (BLUE GRENADIER), though the grenadier, with the other unfortunate name of RAT-TAIL, also provides firm, meaty fillets. The orange roughy is sometimes available fresh in Australia and New Zealand, and can be extremely good, but generally it is sold as skinned and de-fatted fillets, frozen at sea, and it needs a lot of nurturing during cooking to make them interesting.

Other interestingly named and curiously shaped deep-water fish are the RABBITFISH from the Atlantic, the ALFONSINO, and the RIBALDO from the southern Pacific. Alfonsino are abundant in the Pacific Ocean and are very popular in China, where they're known as POH LAP, and Japan, where they're called MADAI. They have thick, scaly skin and white, slightly oily flesh and should be prepared like sea bream. Ribaldo also carries the name of DEEP-SEA COD. While this fish produces thick fillets, it has soft flesh and should be eaten quickly before it deteriorates. It's just the right thing for Thai Fish Cakes (see page 137).

13

drums and croakers

Drums and croakers in North America and the MULLOWAY of Australia are all members of the *Sciaenidae* family. These are distinguished by having an internal muscle used to beat the swim bladder, producing a sound described as either a drumming or croaking that can sometimes even be heard from land. By far the greatest variety of species occurs in North America.

On the East Coast the best eating varieties are the WEAKFISH and the RED DRUM. The weakfish weighs on average 1 to 6 lb (450 g to 2.75 kg). They are either sold whole or in fillets and have white, sweet, and finely textured flesh. The flesh is fragile and the fish needs to be iced quickly after capture. The roe are particularly well favored, too. Weakfish and a closely related fish, the SPOTTED or SPECKLED SEATROUT (also known as the SPOTTED SQUETEAGUE), are often just called trout in the southern states, which can be confusing to those used to the sea-going trout of the salmon family. Highly regarded relations to the weakfish and spotted seatrout are the CORVINAS of Central America.

RED DRUM, sometimes called REDFISH, is caught along the south Atlantic and Gulf coasts. It has moist, white, and heavy-flaked flesh. The best drums from the Pacific are the WHITE SEA BASS from California and the SILVER PERCH, which only grows to about 2¼ lb (1 kg) in size and is therefore a tasty, pan-sized fish. On the East Coast there's also the ATLANTIC CROAKER, which has lean, white meat, and the TOTUAVA, the largest of the drums, which is always sold in steak form for grilling or broiling.

mulloway

Similar species to the drums occur in Australia with the MULLOWAY, the JEWFISH (incorrectly known in the past as the CROAKER or DRUM), and the BLACK JEWFISH (previously known as the SPOTTED CROAKER). These are large fish, common on both eastern and western coasts and usually sold in fillet form. Though not related, I find the flesh of the mulloway similar in texture to the sea bass, and often recommend it when suggesting alternative fish. It's not a commercial fish, being regarded more as a prestige angling fish, but I've written a recipe for Mulloway with Asparagus and a Cream and Caviar Sauce on page 145.

eel and eel-like fish

It is small wonder that the FRESHWATER EEL turns up looking remarkably similar all the world over, when you consider the enormous distances they migrate from the world's seas to rivers, and back again. The EUROPEAN EEL, *Anguilla*, and the AMERICAN EEL, *Anguilla rostrata*, are both born in the Sargasso Sea, which is east of Florida, and, as ELVERS, spend 3 years swimming to Europe or 1 year swimming to North America. The freshwater eels of Australia and New Zealand, the LONGFIN EEL and SHORTFIN EEL, are born in the Coral Sea and take a year to swim to the rivers of eastern Australia and New Zealand.

The eating qualities of eel fall into the three distinct eras in their lives. As elvers, they can fetch a small fortune during the short European season in early March. They are served up by the Spanish in tiny, piping-hot *cazuelas* with olive oil and garlic. The elvers that get away grow into browny-yellow adult eels and it is in this phase that most of them are caught. Then as they start their journey back to the Sargasso Sea to spawn and die, they become more pointed. Having become very fatty, they now stop eating and become sleeker and silvery, ready for the change of habitat on the long voyage home. These SILVER EELS are the best eating and favored by eel smokers for their quality and delicious fat content. Indeed, it is the fattiness of eels that makes them so special—it is of a purity and tastiness unequaled and the recipe for Stir-Fried Eel with Black Beans on page 125 reveals this. The Chinese are the true masters of eel cooking.

moray eel

The other two main types of eel are the Mediterranean MORAY EEL and the CONGER EEL. Moray eel is much sought-after, being firm and almost like Dover sole in quality. There's a mosaic from Pompeii in the National Archeological Museum in Naples, Italy, which shows a selection of the Romans' best-loved Mediterranean fish, including the yellow-speckled moray eel. And it still looks as fresh and ready to be cooked as if it had been caught yesterday. It is a superb fish, firm-fleshed and fresh-tasting and so much more interesting than the conger eel.

conger eel

This appears all over the world in slightly different forms. It's a big, fierce beast and generally caught on a line. Few seem to cook it except for Europeans—notably the northern Spanish, the Bretons of France, and the Cornish of England. It's a common ingredient in Bouillabaisse (see recipe on page 102) and the fish stew Cotriade from Brittany (see page 108). We use it as an essential ingredient in our fish soup (see page 100). I once created a recipe for a pot roast or Poêle of Conger (see page 123) of which I'm still very fond. I wrap the eel in caul fat and cook it in a heavy, lidded casserole with root vegetables.

lamprey

A brief mention must also be made of this eel-like fish that inhabits the estuarine waters of northern Europe. It also lives in American waters, but it's not esteemed, possibly because of its rather horrifying way of feeding: It attaches itself to another fish with the sucking disk, which it has instead of a mouth, bores a hole through the skin with its rasp-like teeth, and sucks the blood out—which, incidentally, doesn't always kill the fish. You sometimes catch a fish, particularly salmon, with a lamprey scar on it. The classic lamprey dish is Lamproie à la Bordelaise, where it is stewed in red wine. Lampreys have no scales and their bones are more like the cartilage in a shark.

elongated fish

There is, of course, no such scientific family as elongated fish, but it seemed an apt grouping of fish that stand out in markets all over the world by virtue of their sinuousness, and which are all treated in much the same way.

barracuda

All barracuda (and there are about six types found in temperate and tropical waters around the world) are what I would call medium quality fish: firm, mild-flavored, with a medium fat content. Because the fish are big, they are free from irritating small bones and are commonly sold in fillet form or in steaks. But beware: Barracuda spoils quickly, so cook it within 24 hours of buying it. Because they're not fantastically well flavored, they are ideal in robustly flavored dishes such as fish curries and habañero-pepper-hot Caribbean dishes. Apart from their cooking qualities, they are thoroughly interesting fish. Fierce, streamlined killers, they have the most amazing array of needle-like teeth, each one of which has its own hole on the opposing jaw, thus allowing the barracuda to close its mouth completely and grip its prey with no chance of escaping. The GREAT BARRACUDA is the biggest fish, reaching up to 6½ feet (2 meters) in length. Unfortunately the larger fish—anything over 5 lb (2.5 kg)—can carry the toxin ciguatera, though these fish are confined to the warmer waters of the western Atlantic, from Florida down to the Caribbean. The toxins, which appear to develop in the fish from eating a type of algae called benthic alga, have a 12 percent fatality rate in unfortunate consumers, because cooking does not destroy the toxins. Fortunately, the toxin doesn't appear in the most popular barracuda for eating, the PACIFIC BARRACUDA or YELLOWTAIL BARRACUDA. The similar STRIPED SEAPIKE from Southeast Asia, the Pacific, and Australia can carry the toxin, but this is rare.

seafood families

silver scabbardfish

I first came upon the SILVER SCABBARDFISH (also called CUTLASS FISH) in the early 80s, in the fish market in Mapusa in Goa, India. I'd never seen anything like them before. Now they're common in specialist fish markets such as Billingsgate in Britain. Back then, though, they looked like strange creatures with their dusty, stainless-steel-like skin, long, flat, sword-shaped bodies, and frightening array of needle-sharp teeth. All scabbardfish are, in fact, very good eating, having firm, white meat that's coarse-textured but delicately flavored, like eels. The tail sections are hard work to eat, being more bone than anything else, but sections of the body are good baked, broiled, pan-fried, or used in soups and stews.

A similar species in the Atlantic, the BLACK SCABBARDFISH, is considered a great delicacy by the Portuguese. It is caught off the island of Madeira at a depth of over 3,280 feet (1000 meters). Fishing for them is a wonder of skill and tradition: the long lines have to be dyed black with a dye made from the bark of a particular Madeiran tree. The fish are fearsome-looking—shiny and black with fierce teeth and vengeful eyes—which might explain why they are of little importance elsewhere.

SOUTHERN FROSTFISH and RIBBON FISH are two other names for the same fish found in Australia and New Zealand, where they are caught as a by-catch of trawling for demersal (bottom-feeding) fish.

garfish

The other main fish in this "elongated" family is the garfish, *Belone belone*. Very similar species occur in northern Europe, Australia, and New Zealand, though the European variety is perhaps more exotic due to its bones being of a bright green hue. These are said to make the fish less popular—I suppose people think they might be poisonous, but this is not so. Their flesh is excellent, firm, fresh-tasting, and slightly oily. It's not a fish that you're likely to get from fishmongers in Britain, but in Australia it's much more common and there they are sold whole or as butterfly fillets—still joined along the back.

A similar fish, which is often considered one and the same, is the NEEDLEFISH, SAURY, or SKIPPER, *Scomberesox saurus*, called BALAOU or AIGUILLE DE MER in French. Though this fish is most common in the Atlantic, west from Madeira across to the Caribbean, where it is eaten fried or grilled, it also swims as far north as Norway in the summer. It's popular in Denmark, fried and served with a sauce verte and boiled potatoes.

Lastly there's the BARRACOUTA, from Australia and New Zealand. With soft, light-tasting flesh, it was widely used in the fish-and-chip trade there, but has largely been replaced by other fish such as flathead and flake (the common name for the GUMMY SHARK and SCHOOL SHARK).

flatfish

In the waters off Great Britain, we have the greatest range of flatfish anywhere in the world and, unfortunately for the rest of the world, the two best flatfish, the DOVER SOLE and TURBOT, occur only on the eastern side of the Atlantic and the Mediterranean.

Flatfish are ideal for those who don't like bones —there are none in the fillets. Being of a largely sedentary nature, all flatfish have delicate white flesh made from muscle used to long inactivity with occasional bursts of energy. Having observed the farming of both turbot and halibut, I would say that they are ideally suited for aquaculture since most of their life is spent motionless on the sea bed, almost camouflaged under the sand. They are waiting for food, which, when it swims nearby, is eaten with great alacrity.

All flatfish begin life as conventional round fish, but, as they grow, the eyes migrate to either the left or right side of the fish, enabling them to see in all directions when on the sea bed. The top and bottom of a flatfish are therefore the two flanks, not the back and belly. Left-sided flatfish are called sinistral and right-sided fish dextral. Most flatfish are right-handed; the left-sided ones are TURBOT, BRILL, MEGRIM, SCALDFISH, and TOPKNOT.

Nowhere in the naming of fish are the common names more confusing than with flatfish. The name of Dover for the most exquisite of soles has nothing to do with its habitation: historically, Dover was where the fish for the London market were landed. Also, the name DOVER SOLE, *Solea solea*, can mean either the EUROPEAN SOLE or PACIFIC FLOUNDER, *Microstomus pacificus*. In fact, this last is a deep-water flatfish that can reach up to 10 lb (4.5 kg); because it is especially slimy, it is only marketed in fillet form. The alternative name for Dover sole, ENGLISH SOLE, doesn't help either, as this is also the name of a good quality flounder, *Parophrys ventulus*, found all the way from northern Mexico to Alaska. TURBOT, *rhombus maximus*, is similarly difficult. Its name in Europe (it's turbot in French, too), is also used for several species of Pacific flounder.

turbot

Turbot is possibly the best tasting fish in the world. It has the perfect combination of firm, thick fillets of moist, white fish. The texture is dense and slightly gelatinous, which means that it remains juicy after cooking and is never dry tasting. It is particularly suited to cooking on the bone in steak or "tronçon" form, cut from good, large fish, weighing from 6½ to 18 lb (3 to 8 kg) so that the pieces are nice and thick. This is one of the few fish I can cook with confidence as the main course for a banquet.

I prefer this exquisite fish served in a simple form, perhaps just broiled, with hollandaise sauce and a slice of lemon. I don't think turbot under 2¼ lb (1 kg) in weight—often called CHICKEN TURBOT—are very interesting. The smallest size worth cooking whole would be about 4½ lb (2 kg). One of the pleasures of eating whole turbot is the gelatinous, fatty flesh near to the side fins, which will have been removed if the fish is filleted.

The price of turbot is now heading into the same bracket as lobster—but deservedly so—and it's rare to find it anywhere else in the world other than Europe. What is sold as "turbot" in the US, for example, is unlikely to be the real thing, but rather the less good GREENLAND TURBOT.

dover sole

Filleting is a fate that falls to far too many DOVER SOLES, which would be better left whole. There are surely no better pan-sized fish than Dover soles when skinned and fried whole à la meunière (dusted with seasoned flour) and finished with a little beurre noisette and lemon (see page 181). An ideal-sized flatfish for eating whole weighs 10 oz to 1¼ lb (300 to 550 g). Larger Dover soles are cheaper than the single-portion-sized ones and produce excellent, firm white fillets. Dover soles are not at their best when eaten immediately after they have been caught, as their natural firmness makes them too tough—they need one or two days after catching for the flavor and texture of the flesh to develop. I always think that eating a Dover sole is like eating a perfect steak. Everything about it is just simple, uncomplicated pleasure, even down to the fact that the fillets are easy to lift off, as the skeleton stays intact after cooking. No wonder they are just as popular in New York as in London and Paris.

flounder, plaice, and dabs

PLAICE and EUROPEAN FLOUNDER have a flavor similar to Dover sole, but, unlike them, are best eaten as soon as possible after being caught, since the fresh "ozone" flavor of both fish quickly dissipates. Although they can be served on the bone, I think plaice and European flounder are only worth eating whole when no more than a couple of days old. Otherwise, they are best filleted, breaded, and deep-fried. This cooking method nurtures the flavor of slightly dull fish. Small whole DABS are good cooked like this, too, and served with tartar sauce.

The Danish have an appetizing way with whole flounder, plaice, or dabs, which they call

13

Bakskuld: they lightly brine the fish, then hot-smoke them and fry them in butter. It's a specialty of Esbjerg in West Jutland, and excellent served with iced aquavit or beer.

In the US, the name flounder refers to a number of fish of rather better eating quality than our European flounder, all of them belonging to the *pleuronectididae* family and many of them called sole. The WINTER FLOUNDER (or BLACKBACK), considered to be the best tasting of the American flounders, has very sweet, fine-flaked, firm, white meat. Although on average they weigh 1 to 2 lb (450 to 900 g), the biggest can weigh up to 6½ lb (3 kg); these are often called sea flounders to distinguish them from the smaller bay fish. The SUMMER FLOUNDER, or FLUKE, also has an excellent flavor. It is usually on the market weighing 1 to 5 lb (450 g to 2.25 kg), but can reach up to 19½ or 22½ lb (9 or 10 kg). SAND DABS, which can be very tiny indeed, are a favorite on the West Coast.

lemon sole

British LEMON SOLE has a longer-lasting flavor than European flounders, plaice, and dabs, and is thus a better bet for broiling whole. Other good pan-sized flatfish in Britain are MEGRIM SOLE (or WHIFF) and WITCH SOLES or TORBAY SOLES, both of which are rather underrated and are therefore good value.

The name lemon sole in the US is a market name for another winter flounder and no more accurate a name than the British name for the fish because it is not a true sole at all. Other good quality American flounders commonly—and incorrectly—called sole include the GRAY SOLE on the East Coast and PETRALE SOLE and REX SOLE on the West Coast.

brill

Brill is similar in shape to turbot, though without the little, hard nodules on the darker side. It tends not to be so big—I've never seen one bigger than 11 lb (5 kg)—and is more oval in shape. It, too, has a great flavor, although softer and less dense in texture than turbot. Like turbot, though, the bigger the fish, the better the eating. I tend to cook brill with slightly more complicated accompaniments than turbot because it is not quite as special. I note that in Gilbert and Sullivan's operetta, *HMS Pinafore*, turbot is described as "ambitious brill."

halibut

Halibut, though a lovely fish, is not quite as fine as turbot. It's the largest of all flatfish and the only one to occur on both sides of the Atlantic—and, indeed, in a very similar form in the Pacific, too. Whole fish can reach up to 250 lb (100 kg) and are therefore always sold in fillet or steak form. It is a remarkably thick, meaty fish, the cooking of which needs to be done with care to avoid dryness. I have a recipe (see page 183) that calls for the halibut to be very gently poached in olive oil, which I think gives it a soft and melting texture. This is similar to the method of slow-cooking salmon in the oven, from the famous Japanese-Australian chef, Tetsuya Wakuda. An interesting fact about farmed halibut is that in the cold months, the fish tend to go into limbo. Fish farmers have discovered that putting a few cod in the tanks encourages the halibut to start feeding earlier in the year. Presumably the cod that accompany halibut in the wild are harbingers of spring.

groupers, sea bass, and barramundi

To those of us living in Europe, groupers represent an exotic family of fish, conjuring up an image of the southern states of the US and the Pacific coast, the Caribbean, and Australasia. The reason for this is that this fish does not occur in any significant numbers in European waters, except for the MEDITERRANEAN GROUPER, (the MÉROU), known in the Britain as the BLACK GROUPER.

Groupers have slightly squat, deep bodies and tend to be rather round and chunky-looking. They are generally excellent eating, and the plus point about them is their versatility: You can grill them or bake them whole, but they also lend themselves to being filleted and served with delicate sauces like the cream and caviar sauce on page 145. Or, try a simple sauce vierge—a warm olive-oil dressing spiked with tomatoes, olives, anchovies, and garlic—as served with the red mullet on page 173. These are customer-friendly fish—they look colorful and attractive, they've got plenty of flavor, and you don't need to be a trained chef to cook them with success.

You can now buy very well-flavored groupers in London. If it's not a fish you are familiar with and you're wondering what to do with it, a tip is to cook it in exactly the same way as you would a sea bass, as they are closely related.

By far the biggest variety of groupers live in American waters. The largest is the ATLANTIC JEWFISH, which can reach weights of up to 675 lb (300 kg); these are now seriously under threat from over-fishing. Groupers are most common around coral reefs and the rocky outcrops of the North American continental shelf. While not so susceptible to trawling, they have suffered considerably from hook-and-line fishing, being large and therefore prized by amateur anglers. A further twist to their fate is that they are hermaphrodites, i.e. they all start life as females and become males as they grow larger.

Over-fishing has led to an acute shortage of males as these are the larger fish and therefore more attractive to anglers. The most popular are the RED GROUPER, SPOTTED CABRILLA, and the YELLOWMOUTH GROUPER. The red grouper can weigh up to 50 lb (22.5 kg), but the average weight in the market is 5 to 15 lb (2.25 to 6.75 kg). Unless you want to feed eight or more people, the most convenient way of buying it is in steak or fillet form. The meat is firm, white, and sweet and is comparable with the far more expensive snapper. A great advantage of the flesh is that it is free from intermuscular bones; however, the skin tends to be tough and strongly flavored so it is usually removed before cooking. The flesh is also often cubed, coated in batter, and deep-fried, or used in the fish chowders of the southern states.

The BLACK SEA BASS, closely related to the grouper, is a very popular fish in the US, and is especially popular with the Chinese and Italians. It has firm, white meat with a delicate flavor—probably produced by its mainly crustacean diet—and can be cooked using most methods.

In Australia, there is a much smaller family of groupers that inhabits the tropical and sub tropical waters, and these are generally called ROCK CODS. The most common members are the CORAL COD, COMMON CORAL TROUT, ESTUARY ROCK COD, and BLACKTIP ROCK COD, this last considered to be one of Australia's best eating fish, with a distinctively flavored, firm, white flesh. But all of these groupers are good eating, with wide and thick fillets.

sea bass

The EUROPEAN SEA BASS is the most sought-after perch species for cooking. A very attractive fish, it has beautiful silvery skin but evil spines, which can cause very painful wounds. It has a dense, slightly soft-textured flesh and a very delicate, superior flavor. It's now farmed widely, though most farmed bass are still too small to be at their best. A good-sized fish is 3 lb 5 oz (1.5 kg). If sold intact, remove the guts as soon as possible, as the stomach is prone to bursting—this would taint the delicate flesh.

The WRECKFISH (also known as STONE BASS) appears in Cornwall in the summer months. Apparently at that time of year the fish follows floating flotsam toward the north from warmer, more southerly waters. It appears on both sides of the Atlantic, but it is a case of feast or famine: you might get two weeks of nothing but wreckfish, and then not see another one for three years! Its flavor is similar to other bass and I've always found it very good value. The same fish in Australia and New Zealand, HAPUKU, is among the most highly priced fish there. What could be a better example of the global nature of so many species of fish?

One of the most prized fish in the US is the STRIPED BASS (also called ROCKFISH). I once caught a 26-lb (12-kg) striped bass in Chesapeake Bay, which left me astonished as to how big this excellent fish grows—and apparently it was not a particularly big one! This was testimony to the successful conservation of a fish, the angling for which is far more profitable to the local community than the previous commercial fishery, which hounded the striped bass close to extinction. Like all perches, this is not a particularly oily fish, falling somewhere between cod and salmon, and it's therefore very versatile since it can be cooked in the same way as either.

barramundi

In Australia, the BARRAMUNDI (also called GIANT SEA PERCH) has an idiosyncratic shape, with a head that is disproportionately large in relation to its deep body. As with sea bass, it is now widely farmed, but is disappointing because of the small size at which the fish are sold. A good-sized fish is 4½ lb (2 kg). The wild fish are very well flavored, with thick, soft fillets that are good cooked in any way. Although a marine species, it is also found in the freshwater creeks and rivers of northern Australia where, presumably, it goes to spawn.

the herring family

herring

The maritime countries of northern Europe have made use of the HERRING in as many diverse culinary ways as the rural people of France have used the pig. Just think of the different ways that herring is served up: kippers, bloaters, buckling, red herring, roll mops, Bismark herring, pickled herring, matjes herring. It's a shame, though, that our taste for oily fish such as herring seems to have disappeared because, fresh out of the sea, there's probably no better tasting fish. It is also becoming increasingly clear that the old adage "Fish is good for you" is true: The herring is rich in beneficial omega-3 polyunsaturated fatty acids, which appear to lower the risk of heart disease. Many people think that the increase in heart disease is due to a decrease in oily fish consumption and point out that the Japanese, great fish eaters, have a far lower rate of heart disease than people in the West. It's also believed that omega-3 is an essential building block for the development of a fetus in the womb.

Though the same species of herring stretches right across the North Atlantic, there are subtle regional differences. NORWEGIAN or ICELANDIC HERRING are those favored by fish

smokers because the larger fish, which weigh about 8 oz (225 g), look more impressive and the greater fat content and bulk leads to a moister product. The BALTIC HERRING is smaller—on average about 5 oz (150 g)—than the Atlantic herring, as are the herring from the North Sea. Wet-cured herring from the Baltic, however, made from smaller, leaner fish, have a distinctive flavor.

There is also an important herring fishery on the Pacific Coast and in Canada, where the fish can weigh up to 1½ lb (675 g), though the average is about 10 oz (300 g). This is the main source of our herring roe, for which there's a recipe on page 159.

One of the problems with cooking all oily fish is that they smell. When perfectly fresh the smell is very appetizing, but there's no denying that as the fish goes stale the smell can become quite off-putting. Assuming you've bought the freshest herring, I think that broiling them whole is preferable to any other way of cooking. But I also like them filleted (it's the bones that so many people find objectionable in herring), dusted with coarsely ground oats, and pan-fried in oil and butter with a slice of bacon.

For a description of the best possible way of eating herring, I offer this account of a Lowestoft drift-trawler crew's breakfast—at which the average consumption was nine herring per person. I found it in an old book called *The Fish Retailer and his Trade* by William Wood, published in 1933: "There is tea, bread and butter in plenty and a wolfish appetite. The herrings have been taken straight from the net and gutted, beheaded and the tails cut off, then they have been slashed across the back with a large jack knife and this slashing seems to hold the secret of the success of this cooking because it allows the boiling fat, into which the herring is plunged, to get a real hold of the flesh. When the cooking is finished, in a few minutes, there is a huge tin dishful of the herrings, crisped and browned and with a flavour that is never approached on shore."

cured herrings

These products are more important economically than the fresh fish to the herring fishing countries.

BISMARK HERRING are filleted, unskinned herring that are cured in vinegar, brine, and sugar, and packed with slices of onion.

BLOATERS are whole, ungutted (and therefore plump-looking), salted herring that are cold-smoked for just 12 hours, leaving them with a slightly gamy flavor.

BUCKLING are hot-smoked, headless, salted herring, available either gutted or ungutted. The smoking renders them ready to eat, like smoked trout, for example with bread and butter, lemon, and horseradish cream.

HARENG SAUR are the French equivalent

of kippers: gutted and salted aboard the boat, the fish are then smoked at a factory close to the landing point.

KIPPERS are fat herring, split from head to tail and air-dried, then cold-smoked.

MATJES HERRING, or "MAIDEN HERRING," are young herring that have been skinned and hand-filleted, then mild-cured in sugar, salt, vinegar, and spices.

PICKLED HERRING is merely the term for gutted herring that has been dry-salted in barrels.

ROLLMOPS are Bismark herring fillets rolled around a pickle or onion slices and secured with a wooden toothpick.

RED HERRING, called GENDARME in French, are little used these days. They are salted and long-smoked whole herring, which turn a deep red color after about three weeks. They were preserved for storing in tropical countries without refrigeration.

sardines and pilchards

Much of what I've said about herring applies to sardines, pilchards, and sprats as well. SARDINES have a certain cachet in Britain, associated as they are with chargrilling and robust local wine around the Mediterranean. But PILCHARDS are devilishly difficult to sell here, even though an enterprising pilchard buyer in Cornwall has renamed them "Cornish sardines" (pilchards are, in fact, adult sardines). The market for sardines for grilling is gradually growing in Britain. Wouldn't it be nice if there were small beach cafés all along the British coast serving little more than local grilled fish? At Saint Jean-de-Luz near Biarritz, one of France's main sardine ports, there's a restaurant that specializes in only two dishes—grilled sardines or grilled tuna with local Basque wine. It's always packed, you get a salad, sardines, and fries. What more could a man ask for?

In my first TV series, I made a film of my son grilling sardines on a beach near my home. I meanwhile drank some red wine and made a tomato, red onion, and basil salad to go with the sardines. I still regard that day as the epitome of what I like best about eating fish.

anchovies and sprats

It's extremely rare to get fresh ANCHOVIES from fishmongers; they're usually all destined for processing. Like SPRATS, they're a bit too small for most people to bother with and, unlike whitebait they can't be eaten whole and are therefore a bit fiddly. There's a technique for eating small oily fish though, which is to nibble along the backbone, then more or less suck the fillets off the bones, almost like a horse nuzzling at oats.

Like all oily fish, anchovies spoil very quickly and so should be iced immediately after they are caught. Indeed, the reason that the flesh around the gut cavities of herring, sardines, and anchovies is often disintegrating when you buy them is because the guts have started to ferment on board the trawlers. For perfect condition, the temperature of oily fish like these should never rise above the temperature of the sea. Sprats keep better in this respect than anchovies, herring, and sardines. If you're lucky enough to get fresh anchovies in good condition, cook them in the same way as you would sardines, or try the excellent Italian recipe for marinated anchovies on page 161. There's a suggestion for a dish in Jane Grigson's *Fish Cookery*, Penguin Books 1973, that strikes me as worth seeking out; it's from Ischia in the Bay of Naples. The anchovies are boned and baked in olive oil flavored with oregano, then lemon juice is squeezed over just before serving.

shad

The SHAD is a similar fish to the herring but much larger and much more bony. The wild fish in Europe tend to weigh about 3 lb (1.3 kg), but commonly reach 5 lb (2.25 kg) in North America. Each fillet has three lines of bones running down it, so shad needs to be dealt with by an accomplished filleter. This can be the only explanation why the fish is not more popular than it is because its taste ranks with the best salmon. The best time to eat shad is in May, when it appears in estuaries in Europe and North America, before going upriver to spawn; you can also buy farmed shad in the Garonne region in France. Cook it in any way that you like to eat salmon. If you're lucky enough to get hold of the great roe of the female shad—described by an excellent seafood cook, Mark Bittman, as "the foie gras of the fish world"—it should be dusted in seasoned flour, gently sautéed, and served still pink.

Not considered great eating in the northern hemisphere, the TARPON is esteemed in West Africa. A southern member of the herring family, it can reach up to 6 feet (2 meters) in length and is a great game fish. The roe are much enjoyed across the Atlantic in Central America.

jacks, pompanos, and trevallys

jacks

The meat of all jacks is dark since they are pelagic (surface swimmers), and travel long distances. Like many other large pelagic fish, such as tuna and swordfish, they should be bled after capture by cutting off or slashing the tail. Jacks are not well represented in Europe, though a species of HORSE MACKEREL (also known as SCAD) occurs all around Britain; it is primarily used as lobster bait. Jacks fetch low prices because of their exterior of

bony platelets; however, with these platelets removed they are rather good cooked à la meunière (see page 181).

A close relative, the BLUEFISH, swims in the Mediterranean as well as the Atlantic. In fact, being a long-distance pelagic fish, it also appears in Australia, where it is called TAILOR. This is a great fighting fish and a voracious eater. Although it is very nutritious, bluefish does not have a good shelf-life. Like other members of this group, it also benefits from having the dark protein line along the fillet removed, since it's rather harsh-tasting. Bluefish is a bit like bonito in flavor. Both fish have dark and coarse flesh and neither is as fine tasting as tuna. Like bonito, too, bluefish is much better undercooked and suits strong accompaniments such as garlic, soy, ginger, and chile.

With the exception of the POMPANO, jacks are not important commercially in America. This is because many of them are not particularly good eating, and some of the larger tropical species occasionally suffer from ciguatera poisoning (see page 235). By far the best eating is the pompano, which is normally sold as a whole fish weighing 1½ to 3 lb (750 g to 1.5 kg) or as skin-on fillets. Its flesh is white but oily, meaty, and sweet with an exquisite flavor. I think it's best broiled, though I once had it braised with tomato, garlic, fish stock, and epazote—a rather pungent herb—in Vera Cruz, Mexico, which was startlingly good.

The AMBERJACK is quite common in the southern states and, when smoked, is quite a delicacy in Florida. Mention, too, should be made of the CREVALLE JACK, a member of the *Caranx* species, which is found in all tropical and sub-tropical seas in the world and is known in Australian waters as a TREVALLY.

trevally

The fillet of this fish family is dark and the darker meat running along the center of the fillet, under the skin, is best removed as its flavor is quite overpowering. There are quite a number of species of trevallys in Indo-Pacific waters; the best-tasting for me are the BLACK POMFRET and the YELLOWTAIL KINGFISH.

cobia

The COBIA, also known as the BLACK KINGFISH, is not truly a jack, but in a family all on its own. It is a prime game fish that is also fished for commercially and is very fine-tasting. It has a very tough skin so it is usually sold in fillet form, and is also often sold smoked.

mahimahi

In a class of its own is the MAHIMAHI, also called the DOLPHINFISH or DORADO. It's much enjoyed all around the Mediterranean,

where it is known as LAMPUKI in Malta and LAMPUGA in Spain. It is very popular on both the Pacific and Atlantic coasts of the US too, and my recipe (see page 138) was inspired by a recent visit to the US and Mexico. Like all the better quality members of this group, mahimahi is excellent served raw as *sashimi*.

mackerel and tuna

Like the jacks and trevallys above, mackerel and tuna are pelagic, long-roaming fish that have dark, oily meat as a result. All species of mackerel and tuna are popular and widely fished commercially, so rather than describe each species, I have grouped them into three broad categories for cooking and eating purposes.

small mackerel

All these small mackerels—the ATLANTIC MACKEREL, CHUB MACKEREL from the Mediterranean, and the BLUE MACKEREL from Australian and New Zealand waters—average out at less than 1 lb 2 oz (500 g) in weight. As with herring, mackerel have to be jumping fresh, and I prefer them broiled or pan-fried. But I do like poached fillets too, and when cooked like this they can take a sauce with some butter in it, as I've suggested for the recipe on page 158. Small mackerel can be cured in many of the ways that herring can—salted or smoked. Try preserving them as Gravlax (see page 66), to produce the Swedish Gravad Mackerel. Like all members of the mackerel and tuna family, these small mackerel are excellent sliced and served raw as sashimi. They are also very good used in an escabèche (see page 163).

large mackerel

The next group comprises all the mackerel ranging from 2¼ to 12½ lb (1 to 5 kg). These are the CERO, CHUB MACKEREL, KING MACKEREL (also called KINGFISH), SPANISH MACKEREL, WAHOO, FRIGATE MACKEREL, KAWAKAWA, SPOTTED MACKEREL, and the BONITO. These again are all good eating, but the flesh tends to be coarser than that of the tunas and doesn't keep as well. While they can be successfully broiled, I think they are particularly good cooked in olive oil confits (see page 144) or poached in oil (as I've done with the halibut on page 183), as well as baked in a tandoori oven or used in Goan-style curries.

large tuna

These are the BLUEFIN TUNA, YELLOWFIN TUNA, SKIPJACK TUNA, and BIGEYE or AHI TUNA, which fetch high prices for the Japanese sashimi market. They are available in all fish shops as dark red, meaty loins, or as steaks that are good for searing or pan-grilling, as in the recipe on page 119. The ALBACORE, also called LONGFIN TUNA, is in this category too, but its meat is much lighter in color, and often called the "chicken of the sea," or WHITE TUNA. It is to my mind a revelation when grilled. Unlike bluefin tuna, it is not in danger of being over-fished.

Tuna belly, which is rich in fat, is much esteemed by the Japanese. In sashimi (their elegant presentation of sliced raw fish) or sushi (vinegared rice topped with raw fish), it provides a flavorful contrast to the leaner loin meat. Being an oily fish, it also lends itself to various types of curing. It is occasionally smoked, though I don't think this works very well. But, when cured and dried and then very thinly sliced, it makes a great addition to crunchy salads made with vegetables such as bulb fennel and Belgian endive. And the Spanish blocks of dried tuna, called MOJAMA, are excellent.

monkfish and stargazers

MONKFISH is in a group of its own—there is no other fish quite like it—although there is a very similar species in North America, sometimes called GOOSEFISH or ANGLERFISH, and another, STARGAZER, in Australia and New Zealand. Monkfish is very popular in these places, just as it is in Europe, because it satisfies a universal desire for firm, meaty, boneless fish. Its flavor is not pronounced, but the small tails have a sweet freshness that, combined with the texture, make it one of my favorite fish. It's particularly suited to pan-grilling and is also great in curries because it remains intact after cooking.

Once the fish is skinned, you'll find the fillets are encased in a thin membrane. You need to remove this or it will cause the tails to distort during cooking (see page 62).

WEEVER is an underrated fish in all parts of the world except for the Mediterranean. Weever has an excellent flavor and firm texture, almost on a par with Dover sole. Maybe its lack of popularity is due to the poisonous spines on the gill covers and the first spine on the dorsal fin, which can give you a sting that's a great deal worse than that of a bee. The pain lasts for about 12 hours, which accounts for the saying, "It's the following tide that takes the pain away."

mullets

red mullet

There's really no similarity between red and gray mullet except for the name and the fact that they can be cooked in much the same way. Both fish appear all over the world. By far my favorite is the RED MULLET, particularly

those species from the Mediterranean. All fish that live on a diet of crustaceans have a flavor somewhat echoing that of shellfish, but none more so than the red mullet. It has a perfect flake and skin that, when broiled, smells of rock pools. If you are lucky enough to get an ungutted red mullet, the liver is something of a delicacy, too. Indeed, the first red mullet I ever ate was broiled with its liver intact; in this form it is known as "becasse de mer." Like the woodcock, it doesn't have a gall bladder, so provided the intestine is removed, the rest will not taste bitter.

The red mullet has the same name in Australia, but is often also called GOATFISH there—this is also the most common name for a very similar species of mullet in North America. There are five different species on both the Atlantic and Pacific coasts of the US, but they are most commonly found in Florida and the Caribbean.

gray mullet

The GRAY MULLET is generally not so well regarded around the world. Unfortunately, they have a reputation for feeding on mud and other undesirable material in estuaries, a habit that is reflected in the flavor. But the mullet in the bays around Padstow, which have a little golden flash on the gill cover, are as good to eat as sea bass.

The gray mullet is either called by this name or STRIPED MULLET in the US. In *The Encyclopedia of Fish Cookery* by A. J. McClane—an excellent book and one that I've referred to a lot when writing this section—the author describes an attempt in Florida to increase gray mullet sales as follows: "The State of Florida chose the seemingly romantic name 'Lisa' to promote sales of the fish. This was no more comprehensible than a plague of bullfrogs. The consumer invariably asked, 'What is a Lisa?' and when the retailer explained that it was a mullet, nothing was accomplished, except to suggest that the fish had to be disguised."

Gray mullet is known as MULLET, SEA MULLET, or DIAMOND-SCALE MULLET in Australia and New Zealand.

puffer fish

I must confess that I have never eaten PUFFER FISH, but I'd certainly like to. Apparently it's one of the most delicate fish in the sea, the creamy white meat being similar to a plump frog's leg.

Puffers, which are known as SEA SQUABS or BLOWFISH in North America, are found from Cape Cod down to Florida, but the largest number of species (38) is found around Japan, and it is from here that the fame of the world's most poisonous fish stems. It seems that the more fatalities that are caused by pufferfish, or FUGU,

as it is known there, the more popular it becomes. There are on average 70 deaths a year, usually in rural areas where people prepare the fish at home. The poison, found in the gut, liver, ovaries, and skin of the fish, is called tetrotoxin. It's similar to curare (the poison used by the Amazonian Indians to tip their arrows), and is 1,250 times deadlier than cyanide.

Kitaoji Rosanjin, the famous Japanese potter and gourmet, wrote: "The taste of fugu is incomparable; if you eat it three or four times you are enslaved; anyone who declines it for fear of death is a really pitiable person." A chef must be licensed to prepare fugu and this requires a written and practical examination that includes eating the fugu he has prepared. Prior to that the chef must have completed at least two years experience working under a master. Death by fugu poisoning is described as terrible: although you can think clearly, you cannot speak or move, and soon cannot breathe. But enthusiasts say consumption of the meat produces a pleasant, warm tingling, a faint echo of the poison. Perhaps eating un-prepared fugu is one of the favored ways of committing hara-kiri (suicide). As the haiku poet Buson wrote:
"I cannot see her tonight.
I have to give her up
So I will eat fugu."

roe fish

Here I've included fish that are most important for their roe (eggs). Some fish, such as LUMPFISH, are only valuable for their roe—which is similar to caviar in appearance, but not in taste—while other fish, such as STURGEON, have tasty flesh as well as roe. Sturgeon has very firm flesh with a high oil content. It is sold in North America as steaks or is preserved in wine vinegar and spices, but it is most often sold smoked.

It is the roe of the BELUGA, OSCIETRA, and SEVRUGA STURGEON that forms the world's most luxurious food—CAVIAR. It is only the sturgeon that live in the Caspian Sea and the rivers that flow into it that matter. Caviar from farmed sturgeon is produced near Bordeaux in France, and in California. Both are good, but bear no comparison to Caspian caviar. The flavor of caviar grows on you: The first time most people taste it it's a little disappointing, but there's something about the salty oiliness of it that makes you give it a second try. And then—like some fiendish drug—it becomes an expensive obsession. Sevruga is the cheapest caviar and Beluga the most expensive, mainly because it comes from the largest of the sturgeons and the eggs are therefore bigger. I think Oscietra is the perfect compromise.

To make caviar, the master caviar-maker

removes the sac of roe from the fish and rubs it through a fine screen, allowing the eggs to pass through whole but removing blood and membrane. The roe is then rinsed and salted. Adding the right amount of salt—between three and five percent—is where the caviar-maker's art lies. The freshest roe requires the least salt and good caviar will always have the label "molossol" or "malossol," which means "little salt." Caviar is now unbelievably expensive due to over-fishing, pollution, and poaching in the Caspian Sea. Let's hope that a recent agreement signed by all the countries that surround the Caspian, prohibiting all open-sea sturgeon fishing (i.e. permitting fishing only in the rivers), can be successfully implemented.

Here are a few tips on how best to enjoy caviar:
• Avoid pasteurized caviar. Only buy fresh and allow about 1 oz (25 g) per person.
• As long as it hasn't been opened, caviar will keep for 6 to 9 months in the coldest part of the refrigerator, but the sooner it's eaten the better.
• Remove the caviar from the refrigerator half an hour before serving. Nestle the can in some crushed ice and use a non-metal spoon to serve it —mother of pearl or even plastic are good—as caviar reacts with metal.
• Serve simply with thin whole-wheat toast, blinis, or good fresh bread.

Some classic accompaniments are blinis brushed with melted butter, or topped with sour cream or crème fraîche. In addition, Russians serve caviar accompanied by minced onions and chopped hard-boiled eggs, both of which are said to bring out the flavor of the fish eggs.

other roe
The roes of some other fish are worthy of note. Both the eggs and the milt of HERRING ROE are delicious. The Japanese lightly salt the roe of the female and use it in sashimi, while the milt, the white seminal fluid of the male, is excellent floured and shallow-fried (see page 159). It's a good idea to disgorge the milt for 10 minutes or so in water, to which lots of lemon juice has been added, before drying and coating it for cooking. I've recently been using lightly smoked herring roe with a lot of success, adding half a teaspoon of it to a cream sauce similar to that on page 145 and serving it with salmon escalopes. I've also mentioned SHAD ROE, sometimes called the "foie gras of the sea," under the entry for the herring family.

If you can get hold of the Greek salted and dried GRAY MULLET ROE (BOTARGO), it is nice sliced into very thin strips and served with olive oil, pepper, and lemon juice as a very pleasant mezze, or added like anchovies to salads to give them piquancy.

SMOKED SALTED COD ROE is now a common substitute for gray mullet roe in the making of the Greek dish, Taramasalata (see page 130).

Lightly salted salmon eggs called KETA are something of a delicacy (see the recipe for Nigiri Sushi on pages 105–6).

salmon and salmon trout

There are six species of SALMON native to the northern hemisphere. There are none in the southern hemisphere, although you wouldn't realize it because the farming of salmon in Tasmania means that ATLANTIC SALMON is just as common there. Atlantic salmon is the fish that is always used for farming. Like it or not, farmed salmon has encouraged more people to eat fish as it is now cheap and readily available. It has lots of flavor and suits cooking in almost any way, though I'm not sure about the current fish-and-chip-shop trend for deep-frying it in batter; it's too oily a fish for that.

There's a great deal of controversy about the farming of salmon because, when it is done unscrupulously, it can have a devastating effect on the wild stocks of other fish as well as salmon, due to the build up of parasites, disease, and chemicals in an overpopulated environment. Some would like to see all salmon farms banned. But when the fish are kept farther out at sea, rather than in the more usual lochs and estuaries, or where the fish densities are kept at a sensible level and the fish are well looked after, far less damage is caused. It is worth paying the price for premium quality farmed salmon, particularly if it is organically farmed. It tastes so much better; the flesh is firmer and not overwhelmingly fatty; and you are less likely to be damaging the environment.

My favorite way to cook salmon and salmon trout is to poach them whole in salted water and serve them with homemade mayonnaise, new potatoes, and a cucumber and mint salad. I'm also particularly fond of seasoning a steak or two of salmon and cooking them gently in butter in a frying pan. I add half a glass of white wine halfway through cooking and let the liquid reduce, then finish the dish with some chopped parsley.

atlantic salmon
WILD ATLANTIC SALMON are still my favorite, but there is a severe shortage, mostly through over-fishing rather than any disasters caused by farming. I mourn the decline of the wild Atlantic salmon and get depressed when I hear that the Rhine in Germany was once teeming with them. We're lucky that we can still buy some wild salmon from the estuary on which our restaurant stands; the lean taste of the wild fish, which has swum so far, is incomparable. Atlantic salmon was also once found in abundance on the east coast of North America, but it has suffered a decline similar to that of the same species in Europe.

pacific salmon
There are six other salmon, all from the Pacific coast of the US, which are in much better shape. The biggest of them all is the CHINOOK SALMON, also called the KING SALMON, which sometimes reaches as much as 125 lb (50 kg). It's a large-flaked fish with a high fat content and soft texture. Next, there's the COHO SALMON, which is smaller—it reaches up to 37½ lb (15 kg). The fillet is lighter in color than the Chinook. The SOCKEYE SALMON's name has nothing to do with the eyes, but is a corruption of an Indian word. Both the male and female sockeye salmon become bright red on spawning. They have very dark, almost orange flesh, with a firm texture and delicate taste. The CHUM SALMON, which weighs up to 37½ lb (15 kg), is, along with pink salmon, cheaper than the others and somewhat coarse in texture. It probably fetches a lower price because its flesh color is often more gray than pink, but it takes to smoking well. The PINK SALMON is the smallest Pacific salmon, never weighing more than 11 lb (5 kg). It is the cheapest salmon of all except the chum, but has a delicate, distinctive flavor and a good pink color.

salmon trout
I'm almost more fond of WILD SALMON TROUT than I am of Atlantic salmon. The small ones that we get at the restaurant, fresh from the sea during the months of May and June, are one of the great pleasures of early summer, as are the spider crabs that arrive on the rocky beaches just below the low-tide mark.

A salmon trout, also known as SEA TROUT, SEWIN, or OCEAN TROUT, is a freshwater brown trout that has gone to sea. On the American West Coast, rainbow trout do the same thing, and are then called STEELHEAD. Why some members of the same species should travel down rivers, through the brackish waters of estuaries, into the sea to feed on shrimp and other crustaceans—which produces the characteristic pink color of the flesh—is unclear. But something in their genetic makeup enables them to develop a silvery sheen and the ability to cope with the osmotic effect of salt in the water. They don't follow the same migratory pattern as salmon, but stay in relatively near-coastal waters before returning up-river to spawn.

Predictably, salmon trout taste somewhere between trout and salmon, being less rich than salmon and slightly less pink. Incidentally, large salmon trout and small salmon look very similar.

The only sure way to tell the difference is to look at the eyes: those of a salmon trout are slightly higher up the head. If you draw an imaginary line from the mouth through to the center of the gill cover, it will bisect the eye of a salmon, but a salmon trout's eye will be above it.

char and smelt

There are a couple of other members of the salmon family that are worthy of note. There are two types of CHAR or ARCTIC CHAR: those that live most of their lives in their sea and swim up northern rivers to spawn, and landlocked char, which can be found in many lakes all over northern Europe (including Lake Windermere in England), Canada, and Alaska. The sea-going variety make by far the best eating and reach up to 30 lb (13 kg) in size. They are fat fish, with firm red flesh when caught in the wild, but less firm or deeply colored when farmed.

The SMELT (also called RAINBOW SMELT or SPARLING), a small member of the salmon family reaching no more than 11 inches (27 cm) in length, is found in both northern Europe and North America. The fish have a characteristic smell of cucumber when very fresh, and generally have light green skin, and soft flesh and bones. They deteriorate incredibly rapidly and like so many oily fish—herring, mackerel, sardines— should be cooked the day they're caught. However, as long as they're chilled straight after catching and frozen soon after, then thawed to a temperature of no more than 34°F (1°C) and cooked from that temperature, they will be almost as good as fresh ones.

The best way to cook the smaller ones is to thread them onto wooden skewers and broil or grill, or fry them in clarified butter. Because of their soft, open texture, they'll take no more than 2 to 3 minutes to cook. They are also particularly nice if left whole, coated in tempura batter, and deep-fried.

smoked salmon

All members of the salmon family can be smoked successfully, but none more so than salmon itself. Cold-smoked salmon, where the fish is subjected to smoke without heat, is now so popular that its luxury status has all but disappeared, and much of the cheap, pre-sliced stuff that you can buy is just pink, flabby, and boring. However, a side of salmon, not necessarily wild, but with a good high fat content, cured maybe with salt and brown sugar and smoked over oak chippings, beech, or whisky barrels for at least 8 hours, is still something very special. Hot-smoked salmon, called BRADAN ROST, is good served on lightly pan-grilled slices of sourdough bread with mixed, small salad leaves and a chive, caper, and crème fraîche dressing.

sea bream, porgies, and snappers

This section looks just at SEA BREAM, not freshwater bream. There are many species, but all bream are firm-fleshed fish, with medium oil content, although smaller ones tend to be a bit bony. They are well-flavored, thanks to a diet of crustaceans, and have a pleasing, compact body shape, which makes them ideal for steaming, broiling, or grilling. One of the unifying features of all bream is that they generally come in one- or two-portion sizes, i.e. 1 lb 2 oz to 2¼ lb (500 g to 1 kg). However, there are plenty of exceptions. I've seen snappers as big as 9 lb (4 kg). Once, while on vacation in Cephalonia, six of us dined on a sumptuous synagrida (the Greek word for the DENTEX), served with Greek salad and potatoes fried in olive oil, and washed down with copious quantities of Robola, a very good local white wine.

red bream

In Padstow, in the 1970s and 80s, we used to have regular landings of RED BREAM, caught very close to the coast near Newquay. They are firm-textured and sweet, with a thick skin and amazingly large scales. Their subtle red color and enormous eyes also make them one of the most attractive fish. I used to serve them baked on a bed of white beans with chile, bay leaf, garlic, olive oil, and orange juice and zest. I recall having a boy working in the kitchen for the summer vacation once. When I asked him to gut the fish, he cut off all their heads, which, owing to the round shape of a bream and his inexperience, meant that half the fillet went with it too. He's now a successful surgeon. Every time I see him he recalls with acute embarrassment the beheading of the red bream. I wish I could go back to those days because there are no red bream left and they were one of my favorite fish.

In fact, all the bream and the closely related PORGY from North America are good eating, but the red bream and the most highly esteemed GILT-HEAD BREAM (daurade in French) are the best in Europe. We buy a lot of local BLACK SEA BREAM, which is reasonably good eating. I like them steamed whole with garlic and ginger, as I've done for the recipe with gray mullet on page 171. And although the scales on bream are always plate-like, once they're removed the skin is often soft and pleasing to eat, particularly when steamed in this way.

In North America, the most highly regarded porgies are the SHEEPSHEAD BREAM and the SCUP, which, when whole, weigh from 12 oz to 3 lb (350 g to 1.5 kg). They have flaky, tender, and very tasty flesh. Interestingly, the EUROPEAN SEA BREAM and the AMERICAN RED PORGY appear to be one and the same fish. As a result of a relatively comprehensive study of the migration of these fish, it is clear that fish appear in different far-flung parts of the world, not generally through a sort of Viking migratory habit, but rather through the eggs drifting on the ocean currents. How else might we explain the presence in Australian and New Zealand waters of the same group of fish, the *Sparidae*? The best-flavored examples of these are the BLACK BREAM, the YELLOWFIN BREAM, the SWEETLIP BREAM, the FRYPAN BREAM, and the SNAPPER. In fact, this snapper, which is one of Australia's most highly regarded fish, is not a true snapper but a bream. Then again, there is another group of fish in Australasia called THREADFIN BREAM, which are not true bream. How confusing!

There is a small group of fish called bream that are actually more closely related to pomfret, (see Thin-Bodied Fish, page 246). These are the wide-ranging RAY'S BREAM, the *Brama brama*, which appear in the southern oceans off New Zealand and yet have also been landed on the beaches of Sussex, England.

snappers

Snappers are a very important fish family in tropical waters and provide one of the best tasting fish the sea has to offer, with their succulent, fantastically flavored white meat. Owing to the wonders of airfreight we can now buy them here in the UK, almost as fresh and lively as fish from the quayside, though I have this rather depressed feeling that the quality could sometimes be better on a lot of supermarket counters. One of my favorites is the RED EMPEROR, also known as BOURGEOIS, EMPEROR, or SNAPPER, from Australia. This is possibly the best fish I know for grilling. I've also had great success pan-grilling large fillets of red emperor. I make a marinade of olive oil, lemon zest, bay leaves, thyme, red pepper flakes, and salt, then I grill or pan-grill the fish, brushing it constantly with this marinade.

A closely related species, from the Indian Ocean and Australia, which is also easy to get in the UK, is the SPANGLED EMPEROR, known as CAPITAINE or BLUE EMPEROR. I cooked this once at a barbecue on Mauritius, and served it with the shrimp and mango salsa on page 147. Unfortunately, it happened to coincide with the only tropical rainstorm of the two-week trip.

In North America, the most sought-after fish in this family is the RED SNAPPER; others with good eating qualities are the MUTTON SNAPPER and YELLOWTAIL SNAPPER. But it's the red snapper that's the snapper for me. When I was 20, I spent two years traveling around the world before I went to university. I was in Acapulco, Mexico, for a couple of months, living— as was the custom then—on five dollars a day

13

(actually more like two dollars: five was luxury!). Such economy meant eating canned frankfurters and sweet American bread from the supermarket, but, with my growing interest in food, also the enchiladas, tamales, and tacos from the street vendors in the back streets around the market. (It also meant sleeping on the beach—at least until I was robbed of all my possessions. Served me right, I suppose.) Every day, what seemed then like absurdly well-off Americans sat at the beachside restaurants eating whole grilled red snapper with tortillas, tomato, and chile peppers. I can remember to this day the smell of those chunky grilled fish and the sight of lots of chilled Mexican beer slipping down … Fish weighing between 1 lb and 3 lb (450 g and 1.5 kg) are great for cooking whole, but any bigger than this and they are best bought filleted.

grunters

The first thing you'd want to know about a fish called a GRUNTER is … why? Well, it's because when they're caught they grind their teeth in panic and the sound is then amplified by their air bladder to make a grunt-like noise. The fish are related to snappers; they have a delicate white flesh but with a slightly softer texture and finer white flake. They tend to be small fish, no more than 1 lb 2 oz (500 g) in size, and are ideal for grilling whole over charcoal. Particularly good is the PORKFISH.

sea catfish

Closely related to the freshwater catfish of the Mississippi, the Danube, and other large rivers of eastern Europe, SEA CATFISH, *Galeichthys felis* has well-flavored, white, medium-firm flesh, which keeps well. The skins of all catfish are thick, slippery, and strong like that of an eel and they therefore have to be skinned in the same way, but it is unusual to buy it in any form other than fillets.

The name catfish is also given to an unrelated species in northern Europe called the WOLFFISH, *Anarhichas lupus*, which is also called SEACAT, OCEAN CATFISH, or ROCK TURBOT. It is of excellent quality. (There is a recipe using this fish on page 138.) It has particularly firm, white fillets. The first time I ate it I thought it tasted a bit like Dover sole, but it deteriorates much more quickly.

In the US, by far the most popular way of cooking freshwater CATFISH is to coat it in cornmeal, often flavored with things such as curry powder, chile powder, and even five-spice powder, and to fry it until crisp and golden. It is traditionally served with hush puppies (onion-flavored cornmeal fritters) and lemon wedges. Interestingly, though the name catfish refers to the "whiskers" or barbels situated near the mouth,

the most striking feature of the American GAFFTOPSAIL CATFISH is the enormous dorsal fin that resembles the sail of an Arabic dhow.

The similar species in Australia and New Zealand, CATFISH and COBBLER, though just as good in quality, are not as well appreciated as the American and European fish. However, there is a growing market in western Australia for cobbler fillets, also known, inevitably, as catfish fillets.

sea creatures

Most of the species in this section are pretty esoteric, and not even known to many people, but they have their enthusiasts. Get talking to a Galician about *percebes*, or a Chinese about sea slugs and you'd think you were talking about a delicacy waiting to take the world by storm. But I think the seafood lover should be familiar with all of these, and most of the time they are very good to eat.

percebes or gooseneck barnacles

The Galicians of northern Spain are mad about these strange brown barnacles, which are correctly classified as crustaceans. They look a bit like the legs of a tortoise, a bit shorter and stumpier than your little finger. They taste something like the claw meat of lobster and are boiled in salted water and eaten plain, often with Albariño, the local wine of Galicia. Percebes fetch big money in Spain because the fishing of them is very dangerous. The fishermen, called "mariscadores," prize them off the rocks at low tide and often risk being swept away by an extra large wave.

jellyfish

Although we don't eat JELLYFISH in the West, the Chinese dry the umbrella part of certain species. They are then rehydrated, cut into strips, and served in a classic Chinese dish, with strips of chicken, cucumber, cilantro, and soy. The jellyfish doesn't have much taste; it's more the texture that is valued. The edible species are *Rhopilema esculenta*, *Stomolophus nomurai*, and, from Australian waters, *Aurelia aurita*, also known as the BLUE JELLYFISH.

sea urchin

The only edible part of a SEA URCHIN is the cluster of creamy or orange-colored roe, also known as corals. Though not common in fishmongers, urchins have many fans. They have a beautiful, fragrant flavor and are to be enjoyed spooned out of the opened and cleaned shell (see page 97) to be eaten raw, folded into hot pasta (see page 218), or used to thicken a fine sauce. The best eating is the MEDITERRANEAN SEA URCHIN, *Paracentrotus lividus*. This is the one with long, black or dark brown spines. The urchin

of northern Europe and North America, the GREEN SEA URCHIN, has a much bigger "test" (shell). In Orkney, they are known as a "Scarrimans Heid," meaning a street child with unruly spiky hair. This same urchin is present in the northern Pacific as well, but there's a bigger species in northern California, which reaches as much as 5 inches (12.5 cm) in diameter. In Australia and New Zealand, the BLACK SEA URCHIN is more like the Mediterranean in shape, but the roe is mostly exported to Asia.

violets

This is a knobby creature with leathery skin that lives anchored to rocks or the sea bed in the Mediterranean. You cut them in half—the skin is violet in color as you are cutting through it, hence the name. The inside, the bit you eat, is bright yellow. It has a very soft texture, like scrambled egg, with a taste of ozone but quite bitter, as raw mussels can sometimes be. Shallot vinegar can offset this.

I've eaten the same sort of creature in New South Wales in Australia, but I haven't been able to track down the name of it in any book. Local fishermen put me on to them. They were nicer than Mediterranean violets, being less bitter.

sea cucumbers

The Chinese hold SEA CUCUMBERS in great esteem. They look like fat slugs lying on the sea bed, about 10 to 14 inches (25 to 35 cm) in length and weighing up to 4½ lb (2 kg) when alive. Once harvested, they are gutted, boiled, and dried, then sometimes smoked. They are then rehydrated in water before cooking. Sea cucumbers have strong, longitudinal muscles and therefore need to be cut thinly crosswise to make them edible. As with jellyfish, the Chinese enjoy their rubbery texture, liking a more comprehensive range of textures in their food than we do in the West.

sea perch

This is a collection of similarly shaped fish with round, deep bodies, tough skins, and large scales, and with the first and second dorsal fins joined, the first fin always being spiny. Their flesh is generally pinkish-white in color, firm but open-textured and therefore slightly flaky when cooked. Because of their medium oil content, they suit every type of cooking, particularly grilling over charcoal, hence the popularity of surfperch in North America and dhufish in Australia at convivial *al fresco* gatherings.

There are 20 types of SURFPERCH on the Pacific coast, ranging from Alaska down to Baja, California. These are not true perch, but are similar in texture, and for cooking purposes we can treat them the same. The best eating are the REDTAIL, the BARRED, and the CALICO SURFPERCH. All are what you might call pan fish as they are never much bigger than 2¼ to 4½ lb (1 to 2 kg), thus they can be pan-fried or cooked whole. The OPALEYE is also sold as perch, being very similar in size and shape.

DRUMMERS are a group of fish in Australia that have a general perch-like appearance. One is the LUDERICK; the other best known fish in this family is the SWEEP. These fish are essentially vegetarian and mainly feed on seaweed. Though they are good table fish, they can be tainted by iodine from eating too much seaweed.

The DHUFISH, also known as JEWFISH, is one of the most sought-after Indian Ocean fish in western Australia, so next time you're in Perth you'll know what to order at Fraser's fish restaurant overlooking the Swan River. Dhufish, and the closely related PEARL PERCH, which is available on the Australia's east coast, have excellent flavor and texture and are among the best fish on the continent.

sea vegetables

carrageen (irish moss)

This red or greenish-brown seaweed grows in short, frilly tufts on the Atlantic coastlines of Europe and North America. It is dried in the open air and bleaches to a creamy pink color. It's traditionally used in Ireland to thicken milk puddings, and to make a vegetarian-friendly alternative to gelatin.

dulse

An edible red seaweed, this occurs in both the northern and southern hemispheres. It is most popular in Ireland, where dried dulse is sold in the pubs of Belfast in little packets, as snacks.

laver

Found around the coasts of North America and Europe, this seaweed is green when young, becoming purple, then dark brown as it ages. It is particularly popular in south Wales where, after harvesting, it is boiled to a purée that is called LAVERBREAD. I think this goes extremely well with the cockles that would often have come from the same beach. (See the recipe on page 207.) Laver is also known as NORI in Japan, and in its dried form, pressed into thin sheets, it is used as the outer wrapping in Nori Sushi.

kelp

This name is given to several large varieties of brown seaweed that grow in the Atlantic and are used by local people in their traditional dishes.

kombu

This name is given to a group of brown seaweeds, of which *Laminaria japonica* is the most common. When dried it is very important in Japanese cooking. Kombu and dried bonito flakes (*katsuobushi*)—a fish from the same family as tuna and mackerel—are the two ingredients needed for making dashi, the classic Japanese stock, which is used in many dishes. Kombu, which is very similar to the kelps that grow in the Atlantic, is very rich in monosodium glutamate.

wakame

By far and away the most popular seaweed in Japan, this is green and frilly-fronded. It is easy to buy dried and can be used raw in salads or cooked in soups, such as the one on page 104.

sea lettuce

The most widely distributed of edible seaweeds in the world, this is used in salads and soups.

sea kale

This member of the cabbage family, which normally grows wild on the pebbly beaches of Europe, is bitter and inedible unless it has grown under sand. These days the young shoots of the new season's sea kale are covered and forced like rhubarb to present an early spring delicacy, which is excellent boiled and served like asparagus, with hollandaise sauce.

salicornia, marsh samphire

SALICORNIA, which is also called MARSH SAMPHIRE and GLASSWORT, grows in muddy estuaries and tidal salt marshes around Europe as well as along the Atlantic and Pacific coasts of North America. It's easy to identify, having unusual light green branches rather than leaves and growing little more than 8 inches (20 cm) tall. It is harvested in the summer months. Contrary to what many think, picking the whole plant will not endanger stocks, as salicornia grows from seed and not from regeneration of the roots. It has a delicious salty, fresh taste, making it an ideal vegetable for serving with fish, and is particularly delicious when served with hollandaise sauce. It should be boiled—without salt in the water—until only just tender.

rock samphire

Gatherers of this European variety of samphire are described in King Lear as plying a "dangerous trade," presumably referring to the need to scramble over the face of high cliffs to collect it. In my part of the world, it grows conveniently out of Cornish stone walls and low rocks by the beach. It has a pungent, aromatic smell, slightly reminiscent of fennel, and in fact belongs to the same family, the *Umbelliferae*. Traditionally it was always pickled. I have had some success in using it as an herb for flavoring a cream sauce, but you have to be very parsimonious with it. To me it is the most evocative of plants, recalling childhood summer vacations strolling down sandy Cornish lanes.

sharks and rays

Here I've grouped all those shark and shark-like fish that have cartilage rather than bones. There are a few other fish with cartilage rather than bone—notably the sturgeon and the lamprey—but these are not related to sharks and rays.

sharks and rays

The great plus of all sharks is that there are no bones in the flesh. All have lots of flavor, many with a slight tartness, particularly the Atlantic sharks—the PORBEAGLE and MAKO—which are excellent eating. Part of the assertive flavor of shark comes from the presence of urea in their flesh. All fish are less salty than the sea around them so, to avoid dehydration, they have to counteract osmosis (the tendency of salt to attract water). Sharks do this by producing urea, which is perfectly acceptable in fresh fish; however, after death urea gradually breaks down into ammonia and becomes repulsive in stale fillets. The advantage of this breakdown is that while quite a few sharks—notably skates and rays—are inedible when just caught, being incredibly tough, the subsequent break up of the urea tenderizes the fish. Skate and ray are at their best 2 to 5 days old: after that point, the smell of the ammonia becomes most unpleasant and no amount of cooking will remove it.

In Britain, most shark appears as PORBEAGLE, if named at all. I wonder sometimes if it's not BLUE SHARK, which is not as nice, having coarser and darker meat with rather an assertive flavor similar to TOPE. Both of these are good for soups and curries, but too powerful for my taste for simple cooking. Most sharks that we can buy in the UK would be between 9 to 45 lb (4 to 20 kg). The larger ones are sold in filleted form, the smaller ones as steaks.

The BLACKTIP SHARK from Florida and the Caribbean has very white meat, a bit drier than mako and TIGER SHARK, but in the US most shark gets marketed as MAKO and sometimes mako gets marketed as swordfish, since the fillet is very similar. Other fine-tasting sharks in the Atlantic are the HAMMERHEAD SHARK, which also swim in Indo-Pacific waters and are the favored shark in Goan Shark Vindaloo (see page 120).

In Australia, the most popular eating sharks are the GUMMY SHARK, the WHISKERY SHARK, and SCHOOL SHARK. The school and gummy sharks are sold in fish-and-chip shops as FLAKE. Australia and New Zealand also have a number of dogfish, skates, and rays, and they have the ANGEL SHARK, which is confusingly also called monkfish. It looks similar to monkfish, but its flavor is more like that of skate or ray; it has small wings like those fish, but without the long, fibrous strands of flesh.

rays

The naming of SKATE and RAY is a little confusing. Alan Davidson, perhaps the world's greatest culinary ichthyologist, suggests that the old distinction should stand, whereby the bigger fish with long snouts are skates, and the smaller fish with rounded heads are rays. In Britain, the best ray for eating is the THORNBACK RAY. The BLONDE RAY is also good.

dogfish

Dogfish are small relatives of the shark family. The best dogfish is the SPUR-DOG, though the LESSER SPOTTED DOGFISH, also called the ROUGH HOUND, MURGY, or MORGAY, is also good. The NURSEHOUND and SMOOTH HOUND are also perfectly enjoyable; the British fish-and-chip trade calls them rock salmon or rock eel. All dogfish are good with Indian masalas, as in the recipe on page 103, but above all I regard them as a vital ingredient in fish soup. Other popular names for dogfish are HUSS and ROCK SALMON, or saumonette in French, probably due to the pinkish-white color of the flesh.

shellfish—bivalves and univalves

bivalves

These are the shellfish that live in two hinged shells. Unlike fish, there is little difference in the taste of CLAMS, MUSSELS, or OYSTERS around the world, although some experts swear that they can taste the water in which they grow. A friend of mine, Johnny Noble, who owns Loch Fyne Oysters in Argyllshire in Scotland, swears that when he's far away from home—say at the Mandarin Hotel in Hong Kong, which stocks his oysters—just one taste can take him back to the bonny banks of the loch. It's a lovely thought and I believe him to be telling the truth. But it rather confounds the idea of a difference between, say, the 20 types of oyster in a big New York oyster bar, where I'm told all the oysters are stored in the same tank.

Because of their similarity in taste, I have grouped all of the bivalves by size: small, medium, and large.

small bivalves

I use small clams for several first courses, including Mussel, Cockle, and Clam Masala (see page 103) and Linguine alle Vongole (page 205), and I find generally that mussels and COCKLES can be used in the same way. The CARPETSHELL CLAM, called *vongole* in Italy, and *palourde* in France, is traditional for Linguine alle Vongole, although I've made it with PIPIS in Australia and been well pleased with it. American LITTLENECK clams are also good. Clams can be used instead of mussels for Moules Marinière (see page 213), if you prefer, although I do think that MUSSELS have the edge for this dish. Though I have a nostalgic affection for the small beach mussels from around Padstow, we find that the best ones to use for all our dishes are rope-grown farmed ones. Suspended in mid-water in estuaries rich in plankton, rope mussels grow very quickly and are not attacked by predators such as crabs and starfish living on the bottom. Because they are always covered with water they are constantly feeding and develop a thinner shell than mussels that live on the shore and have to withstand the attrition of waves. The thin shell ensures that they cook quickly and uniformly, which is particularly advantageous in stir-fries such as the one on page 206.

The technique of opening small clams for serving raw on ice is illustrated on page 89, but you can also steam them open carefully in a covered pan, if you prefer, with a splash of water or wine. The trick is to take them out as soon as the shells pop open, so don't try to do too many at once—just enough to cover the bottom of the pan. You can open cockles by pushing the knuckle end (the hinge of the cockle) against the knuckle of another one and twisting. It's rather satisfying, particularly if, like me, you enjoy gathering cockles and eating the odd one as you do so—only when the beds are pollution-free, of course.

medium bivalves

I wouldn't use medium-sized HARD-SHELL CLAMS (also called QUAHOGS), such as CHERRYSTONES, or SOFT-SHELL CLAMS (STEAMERS) on a fruits de mer or in a pasta dish. I think of them more as a delicacy to be served on their own. I love a bowl of steamers with just drawn butter and the cooking juices.

large bivalves

I prefer to stuff larger mussels, such as the NEW ZEALAND GREENLIP MUSSEL, with garlic breadcrumbs as for Moules Farcies on page 212. And I find that the larger the clam, the more the resistance to eating it whole. I persist in serving RAZOR CLAMS whole—with their fantastic-looking shells that resemble an old cut-throat razor—but some people have an aversion to eating

something that looks like it has come out of the film *Alien*. Razor clams have a wonderful, sweet flavor, which is slightly peppery, I think.

The large CHOWDER CLAMS, SURF CLAMS, and GEODUCKS are best taken out of the shells (see how on page 89), sliced or chopped, and used in chowders and stir-fries.

scallops

At our restaurant, we use SMALL SCALLOPS (or QUEENS), or sometimes BAY SCALLOPS from North America, raw on the fruits de mer. Scallops are also great thinly sliced and served for sashimi, (see page 105), where their sweetness makes a delightful contrast to the oiliness of the sea trout and texture of the brill. One of our most successful dishes is broiled queenies with noisette butter (nut-brown butter) with lemon juice and parsley. You can't get much simpler than that. I think it's the combination of nutty butter and the smell of hot shells (which I always think smell like hot beaches on a sunny day) that gets customers excited.

In North America, it's customary to remove the coral of scallops, whether they be bay scallops or the larger SEA SCALLOPS. I think this is a bit of a shame—a bit like removing the yolk from eggs. Not only are the corals lovely to eat, they can also be used to thicken sauces, just like an egg yolk.

oysters

In Europe, we have two types of oyster: what we call the NATIVE OYSTER, *Ostrea edulis*, and the PACIFIC OYSTER, *Crassostrea gigas*. The native oyster is considered the best: the most famous and revered beds are Colchester, Whitstable, and Helford in England; Galway and Cork in Ireland; Belon and Arachon in France; Ostend in Belgium; Zeeland in Holland; and Limfjord in Denmark. This oyster is also farmed on the Atlantic and Pacific coasts of the US, where it is called FLAT OYSTER or BELON OYSTER. To me, the perfect-sized native oyster is what we in Britain call a number 3, weighing about 3½ oz (90 g).

PACIFIC OYSTERS, also called JAPANESE OYSTERS, are cheaper because they grow faster. They are the variety favored for farming and crop up everywhere—favorites of mine are from Loch Fyne in Scotland and Fowey in Cornwall. The PORTUGESE OYSTER, once considered a separate species, is now acknowledged to be the same as the Pacific.

In the US, the native ATLANTIC OYSTER, *Crassostrea virginica*, which is larger than the European native oyster, ranges from New Brunswick in Canada right down to the Gulf of Mexico. Those from the colder northern waters are held to be the best—they grow more slowly and their shells are more uniform. The most famous beds for these are on Long Island, where grow such evocatively named oysters as Blue Points. There is also the OLYMPIA OYSTER from Washington's Puget Sound.

In Australia and New Zealand, there is the ubiquitous PACIFIC OYSTER and the SYDNEY ROCK OYSTER, *Saccostrea glomerata*. The European native oyster has also been grown in South Australia and Victoria for over 100 years. In northwestern Australia, you'll find pearl meat, a by-product of the pearl oyster fishery there. The adductor muscle of the PEARL LIP OYSTER is white and sweet with a soft texture, and is much sought after by Perth restaurants.

univalves

Univalves are all those mollusks that live in one shell (unlike bivalves, which live in two shells).

There's the PERIWINKLE or WINKLE, which is held in much affection by serious seafood lovers. Periwinkles don't have a great taste, but picking out a bowlful from their shells using your winkle picker, with some shallot vinegar for dipping, provides an enjoyable experience. WHELKS, too, are greatly enjoyed by some. I think the small ones have the best flavor. I like them boiled and served with a choice of mayonnaise or shallot vinegar, or, in the English fashion, with pepper, malt vinegar, and a pint of beer. I've had success by breaking open the shells, removing the meats, and stir-frying them or turning them into fritters. The MUREX is a tough, whelk-like sea snail from the Mediterranean. The attractive shell is much sought after. The TOP-SHELL, known as bodolletti, is popular in Venice, Italy, where it is cooked in a fireproof dish with olive oil, bay leaves, and salt for about 20 minutes.

LIMPETS are reasonable eating in the same way as abalone, if slow-cooked. They must have been very popular in the long past—the house I lived in on Trevose Head seems to have been built on a midden of them. There's also a univalve called the SLIPPER LIMPET, which has become a bit of a pest in Britain. It came originally from America (probably on the keel of a ship), and has since invaded a number of oyster beds, where they smother the oysters in their fight for food. But they're actually good to eat when steamed with a bit of white wine, stuffed like snails with garlic butter, and briefly broiled.

You can deal with CONCH, which are found in the waters off the Florida Keys and in the Caribbean, in the same way I've described for whelks, either stir-frying or using them in fritters.

abalone

By far the most sought-after univalve is the ABALONE (or PAUA, as it's known in New Zealand, ORMER in the Channel Islands, and

ORMEAU in France). It is in the Pacific that the abalone are most prolific. There are three ways of dealing with the toughness of abalone: Slice it very thinly when raw and drop it into hot stock, as the Chinese do; bash it for a minute or so with a mallet to tenderize it, then bread it and fry it; or slow-cook it with oil and aromatics in a low oven for 2 to 3 hours (see the recipe on page 207). Abalone has a similar flavor and texture to cuttlefish or octopus.

The BAILER SHELL from Australia and New Zealand, sought after for its ornamental shell, is now gaining in popularity for its meat as well, which is used in the same way as abalone.

small fry

Here I've grouped together those immature fish that are caught for cooking and eating whole. I've also included a few tiny adult fish, too.

whitebait

The collective term in English for tiny frying fish is WHITEBAIT. These can actually be the fry of any number of species, although they tend to be oily members of the herring family. In Tasmania and New Zealand, whitebait are normally tiny trout, while in the Indian Ocean a similar harvest of tiny fish is called INDIAN BAIT. In the West Indies, they're called PISQUETTES and on the French Mediterranean coast, NONNATS. Curiously, the Americans haven't caught on to this delight yet, although whitebait are available, usually in Chinese markets.

Freshly caught whitebait, deep-fried and served with a little cayenne pepper and lemon wedges, are one of the joys of fish cookery. It's quite easy to get frozen whitebait, but more often than not they seem to have an overpowering and unpleasant flavor, probably because they've been frozen for too long.

sprats, blennys, capelin, gobys, sand eels, silversides, and sand smelts

These small fish are excellent either floured and deep-fried, made into fritters, or skewered, broiled, and sprinkled with chopped herbs (as in the recipe on page 160). SAND EELS, in particular, are good when floured and deep-fried. The larger ones, known locally in Cornwall as LANCES and weighing 2 oz (50 g) or more, need gutting and are therefore better cooked like sprats.

It's a matter of taste whether you remove the guts in small fish (there are instructions on how to do it on page 57, if you wish to). It is a laborious procedure with something like a sprat or anchovy. A lot will depend on the cleanliness of the water in which they were caught.

south american catchall

Here's something of an ichthyophile's treasure, the ICEFISH. It somewhat resembles caviar in appearance but not in taste. Called GUNNARI in French, it is fished off Kerguelen Island in the deeply cold water south of Tierra del Fuego. This fish is often confused with the CHILEAN SEA BASS (Patagonian toothfish), but is quite different from it as it has no hemoglobin, the component of blood that carries oxygen around the body. Instead, the fluid in its body is more like antifreeze and the fish has few innards, so it doesn't go off quickly. It has very firm, lean, white flesh, with no bones, apart from a central spine, like a monkfish. According to those lucky enough to have tasted it, it is delicious. I've seen it on sale in France, and it's very popular in southern Argentina and Chile.

thin-bodied fish

Nothing in the naming of fish is perfect and a family containing a number of thin-bodied fish is clearly not a collection of related species, but rather a group selected by appearance and similar cooking qualities. Round fish have an eye on each side of their head, i.e. on each flank, while flatfish have both eyes on their top flank. The fish I've described here as flat, round fish have very thin but deep bodies. Their design is perfect for concealment, whether for predatory reasons or defence, since they become almost invisible when seen head on.

john dory

The fish that embodies this shape is the JOHN DORY. Some people refer to this lugubrious-looking, big-jawed fish as ugly, but I regard it as splendid, with its expressive face, fierce eyes, and astonishing array of long fins. There is an American john dory in the western Atlantic and another in the Pacific, and there are the closely related OREO DORY from New Zealand.

John dory is a great fish to cook, having very firm, dense, white fillets with a good fresh flavor, ideal for pan-frying, broiling, and pan-grilling whole. It also takes a classic French cream sauce, and we use it in a Mediterranean combination with olives, capers, tomato, rosemary, and new potatoes. (See the recipe on page 168.)

pomfret

Perhaps even better known worldwide than the John Dory is the WHITE POMFRET, which is part of a small family of thin-bodied fish that also includes RAY'S BREAM and BUTTERFISH. These are all very good eating. The pomfret is becoming increasingly popular in the UK. William Black, in the very good seafood book, *Fish*, says, "Supplies of pomfret from the Indian Ocean will almost certainly increase over the coming years, as it's deemed to be one of the under-exploited

13

species. God help it!" Notwithstanding that, the fillets are close-textured and white, and it's great stuffed with a masala paste, like that on page 226, then broiled. Ray's bream is of a very fine quality too; the fish is tinged with pink and formed of long strands, rather like skate.

opah or moonfish

Mention must be made of the OPAH or MOONFISH, a giant, thin-bodied fish that can reach 55 lb (25 kg). I bought some once in Woy Woy in Australia, took it back to where I was staying, and pan-fried the fillets with a lick of olive oil. The flesh was pink and firm. I ate it slightly undercooked and I could have sworn I was eating scallops, it was that good.

Opah, *Lampris guttatus*, can be found in both the Pacific and the Atlantic, but should not be confused with the SUNFISH, which is sometimes also called moonfish, or MOLA MOLA. Sunfish is a thick-skinned, thin, gelatinous-fleshed fish found flopping around on the surface of the seas around Cornwall in the summer months and often gaffed by lobster fisherman and dragged aboard. It's of no culinary value and so much better left where it is, in the sea.

leatherjacket and triggerfish

These two fish, the LEATHERJACKET from Australia and New Zealand (species are also found in the North American sides of the Atlantic and Pacific oceans) and the TRIGGERFISH, which is found in the Atlantic and the Caribbean, closely resemble the john dory. They have thick, leather-like skins and sharp spines just behind the eyes. Both are sold as skinned fillets and have firm flesh. Triggerfish are quite rare in Britain, normally being caught in lobster pots, but I once picked up half a dozen flapping on the beach in Trevose, where I live, flung ashore out of the surf during a winter storm.

us catchall

Here are a few fish unique to the United States, which didn't fit into any other category.

There are nine types of GREENLING found along the Pacific coast, the most popular of which is the LINGCOD, which can grow as large as 65 lb (30 kg). It is not related to the cod, unsurprisingly, but is a bottom-feeding fish usually caught by long line fishing, and produces good, tasty fillets.

The TILEFISH is a member of a small family of fish in both the Atlantic and Pacific oceans. The main Atlantic species is the BLACKLINE TILEFISH. In the Pacific, tilefish are just known as OCEAN WHITEFISH and are much sought after. They eat crabs and other crustacea, and this is reflected in their flavor, which is something like lobster or scallop meat.

The FLYINGFISH, farmed in the Pacific off California as well as in the Caribbean, is considered a delicacy in some parts of the world, especially in the West Indies and in Japan, where their eggs are served in sashimi. They are also extremely nice just dusted with flour and deep-fried.

wrasse

Unfortunately the BALLAN WRASSE that swims off the coast of Great Britain, though of astonishingly beautiful hues of red, green, and gold (and easy to catch from the rocks) is really rather tasteless. As always with fish such as this, it's good for fish soup or fish stews. However, across the world, there are much better flavored members of this family, *Labridae*.

In the US, the TAUTOG or BLACKFISH, HOGFISH, CUNNER, and CALIFORNIA SHEEPHEAD are much better eating, particularly the tautog, which has very firm, white meat. It is especially suitable for chowders and fish stews because it doesn't break up during cooking. The California sheephead feeds on lobster and abalone, and therefore has a good flavor.

parrotfish, maori wrasse, and pigfish

Closely related to the wrasse are the PARROTFISH of the Indian Ocean, which resemble the birds in both color and shape. They appear to have a beak and their teeth are configured somewhat like a parrot's beak in order to crush coral from which they filter out the algae they eat. If you've ever been diving on a coral reef, the sound that fills your ears underwater might well be that of grazing parrotfish. They are extremely highly regarded, with firm, white, and delicate-tasting flesh.

The parrotfish is also present in Australian waters, along with a number of other wrasse, in particular the MAORI WRASSE, much favored by the Chinese for inclusion in the live fish tanks of their restaurants. Have you ever noticed that fish swim to the back of the tank as the chef approaches? There is also the PIGFISH, which has firm, white, flaky flesh and is in great demand within the Indian and Pakistani communities—prices for pigfish in Sydney are among the highest for any Australian fish.

identifying seafood

SHARKS AND RAYS

1 PORBEAGLE SHARK
Lamna nasus

2 DOGFISH
Scyliorhinus canicula

3 THORNBACK RAY
Raja clavata

ROE FISH

4 STURGEON HYBRID
Huso huso x Acipenser ruthenus

EELS AND EEL-LIKE FISH

5 FRESHWATER EEL
Anguilla anguilla

6 EUROPEAN CONGER EEL
Conger conger

MONKFISH AND STARGAZERS

7 MONKFISH
Lophius piscatorius

8 ATLANTIC STARGAZER
Uranoscopus scaber

9 GREATER WEEVER
Trachinus draco

SMALL FRY

10 ATLANTIC SMELT
Osmerus eperlanus

11 ANCHOVY
Engraulis encrasicolus

12 WHITEBAIT
Clupea harengus

HERRING

13 EUROPEAN PILCHARD AND SARDINE
Sardina pilchardus

14 HERRING
Clupea harengus

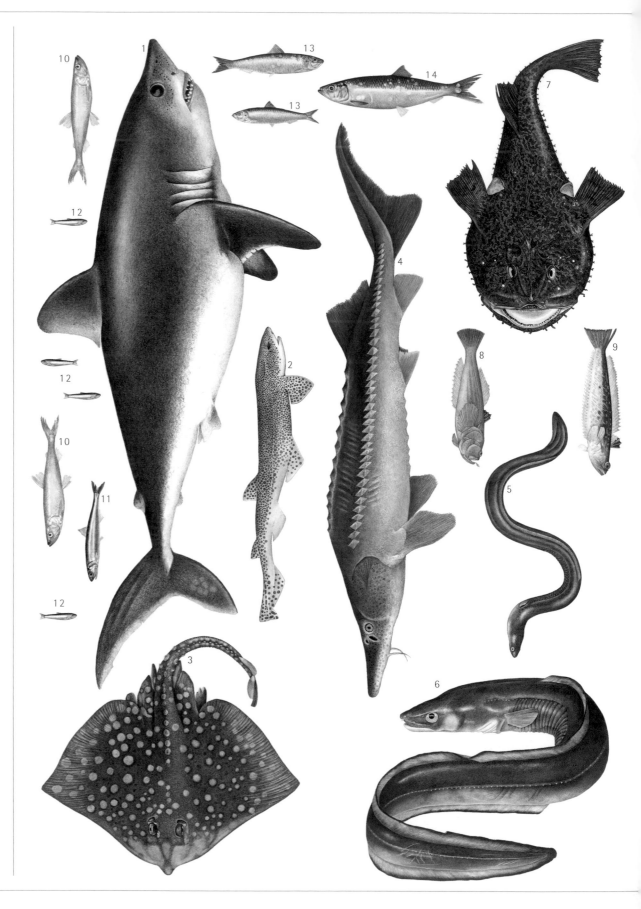

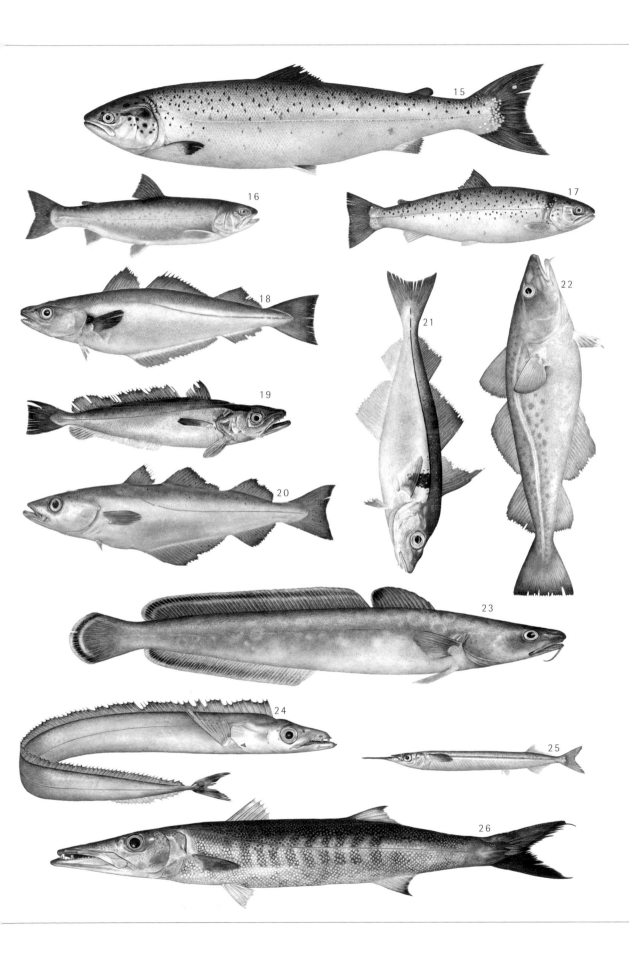

SALMON

15 ATLANTIC SALMON
Salmo salar

16 ARCTIC CHAR
Salvelinus alpinus

17 SALMON TROUT
Salmo trutta

COD AND COD-LIKE FISH

18 WHITING
Merlangius merlangus

19 EUROPEAN HAKE
Merluccius merluccius

20 POLLACK
Pollachius pollachius

21 HADDOCK
Melanogrammus aeglefinus

22 ATLANTIC COD
Gadus morhua

23 LING
Molva molva

ELONGATED FISH

24 SILVER SCABBARD
Lepidopus caudatus

25 EASTERN SEA GARFISH
Hyporhamphus australis

26 EUROPEAN BARRACUDA
Sphyraena sphyraena

BONY-CHEEKED/ SCORPION-LIKE FISH

1 OCEAN PERCH
Sebastes marinus

2 RED GURNARD
Aspitrigla cuculus

3 SAND FLATHEAD
Platycephalus bassensis

GROUPERS, SEA BASS, AND BARRAMUNDI

4 STRIPED BASS
Morone saxatilis

5 EUROPEAN SEA BASS
Dicentrarchus labrax

6 LEOPARD CORAL TROUT
Plectropomus leopardus

7 BARRAMUNDI
Lates calcarifer

JACKS, POMPANOS, AND TREVALLYS

8 MAHIMAHI
Coryphaena hippurus

9 BLUEFISH
Pomatomus saltatrix

10 POMPANO
Trachinotus carolinus

13

SEA BREAM, PORGIES, AND SNAPPERS

11 DENTEX
Dentex maroccanus

12 KEY WEST PORGY
Calamus nodosus

13 SHEEPSHEAD
Archosargus probatocephalus

14 GILT-HEAD BREAM
Sparus aurata

15 RED EMPEROR
Lutjanus sebae

16 SILK SNAPPER
Lutjanus vivanus

DRUMS

17 WEAKFISH
Cynoscion regalis

18 MULLOWAY
Argyrosomus hololepidotus

MULLETS

19 RED MULLET
Mullus surmuletus

20 THICK-LIPPED GRAY MULLET
Chelon labrosus

WRASSE

21 PARROTFISH
Scarus ghobban

identifying seafood

13

SEA CATFISH

1 WOLFFISH
Anarhichas lupus

DEEP-SEA FISH

2 ORANGE ROUGHY
Hoplostethus atlanticus

PUFFERS

3 NORTHERN PUFFER
Spheroides maculatus

MACKEREL AND TUNA

4 NARROW-BARRED
  SPANISH MACKEREL
Scomberomorus commerson

5 SPANISH MACKEREL
Scomberomorus maculatus

6 ATLANTIC MACKEREL
Scomber scombrus

7 ATLANTIC BONITO
Sarda sarda

8 BLUEFIN TUNA
Thunnus thynnus

BILLFISH

9 SWORDFISH
Xiphias gladius

OZ CATCHALL

10 BLUE-EYE COD
Hyperoglyphe antarctica

11 SAND WHITING
Sillago ciliata

US CATCHALL

12 TILEFISH
Lopholatilus chamaeleonticeps

THIN-BODIED FISH

13 JOHN DORY
Zeus faber

14 WHITE POMFRET
Pampus argenteus

15 VELVET LEATHERJACKET
Parika scaber

FLATFISH

16 LEMON SOLE
Microstomus kitt

17 EUROPEAN TURBOT
Psetta maxima

18 PLAICE
Pleuronectes platessa

19 ATLANTIC HALIBUT
Hippoglossus hippoglossus

20a DAB (UNDERSIDE)
20b and 20c DAB (TOP)
Limanda limanda

21 STARRY FLOUNDER
Platichthys stellatus

22 DOVER SOLE
Solea solea

23 BRILL
Scophthalmus rhombus

identifying seafood

CRUSTACEANS

1 EUROPEAN LOBSTER
Homarus gammarus

2 SQUAT LOBSTER
Galathea squamifera

**3 SPINY ATLANTIC
LOBSTER**
Palinurus elephas

4 LANGOUSTINE
Nephrops norvegicus

5 MORETON BAY BUG
Thenus orientalis

6 NORTHERN PINK SHRIMP
Pandalus borealis

**7 BLACK TIGER SHRIMP,
UNCOOKED AND COOKED**
Penaeus monodon

**8 BROWN SHRIMP,
COOKED AND UNCOOKED**
Crangon crangon

9 BLUE CRAB
Callinectes sapidus

10 VELVET CRAB
Liocarcinus puber

11 BLUE SWIMMER CRAB
Portunus pelagicus

12 MUD CRAB
Scylla serrata

13 SPIDER CRAB
Maia squinado

**14 EUROPEAN BROWN
CRAB**
Cancer pagurus

OPPOSITE PAGE

SHELLFISH (BIVALVES)

15 STEAMER CLAM
Mya arenaria

16 POD RAZOR CLAM
Ensis siliqua

17 PIPI
Donax deltoides

**18 WARTY VENUS CLAM,
OPEN AND CLOSED**
Venus verrucosa

**19 SMOOTH VENUS CLAM,
CLOSED AND OPEN**
Callista chione

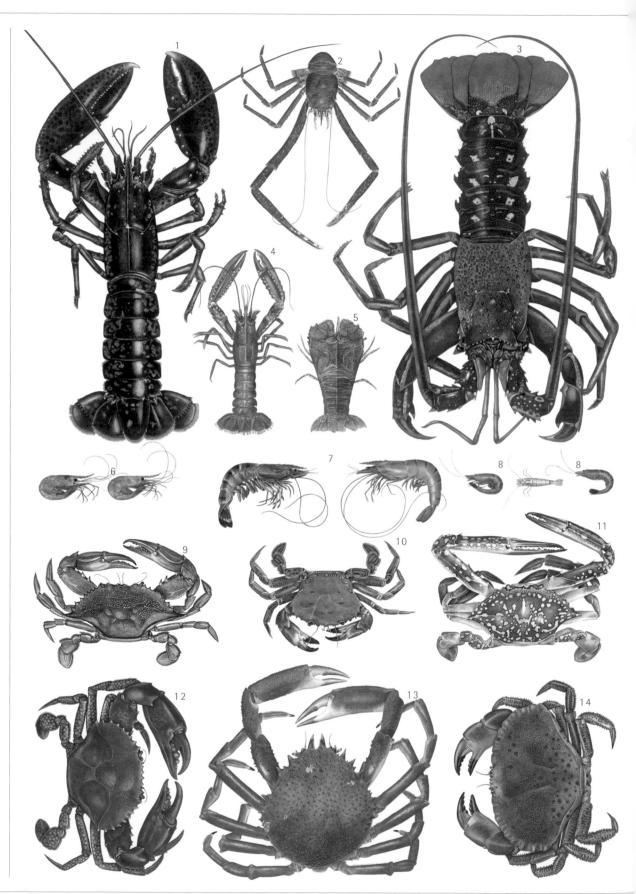

13

20a BLUE MUSSEL, OPEN
20b BLUE MUSSEL, CLOSED
Mytilus edulis

21 EUROPEAN OR FLAT
OYSTER
Ostrea edulis

22 COCKLE, CLOSED AND
OPEN
Cerastoderma edule

23 CARPETSHELL CLAM,
OPEN AND CLOSED
Venerupis decussata

24a GREAT SCALLOP, CLOSED
24b GREAT SCALLOP, OPEN
Pecten maximus

25 CHERRYSTONE CLAM
Mercenaria mercenaria

26 LITTLENECK CLAM,
OPEN AND CLOSED
Mercenaria mercenaria

27 CHOWDER CLAM
Mercenaria mercenaria

28a PACIFIC OYSTER, CLOSED
28b PACIFIC OYSTER, OPEN
Crassostrea gigas

SHELLFISH (UNIVALVES)

29 WHELK
Buccinum undatum

30 PERIWINKLE
Littorina littorea

31 ABALONE
Haliotis tuberculata

CEPHALOPODS

32 OCTOPUS
Octopus vulgaris

33 SQUID
Loligo forbesi

34 CUTTLEFISH
Sepia officinalis

SEA CREATURES

35 GREEN SEA URCHIN
Strongylocentrotus droebachiensis

36 RED SEA URCHIN,
OPEN AND CLOSED
Paracentrotus lividus

37 GOOSENECK
BARNACLES
Pollicipes cornucopia

38 SEA CUCUMBERS
Holothuria scabra

classifying seafood

COMMON NAME	REGION	LATIN NAME	A–Z FAMILY	LATIN FAMILY
Abalone, Atlantic	Eur	Haliotis tuberculata	Shellfish (Univalves)	Haliotidae
Abalone, Green Lip	Anz	Haliotis laevigata	Shellfish (Univalves)	Haliotidae
Albacore, False	USA Atl	Euthynnus alletteratus	Mackerel & Tuna	Scombridae
Alewife	USA Atl	Alosa pseudoharengus	Herring	Clupeidae
Alfonsino	Anz	Beryx splendens	Deep-sea Fish	Berycidae
Amande	Eur	Glycymeris glycemeris	Shellfish (Bivalves)	Glycymeridae
Amberjack, Greater	Eur/USA Atl	Seriola dumerili	Jacks, Pompanos, & Trevallys	Carangidae
Amberjack, Lesser	USA Atl	Seriola fasciata	Jacks, Pompanos, & Trevallys	Carangidae
Amberjack, Pacific	USA Pac	Seriola colburni	Jacks, Pompanos, & Trevallys	Carangidae
Anchovy, Australian	Anz	Engraulis australis	Small Fry	Engraulidae
Anchovy, European	Eur	Engraulis encrasicolus	Small Fry	Engraulidae
Anchovy, North American	USA Atl	Anchoa hepsetus	Small Fry	Engraulidae
Angler Fish	Eur	Lophius piscatorius	Monkfish & Stargazers	Lophiidae
Argentine	Eur/USA Atl	Argentina silus	Salmon	Argentinidae
Bailer Shell	Anz	Livonia mamilla	Shellfish (Univalves)	Volutidae
Baloonfish	Anz	Contusus richei	Puffer Fish	Tetraodontidae
Barnacle, Gooseneck	Eur	Pollicipes cornucopia	Sea Creature	Pollicipidae
Barracouta	Anz	Thyrsites atun	Elongated fish	Gempylidae
Barracuda, European	Eur	Sphyraena sphyraena	Elongated fish	Sphyraenidae
Barracuda, Great	USA/Anz	Sphyraena barracuda	Elongated Fish	Sphyraenidae
Barracuda, Pacific	USA Pac	Sphyraena argentea	Elongated Fish	Sphyraenidae
Barracuda, Slender	Anz	Sphyraena jello	Elongated Fish	Sphyraenidae
Barracuda, Yellowtail	USA Atl	Sphyraena flavicauda	Elongated Fish	Sphyraenidae
Barramundi	Anz	Lates calcarifer	Groupers, Sea Bass, & Barramundi	Centropomidae
Bass, Antarctic Sea	Anz	Dissostichus eleginoides	Deep-sea Fish	Nototheniidae
Bass, Black Sea	USA Atl	Centropristes striatus	Groupers, Sea Bass, & Barramundi	Serranidae
Bass, Channel	USA Atl	Sciaenops ocellatus	Drums	Sciaenidae
Bass, Chilean Sea	Anz	Dissostichus eleginoides	Deep-sea Fish	Nototheniidae
Bass, European Sea	Eur	Dicentrarchus labrax	Groupers, Sea Bass, & Barramundi	Serranidae
Bass, Kelp	USA Pac	Paralabrax clathratus	Groupers, Sea Bass, & Barramundi	Serranidae
Bass, Rock	USA Pac	Paralabrax clathratus	Sea Bream, Porgies, & Snappers	Sparidae
Bass, Spotted Sea	Eur	Dicentrarchus punctatus	Groupers, Sea Bass, & Barramundi	Serranidae
Bass, Stone	Eur/USA Atl	Polyprion americanus	Groupers, Sea Bass, & Barramundi	Serranidae
Bass, Striped	USA Atl	Morone saxatilis	Groupers, Sea Bass, & Barramundi	Serranidae
Bergall	USA Atl	Tautogolabrus adspersus	Wrasse	Labridae
Biddy, Silver	Anz	Gerres subfasciatus	Small Fry	Gerridae
Blackback	USA Atl	Pseudopleuronectes americanus	Flatfish	Pleuronectidae
Blackfish	USA Atl	Tautoga onitis	Wrasse	Labridae
Blenny	Eur	Blennius gattorugine	Small Fry	Blenniidae
Blowfish	USA Atl	Spheroides maculatus	Puffer Fish	Tetraodontidae
Blue-Eye	Anz	Hyperoglyphe antarctica	Australian Catchall	Centrolophidae
Blue-Mouth	Eur	Helicolenus dactylopterus	Bony-Cheeked Fish	Scorpaenidae
Blue-nose	Anz	Sillago ciliata	Australian Catchall	Sillaginidae
Bluefish	USA Atl/Anz	Pomatomus saltatrix	Jacks, Pompanos, & Trevallys	Pomatomidae
Bogue	Eur	Boops boops	Sea Bream, Porgies, & Snappers	Sparidae
Bonefish	USA Atl	Albula vulpes	Herring	Albulidae
Bonito, Arctic	USA Pac	Euthynnus pelamis	Mackerel & Tuna	Scombridae
Bonito, Atlantic	Eur	Sarda sarda	Mackerel & Tuna	Scombridae
Bonito, Australian	Anz	Sarda australis	Mackerel & Tuna	Scombridae
Bonito, Black	USA Atl/Anz	Sarda sarda	Jacks, Pompanos, & Trevallys	Scombridae
Bonito, Oceanic	USA Pac	Euthynnus pelamis	Mackerel & Tuna	Scombridae
Bonito, Pacific	USA Pac	Sarda chiliensis	Mackerel & Tuna	Scombridae
Bonito, Striped	USA Pac	Euthynnus pelamis	Mackerel & Tuna	Scombridae
Bourgeois	Anz	Lutjanus sebae	Sea Bream, Porgies, & Snappers	Lutjanidae
Bream, Annular	Eur	Diplodus annularis	Sea Bream, Porgies, & Snappers	Sparidae
Bream, Black	Anz	Acanthopagrus butcheri	Sea Bream, Porgies, & Snappers	Sparidae
Bream, Black Sea	Eur	Spondyliosoma cantharus	Sea Bream, Porgies, & Snappers	Sparidae
Bream, Bronze	Eur	Pagellus acarne	Sea Bream, Porgies, & Snappers	Sparidae
Bream, European Sea	Eur	Pagrus pagrus	Sea Bream, Porgies, & Snappers	Sparidae
Bream, Frypan	Anz	Argyrops spinifer	Sea Bream, Porgies, & Snappers	Sparidae
Bream, Gilt-Head	Eur	Sparus aurata	Sea Bream, Porgies, & Snappers	Sparidae
Bream, Grunter	Anz	Pomadasys kaakan	Sea Bream, Porgies, & Snappers	Sparidae
Bream, Pikey	Anz	Acanthopagrus berda	Sea Bream, Porgies, & Snappers	Sparidae
Bream, Ray's	Eur/Anz	Brama brama	Sea Bream, Porgies, & Snappers	Sparidae
Bream, Red	Eur	Beryx decadactylus	Sea Bream, Porgies, & Snappers	Sparidae
Bream, Red	Eur	Pagellus bogaraveo	Sea Bream, Porgies, & Snappers	Sparidae
Bream, Red Sea	Eur	Pagellus centrodontus	Sea Bream, Porgies, & Snappers	Sparidae
Bream, Royal	Eur	Sparus aurata	Sea Bream, Porgies, & Snappers	Sparidae
Bream, Saddled	Eur	Oblada melanura	Sea Bream, Porgies, & Snappers	Sparidae
Bream, Sea (UK)	Eur	Pagrus pagrus	Sea Bream, Porgies, & Snappers	Sparidae
Bream, Sheepshead	Eur	Puntazzo puntazzo	Sea Bream, Porgies, & Snappers	Sparidae
Bream, Spanish	Eur	Pagellus acarne	Sea Bream, Porgies, & Snappers	Sparidae
Bream, Striped	Eur	Lithognathus mormyrus	Sea Bream, Porgies, & Snappers	Sparidae
Bream, Sweetlip	Anz	Diagramma labiosum	Sea Bream, Porgies, & Snappers	Haemulidae
Bream, Threadfin	Anz	Nemipterus furcosus	Sea Bream, Porgies, & Snappers	Nemipteridae
Bream, Two-Banded	Eur	Diplodus vulgaris	Sea Bream, Porgies, & Snappers	Sparidae
Bream, White	Eur	Diplodus sargus	Sea Bream, Porgies, & Snappers	Sparidae
Bream, Yellowfin	Anz	Acanthopagrus australis	Sea Bream, Porgies, & Snappers	Sparidae
Brill	Eur	Scopthalmus rhombus	Flatfish	Bothidae
Bug, Balmain	Anz	Ibacus peronii	Crustacean	Scyllaridae
Bug, Moreton Bay	Anz	Thenus orientalis	Crustacean	Scyllaridae
Butterfish	Anz	Scatophagus multifasciatus	Thin-bodied fish	Scatophagidae
Butterfish	USA Atl	Peprilus triacanthus	Thin-bodied fish	Stromateidae
Butterfish	Anz	Coridodax pullus	Thin-bodied fish	Odacidae
Cabezon	USA Pac	Scorpaenichtys marmoratus	Bony-Cheeked Fish	Scorpaenidae
Cabio	USA Atl/Anz	Rachycentron canadum	Jacks, Pompanos, & Trevallys	Rachycentridae
Cabrilla, Spotted	USA Pac	Epinephelus analogus	Groupers, Sea Bass, & Barramundi	Serranidae
Calamari, Northern	Anz	Sepioteuthis lessoniana	Cephalapods	Loliginidae
Calamari, Southern	Anz	Sepioteuthis australis	Cephalapods	Loliginidae
Candlefish	USA Pac	Thaleichthys Pacificus	Small Fry	Osmeridae
Capelin	Eur	Mallotus villosus	Small Fry	Osmeridae
Capitaine	Anz	Lethrinus nebulosus	Sea Bream, Porgies, & Snappers	Lethrinidae
Cardinal Fish	Anz	Epigonus telescopus	Australian Catchall	Apogonidae
Carrageen Moss	Eur/USA Atl	Chrondrus crispus	Seaweed	Rhodophyceae
Catfish, Australian	Anz	Arius thalassinus	Sea Catfish	Arriidae
Catfish, Gafftopsail	USA Atl	Bagre marinus	Sea Catfish	Ariidae
Catfish, Hardhead	USA Atl	Arius felis	Sea Catfish	Arridae
Catfish, Ocean	Eur/USA Atl	Anarhichas lupus	Sea Catfish	Anarhichadidae
Catfish, Sea	USA Atl	Galeichthys felis	Sea Catfish	Arridae
Cavalla	USA Atl	Scomberomorus cavalla	Mackerel & Tuna	Scombridae
Cero	USA Atl	Scomberomorus regalis	Mackerel & Tuna	Scombridae
Char, Arctic	Eur & N. USA	Salvelinus alpinus	Salmon	Salmonidae
Char	Eur	Salvelinus alpinus	Salmon	Salmonidae
Clabbydoo/Clappydoo	Eur/USA Atl	Modiolus modiolus	Shellfish (Bivalves)	Mytilidae
Clam, Bar	USA Atl	Spisula solidissima	Shellfish (Bivalves)	Mactridae
Clam, Butter	USA Atl	Saxidomus giganteus	Shellfish (Bivalves)	Veneridae
Clam, Carpetshell	Eur	Venerupis decussata	Shellfish (Bivalves)	Veneridae
Clam, Cherrystone	USA Atl	Mercenaria mercenaria	Shellfish (Bivalves)	Veneridae
Clam, Clovisse	Eur	Venerupis decussata	Shellfish (Bivalves)	Veneridae
Clam, Coquina	Eur	Donax vitttatus	Shellfish (Bivalves)	Donacidae
Clam, Eastern Razor	USA Atl	Ensis directus	Shellfish (Bivalves)	Solenidae
Clam, Gaper	USA Atl	Mya arenaria	Shellfish (Bivalves)	Myacidae
Clam, Geoduck	USA Pac	Panope geodosa	Shellfish (Bivalves)	Hiatellidae
Clam, Giant Callista	USA Atl	Macrocallista nimbosa	Shellfish (Bivalves)	Veneridae
Clam, Hard	USA Atl	Mercenaria mercenaria	Shellfish (Bivalves)	Veneridae
Clam, Hard-Shell	USA Atl	Mercenaria mercenaria	Shellfish (Bivalves)	Veneridae
Clam, Hen	USA Atl	Spisula solidissima	Shellfish (Bivalves)	Mactridae
Clam, Littleneck	USA Atl	Mercenaria mercenaria	Shellfish (Bivalves)	Veneridae
Clam, Littleneck	USA Atl	Protothaca stamina	Shellfish (Bivalves)	Veneridae
Clam, Longneck	USA Atl	Mya arenaria	Shellfish (Bivalves)	Myacidae
Clam, Palourde	Eur	Venerupis decussata	Shellfish (Bivalves)	Veneridae
Clam, Praire	Eur	Venus vericosa	Shellfish (Bivalves)	Veneridae
Clam, Quahog	USA Atl	Mercenaria mercenaria	Shellfish (Bivalves)	Veneridae
Clam, Razor	Eur	Ensis ensis	Shellfish (Bivalves)	Solenidae
Clam, Skimmer	USA Atl	Spisula solidissima	Shellfish (Bivalves)	Mactridae
Clam, Smooth Venus	Eur	Callista chione	Shellfish (Bivalves)	Veneridae
Clam, Soft-Shell	USA Atl	Mya arenaria	Shellfish (Bivalves)	Myacidae
Clam, Steamer	USA Atl	Mya arenaria	Shellfish (Bivalves)	Myacidae
Clam, Sunray	USA Atl	Macrocallista nimbosa	Shellfish (Bivalves)	Veneridae
Clam, Sunray Venus	USA Atl	Macrocallista nimbosa	Shellfish (Bivalves)	Veneridae
Clam, Surf	USA Atl	Spisula solidissima	Shellfish (Bivalves)	Mactridae
Clam, Surf	Anz	Dosinia caerulea	Shellfish (Bivalves)	Veneridae
Clam, Thin Tellin	Eur	Tellina tenuis	Shellfish (Bivalves)	Scrobiculariidae
Clam, Verni	Eur	Callista chione	Shellfish (Bivalves)	Veneridae
Clam, Vongole	Eur	Venerupis decussata	Shellfish (Bivalves)	Veneridae
Clam, Warty Venus	Eur	Venus verrucosa	Shellfish (Bivalves)	Veneridae
Clam, Wedge Shell	Eur	Donax vitttatus	Shellfish (Bivalves)	Donacidae
Coalfish	Eur	Pollachius virens	Cod & Cod-like	Gadidae
Cobbler	Anz	Cnidoglanis macrocephalus	Sea Catfish	Plotosidae
Cobia	USA Atl/Anz	Rachycentron canadum	Jacks, Pompanos, & Trevallys	Rachycentridae
Cockle, Australian	Anz	Katelysia scalarina	Shellfish (Bivalves)	Veneridae
Cockle, Dog	Eur	Glycymeris glycemeris	Shellfish (Bivalves)	Glycymeridae
Cockle, European	Eur	Cerastoderma edule	Shellfish (Bivalves)	Cardiidae
Cockle, Heart	Eur	Glossus humanus	Shellfish (Bivalves)	Glossidae
Cockle, Spiny	Eur	Acanthocardia aculeata	Shellfish (Bivalves)	Cardiidae
Cod, Atlantic	Eur	Gadus morhua	Cod & Cod-like	Gadidae
Cod, Barramundi	Anz	Cromileptes altivelis	Groupers, Sea Bass, & Barramundi	Serranidae
Cod, Black	Eur	Pollachius virens	Cod & Cod-like	Gadidae
Cod, Black	USA Atl	Anopoploma fimbria	Thin-bodied fish	Anopoplomatidae
Cod, Blue-Eye	Anz	Hyperoglyphe antarctica	Australian Catchall	Centrolophidae
Cod, Coral	Anz	Cephalopholis cyanostigma	Groupers, Sea Bass, & Barramundi	Serranidae
Cod, Deep Sea	Anz	Mora moro	Deep-sea Fish	Moridae

COMMON NAME	REGION	LATIN NAME	A-Z FAMILY	LATIN FAMILY
Cod, Pacific	USA Pac	Gadus macrocephalus	Cod & Cod-like	Gadidae
Cod, Southern Rock	Anz	Pseudophycis bachus	Cod & Cod-like	Ophidiidae
Coley	Eur	Pollachius virens	Cod & Cod-like	Gadidae
Conch	USA Pac	Strombus gigas	Shellfish (Univalves)	Strombidae
Coney	USA Atl	Cephalopholis fulva	Groupers, Sea Bass, & Barramundi	Serranidae
Coquille Saint-Jacques	Eur	Pecten maximus	Shellfish (Bivalves)	Pectinidae
Coral Hind	Anz	Cephalopholis miniata	Groupers, Sea Bass, & Barramundi	Serranidae
Corvina, Californian	USA Pac	Menticirrhus undulatas	Drums	Sciaenidae
Crab, Alaskan King	USA Pac	Paralithodes camtschatica	Crustacean	Lithodidae
Crab, Blue	USA Atl	Callinectes sapidus	Crustacean	Portunidae
Crab, Blue Swimmer	Anz	Portunus pelagicus	Crustacean	Portunidae
Crab, Brown	Eur	Cancer pagurus	Crustacean	Cancridae
Crab, Coral	Anz	Charybdis feriata	Crustacean	Portunidae
Crab, Dungeness	USA Pac	Cancer magister	Crustacean	Cancridae
Crab, Frog	Anz	Ranina ranina	Crustacean	Raninidae
Crab, Giant Tasmanian	Anz	Pseudocarcinus gigas	Crustacean	Portunidae
Crab, Green	Eur	Carcinus maenas	Crustacean	Portunidae
Crab, Horseshoe	USA Atl	Limulus polyphemus	Crustacean	Limulidae
Crab, Jonah	USA Atl	Cancer borealis	Crustacean	Cancridae
Crab, Lady	Eur	Ovalipes ocellatus	Crustacean	Portunidae
Crab, Mangrove	Anz	Scylla serrata	Crustacean	Portunidae
Crab, Mud	Anz	Scylla serrata	Crustacean	Portunidae
Crab, Oyster	Eur	Pinnotheres ostreum	Crustacean	Pinnotheridae
Crab, Pea	Eur	Pinnotheres ostreum	Crustacean	Pinnotheridae
Crab, Queen	USA Atl	Chionocoetes opilio	Crustacean	Majidae
Crab, Red	USA Atl	Geryon quinquedens	Crustacean	Geryyonidae
Crab, Rock	USA Atl	Cancer irroratus	Crustacean	Cancridae
Crab, Sand	Anz	Ovalipes australiensis	Crustacean	Portunidae
Crab, Shore	Eur	Carcinus maenas	Crustacean	Portunidae
Crab, Snow	USA Atl	Chionocoetes opilio	Crustacean	Majidae
Crab, Spanner	Anz	Ranina ranina	Crustacean	Raninidae
Crab, Spider	Eur & USA Atl	Maia squinado	Crustacean	Majidae
Crab, Stone	USA Atl	Menippe mercenaria	Crustacean	Xanthidae
Crab, Tanner	USA Atl	Chionocoetes opilio	Crustacean	Majidae
Crab, Tasmanian King	Anz	Pseodocarcinus gigas	Crustacean	Portunidae
Crab, Velvet	Eur	Liocarcinus puber	Crustacean	Portunidae
Crabeater	USA Atl/Anz	Rachycentron canadum	Jacks, Pompanos, & Trevallys	Rachycentridae
Crawfish	Eur/USA Atl	Palinurus argus	Crustacean	Palinuridae
Crayfish, Seawater	Eur/USA Atl	Palinurus argus	Crustacean	Palinuridae
Creamfish	Anz	Parika scaber	Thin-bodied fish	Balistidae
Crevette Royale	Eur	Aristeus antennatus	Crustacean	Penaeidae
Crevette, Mediterranean	Eur	Penaeus kerathurus	Crustacean	Penaeidae
Crevette, Mediterranean	Eur	Parapenaeus longirostris	Crustacean	Penaeidae
Croaker, Atlantic	USA Atl	Micropogon undulatus	Drums and Croakers	Sciaenidae
Croaker, White	USA Pac	Genyonemus lineatus	Drums and Croakers	Sciaenidae
Croaker, Yellowfin	USA Pac	Umbrina roncador	Drums and Croakers	Sciaenidae
Cunner	USA Atl	Tautogolabrus adspersus	Wrasse	Labridae
Cusk	USA Atl	Brosme brosme	Cod & Cod-like	Gadidae
Cutlass Fish	Eur	Aphanopus carbo	Elongated Fish	Trichiuridae
Cuttlefish	Eur	Sepia officinalis	Cephalapods	Sepiidae
Cuttlefish	Anz	Sepia rex	Cephalapods	Sepiidae
Cuttlefish	Anz	Sepia apama	Cephalapods	Sepiidae
Cuttlefish, Little	Eur	Sepiola rondeleti	Cephalapods	Sepiidae
Cuttlefish, Little	Eur	Sepiola rondeletti	Cephalapods	Sepiidae
Dab	Eur	Limanda limanda	Flatfish	Bothidae
Dab, Long Rough	USA Atl	Hippoglossoides platessoides	Flatfish	Pleuronectidae
Dab, Sand	USA Atl	Hippoglossoides platessoides	Flatfish	Pleuronectidae
Dab, Yellowtail	USA Atl	Limanda ferruginea	Flatfish	Pleuronectidae
Dart	Anz	Trachinotus botla	Jacks, Pompanos, & Trevallys	Carangidae
Daurade Royale	Eur	Sparus auratus	Sea Bream, Porgies, & Snappers	Sparidae
Dentex	Eur	Dentex maroccanus	Sea Bream, Porgies, & Snappers	Sparidae
Dentex	Eur	Dentex dentex	Sea Bream, Porgies, & Snappers	Sparidae
Dhufish	Anz	Glaucosoma hebraicum	Sea Perch	Glaucosomatidae
Dogfish	Eur	Scyliorhinus canicula	Sharks & Rays	Scyliorhinidae
Dogfish, Endeavor	Anz	Centrophorus harrissoni	Sharks & Rays	Squalidae
Dogfish, Greeneye	Anz	Squalus megalops	Sharks & Rays	Squalidae
Dogfish, Lesser-Spotted	Eur	Scyliorhinus canicula	Sharks & Rays	Scyliorhinidae
Dogfish, Spikey	Anz	Squalus megalops	Sharks & Rays	Squalidae
Dogfish, White-Spotted	Anz	Squalus acanthias	Sharks & Rays	Squalidae
Dolphinfish	Eur/USA Atl/Anz	Coryphaena hippurus	Jacks, Pompanos, & Trevallys	Coryphaenidae
Dorado	Eur/USA Atl/Anz	Coryphaena hippurus	Jacks, Pompanos, & Trevallys	Coryphaenidae
Drum, Banded	USA Atl	Larimus fasciatus	Drums and Croakers	Sciaenidae
Drum, Black	USA Atl	Pogonias cromis	Drums and Croakers	Sciaenidae
Drum, Red	USA Atl	Sciaenops ocellatus	Drums and Croakers	Sciaenidae
Dulse	Eur/USA Atl	Palmaria palmata	Seaweed	Rhodophyceae
Eel, American	USA Atl	Anguilla rostrata	Eel & Eel-like	Anguillidae
Eel, Australian Conger	Anz	Conger verreauxi	Eel & Eel-like	Congridae
Eel, Californian Moray	USA Pac	Gymnothorax mordax	Eel & Eel-like	Muraenidae
Eel, Conger	Eur	Conger conger	Eel & Eel-like	Congridae
Eel, Conger	USA Atl	Conger oceanicus	Eel & Eel-like	Congridae
Eel, European	Eur	Anguilla anguilla	Eel & Eel-like	Anguillidae
Eel, Freshwater	Eur	Anguilla anguilla	Eel & Eel-like	Anguillidae
Eel, Longfin	Anz	Anguilla reinhardtii	Eel & Eel-like	Anguillidae
Eel, Monkeyface	USA Pac	Cebidichthys violaceus	Elongated fish	Stichaeidae
Eel, Moray	Eur	Muraena helena	Eel & Eel-like	Muraenidae
Eel, Rock	USA Pac	Xiphister mucosus	Elongated fish	Stichaeidae
Eel, Shortfin	Anz	Anguilla australis	Eel & Eel-like	Anguillidae
Elephant Fish	Anz	Callorhinchus milii	Sharks & Rays	Callorhinchidae
Emperor, Blue	Anz	Lethrinus nebulosus	Sea Bream, Porgies, & Snappers	Lethrinidae
Emperor, Longtail	Anz	Lethrinus olivaceus	Sea Bream, Porgies, & Snappers	Lethrinidae
Emperor, Red	Anz	Lutjanus sebae	Sea Bream, Porgies, & Snappers	Lutjanidae
Emperor, Redspot	Anz	Lethrinus lentjan	Sea Bream, Porgies, & Snappers	Lethrinidae
Emperor, Redthroat	Anz	Lethrinus miniatus	Sea Bream, Porgies, & Snappers	Lethrinidae
Emperor, Sky	Anz	Lethrinus mahsena	Sea Bream, Porgies, & Snappers	Lethrinidae
Emperor, Snubnose	Anz	Lethrinus borbonicus	Sea Bream, Porgies, & Snappers	Lethrinidae
Emperor, Spangled	Anz	Lethrinus nebulosus	Sea Bream, Porgies, & Snappers	Lethrinidae
Emperor, Yellowtail	Anz	Lethrinus mahsena	Sea Bream, Porgies, & Snappers	Lethrinidae
Escolar	Anz	Lepidocybium flavobrunneum	Elongated fish	Gempylidae
Espada	Eur/USA Atl	Lepidopus caudatus	Elongated Fish	Trichiuridae
Eulachon	USA Pac	Thaleichthys Pacificus	Small Fry	Osmeridae
Flake	Anz	Galeorhinus galeus	Sharks & Rays	Carcharhinidae
Flathead	Anz	Platycephalus longispinis	Bony-Cheeked Fish	Platycephalidae
Flathead, Deepwater	Anz	Platycephalus conatus	Bony-Cheeked Fish	Platycephalidae
Flathead, Dusky	Anz	Platycephalus fuscus	Bony-Cheeked Fish	Platycephalidae
Flathead, Rock	Anz	Platycephalus laevigatus	Bony-Cheeked Fish	Platycephalidae
Flathead, Sand	Anz	Platycephalus bassensis	Bony-Cheeked Fish	Platycephalidae
Flathead, Southern	Anz	Platycephalus speculator	Bony-Cheeked Fish	Platycephalidae
Flathead, Tiger	Anz	Neoplatycephalus richardsoni	Bony-Cheeked Fish	Platycephalidae
Flounder	Anz	Pseudorhombus spinosus	Flatfish	Pleuronectidae
Flounder	Eur	Platichthys flesus	Flatfish	Pleuronectidae
Flounder, Bay	Anz	Ammotretis rostratus	Flatfish	Pleuronectidae
Flounder, Greenback	Anz	Rhombosolea tapirina	Flatfish	Pleuronectidae
Flounder, Pacific	USA Pac	Microstomus Pacificus	Flatfish	Pleuronectidae
Flounder, Rusty	USA Atl	Limanda ferruginea	Flatfish	Pleuronectidae
Flounder, Southern	USA Atl	Paralichthys lethostigmus	Flatfish	Bothidae
Flounder, Starry	USA Pac	Platichthys stellatus	Flatfish	Pleuronectidae
Flounder, Summer	USA Atl	Paralichthys dentatus	Flatfish	Bothidae
Flounder, Winter	USA Atl	Pseudopleuronectes americanus	Flatfish	Pleuronectidae
Fluke	Eur	Platichthys flesus	Flatfish	Pleuronectidae
Fluke, Northern	USA Atl	Paralichthys dentatus	Flatfish	Bothidae
Flyingfish	USA Atl	Exocoetus volitans	US Catchall	Exocetidae
Forkbeard	Eur	Phycis blennoides	Cod & Cod-like	Gadidae
Frostfish, Southern	Anz	Lepidopus caudatus	Elongated fish	Trichiuridae
Fugu Fish	Anz	Takifugu rubripes	Puffer Fish	Tetraodontidae
Fugu Fish	Anz	Takifugu porphyreus	Puffer Fish	Tetraodontidae
Garfish	Eur	Belone belone	Elongated Fish	Belonidae
Garfish, Eastern Sea	Anz	Hyporhamphus australis	Elongated fish	Hemiramphidae
Garfish, River	Anz	Hyporhamphus regularis	Elongated fish	Hemiramphidae
Garfish, Shortnosed	Anz	Hyporhamphus quoyi	Elongated fish	Hemiramphidae
Garfish, Snubnose	Anz	Arrhamphus sclerolepis	Elongated fish	Hemiramphidae
Garfish, Southern	Anz	Hyporhamphus melanochir	Elongated fish	Hemiramphidae
Garfish, Tropical	Anz	Hyporhamphus affinis	Elongated fish	Hemiramphidae
Gemfish	Anz	Rexea solandri	Elongated fish	Gempylidae
Globefish	USA Atl	Spheroides maculatus	Puffer Fish	Tetraodontidae
Goatfish	USA Atl	Mullus auratus	Mullets	Mullidae
Goatfish, Goldband	Anz	Upeneus moluccensis	Mullets	Mullidae
Goatfish, Indian	Anz	Parupeneus indicus	Mullets	Mullidae
Goatfish, Yellowspot	Anz	Parupeneus indicus	Mullets	Mullidae
Goby	Eur	Gobius niger	Small Fry	Gobiidae
Goosefish	USA Atl	Lophius americanus	Monkfish & Stargazers	Lophiidae
Greenbone	Anz	Coridodax pullus	Thin-bodied fish	Odacidae
Grenadier	Eur/USA Atl	Macrourus berglax	Deep-sea Fish	Macrouridae
Grenadier, Blue	Anz	Macruronus novaezelandiae	Deep-sea Fish	Macrouridae
Grenadier, Roughhead	Eur/USA Atl	Macrourus berglax	Deep-sea Fish	Macrouridae
Grenadier, Roundnose	Eur/ Usa Atl	Coryphaenoides rupestris	Deep-sea Fish	Macrouridae
Groper, Baldchin	Anz	Choerodon rubescens	Wrasse	Labridae
Groper, Blue	Anz	Achoerodus gouldii	Wrasse	Labridae
Grouper	Eur	Epinephelus guaza	Groupers, Sea Bass, & Barramundi	Serranidae
Grouper, Black	USA Atl	Epinephelus marginatus	Groupers, Sea Bass, & Barramundi	Serranidae
Grouper, Blue Spotted	USA Atl	Cephalopholis taeniops	Groupers, Sea Bass, & Barramundi	Serranidae
Grouper, Malabar	USA Atl	Epinephelus malabaricus	Groupers, Sea Bass, & Barramundi	Serranidae
Grouper, Nassau	USA Atl	Epinephelus striatus	Groupers, Sea Bass, & Barramundi	Serranidae
Grouper, Red	USA Atl	Epinephelus morio	Groupers, Sea Bass, & Barramundi	Serranidae
Grouper, Red	USA Atl	Cephalopholis taeniops	Groupers, Sea Bass, & Barramundi	Serranidae
Grouper, Warsaw	USA Atl	Epinephelus nigritus	Groupers, Sea Bass, & Barramundi	Serranidae
Grouper, Yellowmouth	USA Atl	Mycteroperca interstitialis	Groupers, Sea Bass, & Barramundi	Serranidae
Grunt, White	USA Atl	Haemulon plumieri	Sea Bream, Porgies, & Snappers	Pomadasyidae
Gurnard, Butterfly	Anz	Lepidotrigla vanessa	Bony-Cheeked Fish	Triglidae

classifying seafood (continued)

COMMON NAME	REGION	LATIN NAME	A–Z FAMILY	LATIN FAMILY
Gurnard, Gray	Eur	Eutrigla gurnardus	Bony-Cheeked Fish	Triglidae
Gurnard, Red	Eur	Aspitrigla cuculus	Bony-Cheeked Fish	Triglidae
Gurnard, Red	Anz	Chelidonichthys kumu	Bony-Cheeked Fish	Triglidae
Gurnard, Tub	Eur	Trigla lucerna	Bony-Cheeked Fish	Triglidae
Haddock	Eur/USA Atl	Melanogrammus aeglefinus	Cod & Cod-like	Gadidae
Hake	Eur	Merluccius merluccius	Cod & Cod-like	Gadidae
Hake, Blue	Anz	Macruronus novaezelandiae	Deep-sea Fish	Macrouridae
Hake, Pacific	USA Pac	Merluccius productus	Cod & Cod-like	Gadidae
Hake, Red	USA Atl	Urophycis chuss	Cod & Cod-like	Gadidae
Hake, Silver	USA Atl	Merluccius bilinearis	Cod & Cod-like	Gadidae
Hake, South African	Anz/South Africa	Merluccius capensis	Cod & Cod-like	Gadidae
Hake, Southern	Anz	Merluccius australis	Cod & Cod-like	Gadidae
Hake, Squirrel	USA Atl	Urophycis tenuis	Cod & Cod-like	Gadidae
Hake, White	USA Atl	Urophycis tenuis	Cod & Cod-like	Gadidae
Halibut	USA Atl	Hippoglossus hippoglossus	Flatfish	Pleuronectidae
Halibut, Australian	Anz	Psettodes erumei	Flatfish	Psettodidae
Halibut, Californian	USA Pac	Paralichthys californicus	Flatfish	Bothidae
Halibut, Greenland	Usa Atl	Reinhardtius hippoglossoides	Flatfish	Pleuronectidae
Halibut, Pacific	USA Pac	Hippoglossus stenolepis	Flatfish	Pleuronectidae
Hapuku	Anz	Polyprion oxygeneios	Groupers, Sea Bass, & Barramundi	Serranidae
Hardhead	USA Atl	Micropogon undulatus	Drums and Croakers	Sciaenidae
Hardtail	USA Atl	Caranx crysos	Jacks, Pompanos, & Trevallys	Carangidae
Harvestfish	USA Atl	Peprilus alepidotus	Thin-bodied fish	Stromateidae
Heart Shell	Eur	Glossus humanus	Shellfish (Bivalves)	Glossidae
Herring	Eur/USA Atl	Clupea harengus	Herring	Clupeidae
Herring, Australian	Anz	Arripis georgianus	Herring	Clupeidae
Herring, Pacific	USA Pac	Clupea harengus pallasii	Herring	Clupeidae
Hind, Red	USA Atl	Epinephelus guttatus	Groupers, Sea Bass, & Barramundi	Serranidae
Hind, Speckled	USA Atl	Epinephelus drummondhayi	Groupers, Sea Bass, & Barramundi	Serranidae
Hins, Rock	USA Atl	Epinephelus adscensionis	Groupers, Sea Bass, & Barramundi	Serranidae
Hogfish	USA Atl	Lachnolaimus maximus	Wrasse	Labridae
Hoki	Anz	Macruronus novaezelandiae	Deep-sea Fish	Macrouridae
Hussar	Anz	Lutjanus adetii	Sea Bream, Porgies, & Snappers	Lutjanidae
Icefish	Anz	Chamsocephalus gunnari	Deep-sea Fish	Channichthyidae
Imperador	Anz	Beryx decadactylus	Bony-Cheeked Fish	Berycidae
Inanga	Anz	Galaxias maculatus	Small Fry	Galaxiidae
Inkfish	USA Pac	Loligo opalescens	Cephalapods	Loliginidae
Jack, Almaco	USA/Anz	Seriola rivoliana	Jacks, Pompanos, & Trevallys	Carangidae
Jack, Common	Eur	Caranx hippos	Jacks, Pompanos, & Trevallys	Carangidae
Jack, Crevalle	USA Atl	Caranx hippos	Jacks, Pompanos, & Trevallys	Carangidae
Jack, Mangrove	Anz	Lutjanus argentimaculatus	Sea Bream, Porgies, & Snappers	Lutjanidae
Jack, Silver	Anz	Lutjanus argentimaculatus	Sea Bream, Porgies, & Snappers	Lutjanidae
Jack, Yellow	USA Atl	Caranx bartholomaei	Jacks, Pompanos, & Trevallys	Carangidae
Jackmackerel	USA Atl	Trachurus symmetricus	Jacks, Pompanos, & Trevallys	Carangidae
Jackmackerel	Anz	Trachurus declivis	Jacks, Pompanos, & Trevallys	Carangidae
Jacknife, Atlantic	USA Atl	Ensis directus	Shellfish (Bivalves)	Solenidae
Jellyfish	Anz	Aurelia aurita	Sea Creature	Schyphoza
Jellyfish, Blue	Eur/Anz	Aurelia aurita	Sea Creature	Ulmariidae
Jewfish	Anz	Johnius borneensis	Drums and and Croakers	Sciaenidae
Jewfish	USA Atl	Epinephelus itajara	Groupers, Sea Bass, & Barramundi	Serranidae
Jewfish, Atlantic	Eur	Epinephelus guaza	Groupers, Sea Bass, & Barramundi	Serranidae
Jewfish, Black	Anz	Protonibea diacanthus	Drums and Croakers	Sciaenidae
Jobfish	Anz	Aprion virescens	Sea Bream, Porgies, & Snappers	Lutjanidae
John Dory	Eur/Anz	Zeus faber	Thin-bodied fish	Zeidae
Kahawai	Anz	Arripis trutta	Sea Bream, Porgies, & Snappers	Arripidae
Kawakawa	USA Pac/Anz	Euthynnus affinis	Mackerel & Tuna	Scombridae
Kelp, Japanese	Anz	Laminaria japonica	Seaweed	Laminariacea
Kingfish	Anz	Seriola dorsalis	Jacks, Pompanos, & Trevallys	Carangidae
Kingfish	USA Atl	Scomberomorus cavalla	Mackerel & Tuna	Scombridae
Kingfish, Black	USA Atl/Anz	Rachycentron canadum	Jacks, Pompanos, & Trevallys	Rachycentridae
Kingfish, Northern	USA Atl	Menticirrhus saxatilis	Drums and Croakers	Sciaenidae
Kingfish, Southern	USA Atl	Menticirrhus americanus	Drums and Croakers	Sciaenidae
Kingfish, Yellowtail	Anz	Seriola lalandi	Jacks, Pompanos, & Trevallys	Carangidae
Knifejaw	Anz	Oplegnathus woodwardi	Thin-bodied fish	Oplegnathidae
Kombu	Anz	Laminaria japonica	Seaweed	Laminariacea
Lamprey	Eur/USA Atl	Petromyzon marinus	Eel & Eel-like	Petromyzonidae
Langoustine	Eur	Nephrops norvegicus	Crustacean	Nephropidae
Latchet	Anz	Pterygotrigla polyommata	Bony-Cheeked Fish	Triglidae
Laver	Eur	Porphyra purpurea	Seaweed	Rhodophyceae
Leatherjacket, Potbelly	Anz	Pseudomonacanthus peroni	Thin-bodied fish	Monacanthidae
Leatherjacket, Velvet	Anz	Parika scaber	Thin-bodied fish	Balistidae
Lemonfish	Anz	Mustelus lenticulatus	Sharks & Rays	Triakidae
Limpet	Eur	Patella vulgata	Shellfish (Univalves)	Patellidae
Limpet, Slipper	Eur	Crepidula fornicata	Shellfish (Univalves)	Calyptraeidae
Ling	Eur	Molva molva	Cod & Cod-like	Gadidae
Ling, Boston	USA Atl	Urophycis tenuis	Cod & Cod-like	Gadidae
Ling, Pink	Anz	Genypterus blacodes	Cod & Cod-like	Ophidiidae

COMMON NAME	REGION	LATIN NAME	A–Z FAMILY	LATIN FAMILY
Ling, Rock	Anz	Genypterus tigerinus	Cod & Cod-like	Ophidiidae
Lingcod	USA Pac	Ophiodon elongatus	US Catchall	Hexagramidae
Lobster, American	USA Atl	Homarus americanus	Crustacean	Nephropidae
Lobster, Bay	Anz	Thenus orientalis	Crustacean	Scyllaridae
Lobster, Eastern Rock	Anz	Jasus verreauxi	Crustacean	Palinuridae
Lobster, European	Eur	Homarus gammarus	Crustacean	Nephropidae
Lobster, European	Eur	Homarus vulgaris	Crustacean	Nephropidae
Lobster, Flat	Eur	Scyllarus arctus	Crustacean	Scyllaridac
Lobster, Norway	Eur	Nephrops norvegicus	Crustacean	Nephropidae
Lobster, Pink Spiny	Africa	Palinurus mauritanicus	Crustacean	Palinuridae
Lobster, Rock	Eur	Palinurus elephas	Crustacean	Palinuridae
Lobster, Shovel-nosed	USA Atl	Scyllarides nodifer	Crustacean	Scyllaridae
Lobster, Slipper	Eur	Scyllarus arctus	Crustacean	Scyllaridae
Lobster, Slipper	Eur	Scyllarus latus	Crustacean	Scyllaridae
Lobster, Slipper	USA Atl	Scyllarides nodifer	Crustacean	Scyllaridae
Lobster, Slipper	USA Atl	Scyllarides aequinoctialis	Crustacean	Scyllaridae
Lobster, Slipper	USA Atl	Scyllarides depressus	Crustacean	Scyllaridae
Lobster, Slipper	Anz	Scyllarides squammosus	Crustacean	Scyllaridae
Lobster, Southern Rock	Anz	Jasus edwardsii	Crustacean	Palinuridae
Lobster, Spanish	USA Atl	Scyllarides nodifer	Crustacean	Scyllaridae
Lobster, Spiny	Eur	Palinurus elephas	Crustacean	Palinuridae
Lobster, Spiny	USA Atl	Palinurus argus	Crustacean	Palinuridae
Lobster, Squat	Eur	Galathea squamifera	Crustacean	Scyllaridae
Lobster, Tropical Rock	Anz	Panulirus ornatus	Crustacean	Palinuridae
Lobster, Western Rock	Anz	Panulirus cygnus	Crustacean	Palinuridae
Lobsterette	USA Atl	Metanephrops binghami	Crustacean	Nephropidae
Longfin	Anz	Caprodon longimanus	Groupers, Sea Bass, & Barramundi	Serranidae
Longtom, Stout	Anz	Tylosurus gavialoides	Elongated fish	Belonidae
Lookdown	USA Atl/Anz	Alectis indicus	Jacks, Pompanos, & Trevallys	Carangidae
Lotte	Eur	Lophius piscatorius	Monkfish & Stargazers	Lophiidae
Luderick	Anz	Girella tricuspidata	Sea Perch	Kyphosidae
Lumpfish	Eur/USA Atl	Cyclopterus lumpus	Roe-Fish	Cyclopteridae
Mackerel, School	Anz	Scomberomorus queenslandicus	Mackerel & Tuna	Scombridae
Mackerel, Atlantic	Eur/USA Atl	Scomber scombrus	Mackerel & Tuna	Scombridae
Mackerel, Blue	Anz	Scomber australasicus	Mackerel & Tuna	Scombridae
Mackerel, Bullet	Eur	Auxis rochei	Mackerel & Tuna	Scombridae
Mackerel, Chub	Eur	Scomber colias	Mackerel & Tuna	Scombridae
Mackerel, Chub	USA Pac	Scomber japonicus	Mackerel & Tuna	Scombridae
Mackerel, Frigate	Anz	Auxis thazard	Mackerel & Tuna	Scombridae
Mackerel, Frigate	Eur	Auxis rochei	Mackerel & Tuna	Scombridae
Mackerel, Gray	Anz	Scomberomorus semifasciatus	Mackerel & Tuna	Scombridae
Mackerel, Horse	Eur	Trachurus mediterraneus	Jacks, Pompanos, & Trevallys	Carangidae
Mackerel, Narrow-Barred Spanish	Anz	Scomberomorus commerson	Mackerel & Tuna	Scombridae
Mackerel, Painted	USA Atl	Scomberomorus regalis	Mackerel & Tuna	Scombridae
Mackerel, Shark	Anz	Grammatorcynus bicarinatus	Mackerel & Tuna	Scombridae
Mackerel, Snake	Eur	Ruvettus pretiosus	Elongated fish	Gempylidae
Mackerel, Spotted	Anz	Scomberomorus munroi	Mackerel & Tuna	Scombridae
Mackerel, Spanish	USA Atl	Scomberomorus maculatus	Mackerel & Tuna	Scombridae
Mahimahi	Eur/USA Atl/Anz	Coryphaena hippurus	Jacks, Pompanos, & Trevallys	Coryphaenidae
Mackerel, King	USA Atl	Scomberomorus cavalla	Mackerel & Tuna	Scombridae
Maomao, Blue	Anz	Scorpis aequipinnis	Sea Perch	Kyphosidae
Maomao, Pink	Anz	Caprodon longimanus	Groupers, Sea Bass, & Barramundi	Serranidae
Marbré	Eur	Lithognathus mormyrus	Sea Bream, Porgies, & Snappers	Sparidae
Marlin, Black	USA Pac/Anz	Makaira indica	Billfish	Istiophoridae
Marlin, Blue	USA Atl	Makaira nigricans	Billfish	Istiophoridae
Marlin, Blue	Anz	Makaira mazara	Billfish	Istiophoridae
Marlin, Striped	USA Pac/Anz	Tetrapturus audax	Billfish	Istiophoridae
Marlin, White	USA Atl	Makaira albida	Billfish	Istiophoridae
Meagre	Eur	Argyrosomus regius	Drums and Croakers	Sciaenidae
Mérou	Eur	Epinephelus guaza	Groupers, Sea Bass, & Barramundi	Serranidae
Mirror Dory	Anz	Zenopsis nebulosus	Thin-bodied fish	Zeidae
Moki	Anz	Latridopsis ciliaris	Australian Catchall	Latrididae
Moki, Blue	Anz	Latridopsis ciliaris	Australian Catchall	Latrididae
Monkfish	Eur	Lophius piscatorius	Monkfish & Stargazers	Lophiidae
Moonfish	Eur/Anz	Lampris guttatus	Thin-bodied fish	Lamprididae
Morgay	Eur	Scyliorhinus caniculla	Sharks & Rays	Scyliorhinidae
Morwong	Anz	Nemadactylus macropterus	Australian Catchall	Cheilodactylidae
Morwong, Banded	Anz	Cheilodactylus spectabilis	Australian Catchall	Cheilodactylidae
Morwong, Blue	Anz	Nemadactylus valenciennesi	Australian Catchall	Cheilodactylidae
Morwong, Gray	Anz	Nemadactylus douglasii	Australian Catchall	Cheilodactylidae
Morwong, Red	Anz	Cheilodactylus fuscus	Australian Catchall	Cheilodactylidae
Mullet, Diamond-Scale	Anz	Liza vaigiensis	Mullets	Mugilidae
Mullet, Golden Gray	Eur	Liza aurata	Mullets	Mugilidae
Mullet, Green-Backed Gray	USA Pac	Liza subviridis	Mullets	Mugilidae
Mullet, Gray	Eur/USA Atl	Mugil cephalus	Mullets	Mugilidae
Mullet, Red	Eur	Mullus surmuletus	Mullets	Mullidae
Mullet, Red	Eur	Mullus barbatus	Mullets	Mullidae

COMMON NAME	REGION	LATIN NAME	A-Z FAMILY	LATIN FAMILY
Mullet, Red	Anz	Parupeneus indicus	Mullets	Mullidae
Mullet, Sea	Anz	Mugil cephalus	Mullets	Mugilidae
Mullet, Southern Red	Anz	Upeneichthys vlamingii	Mullets	Mullidae
Mullet, Striped	USA Atl	Mugil cephalus	Mullets	Mugilidae
Mullet, Thick-Lipped Gray	Eur	Chelon labrosus	Mullets	Mugilidae
Mullet, Thin-Lipped Gray	Eur	Liza ramada	Mullets	Mugilidae
Mullet, White	USA Atl	Mugil curema	Mullets	Mugilidae
Mullet, Yelloweye	Anz	Aldrichetta forsteri	Mullets	Mugilidae
Mulloway	Anz	Argyrosomus hololepidotus	Drums and Croakers	Sciaenidae
Murex	Eur	Murex brandaris	Shellfish (Univalves)	Muricidae
Murgy	Eur	Scyliorhinus canicula	Sharks & Rays	Scyliorhinidae
Mussel	Eur/USA At/Anz	Mytilus edulis	Shellfish (Bivalves)	Mytilidae
Mussel, Blue	USA Atl	Mytilus edulis	Shellfish (Bivalves)	Mytilidae
Mussel, Californian	USA Pac	Mytilus californianus	Shellfish (Bivalves)	Mytilidae
Mussel, Fan	Eur	Pinna fragilis	Shellfish (Bivalves)	Pinnidae
Mussel, Greenlip	Anz	Perna canaliculus	Shellfish (Bivalves)	Mytilidae
Mussel, Horse	Eur/USA Atl	Modiolus modiolus	Shellfish (Bivalves)	Mytilidae
Mussel, Mediterranean	Eur	Mytilus galloprovincialis	Shellfish (Bivalves)	Mytilidae
Mutton-Fish	USA Atl	Macrozoarces americanus	Cod & Cod-like	Gadidae
Needlefish	Eur	Scomberesox saurus	Elongated fish	Scomberesocidae
Norway Haddock	Eur	Sebastes viviparus	Bony-Cheeked Fish	Scorpaenidae
Nursehound	Eur	Scyliorhinus stellaris	Sharks & Rays	Scyliorhinidae
Oblade	Eur	Oblada melanura	Sea Bream, Porgies, & Snappers	Sparidae
Ocean Perch	USA	Sebastes marinus	Bony-Cheeked Fish	Scorpaenidae
Octopus	Eur	Octopus macropus	Cephalapods	Octopodidae
Octopus, Common	Eur/USA Atl	Octopus vulgaris	Cephalapods	Octopodidae
Octopus, Curled	Eur	Eledone cirrosa	Cephalapods	Octopodidae
Octopus, Gloomy	Anz	Octopus tetricus	Cephalapods	Octopodidae
Octopus, Lesser	Eur	Eledone cirrosa	Cephalapods	Octopodidae
Octopus, Maori	Anz	Octopus maorum	Cephalapods	Octopodidae
Octopus, Pacific	USA Pac	Octopus dofleini	Cephalapods	Octopodidae
Octopus, Pale	Anz	Octopus pallidus	Cephalapods	Octopodidae
Octopus, Southern	Anz	Octopus australis	Cephalapods	Octopodidae
Opah	Eur	Lampris guttatus	Thin-bodied fish	Lamprididae
Opaleye	USA Pac	Girella nigricans	Sea Perch	Kyphosidae
Oreo, Black	Anz	Allocyttus niger	Thin-bodied fish	Zeidae
Oreo, Smooth	Anz	Pseudocyttus maculatus	Thin-bodied fish	Zeidae
Ormer	Eur	Haliotis tuberculata	Shellfish (Univalves)	Haliotidae
Oyster, American Blue Point	USA Atl	Crassostrea virginica	Shellfish (Bivalves)	Ostreidae
Oyster, European	Eur	Ostrea edulis	Shellfish (Bivalves)	Ostreidae
Oyster, Japanese	USA Pac	Ostrea lurida	Shellfish (Bivalves)	Ostreidae
Oyster, New Zealand	Anz	Saccostrea glomerata	Shellfish (Bivalves)	Ostreidae
Oyster, Olympia	USA Pac	Ostrea lurida	Shellfish (Bivalves)	Ostreidae
Oyster, Pacific	USA Pac/Anz	Crassostrea gigas	Shellfish (Bivalves)	Ostreidae
Oyster, Portuguese	Eur	Crassostrea angulata	Shellfish (Bivalves)	Ostreidae
Oyster, Sydney Rock	Anz	Saccostrea glomerata	Shellfish (Bivalves)	Ostreidae
Pageot	Eur	Pagellus erythrinus	Sea Bream, Porgies, & Snappers	Sparidae
Pagre	Eur	Pagrus pagrus	Sea Bream, Porgies, & Snappers	Sparidae
Pandora	Eur	Pagellus erythrinus	Sea Bream, Porgies, & Snappers	Sparidae
Pandora, Common	Eur	Pagellus erythrinus	Sea Bream, Porgies, & Snappers	Sparidae
Parore	Anz	Girella tricuspidata	Sea Perch	Kyphosidae
Parrotfish	Anz	Scarus ghobban	Wrasse	Scaridae
Paua	Anz	Haliotis iris	Shellfish (Univalves)	Haliotidae
Pen Shell	Eur	Pinna fragilis	Shellfish (Bivalves)	Pinnidae
Percebes	Eur	Pollicipes cornucopia	Sea Creature	Pollicipidae
Perch, Coral	Anz	Scorpaena cardinalis	Bony-Cheeked Fish	Scorpaenidae
Perch, Crimson Sea	Anz	Lutjanus erythropterus	Sea Bream, Porgies, & Snappers	Lutjanidae
Perch, Giant Sea	Anz	Lates calcarifer	Groupers, Sea Bass, & Barramundi	Centropomidae
Perch, Longfin	Anz	Caprodon longimanus	Groupers, Sea Bass, & Barramundi	Serranidae
Perch, Ocean	Anz	Helicolenus barathri	Bony-Cheeked Fish	Scorpaenidae
Perch, Pacific Ocean	USA Pac	Sebastes alutus	Bony-Cheeked Fish	Scorpaenidae
Perch, Pearl	Anz	Glaucosoma scapulare	Sea Perch	Glaucosomatidae
Perch, Saddletail Sea	Anz	Lutjanus malabaricus	Sea Bream, Porgies, & Snappers	Lutjanidae
Perch, Sea	USA Atl	Morone americanus	Groupers, Sea Bass, & Barramundi	Serranidae
Perch, Silver	USA Atl	Bairdiella chrysura	Drums and Croakers	Sciaenidae
Perch, White	USA Atl	Morone americanus	Groupers, Sea Bass, & Barramundi	Serranidae
Periwinkle	Anz	Turbo undulatus	Shellfish (Univalves)	Turbinidae
Periwinkle	Eur	Littorina littorea	Shellfish (Univalves)	Lacunidae
Permit	USA Atl	Trachinotus falcatus	Jacks, Pompanos, & Trevallys	Carangidae
Petoncle	Eur	Pecten opercularis	Shellfish (Bivalves)	Pectinidae
Piddock	Eur	Pholas dactylus	Shellfish (Bivalves)	Pholadidae
Pigfish	USA Atl	Orthopristis chyrsoptera	Sea Bream, Porgies, & Snappers	Pomadasyidae
Pigfish	Anz	Bodianus unimaculatus	Wrasse	Labridae
Pike	Anz	Sphyraena novaehollandiae	Elongated Fish	Sphyraenidae
Pilchard	Anz	Sardinops neopilchardus	Herring	Clupeidae
Pilchard	Eur	Sardina pilchardus	Herring	Clupeidae
Pilot Fish	Eur	Naucrates ductor	Jacks, Pompanos, & Trevallys	Carangidae
Piper	Eur	Trigla lyra	Bony-Cheeked Fish	Scorpaenidae

COMMON NAME	REGION	LATIN NAME	A-Z FAMILY	LATIN FAMILY
Piper	Anz	Hyporhamphus ihi	Elongated fish	Hemiramphidae
Pipi	Anz	Donax deltoides	Shellfish (Bivalves)	Donacidae
Plaice	Eur	Pleuronectes platessa	Flatfish	Pleuronectidae
Plaice, American	USA Atl	Hippoglossoides platessoides	Flatfish	Pleuronectidae
Plaice, Canadian	USA Atl	Hippoglossoides platessoides	Flatfish	Pleuronectidae
Pod Razor	Eur	Ensis siliqua	Shellfish (Bivalves)	Solenidae
Pollack	Eur	Pollachius pollachius	Cod & Cod-like	Gadidae
Pollock	USA Atl	Pollachius virens	Cod & Cod-like	Gadidae
Pomfret, Atlantic	Eur/Anz	Brama brama	Thin-bodied fish	Bramidae
Pomfret, Black	Anz	Parastromateus niger	Jacks, Pompanos, & Trevallys	Carangidae
Pomfret, White	USA Atl	Pampus argenteus	Thin-bodied fish	Stromateidae
Pompano, African	USA Atl/Anz	Alectis ciliaris	Jacks, Pompanos, & Trevallys	Carangidae
Pompano, Californian	USA Pac	Peprilus simillimus	Jacks, Pompanos, & Trevallys	Carangidae
Pompano, Florida	USA Atl	Trachinotus carolinus	Jacks, Pompanos, & Trevallys	Carangidae
Pompano, Pacific	USA Pac	Peprilus simillimus	Jacks, Pompanos, & Trevallys	Carangidae
Pompano, Round	Eur/USA Atl	Trachinotus ovatus	Jacks, Pompanos, & Trevallys	Carangidae
Porae	Anz	Nemadactylus douglasii	Australian Catchall	Cheilodactylidae
Porgy, European	Eur	Sparus pagrus	Sea Bream, Porgies, & Snappers	Sparidae
Porgy, Jolthead	USA Atl	Calamus bajonado	Sea Bream, Porgies, & Snappers	Sparidae
Porgy, Key West	USA Atl	Calamus nodosus	Sea Bream, Porgies, & Snappers	Sparidae
Porgy, Knobbed	USA Atl	Calamus nodosus	Sea Bream, Porgies, & Snappers	Sparidae
Porgy, Northern	USA Atl	Stenotomus chrysops	Sea Bream, Porgies, & Snappers	Sparidae
Porgy, Red	USA Atl	Stenotomus chrysops	Sea Bream, Porgies, & Snappers	Sparidae
Porgy, Red	USA Atl/Eur	Pagrus pagrus	Sea Bream, Porgies, & Snappers	Sparidae
Porgy, Whitebone	USA Atl	Calamus leucosteus	Sea Bream, Porgies, & Snappers	Sparidae
Porkfish	USA Atl	Anisotremus virginicus	Sea Bream, Porgies, & Snappers	Pomadasyidae
Pout, Eel	Eur	Zoarces viviparus	Cod & Cod-like	Zoarcidae
Pout, Ocean	USA Atl	Macrozoarces americanus	Cod & Cod-like	Zoarcidae
Prawn, Banana	Anz	Fenneropenaeus merguiensis	Crustacean	Penaeidae
Prawn, Bay	Anz	Metapenaeus bennettae	Crustacean	Penaeidae
Prawn, Black Tiger	Anz	Penaeus monodon	Crustacean	Penaeidae
Prawn, Common	Eur	Palaemon serratus	Crustacean	Palaemonidae
Prawn, Deep-water	Eur/USA Atl	Pandalus borealis	Crustacean	Pandalidae
Prawn, Dublin Bay	Eur	Nephrops norvegicus	Crustacean	Nephropidae
Prawn, Endeavour	Anz	Metapenaeus ensis	Crustacean	Penaeidae
Prawn, Giant Tiger	Anz	Penaeus monodon	Crustacean	Penaeidae
Prawn, Indian White	Anz	Penaeus indicus	Crustacean	Penaeidae
Prawn, King	Anz	Melicertus latisulcatus	Crustacean	Penaeidae
Prawn, Kuruma	Anz	Marsupenaeus japonicus	Crustacean	Penaeidae
Prawn, Mediterranean	Eur	Aristeus antennatus	Crustacean	Penaeidae
Prawn, Redspot King	Anz	Melicertus longistylus	Crustacean	Penaeidae
Prawn, Royal Red	Anz	Haliporoides sibogae	Crustacean	Solenoceridae
Prawn, School	Anz	Metapenaeus macleayi	Crustacean	Penaeidae
Prawn, Tiger	Anz	Penaeus esculentus	Crustacean	Penaeidae
Puffer Fish	USA Atl	Spheroides maculatus	Puffer Fish	Tetraodontidae
Rabbitfish	Eur/USA Atl	Chimaera monstosa	Deep-sea Fish	Siganidae
Rabbitfish	Eur	Siganus rivulatus	Puffer Fish	Siganidae
Rabbitfish	Anz	Siganus nebulosus	Puffer Fish	Siganidae
Rajafish	USA	Raja batis	Sharks & Rays	Rajidae
Rascasse	Eur	Scorpaena scrofa	Bony-Cheeked Fish	Scorpaenidae
Rat-Tail	Eur/USA Atl	Macrourus berglax	Deep-sea Fish	Macrouridae
Ray, Blonde	Eur	Raja brachyura	Sharks & Rays	Rajidae
Ray, Spotted	Eur	Raja montagui	Sharks & Rays	Rajidae
Ray, Starry	USA Atl	Raja radiata	Sharks & Rays	Rajidae
Ray, Thornback	Eur	Raja clavata	Sharks & Rays	Rajidae
Redfish	Eur/USA Atl	Sebastes marinus	Bony-Cheeked Fish	Scorpaenidae
Redfish	Anz	Centroberyx affinis	Bony-Cheeked Fish	Berycidae
Redfish, Bight	Anz	Centroberyx gerrardi	Bony-Cheeked Fish	Berycidae
Ribaldo	Anz	Mora moro	Deep-sea Fish	Moridae
Ribbonfish	Anz	Lepidopus caudatus	Elongated Fish	Trichiuridae
River Roman	Anz	Lutjanus argentimaculatus	Sea Bream, Porgies, & Snappers	Lutjanidae
Rock Cod, Blacktip	Anz	Epinephelus fasciatus	Groupers, Sea Bass, & Barramundi	Serranidae
Rock Cod, Estuary	Anz	Epinephelus coioides	Groupers, Sea Bass, & Barramundi	Serranidae
Rock Cod, Red	Anz	Scorpaena cardinalis	Bony-Cheeked Fish	Scorpaenidae
Rock Cod, White-spotted	Anz	Epinephelus multinotatus	Groupers, Sea Bass, & Barramundi	Serranidae
Rock Cod, Yellow-spotted	Anz	Epinephelus areolatus	Groupers, Sea Bass, & Barramundi	Serranidae
Rock Turbot	Eur/USA Atl	Anarhichas lupus	Sea Catfish	Anarhichadidae
Rockcod, Coral	Anz	Cephalopholis miniata	Groupers, Sea Bass, & Barramundi	Serranidae
Rockfish, Brown	USA Pac	Sebastes auriculatus	Bony-Cheeked Fish	Scorpaenidae
Rockfish, Golden Eye	USA Pac	Sebastes ruberrimus	Bony-Cheeked Fish	Scorpaenidae
Rockfish, Olive	USA Atl	Morone saxatilis	Groupers, Sea Bass, & Barramundi	Serranidae
Rockling	Eur/USA Atl	Gaidropsarus vulgaris	Cod & Cod-like	Gadidae
Roker	Eur	Raja clavata	Sharks & Rays	Rajidae
Roosterfish	USA Pac	Nematistius pectoralis	US Catchall	Nematistiidae
Rouget (de roche)	Eur	Mullus surmuletus	Mullets	Mullidae
Rough Hound	Eur	Scyliorhinus canicula	Sharks & Rays	Scyliorhinidae
Roughjacket	USA Pac	Platichthys stellatus	Flatfish	Pleuronectidae
Roughy, Darwin's	Anz	Gephyroberyx darwinii	Deep-sea Fish	Trachichthyidae

classifying seafood (continued)

COMMON NAME	REGION	LATIN NAME	A-Z FAMILY	LATIN FAMILY
Roughy, Orange	Anz	Hoplostethus Atlanticus	Deep-sea Fish	Trachichthyidae
Rudderfish	Anz	Centrolophus niger	Australian Catchall	Centrolophidae
Rudderfish	Eur/USA Atl	Seriola dumerili	Jacks, Pompanos, & Trevallys	Carangidae
Rudderfish, Banded	Anz	Seiola zouata	Australian Catchall	Centrolophidae
Runner, Blue	USA Atl	Caranx crysos	Jacks, Pompanos, & Trevallys	Carangidae
Runner, Rainbow	USA Atl	Elagatis bipinnulatus	Jacks, Pompanos, & Trevallys	Carangidae
Sablefish	USA Atl/Pac	Anopoploma fimbria	Thin-bodied fish	Anopoplomatidae
Saber Fish	Eur/USA Atl	Lepidopus caudatus	Elongated Fish	Trichiuridae
Sailfish	Eur/USA/Anz	Istiophorus platypterus	Billfish	Istiophoridae
Saithe	Eur	Pollachius virens	Cod & Cod-like	Gadidae
Salema	Eur	Sarpa salpa	Sea Bream, Porgies, & Snappers	Sparidae
Salmon, Atlantic	Eur	Salmo salar	Salmon	Salmonidae
Salmon, Australian	Anz	Arripis trutta	Sea Bream, Porgies, & Snappers	Arripidae
Salmon, Blueback	USA Pac	Oncorhynchus nerka	Salmon	Salmonidae
Salmon, Chinook	USA Pac	Oncorhynchus tshawytscha	Salmon	Salmonidae
Salmon, Chum	USA Pac	Oncorhynchus keta	Salmon	Salmonidae
Salmon, Coho	USA Pac	Oncorhynchus kisutch	Salmon	Salmonidae
Salmon, King	USA Pac	Oncorhynchus tshawytscha	Salmon	Salmonidae
Salmon, Pink	USA Pac	Oncorhynchus gorbuscha	Salmon	Salmonidae
Salmon, Rock	Eur	Scyliorhinus canicula	Sharks & Rays	Scyliorhinidae
Salmon, Silver	USA Pac	Oncorhynchus kisutch	Salmon	Salmonidae
Salmon, Sockeye	USA Pac	Oncorhynchus nerka	Salmon	Salmonidae
Samphire, Marsh	Eur	Salicornia europea	Seaweed	Chenopodiaceae
Samphire, Rock	Eur	Crithmum maritimum	Seaweed	Umbelliferae
Samson Fish	Anz	Seriola hippos	Jacks, Pompanos, & Trevallys	Carangidae
Sand Gaper	USA Atl	Mya arenaria	Shellfish (Bivalves)	Myacidae
Sand Eel	USA Atl	Ammodytes americanus	Small Fry	Ammodytidae
Sand Eel	Eur	Ammodytes tobianus	Small Fry	Ammodytidae
Sand-Lance	Eur	Ammodytes tobianus	Small Fry	Ammodytidae
Sardine	Eur	Sardina pilchardus	Herring	Clupeidae
Saupe	Eur	Sarpa salpa	Sea Bream, Porgies, & Snappers	Sparidae
Saury, Atlantic	Eur	Scomberesox saurus	Elongated Fish	Scomberesocidae
Scabbardfish, Black	Eur	Aphanopus carbo	Elongated fish	Trichiuridae
Scabbardfish, White/Silver	Eur/USA Atl	Lepidopus caudatus	Elongated Fish	Trichiuridae
Scad	Eur	Trachurus trachurus	Jacks, Pompanos, & Trevallys	Carangidae
Scad, Yellowtail	Anz	Trachurus novaezelandiae	Jacks, Pompanos, & Trevallys	Carangidae
Scaldfish	Eur	Arnoglossus laterna	Flatfish	Bothidae
Scallop, Atlantic Sea	USA Atl	Placopecten magellicanus	Shellfish (Bivalves)	Pectinidae
Scallop, Ballot's Saucer	Anz	Amusium balloti	Shellfish (Bivalves)	Pectinidae
Scallop, Bay	USA Atl	Argopecten irradians	Shellfish (Bivalves)	Pectinidae
Scallop, Calico	USA Atl	Argopecten gibbus	Shellfish (Bivalves)	Pectinidae
Scallop, Commercial	Anz	Pecten fumatus	Shellfish (Bivalves)	Pectinidae
Scallop, Doughboy	Anz	Mimachlamys asperrima	Shellfish (Bivalves)	Pectinidae
Scallop, Fan	Anz	Annachlamys flabellata	Shellfish (Bivalves)	Pectinidae
Scallop, Great	Eur	Pecten maximus	Shellfish (Bivalves)	Pectinidae
Scallop, Mediterranean	Eur	Pecten jacobaeus	Shellfish (Bivalves)	Pectinidae
Scallop, Northern Saucer	Anz	Amusium pleuronectes	Shellfish (Bivalves)	Pectinidae
Scallop, Queen	Eur	Chlamys opercularis	Shellfish (Bivalves)	Pectinidae
Scallop, Queen	Anz	Equichlamys bifrons	Shellfish (Bivalves)	Pectinidae
Scallop, Rock	USA Pac	Hinnites giganteus	Shellfish (Bivalves)	Pectinidae
Scampi	Anz	Metanephrops boschmai	Crustacean	Nephropidae
Scampi	Eur	Nephrops norvegicus	Crustacean	Nephropidae
Scorpion Fish	Eur	Scorpaena scrofa	Bony-Cheeked Fish	Scorpaenidae
Scorpion Fish, Californian	USA Pac	Scorpaena guttata	Bony-Cheeked Fish	Scorpaenidae
Scorpion Fish, Spotted	USA Atl	Scorpaena plumieri	Bony-Cheeked Fish	Scorpaenidae
Scourer	Eur	Ruvettus pretiosus	Elongated Fish	Gempylidae
Sculpin	USA Atl	Myxocephalus scorpius	Bony-Cheeked Fish	Scorpaenidae
Sculpin, Longhorn	USA Atl	Myxocephalus octodecemspinosus	Bony-Cheeked Fish	Scorpaenidae
Scup	USA Atl	Stenotomus chrysops	Sea Bream, Porgies, & Snappers	Sparidae
Sea Cucumber	Anz	Holothuria scabra	Sea Creature	Holothuriidae
Sea Devil	Eur	Lophius piscatorius	Monkfish & Stargazers	Lophiidae
Sea Lettuce	Eur	Ulva lactuca	Seaweed	Chlorophyceae
Sea Robin	USA Atl	Prionotus carolinus	Bony-Cheeked Fish	Triglidae
Sea Scorpion	USA Atl	Myxocephalus scorpius	Bony-Cheeked Fish	Scorpaenidae
Sea Squab	USA Atl	Spheroides maculatus	Puffer Fish	Tetraodontidae
Sea Urchin	Anz	Heliocidaris erythrogramma	Sea Creature	Echinoidea
Sea Urchin, Black	Eur	Arbacia lixula	Sea Creature	Echinoidea
Sea Urchin, Green	Eur/USA Atl	Strongylocentrotus droebachiensis	Sea Creature	Strongylocentrotidae
Sea Urchin, Mediterranean	Eur	Paracentrotus lividus	Sea Creature	Echinoidea
Sea-wing	Eur	Pinna fragilis	Shellfish (Bivalves)	Pinnidae
Seabass, White	USA Pac	Atractoscion nobilis	Drums and Croakers	Sciaenidae
Seabass, White	USA Atl	Sciaenops ocellatus	Drums and Croakers	Sciaenidae
Seacat	Eur/USA Atl	Anarhichas lupus	Sea Catfish	Anarhichadidae
Seaperch, Brownband	Anz	Lutjanus vitta	Sea Bream, Porgies, & Snappers	Lutjanidae
Seaperch, Darktail	Anz	Lutjanus lemniscatus	Sea Bream, Porgies, & Snappers	Lutjanidae
Seaperch, Fingermark	Anz	Lutjanus johnii	Sea Bream, Porgies, & Snappers	Lutjanidae
Seaperch, Moses	Anz	Lutjanus russelli	Sea Bream, Porgies, & Snappers	Lutjanidae

COMMON NAME	REGION	LATIN NAME	A-Z FAMILY	LATIN FAMILY
Seaperch, Stripey	Anz	Lutjanus carponotatus	Sea Bream, Porgies, & Snappers	Lutjanidae
Seapike	Anz	Sphyraena barracuda	Elongated Fish	Sphyraenidae
Seapike, Striped	Anz	Sphyraena obtusata	Elongated Fish	Sphyraenidae
Seatrout, Spotted	USA Atl	Cynoscion nebulosus	Drums and Croakers	Sciaenidae
Sergeant Fish	USA Atl/Anz	Rachycentron canadum	Jacks, Pompanos, & Trevallys	Rachycentridae
Sewin	Eur	Salmo trutta	Salmon	Salmonidae
Shad, Allis (Allice)	Eur	Alosa alosa	Herring	Clupeidae
Shad, American	USA Atl	Alosa sapidissima	Herring	Clupeidae
Shad, Hickory	USA Atl	Pomolobus mediocris	Herring	Clupeidae
Shad, Twaite	Eur	Alosa fallax	Herring	Clupeidae
Shark, Australian Angel	Anz	Squatina australis	Sharks & Rays	Squatinidae
Shark, Blacktip	USA Atl	Carcharhinus limbatus	Sharks & Rays	Carcharhinidae
Shark, Blacktip	Anz	Carcharhinus dussumieri	Sharks & Rays	Carcharhinidae
Shark, Blue	Eur.Anz	Prionace glauca	Sharks & Rays	Carcharhinidae
Shark, Blue Whaler	Anz	Prionace glauca	Sharks & Rays	Carcharhinidae
Shark, Bronze Whaler	Anz	Carcharhinus obscurus	Sharks & Rays	Carcharhinidae
Shark, European Angel	Eur	Squatina squatina	Sharks & Rays	Squatinidae
Shark, Gummy	Anz	Mustelus antarcticus	Sharks & Rays	Triakidae
Shark, Hammerhead	Eur/USA Atl	Sphyrna zygaena	Sharks & Rays	Sphyrnidae
Shark, Mako	Eur/USA Atl	Isurus oxyrinchus	Sharks & Rays	Lamnidae
Shark, North American Angel	USA Atl	Squatina dumerili	Sharks & Rays	Squatinidae
Shark, Porbeagle	Eur/USA Atl	Lamna nasus	Sharks & Rays	Lamnidae
Shark, Sand	USA Atl	Mustelus canis	Sharks & Rays	Triakidae
Shark, School	Anz	Galeorhinus galeus	Sharks & Rays	Carcharhinidae
Shark, Shortfin Mako	Eur/USA Atl	Isurus oxyrinchus	Sharks & Rays	Lamnidae
Shark, Tiger	USA Atl/Pac	Galeocerdo cuvieri	Sharks & Rays	Carcharhinidae
Shark, Whiskery	Anz	Furgaleus macki	Sharks & Rays	Triakidae
Sheephead, California	USA Pac	Pimelometopon pulchrum	Wrasse	Labridae
Sheepshead	USA Atl	Archosargus probatocephalus	Sea Bream, Porgies, & Snappers	Sparidae
Shrimp, Brown	USA Atl	Penaeus aztecus aztecus	Crustacean	Penaeidae
Shrimp, Brown	Eur	Crangon crangon	Crustacean	Crangonidae
Shrimp, Caribbean White	USA Atl	Penaeus schmitti	Crustacean	Penaeidae
Shrimp, Coon-Stripe	USA Pac	Pandalus danae	Crustacean	Pandalidae
Shrimp, Pink	Eur/USA Atl/Pac	Pandalus borealis	Crustacean	Pandalidae
Shrimp, Rock	USA Atl	Sicyonia brevirostris	Crustacean	Scyoniidae
Shrimp, Royal Red	USA Atl	Hymenopenaeus robustus	Crustacean	Penaeidae
Shrimp, Side-Stripe	USA Pac	Pandalopsus dispar	Crustacean	Pandalidae
Shrimp, Spot	USA Pac	Pandalus platyceros	Crustacean	Pandalidae
Shrimp, White	USA Atl	Penaeus setiferus	Crustacean	Penaeidae
Silverside	USA Atl	Menidia menidia	Small Fry	Atherinidae
Silverside	Eur	Atherina presbyter	Small Fry	Atherinidae
Skate & Ray	Anz	Raja batis	Sharks & Rays	Rajidae
Skate, Barndoor	USA Atl	Raja laevis	Sharks & Rays	Rajidae
Skate, Big/Large	USA Pac	Raja binoculata	Sharks & Rays	Rajidae
Skate, California	USA Pac	Raja inornata	Sharks & Rays	Rajidae
Skate, Common	Eur	Raja batis	Sharks & Rays	Rajidae
Skate, Clearnose	USA Atl	Raja eglanteria	Sharks & Rays	Rajidae
Skate, Thorny	USA Atl	Raja radiata	Sharks & Rays	Rajidae
Skipjack	USA Pac	Euthynnus pelamis	Mackerel & Tuna	Scombridae
Skipper	Eur	Scomberesox saurus	Elongated fish	Scomberesocidae
Smelt, Atlantic	Eur	Osmerus eperlanus	Small Fry	Osmeridae
Smelt, Rainbow	USA Atl	Osmerus mordax	Small Fry	Osmeridae
Smelt, Sand	Eur	Atherina presbyter	Small Fry	Atherinidae
Smelt, Silver	Eur/USA Atl	Argentina silus	Salmon	Argentinidae
Smelt, Surf	USA Pac	Hypomesus pretiosus	Small Fry	Osmeridae
Smooth Hound	Eur	Mustelus mustelus	Sharks & Rays	Triakidae
Smooth Hound	Anz	Mustelus lenticulatus	Sharks & Rays	Triakidae
Snapper	Anz	Pagrus auratus	Sea Bream, Porgies, & Snappers	Sparidae
Snapper, American Red	USA Atl	Lutjanus campechanus	Sea Bream, Porgies, & Snappers	Lutjanidae
Snapper, Cubera	USA Atl	Lutjanus cyanopterus	Sea Bream, Porgies, & Snappers	Lutjanidae
Snapper, Emperor	Anz	Lutjanus sebae	Sea Bream, Porgies, & Snappers	Lutjanidae
Snapper, Goldband	Anz	Pristipomoides multidens	Sea Bream, Porgies, & Snappers	Lutjanidae
Snapper, Gray	USA Atl	Lutjanus griseus	Sea Bream, Porgies, & Snappers	Lutjanidae
Snapper, Humpback Red	Anz	Lutjanes gibbus	Sea Bream, Porgies, & Snappers	Lutjanidae
Snapper, King	Anz	Pristipomoides filamentosus	Sea Bream, Porgies, & Snappers	Lutjanidae
Snapper, Lane	USA Atl	Lutjanus synagris	Sea Bream, Porgies, & Snappers	Lutjanidae
Snapper, Mangrove	USA Atl	Lutjanus griseus	Sea Bream, Porgies, & Snappers	Lutjanidae
Snapper, Mutton	USA Atl	Lutjanus analis	Sea Bream, Porgies, & Snappers	Lutjanidae
Snapper, Red	USA Atl	Lutjanus campechanus	Sea Bream, Porgies, & Snappers	Lutjanidae
Snapper, Ruby	Anz	Etelis coruscans	Sea Bream, Porgies, & Snappers	Lutjanidae
Snapper, Schoolmaster	USA Atl	Lutjanus apodus	Sea Bream, Porgies, & Snappers	Lutjanidae
Snapper, Silk	USA Atl	Lutjanus vivanus	Sea Bream, Porgies, & Snappers	Lutjanidae
Snapper, Two-Spot	Anz	Lutjanes bohar	Sea Bream, Porgies, & Snappers	Lutjanidae
Snapper, Vermillion	USA Atl	Rhomboplites aurorubens	Sea Bream, Porgies, & Snappers	Lutjanidae
Snapper, Yellowtail	USA Atl	Ocyurus chrysurus	Sea Bream, Porgies,, & Snappers	Lutjanidae
Snoek	Anz	Thyrsites atun	Elongated fish	Gempylidae
Snook	Anz	Sphyraena novaehollandiae	Elongated Fish	Sphyraenidae

COMMON NAME	REGION	LATIN NAME	A-Z FAMILY	LATIN FAMILY
Snook	USA Atl	Centropomus undecimalis	Groupers, Sea Bass, & Barramundi	Centropomidae
Snook, Black	USA Pac	Centropomus nigrescens	Groupers, Sea Bass, & Barramundi	Centropomidae
Sole	Anz	Synaptura nigra	Flatfish	Pleuronectidae
Sole, Butter	USA Pac	Isopsetta isolepis	Flatfish	Pleuronectidae
Sole, California	USA Pac	Parophrys ventulus	Flatfish	Pleuronectidae
Sole, Dover	Eur	Solea solea	Flatfish	Soleidae
Sole, English	USA Pac	Parophrys ventulus	Flatfish	Pleuronectidae
Sole, French	Eur	Solea lascaris	Flatfish	Soleidae
Sole, Lemon	Eur	Microstomus kitt	Flatfish	Pleuronectidae
Sole, Megrim	Eur	Lepidorhombus whiffiagonis	Flatfish	Bothidae
Sole, Petrale	USA Pac	Eopsetta jordani	Flatfish	Pleuronectidae
Sole, Thickback	Eur	Microchirus variegatus	Flatfish	Soleidae
Sole, Torbay	Eur	Glyptocephalus cynoglossus	Flatfish	Pleuronectidae
Sole, Witch	Eur	Glyptocephalus cynoglossus	Flatfish	Pleuronectidae
Sparling	Eur	Osmerus eperlanus	Small Fry	Osmeridae
Spearfish, Mediterranean	Eur	Tetrapturus albidus	Billfish	Istiophoridae
Spearfish, Shortbill	USA Pac	Tetrapturus angustirostris	Billfish	Istiophoridae
Spot	USA Atl	Leiostomus xanthurus	Drums and Croakers	Sciaenidae
Sprat	Eur	Sprattus sprattus	Herring	Clupeidae
Sprat	Anz	Sprattus antipodum	Herring	Clupeidae
Sprat, Sandy	Anz	Hyperlophus vittatus	Herring	Clupeidae
Spur-Dog	Eur/USA/Anz	Squalus acanthias	Sharks & Rays	Squalidae
Squeteague, Spotted	USA Atl	Cynoscion nebulosus	Drums and Croakers	Sciaenidae
Squid, Arrow	Anz	Nototodarus gouldi	Cephalapods	Loliginidae
Squid, Bone	USA Atl	Loligo pealei	Cephalapods	Loliginidae
Squid, California	USA Pac	Loligo opalescens	Cephalapods	Loliginidae
Squid, Common	Eur	Loligo forbesi	Cephalapods	Loliginidae
Squid, European	Eur	Loligo vulgaris	Cephalapods	Loliginidae
Squid, Flying	Eur	Todarodes saggittatus	Cephalapods	Loliginidae
Squid, Flying	USA Pac	Todarodes Pacificus	Cephalapods	Loliginidae
Squid, Long-finned	USA Atl	Loligo pealei	Cephalapods	Loliginidae
Squid, Miter	Anz	Loligo chinensis	Cephalapods	Loliginidae
Squid, Winter	USA Atl	Loligo pealei	Cephalapods	Loliginidae
St. Peter's Fish	Eur	Zeus faber	Thin-bodied fish	Zeidae
Stargazer	Eur	Uranoscopus scaber	Monkfish & Stargazers	Uranoscopidae
Stargazer	Anz	Kathetostoma canaster	Monkfish & Stargazers	Uranoscopidae
Stargazer, Giant	Anz	Kathetostoma giganteum	Monkfish & Stargazers	Uranoscopidae
Sturgeon	Eur	Acipenser sturio	Roe Fish	Acipenseridae
Sturgeon	Eur	Acipenser gueldenstaedti colchicus	Roe-Fish	Acipenseridae
Sturgeon	USA Atl	Acipenser oxyrhynchus	Roe-Fish	Acipenseridae
Sturgeon, Beluga	Eur	Huso huso	Roe-Fish	Acipenseridae
Sturgeon, Sevruga	Eur	Acipenser stellatus	Roe-Fish	Acipenseridae
Sunfish	Eur/USA	Mola mola	Thin-bodied fish	Molidae
Surfperch, Barred	USA Pac	Amphistichus argenteus	Sea Perch	Embiotocidae
Surfperch, Calico	USA Pac	Amphistichus koelzi	Sea Perch	Embiotocidae
Surfperch, Redtail	USA Pac	Amphistichus rhodoterus	Sea Perch	Embiotocidae
Swallowtail	Anz	Centroberyx lineatus	Bony-Cheeked Fish	Berycidae
Sweep	Anz	Scorpis lineolatus	Sea Perch	Scorpididae
Swellfish	USA Atl	Spheroides maculatus	Puffer Fish	Tetraodontidae
Swordfish	Eur/USA Atl/Anz	Xiphias gladius	Billfish	Xiphiidae
Tailor	Anz	Pomatomus saltatrix	Jacks, Pompanos, & Trevallys	Pomatomidae
Tarpon	USA Atl	Megalops Atlanticus	Herring	Elopidae
Tarwhine	Anz	Rhabdosargus sarba	Sea Bream, Porgies, & Snappers	Sparidae
Tautog	USA Atl	Tautoga onitis	Wrasse	Labridae
Tellin	Eur	Scrobicularia plana	Shellfish (Bivalves)	Scrobiculariidae
Teraglin	Anz	Atractoscion aequidens	Drums and Croakers	Sciaenidae
Terakihi	Anz	Nemadactylus macropterus	Australian Catchall	Cheilodactylidae
Threadfin, Blue	Anz	Eleutheronema tetradactylum	Sea Bream, Porgies, & Snappers	Sparidae
Threadfin, Indian	USA Atl/Anz	Alectis indicus	Jacks, Pompanos, & Trevallys	Carangindae
Threadfin, King	Anz	Polydactylus sheridani	Sea Bream, Porgies, & Snappers	Sparidae
Threadfin, Pacific	Anz	Polydactylus approximans	Sea Bream, Porgies, & Snappers	Sparidae
Tilefish	USA Atl	Lopholatilus chamaeleonticeps	US Catchall	Branchiostegidae
Tilefish, Blackline	USA Atl	Caulotilus cyanops	US Catchall	Branchiostegidae
Tilefish, Sand	USA Atl	Malacanthus plumieri	US Catchall	Branchiostegidae
Tomcod	USA Atl	Microgadus tomcod	Cod & Cod-like	Gadidae
Toothfish, Patagonian	Anz	Dissostichus eleginoides	Deep-sea Fish	Nototheniidae
Top-Shell	Eur	Monodonta turbinata	Shellfish (Univalves)	Trochidae
Tope	Eur	Galeorhinus galeus	Sharks & Rays	Carcharhinidae
Topknot	Eur	Zeugopterus punctatus	Flatfish	Bothidae
Torsk	Eur/USA	Brosme brosme	Cod & Cod-like	Gadidae
Totuava	USA Pac	Cynoscion macdonaldi	Drums and Croakers	Sciaenidae
Trevalla, Blue-Eye	Anz	Hyperoglyphe antarctica	Australian Catchall	Centrolophidae
Trevally	Anz	Carangoides gymnostethus	Jacks, Pompanos, & Trevallys	Carangidae
Trevally, Bigeye	Anz	Caranx sexfasciatus	Jacks, Pompanos, & Trevallys	Carangidae
Trevally, Blue-Spotted	Anz	Caranx bucculentus	Jacks, Pompanos, & Trevallys	Carangidae

COMMON NAME	REGION	LATIN NAME	A-Z FAMILY	LATIN FAMILY
Trevally, Bluefin	Anz	Caranx melampygus	Jacks, Pompanos, & Trevallys	Carangidae
Trevally, Giant	Anz	Caranx ignobilis	Jacks, Pompanos, & Trevallys	Carangidae
Trevally, Orange-spotted	Anz	Carangoides bajad	Jacks, Pompanos, & Trevallys	Carangidae
Trevally, Silver	Anz	Pseudocaranx dentex	Jacks, Pompanos, & Trevallys	Carangidae
Triggerfish	Eur/USA Atl	Balistes carolinensis	Thin-bodied fish	Balistidae
Trout, Bar-Cheeked Coral	Anz	Plectropomus maculatus	Groupers, Sea Bass, & Barramundi	Serranidae
Trout, Bluespot	Anz	Plectropomus laevis	Groupers, Sea Bass, & Barramundi	Serranidae
Trout, Common Coral	Anz	Plectropomus leopardus	Groupers, Sea Bass, & Barramundi	Serranidae
Trout, Coronation	Anz	Variola louti	Groupers, Sea Bass, & Barramundi	Serranidae
Trout, Leopard Coral	Anz	Plectropomus leopardus	Groupers, Sea Bass, & Barramundi	Serranidae
Trout, Ocean	Eur	Salmo trutta	Salmon	Salmonidae
Trout, Salmon	Eur	Salmo trutta	Salmon	Salmonidae
Trout, Sea	Eur	Salmo trutta	Salmon	Salmonidae
Trout, Silver	Eur	Salmo trutta	Salmon	Salmonidae
Trumpeter	Anz	Latridopsis forsteri	Australian Catchall	Latrididae
Trumpeter, Bastard	Anz	Latridopsis forsteri	Australian Catchall	Latrididae
Trumpeter, Striped	Anz	Latris lineata	Australian Catchall	Latrididae
Tuna	Anz	Cybiosarda elegans	Mackerel & Tuna	Scombridae
Tuna, Albacore	Eur/USA At/Anz	Thunnus alalunga	Mackerel & Tuna	Scombridae
Tuna, Bigeye	Eur/USA At/Anz	Thunnus obesus	Mackerel & Tuna	Scombridae
Tuna, Blackfin	USA Atl	Thunnus Atlanticus	Mackerel & Tuna	Scombridae
Tuna, Bluefin	Eur, USA Atl	Thunnus thynnus	Mackerel & Tuna	Scombridae
Tuna, Bullet	Eur	Auxis rochei	Mackerel & Tuna	Scombridae
Tuna, Long-Fin	Eur/USA Atl	Thunnus alalunga	Mackerel & Tuna	Scombridae
Tuna, Skipjack	USA Pac	Euthynnus pelamis	Mackerel & Tuna	Scombridae
Tuna, Skipjack	Anz	Katsuwonus pelamis	Mackerel & Tuna	Scombridae
Tuna, Slender	Anz	Allothunnus fallai	Mackerel & Tuna	Scombridae
Tuna, Southern Bluefin	Anz	Thunnus maccoyii	Mackerel & Tuna	Scombridae
Tuna, White	Eur/USA Atl/Anz	Thunnus alalunga	Mackerel & Tuna	Scombridae
Tuna, Yellowfin	Eur/USA/Anz	Thunnus albacares	Mackerel & Tuna	Scombridae
Tunny, Little	USA Atl	Euthynnus alletteratus	Mackerel & Tuna	Scombridae
Turban Shell	Anz	Turbo undulatus	Shellfish (Univalves)	Turbinidae
Turbot	Eur	Psetta maxima	Flatfish	Bothidae
Turbot, Diamond	USA Pac	Hypsopsetta guttulata	Flatfish	Pleuronectidae
Turrum	Anz	Carangoides fulvoguttatus	Jacks, Pompanos, & Trevallys	Carangidae
Tusk	Eur	Brosme brosme	Cod & Cod-like	Gadidae
Tusk	Anz	Dannevigia tusca	Cod & Cod-like	Ophidiidae
Tuskfish	Anz	Choerodon venustus	Wrasse	Labridae
Violet	Eur	Microcosmus suculatus	Sea Creature	Pyuridae
Wahoo	USA Atl/Anz	Acanthocybium solanderi	Mackerel & Tuna	Scombridae
Wakame	Anz	Undaria pinnatifida	Seaweed	Laminariacea
Warehou, Blue	Anz	Seriolella brama	Australian Catchall	Centrolophidae
Warehou, Silver	Anz	Seriolella punctata	Australian Catchall	Centrolophidae
Warehou, White	Anz	Seriolella caerulea	Australian Catchall	Centrolophidae
Weakfish, Gray	USA Atl	Cynoscion regalis	Drums and Croakers	Sciaenidae
Weever	Eur	Trachinus draco	Monkfish & Stargazers	Trachinidae
West Australian Jewfish	Anz	Glaucosoma hebraicum	Sea Perch	Glaucosomatidae
Westralian Jewfish	Anz	Glaucosoma hebraicum	Sea Perch	Glaucosomatidae
Whelk	Eur/USA Atl	Buccinum undatum	Shellfish (Univalves)	Buccinidae
Whelk, Channeled	USA Atl	Busycon canaliculatum	Shellfish (Univalves)	Melongenidae
Whelk, Knobbled	USA Atl	Busycon carica	Shellfish (Univalves)	Melongenidae
Whiff	Eur	Lepidorhombus whiffiagonis	Flatfish	Bothidae
Whiptail	Anz	Macruronus novaezelandiae	Deep-sea Fish	Macrouridae
Whitebait	Eur	Clupea harengus	Small Fry	Clupeidae
Whitebait	Anz	Lovettia sealii	Small Fry	Galaxiidae
Whitefish	Eur	Coregonus lavaretus	Salmon	Coregonidae
Whitefish, Ocean	USA Pac	Caulotilus princeps	US Catchall	Branchiostegidae
Whiting	Eur	Merlangius merlangus	Cod & Cod-like	Gadidae
Whiting, Blue	Eur/USA Atl	Micromesistius poutassou	Cod & Cod-like	Gadidae
Whiting, Eastern School	Anz	Sillago flindersi	Australian Catchall	Sillaginidae
Whiting, King George	Anz	Sillaginodes punctata	Australian Catchall	Sillaginidae
Whiting, Sand	Anz	Sillago ciliata	Australian Catchall	Sillaginidae
Whiting, Stout	Anz	Sillago robusta	Australian Catchall	Sillaginidae
Whiting, Trumpeter	Anz	Sillago maculata	Australian Catchall	Sillaginidae
Whiting, Western School	Anz	Sillago bassensis	Australian Catchall	Sillaginidae
Whiting, Yellowfin	Anz	Sillago schomburgkii	Australian Catchall	Sillaginidae
Winkle	Eur	Littorina littorea	Shellfish (Univalves)	Lacunidae
Wolffish	Eur/USA Atl	Anarhichas lupus	Sea Catfish	Anarhichadidae
Wrasse, Ballan	Eur	Labras bergylta	Wrasse	Labridae
Wrasse, Crimsonband	Anz	Notolabrus gymnogenis	Wrasse	Labridae
Wreckfish	Eur/USA Atl	Polyprion americanus	Groupers, Sea Bass, & Barramundi	Serranidae
Yellowtail	Anz	Seriola lalandi	Jacks, Pompanos, & Trevallys	Carangidae
Yellowtail, California	USA Pac/Anz	Seriola dorsalis	Jacks, Pompanos, & Trevallys	Carangidae
Yellowtail, Japanese	Japan	Seriola guigueradiata	Jacks, Pompanos, & Trevallys	Carangidae
Yellowtail, Southern	Anz	Seriola grandis	Jacks, Pompanos, & Trevallys	Carangidae

key to abbreviations

Anz – Australia/New Zealand; Eur – Europe; USA Atl – U.S. East Coast; USA Pac – U.S. West Coast

index

Illustrations are shown by *italic* numbers.

acknowledgments

I would like to thank Debbie Major who helped me put this book together, James Murphy who took the wonderful pictures, and Paul Welti and Lisa Pettibone for their inspired design work. Thanks to Charlotte Knox for her beautiful illustrations, to my Commissioning Editor Viv Bowler for her quiet insistence, and Rachel Copus for her accurate editing. I would also like to thank Myrtle Allen, Betsy Apple, Simon Hopkinson, Tetsuya Wakuda, and Patricia Wells for allowing me to use their recipes in this book. Lastly, a big thanks to our fishmonger, Nick Jenkins, for help with the fish preparation techniques—he's the one with the tough hands!